AF767535

PRAISE FOR *THE INVENTORY TOOLKIT*

'Essential reading for companies with complex operations and supply chains that cannot rely on traditional techniques alone. The KCM methodology will cater for demand variation and recognise the need to categorise demand to fully optimize inventory.'
Colin Mills, CEO, Acenta Steel Ltd

'Increasingly within organizations inventory management is treated as a "black box" activity, hidden within the computer algorithms. Practitioners however need to understand the foundational basics of what occurs within the "black box", otherwise sub-optimization and margin erosion can occur within an organization. *The Inventory Toolkit* provides an accessible insight into how effective inventory management needs to pervade a business, connecting strategy to shop floor. It provides insights into the tools, approaches and algorithms used in the inventory "black box". It also provides a useful perspective for anyone reviewing or implementing modern inventory management approaches.'
Professor Richard Wilding OBE, Professor of Supply Chain Strategy, Cranfield School of Management

'*The Inventory Toolkit* provides an invaluable and practical set of tools which will help you drive strong, achievable and ongoing improvements to a business's key performance indicators. Geoff Relph and Catherine Milner use theory balanced with insightful case studies from a number of businesses to demonstrate how the user can make informed decisions in key areas such as managing and controlling cost and understanding the different impacts of both good and bad inventory. The book will be of value to those in further education as well as those already in business.'
Paul Buxton, guest lecturer at WMG, University of Warwick

'Every inventory manager worth their salt should be working with this book. It has a thorough explanation of the history of inventory management analysis tools, what they do and how to use them. The Excel examples with formulas are excellent and raises the bar for inventory analysis texts.'
Sophie Damoglou, Stock and Logistics Manager, Icomera UK Ltd

'Rightsizing inventory buffers is critical for companies to deliver desired customer service levels at lowest supply chain cost. *The Inventory Toolkit* provides a practical approach to achieve this. An essential read for all operations management professionals.'
Professor Janet Godsell, Professor of Operations and Supply Chain Strategy, University of Warwick

'*The Inventory Toolkit* is an insightful and practical read. There are tips and tools that can be implemented to support and improve inventory control, as well as practical examples from across our industry. A very interesting read for anyone looking at their end-to-end supply chain with a view to optimizing inventory control.'
Paul Daniel, guest lecturer at WMG, University of Warwick

2nd Edition

The Inventory Toolkit

Business systems solutions

Geoff Relph
Catherine Milner

KoganPage

Publisher's note

Every possible effort has been made to ensure that the information contained in this book is accurate at the time of going to press, and the publishers and authors cannot accept responsibility for any errors or omissions, however caused. No responsibility for loss or damage occasioned to any person acting, or refraining from action, as a result of the material in this publication can be accepted by the editor, the publisher or the authors.

First published in Great Britain and the United States in 2015 by Kogan Page Limited as *Inventory Management*
Second edition published 2019

Apart from any fair dealing for the purposes of research or private study, or criticism or review, as permitted under the Copyright, Designs and Patents Act 1988, this publication may only be reproduced, stored or transmitted, in any form or by any means, with the prior permission in writing of the publishers, or in the case of reprographic reproduction in accordance with the terms and licences issued by the CLA. Enquiries concerning reproduction outside these terms should be sent to the publishers at the undermentioned addresses:

2nd Floor, 45 Gee Street
London
EC1V 3RS
United Kingdom

122 W 27th St, 10th Floor
New York, NY 10001
USA

4737/23 Ansari Road
Daryaganj
New Delhi 110002
India

www.koganpage.com

© Geoff Relph and Catherine Milner, 2015, 2019

The right of Geoff Relph and Catherine Milner to be identified as the authors of this work has been asserted by them in accordance with the Copyright, Designs and Patents Act 1988.

ISBNs

Hardback 978 1 78966 007 4
Paperback 978 0 7494 8212 1
Ebook 978 0 7494 8213 8

British Library Cataloguing-in-Publication Data

A CIP record for this book is available from the British Library.

Library of Congress Cataloging-in-Publication Number

2019013111

Typeset by Hong Kong FIVE Workshop
Print production managed by Jellyfish
Printed and bound by CPI Group (UK) Ltd, Croydon, CR0 4YY

This book is dedicated to June and Simon,
our patient other halves.

Our thanks to all the staff at Kogan Page for their help and support during the process of writing this book.

Also our thanks to all the case study sources for granting permission to quote them in the book.

CONTENTS

Introduction

What this book is about

This book is intended as a manual for operations management professionals who are looking to improve the effectiveness of the inventory management and production planning and control functions within their organizations. We hope you will find it a useful guide.

You will know that the availability of software is such that from small businesses upwards planning and control systems systems are now used to manage companies' materials and production. To do this, three decisions need to be made:

1 How much to buy and how often.

2 How to protect against variations in supply and demand.

3 How long it will take to make/deliver the item.

All these decisions affect the inventory level that the system and the planners will deliver. What is a little disturbing is that, despite many decades of research, business systems still provide very little support to the planners in the form of optimizing techniques. Research by Relph (2006) showed that:

- only 50 per cent of business systems provided automatic mathematical models for determining cycle and safety stock; and
- even when offered they were rarely used by planners.

If the reader is concerned that their company is not managing their planning parameters well and that they are 'lagging behind' their competitors, these conclusions offer a crumb of comfort: you are not alone. This book is here to help you.

In our many years of experience, we have come across numerous companies that have struggled with the problem of managing their planning parameters. The inventory budget is set in the boardroom as a simple financial amount or percentage, but operations managers know that the decisions of what inventory to hold must be taken at a detail level – what items, where, when, what quantity? Thus, achieving eg a 20 per cent inventory reduction is simple to say (or be told to deliver) but complex to put into action.

This book is based on our many years of operational, consulting and academic experience working with small and large companies. It sets out tools and techniques that have been used successfully to help companies:

- simplify this complex task of managing many thousands of parameters; and
- achieve inventory targets set by senior management.

The book will provide:

- a step-by-step guide on how to simplify the approach to determining the optimal parameters for each item; and
- a simple linkage between the business budget decisions and the item-level parameter settings.

'You do the maths' exercises

In Chapters 2 to 7 we have provided 'You do the maths' exercises. They are designed to enable the reader to review the key points covered in each chapter by working through a relevant exercise, and to reinforce the tools and techniques covered. All the 'You do the maths' exercises in Chapters 2 to 5 are based around a common set of products (Control Boxes) and which we consider to be typical of most batch manufacturing companies.

How the book works

There are a number of threads in the book that look at the problem of inventory management theoretically and philosophically as well as on a practical level. It gives a general narrative of issues, current thinking and best practice, examples of theory/formulae, and worked examples which are developed throughout the book. Each technique is explained and, where possible, formulae are shown in both academic form as well as being expressed in an Excel format. Reading this book, you will be able to create Excel models to test and gain an understanding of each tool. The tools will build into a comprehensive working model that will enable you to analyse and plan inventory. We believe that the best tool to use in each case will depend on the individual circumstances. Traditional techniques can be used to great effect by knowledgeable people. We show how these techniques developed from Pareto, to exchange curve and *k*-curve which are techniques designed to optimize inventory volumes by grouping items into categories and from there identifying their ideal order frequencies and quantities.

The development of the model through Chapters 4 to 6 will show how high-level targets can be broken down and developed into a coherent plan.

All the Excel sheets that we work through in the book are available to download on the Kogan Page website.

In the Excel sheets reproduced in this book, cells displaying the result of a formula are shown with a grey fill. The formula to be entered in each cell is shown below the Excel sheet.

The planner

We often refer to the role of the 'planner'. Terminology varies between organizations, but in this book the term includes buyers, supply chain analysts, purchasing officers or whoever is responsible for planning the purchasing or management of inventory.

The use of Excel

The book can be read without the added use of Excel should you so wish. We believe there is great value in the reading of the book without investigating the calculations in any depth. However, there is the additional benefit, should you wish to use it, of creating a plan using the step-by-step Excel exercises.

The use of Excel within business is both a blessing and a curse. The ease with which data can be extracted and manipulated means that often planners prefer to plan with Excel and as a result do not use the planning system, for example in Materials Requirements Planning (MRP). The intention in this book is to allow the reader to create a plan whose results can be transferred back into the planning system, which will encourage more effective use of it. There is a presumption that you will be familiar with Excel and have a good working knowledge of the basic features and some knowledge of more advanced features.

You should be comfortable using the following Excel features:

- VLOOKUP;
- CHOOSE;

- DSUM;
- Complex IF statements;
- FILTER; and
- pivot tables.

The use of the formulae is entirely the reader's responsibility: no liability for use/misuse will be accepted. If the reader does not understand what the function is doing, they should not use it in a business situation unless they have fully understood the input and output of the model. The examples are intended to assist in guiding the user in the correct use of the tools.

How the book is arranged

Chapter 1 Introduction to inventory management. This chapter looks at the essentials of inventory management, and breaks it down into the three key components: planning, control, and balancing. The chapter introduces how business planning and control systems (eg MRP) are used to support the management of inventory. The journey through the book is discussed and five milestones are introduced. The chapter concludes with surfacing the supply/demand planning dilemma.

Chapter 2 Business systems and business. This chapter begins by looking at a brief history of business systems and why we need them today. It then considers the basic business processes and the guidelines for implementation and management of the business systems.

Chapter 3 Inventory balancing and control. Inventory balancing and control are considered. They operate both at a tactical and, primarily, at an operational (or transactional) level. Inventory balancing is the routine management of the supply-demand relationship, returning inventory levels that have veered away from the plan back to where they should be (eg managing overage and backlog). Inventory control is both the management of the physical inventory, and ensuring that the physical inventory is correctly reflected in the system records (eg holding and moving inventory).

Chapter 4 The complexity of inventory management within business systems. The essence of this chapter is to examine why inventory management has become so complex, where the real problems lie and what the simple approaches are to successful management. At the end of this chapter the reader will have a good understanding of the problems facing an operations manager and the planner.

Chapter 5 Stack and flow inventories. In simplistic terms, inventory is either being stored (Stacked) or is being processed (Flowing). When the inventory is stationary (ie in a stack) we need to optimize, as it may not be adding value. When it is moving (ie flowing) we need to maximize the speed of progress and to ensure there are a minimum of non-value add process steps. Techniques that are designed to help identify and manage inventory stack and flow are examined.

Chapter 6 Traditional thinking in inventory optimization. This is the first of the technical chapters that look in detail at the current tools available for planning the optimum inventory level. It covers the planning of the cycle stock and safety stock and concludes by looking at techniques that can be used for aggregate planning. In this chapter the reader will begin to build working inventory models that can be utilized within their own businesses.

Chapter 7 k-*curve methodology.* This chapter will show how the economic order quantity (EOQ) and Pareto techniques were combined to create the *k*-curve methodology. It shows how *k*-curve methodology builds on traditional approaches and addresses the weakness of EOQ and Pareto approaches. As with Chapter 4, the reader will be able to build inventory models: these can be experimented with to aid understanding and appreciation of the techniques.

Chapter 8 The practical application of k-*curve.* This chapter builds on Chapter 7 to show how the *k*-curve approach can be used as part of an inventory planning process. It takes as an example the case of planning a 20 per cent reduction of a company with £9 million inventory spread across 5,000 parts with a turnover just short of £100 million. By the end of the chapter the reader should be able to apply the technique to their own business data.

Chapter 9 Case study examples of k-*curve planning approach.* Illustrated by case studies of successful implementations, Chapter 9 looks at the issues of implementing *k*-curve successfully: what are the steps and who needs to be involved? The relevance of the *k*-curve approach to the pressures of business operations today is discussed. The business drive to reduce inventory and cost is reviewed and shows how these are often in conflict with the desire to increase customer service. Techniques are detailed to show how to decide when inventory reduction has gone far enough.

Chapter 10 Review, summary and what to do next. This chapter briefly revisits some of the key messages, covering the three pillars of inventory management, which is discussed throughout the book. The business planning and control systems (MRP, ERP, etc) are reviewed, within which the instructions for the aligned inventory plans must be structured (ie management of parameters), which result in the purchase and production orders being raised and transacted. The impact of new technology on the future of inventory management is considered, together with a final review of all the tools that have been introduced throughout the whole book, and which finally comprise the inventory management toolkit. The book will conclude with a review of the tools and techniques used throughout this book and suggested next steps for anyone eager to improve their inventory management and put the messages of this book into effect.

We really hope this book will help you make a difference in your business.

Reference

Relph, G J (2006) Inventory Management in Business Systems, PhD thesis, Manchester University

Introduction to inventory management 01

Introduction

Almost all organizations use computer systems of one sort or another to help manage their business. Most of them also have a good deal of cash tied up in inventory, from which they need to get a good return on the ongoing investment. This chapter brings together these two fundamental business concerns – effective use of business systems and getting value from money tied up in them. The main question is how to optimize inventory within the business system. No distinction is made in this book between the use of the words 'inventory' and 'stock'.

Inventory (or stock) covers all the goods and materials that an organization owns or holds, and to which a business intends to add value before selling. The dichotomy of inventory is that inventory held ties up working capital (because it costs money and therefore less is better) but it is necessary to have something to add value to and sell (because we need the inventory to ensure product availability and therefore more is perceived as better).

The dichotomy of inventory is that inventory held ties up working capital (because it costs money and therefore less is better) but it is necessary to have something to add value to and sell (because we need the inventory to ensure product availability and therefore more is perceived as better).

Business systems are designed to help to manage inventory but need to be given precise instructions to do so. The problem comes when these instructions are generalized or delegated ad hoc to individuals within the organization and not coordinated or aligned to the business goals. Many businesses fail to effectively synchronize the vision and strategy of their business with the detailed inventory management decisions needed to define the system parameters. This is precisely the challenge that this book sets out to meet.

This challenge is confirmed by (Jonsson and Mattsson, 2006), whose analysis of companies from 1993 to 2006 stated:

> It could be thus concluded that a common way of determining parameters such as order quantities and safety stocks is by general judgement and experience. Only a minority of companies applied formal calculations and optimizations. Parameters used in materials planning methods are reviewed rather infrequently, typically once a year or less in over half the companies.

Availability of software is such that from small businesses upwards these systems will be used to manage the company. The systems will need to use either simple re-order point (ROP) logic (based on historical usage) or Material Requirements Planning (MRP) logic (based on forecast of future demand) for purchasing and inventory planning. Whichever one is used, three decisions need to be made:

1. what quantity and how often to purchase raw material;
2. how to protect against variations in supply and demand;
3. how long it will take to make/deliver the item.

All these decisions produce inventory. And inventory costs money.

The inventory budget is typically set in the boardroom as a financial amount as part of a business plan. The decisions of what inventory to hold must be taken at a detail level – what items, where, when, what quantity? Determining the link between the boardroom budget and the item-level decisions has been the challenge for operations managers and planning teams for a long time.

It is this critical linkage that this book sets out to examine. We first consider the issues facing operations managers, then move on to review the tools and techniques used today. Finally, we show how they can be extended to utilize the proven *k*-curve methodology (KCM).

k-*curve methodology*

k-curve methodology (KCM) is a practical way of implementing the *k*-curve technique, ie the optimization of inventory volumes by grouping items into categories and thereby the identification of their ideal order frequencies and quantities. The relationship between the order size and frequency on one hand and the capability of the business to manage the resulting activity on the other is a critical factor in KCM.

KCM was conceived in the 1990s through research between IBM and Aston University. The approach was used by IBM in its manufacturing plant in Havant, and subsequently used by the IBM consultants working with IBM's major clients. The IBM research centre in Zurich developed software to support the consulting teams in early 2000. When Geoff Relph left IBM and set up Inventory Matters, he continued the research work and used KCM to support his clients in the understanding and management of inventory. Inventory Matters' own software was developed in 2007.

This book provides a step-by-step guide on how KCM achieves the linkage between the business budget decisions and the detail level on parameter settings at item level. The reader will be able to construct a working KCM model that will, in a simplified form, enable you to analyse and plan inventory using this approach. This chapter sets the stage:

- We first discuss the fundamental principles of inventory management.
- Second, we examine the issues and relationships between the business systems designed to manage inventory and the problems of achieving the business goal.
- And finally, we examine the essential costs and the need for flexibility within business operations.

Inventory and inventory management

Inventory is the stock of any item held in an organization. The aim is, naturally, to have the right amount, in the right place, at the right time and the right cost.

Inventory management sets out to achieve just that. It is the process of directing and administering the holding, moving and converting of raw materials through value-adding processes to deliver finished products to the customer. The efficient and effective management of inventory (or stock) is important to almost every organization. The ordering and managing of inventory is nothing new; it is known to date back at least as far as the ancient Egyptians, as shown by inventory management records on papyrus fragments held by the Louvre in France:

> The solar temple... sent goods from various agricultural centres or services to the funerary temple... Three columns [in the table] were devoted to each product: the expected quantities to be delivered, the actual amount delivered, and the remainder due. (Bernadette Letellier)

In simple terms, inventory management:

- is the set of policies and controls that monitor levels of inventory;
- determines what levels of each product should be maintained;
- identifies when stock should be replenished;
- decides how large orders should be.

Figure 1.1 Optimum inventory tightrope

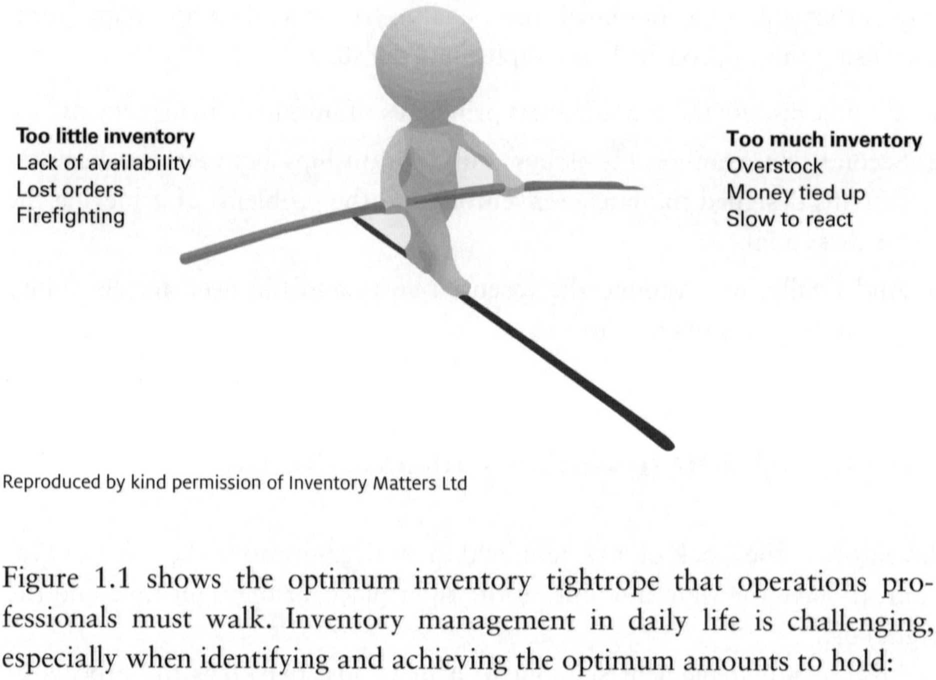

Reproduced by kind permission of Inventory Matters Ltd

Figure 1.1 shows the optimum inventory tightrope that operations professionals must walk. Inventory management in daily life is challenging, especially when identifying and achieving the optimum amounts to hold:

- Holding *too little inventory* of the required products often leads to customer orders being unfulfilled on time, or perhaps lost altogether. This can put the business at risk since *lost orders* may lose a customer altogether, and dissatisfied customers often complain about lack of availability. If this dissatisfaction spreads, the long-term impact causes a reduction in profitability. Another problem when too little inventory is held is the time and energy then needed to manage the shortage. *Fire-fighting*, although often accompanied by a feeling of success, uses a great deal of time and energy. Wherever possible, the upfront management of inventory to ensure that sufficient product is being held is a far more valuable use of time.

- Holding *too much inventory* – being 'over-stock'– is also problematic. Money is not only tied up in the purchase of unnecessary stock but is also spent on the holding and managing of that inventory. If too much working capital is tied up for too long then cash flow may be affected, and buying-in of inventory of other much-needed products may be compromised.
- *Over-stock* also impacts on the space where inventory is held, whether on the shop-floor or in a warehouse. The over-stock items need space to be stored, space that cannot then be used for the normally rotating products, and in extreme situations additional warehousing space may need to be bought.
- Another problem when too much inventory is being held is that an organization will find it more *difficult to react to changes* quickly. The change may be due to demand in the marketplace, where requirements may change very quickly. Alternatively, the change may be in engineering or design, which may happen because of health and safety or quality reasons, or due to an upgrade in development. When large amounts of inventory are held, the number of parts that need to have changes made to them is correspondingly large and changes cannot be made through the system quickly.

For every part held within an organization there is an ideal quantity of inventory which lies within an optimum range. The ideal range is based on a wide range of factors, for example demand, variability of the demand, unit cost of the item, size of the product, shelf-life (if any) and the time it takes to supply/manufacture the product. Determining this ideal is explored further in later chapters when the inventory saw-tooth and the economics of stock balancing are discussed.

It is quite usual for demand to vary within an expected range in many businesses. Unexpected changes in customer demand or product supply will affect inventory plans, which in turn may push inventory holdings out of the ideal range. The sooner a business knows about changes in supply or demand, either within its own organization or elsewhere in its supply chain, the quicker it can react and calculate the impact of those variations, and the closer it will be able to stay to the new ideal volumes.

The three pillars of inventory management

Inventory can be held in many places within an organization – for example, raw materials, components and finished goods in warehouses, work in progress and feed-stock on the shop floor. Wherever it is held it needs to be managed.

Inventory management has three key pillars, as shown in Figure 1.2:

- **Inventory Planning:** determining the optimum level.
- **Inventory Control:** managing the integrity of the stock.
- **Inventory Balancing:** balancing the on-going supply/demand relationship.

Figure 1.2 The three pillars of inventory management: plan, control and balance

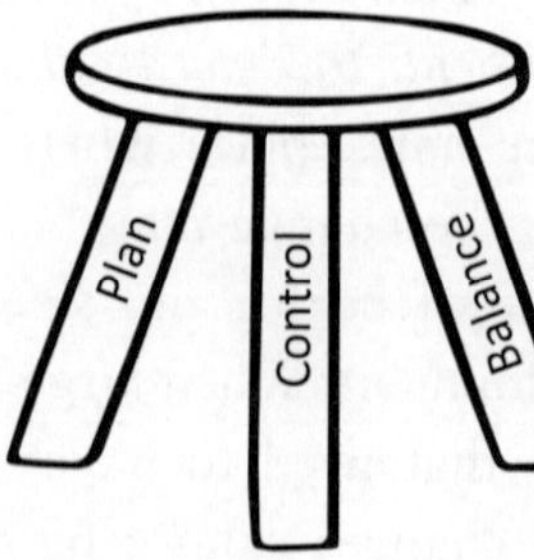

Reproduced by kind permission of Inventory Matters Ltd

Inventory planning

Inventory planning is about determining the optimum levels of inventory both for today and the future:

- The purpose of creating the plan is to identify the optimum inventory levels. This will involve understanding demand patterns, what value-add is needed for each product (eg manufacturing requirements, retail volumes and sales locations, military and medical consumption levels), and deciding what inventory categories each product should be in.
- The inventory plan must aim to match the high-level business needs with what is possible at the detailed item level, ie in order to meet the expected demand for the products to be sold by the business, what products should be held, where and in what volumes, and at what cost?

- A key feature of the plan is to identify and manage the parameters that need to be set within the business systems, which are needed to balance future stock levels (eg order frequencies, safety stock policies, minimum order quantities and lead times).

Inventory planning is the main focus area of this book.

Inventory control

Inventory control is about managing the integrity of the stock. Data accuracy is essential:

- Inventory moves through a physical process. The physical movements need to be tracked by system transactions to accurately reflect where inventory is in the process and in what quantities.
- It is necessary to ensure that the system records of each product match the physical inventory held.

Inventory control is also, obviously, about the management of the physical inventory. This is a critical and essential part of inventory management. As Gwynne Richards (2013) says: 'Warehouses are now seen as a vital cog within today's supply chain' and this is well covered in his book *Warehouse Management*. Important warehouse topics include:

- Warehouse locations: regional and local warehouses and movement of products in between.
- Warehouse routine management, including:
  - order-picking strategies, systems and sequencing;
  - storage and material handling equipment, and location numbering;
  - packaging and labelling: hazardous goods information, degree of automation, bar coding and radio frequency identification (RFID);
  - sustainability: how to introduce and use environmentally friendly methods to save energy;
  - stock checking and audits: perpetual checks and annual checks; external audits;
  - key performance measures;
  - outsourcing options, including:
    use of consignment stocks;

use of an external company to assist in managing inventory, eg vendor-managed inventory (VMI).

- Transportation:
  - transportation options and costs:
    road, rail, sea, air;
    comparing and calculating emissions;
    multimodal options.
  - national infrastructure and its impact on transport choices;
  - load calculations and pallet configuration;
  - safety, risks and good practice;
  - outsourcing considerations and costings:
    third- and fourth-party logistics providers (3PL and 4PL);
    benefits and risks.

Inventory control is a large topic in itself. For those who wish to focus on this in more detail later, it can be read about in more detail in Gwynne Richards' book and elsewhere.

In Chapter 3 of this book we cover the key points of inventory control, since both excellent data integrity and good management of the physical stock are of fundamental importance in inventory management.

Inventory balancing

Inventory balancing is required to manage the success of the inventory plan on a daily or weekly basis:

- Is the rate of supply (eg goods-in) as expected?
- Is the rate of demand (eg goods-out) as expected?
- Is the flow of inventory through the process as expected?
- Is the process in balance from the supply to the through-put to the fulfilment of customer demand?

Inventory balancing is about managing the supply/demand relationship:

- The daily managing of the ongoing supply/demand relationship.
- Is the inventory flowing properly today?
- Is the plan working?

Inventory balancing is normally managed by the business systems. When systems manage inventory balancing well, they are based on:

- good inventory planning, for example clear categorization of parts and correct setting of parameters;
- good inventory control, for example accurate data and good management of the physical stock;
- good performance measurements, for example good exception management.

Inventory balancing examples will be used in later chapters in this book to show how the business systems calculations are made within the planning engine (MRP/MPS – material requirements planning/master production schedule).

Key performance indicators (KPIs) for inventory planning, balancing and control

Key performance indicators (KPIs) measure and monitor a company's strategic and operational performance towards set targets. Financial, management, customer and growth KPIs are set to focus a company on achieving its strategic aims, which are then cascaded down to the operational level to ensure daily performance remains in line with strategy. A 'balanced scorecard' and the supply chain operations reference model (SCOR) are both useful structures to use when setting KPIs (Rushton, Croucher and Baker, 2017).

A fundamental performance KPI used by many companies is On Time In Full (OTIF), which identifies what percentage of customer orders are delivered to the correct location on time and in full. It is an important KPI which demonstrates both a good degree of customer focus and good cooperation between many departments. Its relevance to inventory management is clear, since planning is carried out to achieve the known and forecast customer demand, and control and balancing work to the inventory plan.

Key differences between the three aspects of inventory management are illustrated with example inventory tasks broken into the areas of planning, balancing and control, with their related key performance indicators (KPIs) listed in Table 1.1. For example, in inventory balancing, one essential task given is 'manage supply demand' and the KPI given which relates to that is '% availability'. This therefore relates to the OTIF KPI, which in turn will relate to customer satisfaction.

Table 1.1 Example tasks and related key performance indicators in each of the three areas of inventory planning, balancing and control

Inventory Planning	Tasks	KPI
Example:		
Maintain optimum stock	Set maximum levels	Depot availability Stock holding (case / £) Warehouse space requirement
	Set minimum levels	Depot availability
	Safety stock levels	Safety stock investment
	Set lead-times	Replenishment times
	Set (MOQ) Minimum Order Quantities	Purchase spend
	Order pattern/frequency	Number of receipts planned/day
	Vehicle fill	Weeks of cover
	Promotion planning	No of promotions
	Seasonal planning	No of promotions Depot space requirements

Inventory Control	Tasks	KPI
Example:		
Ensure stock accuracy	Book-stock	Accuracy of count
	Missed picks Damage	Reduction in WoW %
	Store returns	Booked back on stock within xx hours
	Shrinkage	Stock write-off
	Pick rate	Cases picked / shift

Table 1.1 *continued*

Inventory Control	Tasks	KPI
	Stock Check Accuracy	% Loss / Gain adjustments
	Intake Accuracy	Missed picks Supplier compliance to delivery specification
	Scanning Errors	% Loss / Gain adjustments
	Receipt Damage	Returns / Claims
	Bulk Capacity – stock in right place	Internal Stock Movements

Inventory Balancing	Tasks	KPI
Example:		
Manage the supply demand	Cancellation of orders eg weather	Non-moving stock levels
	Non-moving stocks	Aged Inventory > x days
	Forecast error/bias	No of exceptions Trigger levels for exceptions
	Constraints	Short coded cases (life)
	Minimum Order Quantities	Shortages to stores
	Overstock management	% Space available No of short codes Promotion of overstock
	Manage Supply and Demand	% Availability
	Manage out of ordinary	Exception management

Reproduced by kind permission of Inventory Matters Ltd

Inventory planning pyramid

Inventory reduction is seen as a good route to:

- increase profitability;
- reduce costs; and
- become more agile and responsive.

An instruction from senior management within a company to 'reduce inventory by 25 per cent' gives a clear direction of what is wanted, but often without a clear indication of how it can be achieved.

The relationship between these different views, and the process flows that link them, is shown in the inventory planning pyramid in Figure 1.3.

The following areas of a company will be interested in inventory availability and cost and therefore affected in different ways by a significant reduction in it:

Figure 1.3 The inventory planning pyramid

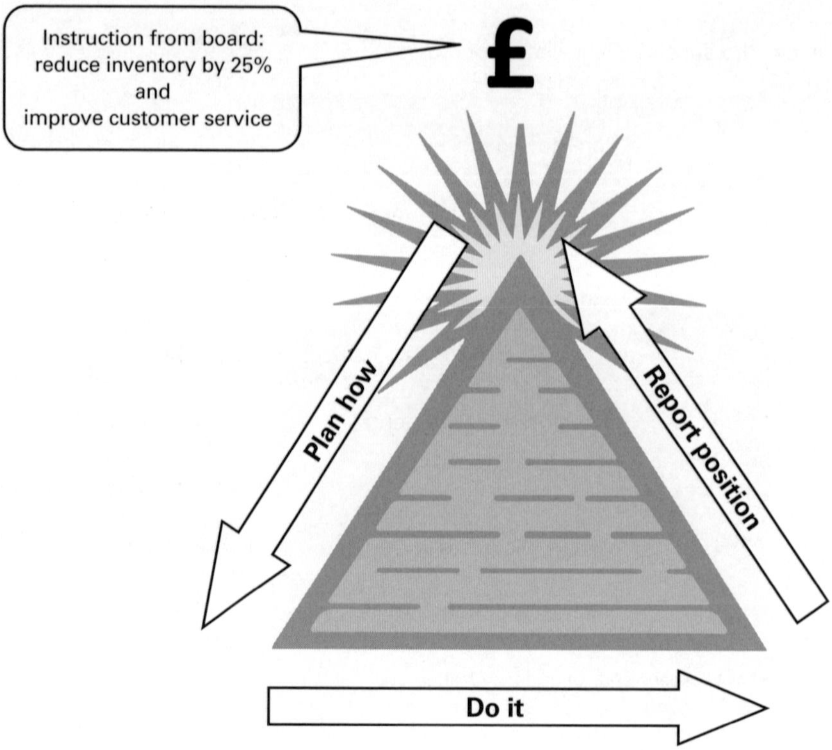

Reproduced by kind permission of Inventory Matters Ltd

- sales and marketing;
- customer service;
- after sales;
- warehousing and logistics;
- manufacturing;
- finance.

We will now look at this important relationship and the process steps in the inventory planning pyramid in more detail.

Report position

The first step in the inventory planning pyramid is to 'report the current position':

- Has the previous plan achieved the required reduction?
- What is the impact on customer service and product availability?
- Are there critical inventory items that were needed, and why?
- What items am I short of, what do I have too much of?
- What do my customers want?

As shown in Figure 1.4, by breaking down the inventory planning pyramid, this first step will include identifying the stock data from the MRP system.

Instruction from the board

Senior management should view good inventory management as a critical part of effectively managing a business. However, a call from the board to reduce inventory volumes and costs often lacks any real understanding of the impact at a part level, and the resulting impact this might have on product availability for customers. This is the responsibility of the operations management people, who must consider how this could be done and report back on the consequences of any reductions.

Plan how

The next step in the inventory planning pyramid is to plan how to achieve the reduction. To plan this reduction the operations manager will need to

Figure 1.4 Breaking down the inventory planning pyramid

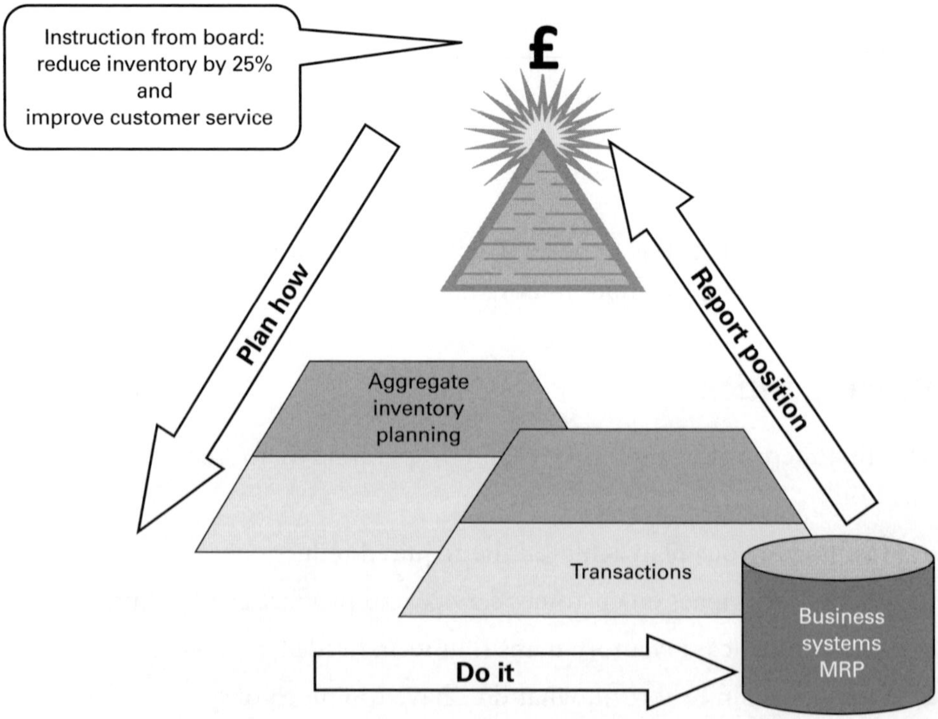

decide which of the many parts (often 10,000 and frequently more) can have their stock levels reduced. This will involve a detailed understanding of not only the part's value, but any issues related to its supply and demand, and its relative importance to the business. We will look in detail at ways of doing this in Chapters 4, 5 and 6.

Do it

Once the 'plan how' is decided, the next step can be started. To do this, instructions need to be given to the planning and control systems within the business system, for example, the production schedule via MPS or the manufacturing/materials plan via MRP or MRPII. The MPS or MRP use these instructions to perform a series of planning calculations. Systems often give planners the opportunity to try this out in a what-if scenario:

- The instructions are given through the setting of system parameters (for example, lead time, minimum batch size, safety stock) which result in suggested order quantities.

- The planning system uses these parameter settings to calculate orders and thus volume of inventory that will be produced as a consequence.
- The ability of the system and the business processes to continue to satisfy customers with the reduction in inventory levels can be measured with key performance indicators (KPIs) such as stock availability measured against demand, non-compliance, etc.

This book sets out the process and tools needed to enable the use of the inventory planning pyramid. Figure 1.5 shows the four steps in the pyramid which can be used to link the high-level financial instruction to reduce inventory with the detailed implications of that reduction at an item-by-item and parameter-by-parameter level.

We have also talked about the process flow in the planning pyramid. Managing processes well is of fundamental importance in a successful business.

We will examine the way in which companies can effectively manage the relationship between their processes, their organization (and people), and their technology (or systems) in Chapters 2 and 3.

Figure 1.5 Translating financial saving to detailed items in the inventory planning pyramid

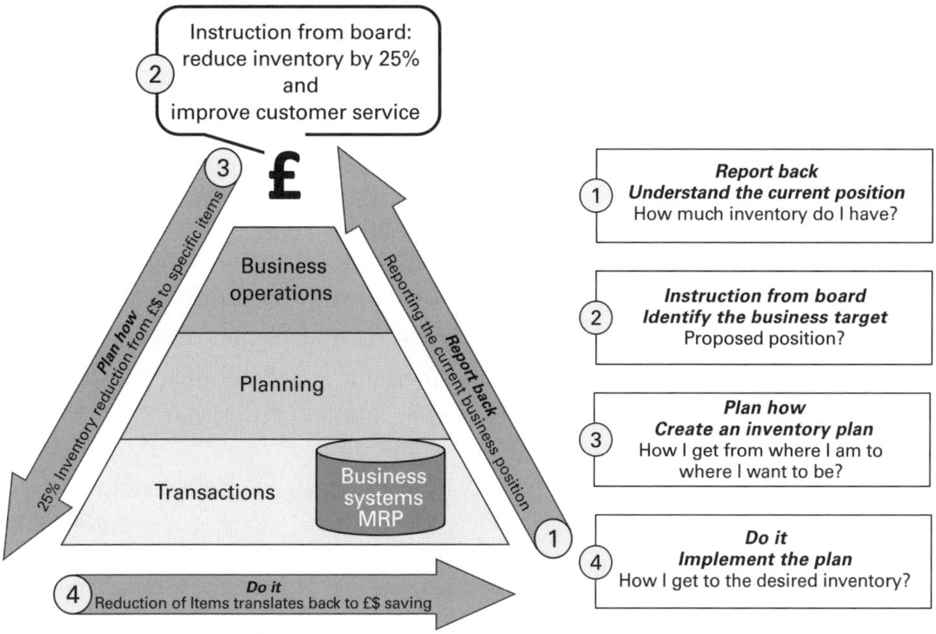

Understanding the inventory planning pyramid allows a company to address the following questions, and determine 'how' to carry it out and what the implications are likely to be:

- Does your company have too much money tied up in stock?
- Does it make sense to reduce your inventory by 25 per cent?
- Would you like to understand where you'd be at risk?

Management of inventory in business systems

As we have already said, all organizations plan and most use business systems to help them. It is essential to be able to create the best inventory plans in such a way that they work with the business systems in an organization. These planning and control systems help manage all three elements of the three inventory pillars of planning, control and balancing.

Planning

Materials requirement planning is the principal tool used to execute the inventory plan. It utilizes BOMs (bills of materials) to define what is needed and the MPS to define what is wanted and when. When the optimal parameters are defined (by the planners) the MRP system will drive the business towards the optimal inventory.

Control

By capturing all the transactions made (ordering products, receiving goods, moving through processes, storing locations within the process) the systems enable the control needed to facilitate tracking and finding stock. Accurate records ensure that when the MRP is planned it is based on an accurate foundation of what is in stock, what is needed and what is on order.

Balancing

As the demand (inevitably) changes, these MRP planning systems will recalculate requirements. MRP has to take account of the differences with the original plan, and to make adjustments to the stock levels and order due dates in order to reflect the increase and decrease in demand. The system will output instructions to the planners detailing which orders are to be brought forward, pushed back and, if needed, cancelled.

An overview of the importance of inventory management within business systems is considered here, with Chapter 2 looking at the planning engine within business systems in more detail.

A good, well-installed system will help people within a business to make speedier and better-informed decisions. Vollmann *et al* (2005: 4) say that the 'system does not make the decisions or manage the operations – managers perform those activities. The system provides the support for them to do so wisely.'

As shown in the inventory planning pyramid in Figure 1.5, it is essential to be able to link between the different levels within a business:

- Communicating in a meaningful way is essential from the very top of an organization to the shop floor and back again. This is no different whether the message being communicated is about new products, business success and direction, profitability or cost of inventory held. The difference with inventory is often that the communication on inventory from the top of a business is in a different language to that used by planners and on the shop floor, and needs translating from financial amounts into parts held, and back again. The inventory communication goes from company vision to strategy to tactical planning to operational planning to transactional execution and back again.
- The ability to communicate the inventory requirements and implications between the different levels in a meaningful way is essential for businesses and is a key topic for this book.

Process flow

Organizations tend to follow the same process flow (see Figure 1.6) ie forecast, plan and execute:

- Forecast: deciding what future demand and requirements are anticipated and need to be met.
- Plan: the determination of how to do it.
- Execute: putting the plan into action and ensuring that what is achieved will correctly meet the business need.

Figure 1.6 Process flow from forecast to execute

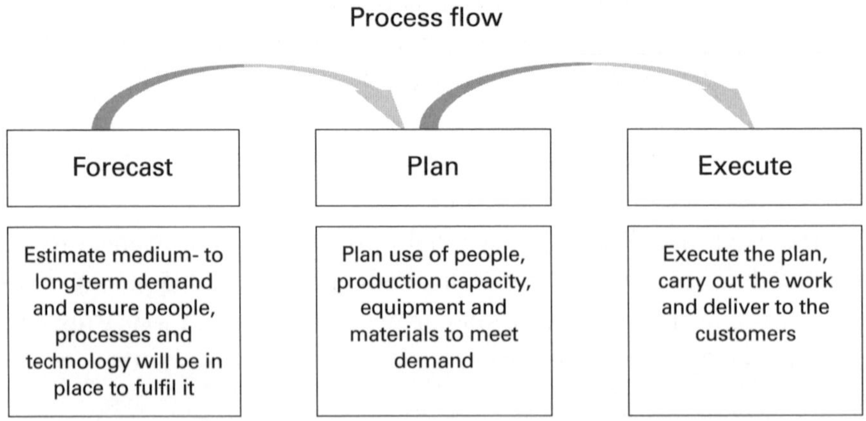

Transactions within the planning engine

Many of the transactions within the planning engine of a business system are involved with inventory. Accurate data and careful management of these activities is essential to allow the planning engine to calculate a meaningful output.

Vollmann, Berry and Whybark (1998: 2) identified inventory-related tasks within the planning engine:

- Production planning: plan when materials need to arrive and in what quantities.
- Maintain necessary inventory levels: inventories of raw materials, work in progress, and finished goods at the appropriate levels and in the correct locations need to be managed.
- Track and record resources: accurate and up-to-date information on customers' orders, people, material, equipment, tooling, etc.
- Communicate with stakeholders: keep customers and suppliers informed on specific issues as well as managing long-term relationships; communicate appropriately with other stakeholders.
- Build in flexibility: uncertainty in demand may be hard to anticipate. Customer requirements need to be understood and orders met nevertheless.
- Respond when issues arise: identify and carry out the correct response when unexpected problems arise.

- Communicate with other functions: provide information 'to other functions on the physical and financial implications of the manufacturing activities'.

This list gives a clear idea why it is essential that good inventory planning and inventory control is in place before the system performs its calculations and transactions.

Business planning systems

The planning engine within a business system calculates production requirements based on the known or estimated future demand. The planning engine may be based on a re-order point (ROP) calculation, or on a manufacturing requirement planning calculation.

The business system may be called an enterprise requirement planning (ERP) system. The key elements and the differences between ERP, MRPI and MRPII are shown in Figure 1.7.

Re-order point logic, according to the APICS body of knowledge, is defined as:

> A re-order point is calculated for each independent demand item. When inventory levels drop to the re-order point, a signal is sent to replenish inventory in a fixed quantity amount. The reorder point is equal to the expected demand during lead time plus safety stock to cover demand in excess of expectations.
>
> (APICS, 2016)

The difference between MRP logic and ROP is that MRP is time-phased and based on future demand, whereas ROP is based on an average of past demand.

Business planning systems are discussed further in Chapter 2.

Lean and JIT

Lean and 'just in time' (JIT) processes are not based on business systems but are philosophies, processes or techniques used by companies. Lean and JIT were popularized in the 1980s when exported from Japan following their success at reinvigorating the Japanese industry post-WWII. Lean and JIT are process-driven approaches, although transactions such as Kanban triggers are not incorporated into some ERP systems. Where JIT production techniques are employed there tends to be a reduced need for all operations to be

Figure 1.7 MRP to MRPII to ERP

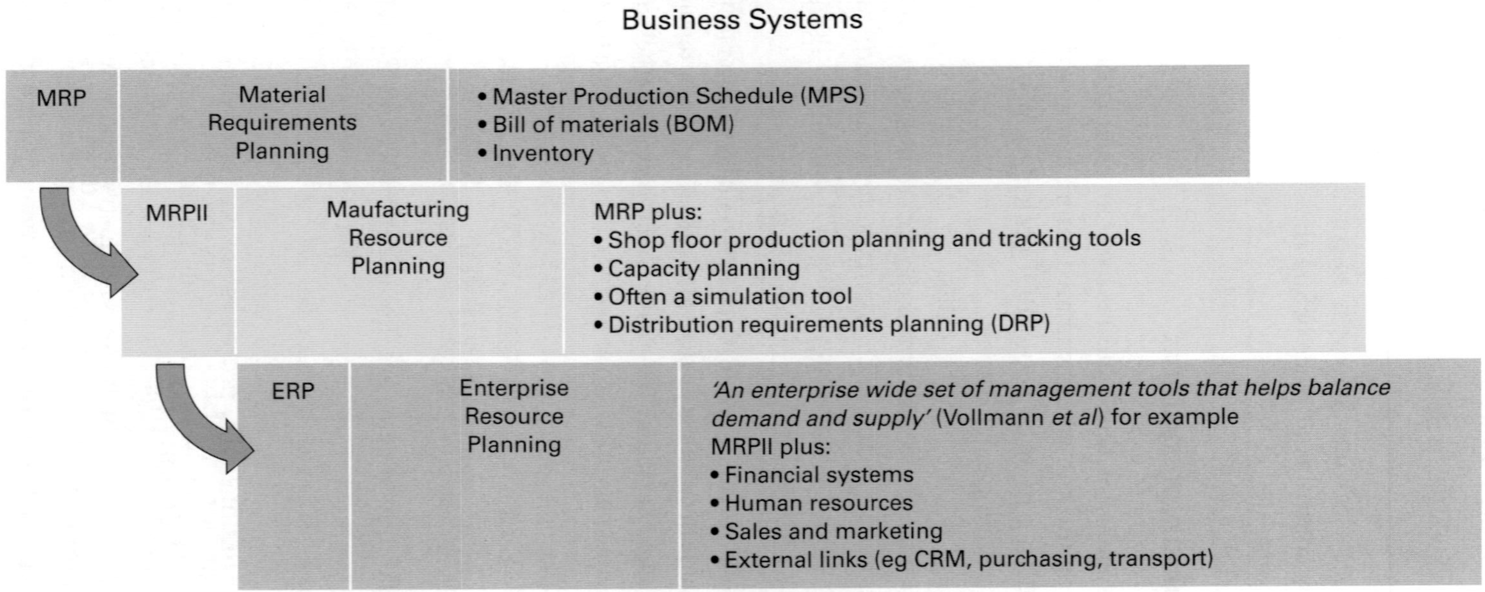

recorded within the business system, although some recording will still be necessary. The processes are designed to self-regulate the management of inventory levels and movement. The effect that Lean and JIT have on inventory will be considered in more detail in Chapter 2.

The cost of inventory and the ability to react to change

Cost of inventory

Inventory has four main costs:

- Unit price cost of the inventory: this is the price paid per unit for the volume of product bought. It is fairly common for large orders to attract a reduction in the unit price paid. 'Price breaks' are often offered for different order volumes (for example, to buy a quantity of 100 t-shirts @ £8.00, 500 @ £5.00, 1,000 @ £4.00). Unit price is a reasonably obvious number because it is the price paid when the items arrive or leave the business.
- Cost of ordering inventory/cost of set-up:
  - Cost of ordering inventory: there is a cost associated with order placement, including the cost of placing the order as well as the cost of packaging and transporting the order, and the cost of receiving or issuing materials. This is less easy to calculate than the unit price cost, and is explored further in Chapter 6 when economic order quantity is discussed (EOQ).
  - Cost of set-up: there is a cost to set up a machine or workstation when changing over from producing product A to product B. This set-up time will take x minutes or hours, and the cost of set-up is then allocated to the number of items in the production run (for example, if the set-up time is two hours and the production run is 120, one set-up minute has been spent per item; alternatively, if the set-up time is two hours and the production run is 12, 10 set-up minutes have been spent per item). A common approach used to improve/reduce the set-up times is known as SMED (Single Minute Exchange of Die), developed by Shigeo Shingo.
- Cost of holding inventory: the cost of holding inventory is more difficult again to calculate. This cost includes warehousing and handling costs

(renting, heating, lighting, insurance, and personnel), the cost of having the money tied up in inventory (working capital costs), risk costs (eg obsolescence, deterioration, shrinkage or evaporation) and opportunity costs (the lost opportunity to invest elsewhere, etc).

- Cost of shortage: there is another inventory cost that may be considered: the cost of shortage or lost sales. This cost is the loss of the revenue opportunity when a business has been unable to meet demand, and the known or estimated unmet demand is allocated a cost. The evaluation of this cost is very difficult because it is not always possible to know when you have failed to deliver. This is considered in Chapter 6 where safety stock considerations are discussed.

The supply/demand dilemma

It is very important for businesses to be able to react to changes in the marketplace within their supply chains. This is possible where: there is a desire to make changes; there are clear market signals; there is good information available within the supply chain; and when optimum amounts of inventory are held.

The ability to react to change

An example of this was demonstrated in the automotive industries in the US Great Depression of the late 1920s and 1930s. General Motors was able to remain profitable during this time, while Ford was losing money during the 1930s 'because it was disorganized' (Sloan, 2013):

> What accounts for this exceptional record [of GM paying dividends throughout the 1930s] in a period when many durable-goods producers failed or came close to bankruptcy? ... I think that... we had simply learned how to react quickly. This was perhaps the greatest pay-off of our system of financial and operating controls. (Sloan, 2013)

This lesson is one that repeated itself with the economic downturn in 2008 and the severe impact on the automotive industries in the United Kingdom. The following quotes show how purchasing of cars fell drastically at this time and how the car manufacturers reacted:

> From end Jan 2009 'carmaker Honda... shut its British factory for four months' because in December 2008 'In Britain, the number of cars rolling off production lines nearly halved'. (Kollewe, 2009)

This second quote shows how Toyota dealt with the economic downturn in a slightly different way:

> [Toyota] put its European workforce on a three-day week as it forecasts the biggest slump in car sales for 35 years ... Thierry Dombreval, chief operating officer, said it would be 'foolish' to take short-term decisions to close plants needed in the longer term. 'These are assets for the future'. (Gow, 2009)

In addition to taking a long-term view, Toyota was also aware that they wanted to avoid building inventory levels too high, since they were confident that they would easily be able to increase production levels once sales started to take off again.

Both car companies reacted to the change in demand from the market by reducing the rate at which they were producing their end products. Since the products were not selling, they had an urgent need to stop building up excess stocks of inventory. This reaction to the economic shock of 2008 was repeated across a wide range of industries. The industries have, over the past 50 years, developed very tight and reactive supply chains which have increased their capabilities to react to economic shocks.

An example of a non-automotive company that worked hard to reduce their number of suppliers and create truly strategic partnerships is Boeing with the Dreamliner. The strategic decision to involve suppliers in the design and production of the Boeing 787 Dreamliner was made partly as a way of reducing design time, reducing costs and ensuring total commitment from a single-source supplier. There was, however, an unexpected consequence when there was a major production disruption following the 2011 earthquake in Japan. The Japanese manufacturers at that time were producing '35 per cent of the 787, 20 per cent of the 777, and 15 per cent of the 767. What they build can't be duplicated anywhere else, and Boeing can't call in a new supplier to make one piece if it runs short' (Ray, 2011).

The natural disaster demonstrated one of the risks of running a Lean supply chain: when this happens the low volumes of inventory held means that there is a very small buffer of components and sub-assemblies to keep production going. The benefits of a single source supplier need to be balanced with a good risk analysis of what to do if it all goes wrong.

This example shows how at the strategic level the drive for Lean business can expose a business's ability to cope with catastrophic shocks. This dilemma is summarized in Figure 1.8.

Figure 1.8 Supply demand planning dilemma

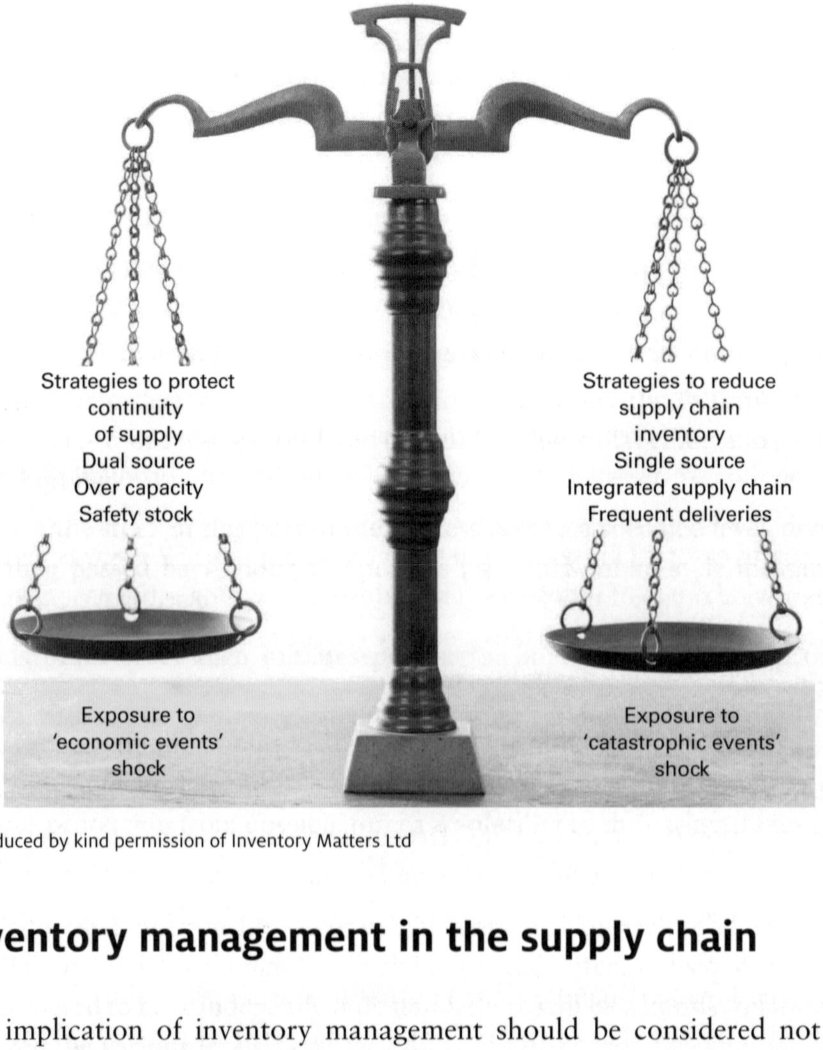

Reproduced by kind permission of Inventory Matters Ltd

Inventory management in the supply chain

The implication of inventory management should be considered not just within a single organization but across the whole supply chain. Managing the steps in the journey of inventory throughout the supply chain is the responsibility of many different organizations (ie the sequence of steps from initial raw material via a series of value-adding processes to end customer and beyond) but the information on the steps in the journey can be shared.

The supply chain, logistics and operations management are all linked:

- Operations management is the organizing of value-adding activity within a business.
- Logistics is the placement of inventory throughout the supply chain at the right time and in the right place: transporting and warehousing of stock

has to be managed both within an organization (eg bins of nuts and bolts at a work station, or work in progress awaiting machine availability) and between organizations (eg tins of tomatoes being transported – in one or many stages – from a manufacturer to a retailer).

- The supply chain is the linking of the businesses and the processes involved with producing a product from the raw material to the end customer, and beyond to recycling or disposal for many products. Supply chain management, therefore, is the management of this supply chain, defined by Mentzer (2001) as:

> The systemic, strategic coordination of the traditional business functions and the tactics across these business functions within a particular company and across businesses within the supply chain, for the purposes of improving the long-term performance of the individual companies and the supply chain as a whole.

Sharing supply and demand information throughout the supply chain can have huge implications on the cost of creating a product.

Inventory management in the extended supply chain and the 'Beer Game'

We know that sharing supply and demand information throughout the supply chain can have huge implications and benefits for the cost of creating and manufacturing a product. The importance of developing the view of inventory management beyond the walls of a single organization and into the extended supply chain is well understood. One place where this was demonstrated was in research by Kevin Permenter of the Aberdeen Group in 2013, which focused on supply chain collaboration in consumer markets: these were identified as having a particularly high market pressure to perform well, in addition to an increasingly complex global customer-supplier network. One of the respondents to the 'Supply Chain Collaboration in the Consumer Markets' research is quoted in support of extended collaboration as saying:

> It is a no-brainer that collaboration can decrease material or distribution costs... and working with our suppliers and partners to react quickly and proactively to deal with packaging disclosure changes has been a huge boon to our cost structure. (Permenter, 2013)

The research concludes that collaboration – in both the external and the internal supply chains – and the speedy sending and receiving of information between the customers and suppliers along the supply chain are the way forward.

It is also possible to find examples of where increased collaboration along the supply chain has resulted in major problems for some or all of those involved. One example is the company GTAT, which was driven to bankruptcy and ceased trading on 15 October 2014 (Arthur, 2014), when it failed to deliver Sapphire screens to Apple. Another example is the Boeing Dreamliner. The message here is that extended collaboration along the supply chain needs to be entered into carefully by all parties, with an understanding of the risks as well as the benefits.

Less controversial is the benefit of speedy exchange of information up and down the supply chain. Despite being less controversial, a true understanding of the dangers of not taking this seriously may be hard to achieve within an organization. Alick Chia, MD of global company SKF Logistics, addressed this issue when he spoke about 'Logistics Challenges Today' at the Singapore Institute of Management on 27 November 2014, saying that he had used 'The Beer Game' to great effect in his company to instil a real understanding of the importance of communicating along the extended supply chain and the perils of not doing so.

The Beer Game was developed by the Massachusetts Institute of Technology (MIT) in the 1960s to demonstrate the impact of the Bullwhip or Forrester Effect (first documented by JW Forrester and identified by him in the 1950s), that is:

> An extreme change in the supply position upstream in a supply chain generated by a small change in demand downstream in the supply chain. Inventory can quickly move from being backordered to being excess. This is caused by the serial nature of communicating orders up the chain with the inherent transportation delays of moving product down the chain. The bullwhip effect can be eliminated by synchronizing the supply chain. (APICS, 2016)

The Beer Game, which has had several spin-off games, is a training technique developed to demonstrate the Forrester Effect. It gives the participants in the game first-hand experience of the confusion that can arise along a simple supply chain where demand varies only slightly but where there is a lack of communication. This results in wildly varying amounts of inventory being built and held and normally a feeling of chaos, mistrust and bewilderment.

A spin-off Beer Game developed by the Warwick Manufacturing Group (WMG) at Warwick University doesn't stop at the end of the initial stage, by which point confusion has normally reigned, but has interesting second and third stages:

- In the second stage, the teams are rearranged to gather together a single member of each of the 'companies' from the game's first stage. The new teams then collaborate in managing the supply chain, calculating the inventory and production needed with the variation in demand from the end customer.
- In the final stage, there is a further degree of control. The variation in demand is input directly into an Excel program which calculates the requirements along the whole supply chain to meet the change in demand. This final stage takes minutes to calculate, compared with the hour or more that the first stage of the game will have taken. It also demonstrates one of the benefits of using a computer system to assist in managing the information flow along the supply chain.

The benefits of sharing supply and demand information throughout the supply chain, with collaboration where there is sufficient trust and ability, are available to those companies who can make it work. The question of 'what do we have to do?' can be added to 'how do we do it?' by electronic communications between business systems. The Beer Game helps people experience the problems of the Forrester Effect for themselves in a risk-free environment, to perhaps assist towards greater integration in the extended supply chain.

Five milestones

Throughout this book we discuss many facets of inventory management in business systems.

The journey through the book has five key milestones:

1 We consider the business needs as they relate to inventory, together with and separately from systems.
   - The business needs:

     inventory available at the right place, time, quantity and quality, and at minimal cost;

     inventory to be well managed – ie planned, controlled and balanced.

- The systems:

    are used to communicate and coordinate throughout the business;

    assist planning and manage the product and service complexity;

    are used to control: the physical items (in the warehousing etc); data so that it matches the actual physical parts;

    are used to balance real-time progress and situations.

2 Inventory is considered in the way that it impacts the business at strategic, tactical and operational levels, as well as in many parts of the business from commercial to production and customer service to operations.

3 How to plan inventory as effectively as possible is examined, together with key measurements.

4 The inventory management toolbox is developed throughout the book, and the right tools and techniques are reviewed.

5 People are seen throughout the book as central to managing inventory. We also review how to ensure that systems support and assist people to work in alignment and focus together on the business needs.

Summary

Chapter 1 has given an overview of the three pillars of inventory management: planning, controlling and balancing. We have outlined what inventory and inventory management are, the importance of good inventory planning and why it is essential to be able to translate the high-level financial inventory needs of the business into what this means at an item level, and back again. On a practical level in most businesses, it means that the results of inventory planning decisions need to be routinely fed into the business systems. We have outlined the types of systems available and how using these business systems on a daily basis to execute both purchase and works orders can ensure inventory is well managed and optimum levels achieved. We have looked at the costs that are involved when making these inventory management decisions and the supply-demand dilemma that faces every business when planning inventory. Finally, we have outlined the five key milestones on the journey to excellent inventory management which will be taken through the book. The following chapters discuss how all this can be carried out in practice.

References

APICS (2016) *APICS Dictionary*, 15th edn, APICS, Chicago

Arthur, C (2014) The desperate struggle at the heart of the brutal Apple supply chain, Guardian [online] www.theguardian.com/technology/2014/nov/14/sapphire-gt-advanced--brutal-apple-supply-chain [accessed April 2019]

Chia, A (2014, 27 November) Logistics Challenges Today, interview with C Milner, Singapore Institute of Management

Gow, D (2009) Toyota's European workers face three-day week, Guardian [online] www.theguardian.com/business/2009/mar/03/toyota-car-crisis-europe [accessed April 2019]

Jonsson, P and Mattsson, S (2006) A longitudinal study of materials planning applications in manufacturing companies, *International Journal of Operations Production Management*, **26**, pp. 971–95

Kollewe, J (2009) Honda shuts UK factory for four months, *Guardian* [online] www.theguardian.com/business/2009/jan/30/honda-swindon-shutdown [accessed April 2019]

Letellier, B (nd) Inventory and accounts from a temple of Abusir, *Louvre* [online] from www.louvre.fr/en/oeuvre-notices/inventory-and-accounts-temple-abusir [accessed April 2019]

Mentzer, J T (2001) Defining supply chain management, *Journal of Business Logistics*, **22** (2), pp. 1–25

Permenter, K (2013) Supply chain collaboration in the consumer markets, CH Robinson white paper – Aberdeen Group Research

Ray, S A (2011) The downside of just-in-time inventory, *Business Week* [online] www.bloomberg.com/news/articles/2011-03-24/the-downside-of-just-in-time-inventory [accessed April 2019]

Richards, G (2013) *Warehouse Management: A complete guide to improving efficiency and minimizing costs in the modern warehouse*, p7, Kogan Page, London

Rushton, A, Croucher, P and Baker, P (2017) *The Handbook of Logistics and Distribution Management*, Kogan Page, London

Sloan, A P (2013) *Critical Evaluations in Business Management*, ed M Wood and J Wood, Routledge

Vollmann, T E, Berry, W L and Whybark, D C (1998) *Manufacturing Planning and Control Systems* (4th edn) Irwin/McGraw-Hill, Bolton

Vollmann, T, Berry, T, Whybark, D C and Jacobs, F R (2005) *Manufacturing Planning and Control for Supply Chain Management* (5th edn) McGraw Hill, Singapore

Business systems and business 02

Introduction

Inventory management doesn't exist separately in a business but is integral to the organization. In this chapter we look at how businesses utilize their systems and the basic architectures that are used to help to understand and design effective organizations.

Inventory management and business systems exist within the wider context of the business itself. At the highest level a business will have a vision and a mission statement. These need to be translated into strategic, tactical and operational actions, as well as considering their influence on the key business elements of process, organization (including people) and technology. The technology or business systems architecture that manages the business activities has three simple steps – forecast, plan and execute. We look at how these simple steps evolved as systems have developed from MRP to the all-encompassing ERP. We will also examine the importance of the sales and operations planning process and where responsibility for inventory rests within an organization. The chapter will conclude by looking at business system development, how Lean and JIT processes interact with the business systems and the part inventory plays in the business processes and business systems.

The business

An organization exists to deliver something – perhaps an aeroplane, or a packet of peas, a music festival, a guide dog, healthcare, sports facilities, or the defence of the realm – to someone or to another organization. They all add value to a raw material to create products or services for a customer, whether they belong to the public sector, the private sector or if they're a charity.

Vision, mission and action plan

All organizations have a vision, a mission and an action plan at their start and foundation. These are essential to keep a business focused in a clear direction. A company's vision (what) and mission (how) statements tell us what the company intends to be and to do today and in the future. A clear strategy and high-level action plan are necessary to identify what objectives need to be achieved in what markets and in what timescales.

Some examples of several well-known companies' vision and mission statements are given in Figure 2.1.

Figure 2.1 Examples of vision and mission

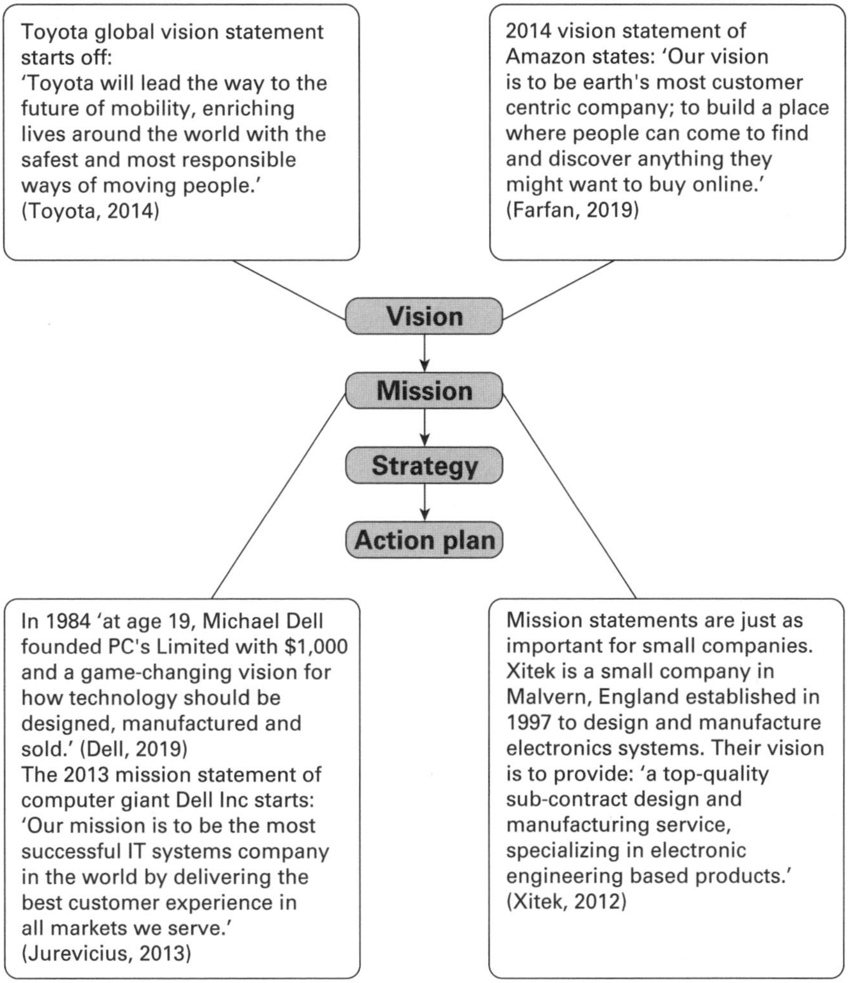

Working at strategic, tactical, operational and transactional levels

Organizations manage long-, medium- and short-term objectives and needs by operating at strategic, tactical and operational levels. Figure 2.2 shows how purchasing activities work at:

- a strategic level (eg what products and items need to be brought in for the business to be able to sell the goods it intends to sell; whether strategic supplier partnerships are to be created);
- a tactical level (eg supplier specification, partnership agreements, what level of automation is desirable and achievable, how the order process will flow with the suppliers, and longer-term price, quantity and delivery schedule agreements); and
- operational and transactional levels (eg order placement and payment).

Figure 2.2 Purchasing at strategic, tactical and operational levels

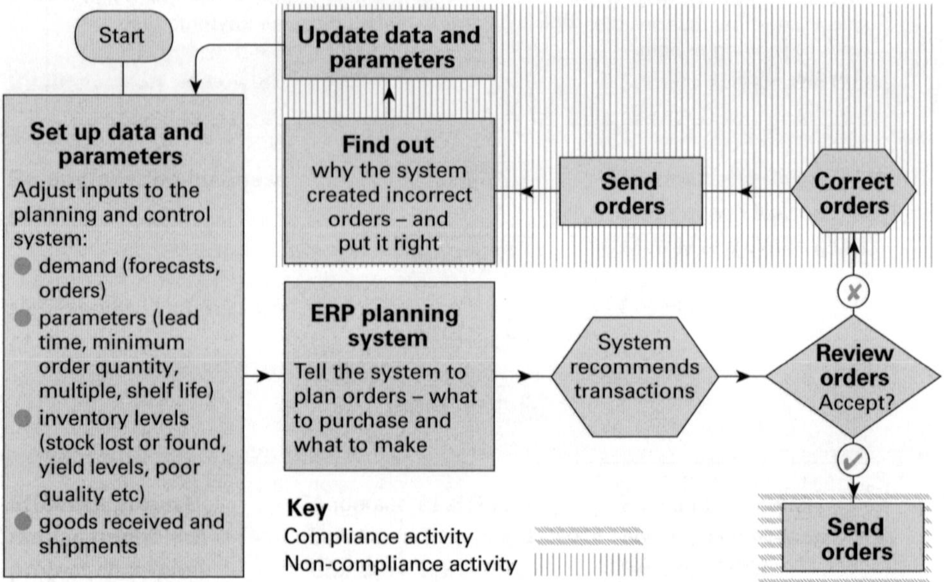

Reproduced by kind permission of Inventory Matters Ltd

Inventory management at strategic, tactical, operational and transactional levels

Inventory management will also be affected by strategic, tactical and operational decisions and activities. As shown in Chapter 1 in the inventory planning pyramid, there is an involvement at a strategic level in setting the inventory holding budget. There are also key decisions at a strategic level that are critical to inventory management, for example selection of strategic supplier partnerships, risk management and meeting industry regulatory requirements. As discussed in Chapter 1, the supply demand dilemma requires careful consideration as there is no right answer. Often inventory is purchased to 'protect' against a future risk that never materializes. Catastrophic or economic shocks can never be truly planned for and survival is often the result of the dedication of the staff within the business to react swiftly and creatively. The legacy of each shock/risk will drive the organization to either invest in inventory or drive the inventory down, focusing on Lean supply. This see-saw is reflected at all three levels: at the strategic level it is the choice to be single or dual source; at the tactical level it will be whether the sales department, who tend to be optimistic, or production department, who tend to be pessimistic, will drive the manufacturing volumes; and at an operational level it will be whether the planner adds to or reduces the safety stock on individual parts.

Business performance measures (what measurements are reported and what the figures show) will indicate how successful the inventory planning is and how well the strategic, tactical and operations plans are being adhered to. However, they do not always show the underlying detail crucial when wanting to change direction. The translation from strategic measures into detail operational measure is achieved by a number of management tools, such as Hosin Kanri, which are discussed in more detail in Chapter 8.

The choice of business systems and how they are implemented will be very important for inventory management. Decisions made during implementation will impact how inventory planning is carried out at a tactical level; for example, a decision at the implementation stage whether inventory replenishment should be calculated using a fixed quantity or a fixed interval method. The reason for choosing the latter of these two options is discussed in more detail in a later chapter.

In addition, the decisions made in the strategic and tactical levels in the development of the action plan will determine the type and number of transactions (eg purchase order (PO) placement) carried out: for example, whether the POs will be created completely automatically or have some manual involvement, or whether a form of supplier replenishment – eg vendor-managed inventory (VMI) – is used instead, removing the need for PO transactions.

Completely automatic creation of POs aims to increase both data accuracy and speed of placing the orders. The following considerations are important:

- a system that is capable of handling automatic order placing;
- a process that enables automatic order placing and does not require additional human input or checking;
- established supplier partnerships with agreed pricing, lead times etc; and
- a process that alerts the user if a problem arises.

Semi-automatic creation of POs allows for the order to be raised automatically but it is only sent when the user actions it. A benefit of this manual intervention is that orders can be changed before sending if necessary. However, the underlying cause of the mistakes must also be rectified, and making this correction is all too easy to put off until later, as shown in Figure 2.2. Meanwhile, more incorrect orders may be raised due to the same mistake. An example is that a delivery lead time may need to be decreased in the system, causing purchase orders for parts to be raised too early.

The volume of transactions is a critical measure when considering the capability of the business process and of the system, and will be revisited in later chapters.

Inventory is the responsibility of the whole organization, including:

- Board – visions and mission, strategic, long-term implications.
- Senior management – tactical importance, translating strategic decisions into medium- to long-term plans.
- Management – operational, medium-term plans.
- Planners – operational, short to medium-term actions.
- Systems – transactional, consequences of all the above levels of inventory management, translation into a high level of detail.

Process, organization (including people) and technology

For an organization to be successful it will need to manage business processes, the organization (eg people and products) and technology (eg business systems such as enterprise resource planning (ERP) systems). All three need to be present, and much like the three-legged stool in Figure 2.3, if one leg were missing it would be impossible for the stool to remain standing.

Figure 2.3 Process, organization and technology (POT)

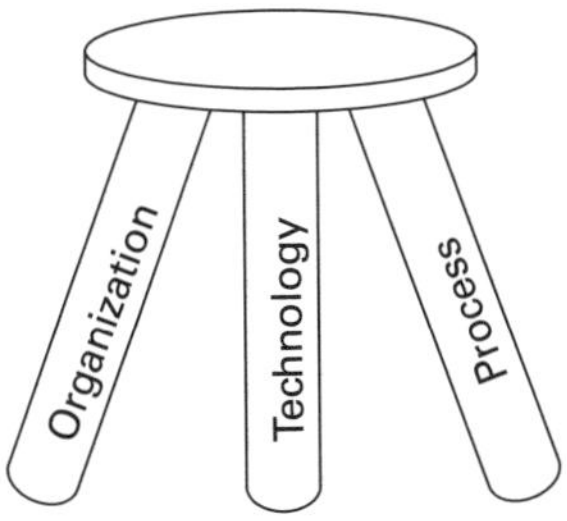

Reproduced by kind permission of Inventory Matters Ltd

The following paragraphs consider process, organization and technology in more detail.

A process is:

- a series of connected actions with an end goal;
- the way in which raw materials are converted into more valuable items;
- where inputs are transformed into outputs; and
- a way of describing something we do and the deliverables we produce.

Processes should not be considered to be static since the environment a business works in is constantly changing: process review should be carried out routinely (for example, comparing 'our' business with best practice in operations management), and change made where necessary.

Organization is concerned with:

- people with the right abilities and experiences; training where new skills are needed;
- product: R&D, engineering, design, manufacture; and
- culture: the values and practices of an organization and how its people interact with each other and with customers and suppliers. Companies with 'adaptive' cultures find change easier to manage.

Technology includes:

- the systems and hardware needed for effective and efficient business management; and
- ERP, financial control, engineering management, planning and control.

These are looked at in more detail in the following section.

Business system development

According to Klassen and Menor:

> Offering desirable customer service at a reasonable cost requires an efficient flow of materials and services while simultaneously managing the organization's resources that direct and form these flows. Effective planning and coordination ensures that all resources required to deliver services or produce goods are available in the right quantity and quality at the right time. (Klassen, 2005)

It is not an easy task for most organizations to deliver goods or services in the right quantity, right place and right time at reasonable cost. This has driven the need for business systems.

A brief history of planning systems

Business system development initially grew because of the need to manage manufacturing (the timeline is shown in Table 2.1). As we saw in Chapter 1, inventory management was used in ancient Egypt to record stocks and overdue orders of food and goods. From the early 20th century onwards, more sophisticated methods were developed:

Table 2.1 An overview of business system evolution

Timeline	Development
Early 1900s–1920s	Re-order point and economic order quantity
1960s	Early computer-based production planning; Toyota Production System/Just In Time developments continue
1970s	Material Requirements Planning (MRPI)
1980s	Manufacturing Resource Planning (MRPII) Lean Manufacturing introduced in James Womack's book
1990s	Enterprise Resource Planning (ERP)
2000s	Cloud-based ERP systems, Software as a Service, Customer Resources Management
2010s	ERP developments continue: integration (eg with SCM, CRM), platforms and connectivity (eg web options and mobile devices)

- Re-order point/re-order-quantity (ROP/ROQ) methods were used by early manufacturing industry.
- Economic Order Quantity (EOQ): the model and formula, originally developed by Ford Whitman Harris in 1913, was used in the 1920s by Wilson.

From the 1960s, computers started to be used in production planning. Over the following decade, Material Requirements Planning (MRPI) was championed by Joseph Orlicky. MRPI was designed to plan manufacturing, inventory, purchasing and shipments to customers. Forecast or actual demand was used to plan production of finished products (known as 'independent demand'), and bills of materials identified the relationship of the finished products to all the components and items required to create the final product. MRPI was first used in 1964 by Black and Decker.

In the 1980s, Oliver Wight developed MRPI further into MRPII (Manufacturing Resource Planning), which introduced capacity planning and master scheduling. MRPII also started to link with other areas of an organization such as cost accounting.

In the 1990s, MRPII continued to link with other areas of the business – human resources, financial management – to create Enterprise Resource Planning (ERP). ERP is defined by APICS (APICS, 2016) as:

> Framework for organizing, defining, and standardizing the business processes necessary to effectively plan and control an organization so the organization can use its internal knowledge to seek external advantage.

ERP systems were not all developed from the basis of the MRPII production systems. There were already sophisticated financial control packages in existence, as well as maintenance or human resources systems, and software development companies built out from their strengths in their various offerings. By the mid-1990s there were several ERP systems which addressed and linked these core functions together in a single system, typically having the following: a common database which is shared by and built to support all applications and an integrated system operating in 'real time'.

ERP is 'not a revolutionary conceptual breakthrough' according to Hicks and Stecke (1995). It has been attributed to the Gartner Group of Stamford, Connecticut, US. Hicks and Stecke go on to say about ERP that:

> It is not a major technological advance, nor is it even a truly new idea. It is however, a pretty useful paradigm, and it stems from the recognition that you can't make good decisions in a vacuum.

> Essentially, ERP is concerned with making sure that a firm's manufacturing decisions are not made without taking into account their impact on the supply chain, both upstream and downstream. (Hicks and Stecke, 1995)

Figure 2.4 ERP systems application architecture (Slack *et al*, 2010)

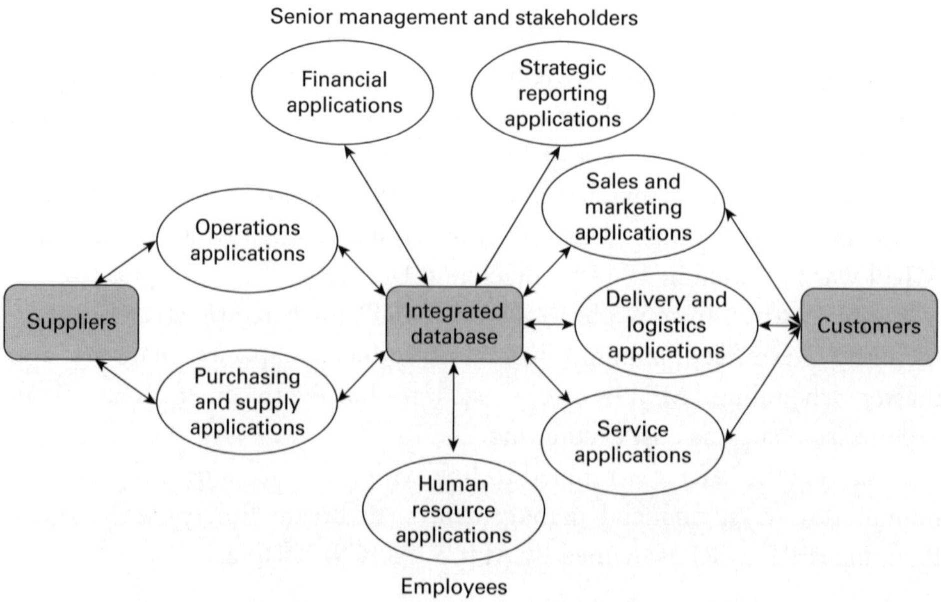

The development of ERP cloud applications was a natural consequence of the globalization of commerce. Cloud-based ordering between systems without human intervention has already started, as well as production being managed by computer-based order release onto the shop floor. In fact, many scheduling systems used by servicing companies and taxi firms utilize computerized or intelligent scheduling to direct the engineer/taxi driver to the next job at the point that they become free, rather than being planned on the day or even a couple of hours ahead.

In the first decade of the 21st-century ERP moved from just being offered as an 'on-premise' system (ie installed and maintained on the customer's own sites), to being offered through the internet. Often called 'cloud ERP' this comes in many forms, all accessible to many users in similar or diverse locations. Cloud ERP aims to benefit users with lower upfront and operating costs, with faster implementation and upgrades, as well as with improved accessibility and mobility. The major ERP software suppliers (SAP, Infor,

Oracle, Microsoft) all offer various forms of cloud-based ERP packages as well as 'on-premise' or hosted ERP. There are now a number of ERP cloud packages which were originally developed in the cloud (rather than starting as 'on-premise' packages), such as that offered on the Salesforce platform: Salesforce originated as a customer relationship management (CRM) package. The move from on-site to cloud-based applications has enabled businesses to implement systems faster and at lower costs, however it is still important to heed the warnings of Wilson (2003) and Oliver Wight International Inc (2010) who both focus on avoiding the technology trap by getting the business process right before implementing technology. This is discussed in more depth in Chapter 3.

The development of Just in Time (JIT) occurred differently to the MRPI ERP journey. JIT started in Toyota as the Toyota Production System (TPS) and was developed from 1949 into the 1970s. JIT is based on the elimination of waste. A JIT production system is often called a 'pull system', ie parts are only made when existing stock has been consumed by upstream processes. This is in direct contrast to MRP or 'push' where the product is made to a planned date even if the requirement has changed in the meantime. JIT uses stocks that is delivered to the production line 'just in time' but more importantly in direct response to the customer demand. The phrase 'sell one make one' is often used to describe the real benefit of JIT. The automotive industry is a well-known user of JIT.

Taiichi Ohno, Shigeo Shingo and Eiji Toyoda are jointly credited with developing the TPS (Strategos Inc, 2019). TPS is both a management philosophy and a way of working. In post-WWII Japan industry had been devastated and visionaries like Toyoda Kiichiro, president of Toyoda Motor Company said: 'Catch up with America in three years. Otherwise, the automobile industry of Japan will not survive' (Ohno, 1988). Ohno decided that establishing production flow and a way to maintain a constant supply of raw materials was the way of Japanese production.

The concept of Lean manufacturing was well suited to both the culture of Japan as well as the physical infrastructure as described in the book *The Machine that Changed the World* by James Womack, first published in 1990. Lean manufacturing is based on waste elimination and follows the JIT philosophy closely, introducing 'tools' to assist in the elimination of waste. The US and the Western economies still find it difficult to migrate away from the 'large batch' mentality and move to the JIT approach.

Choosing the most appropriate system

The choice of whether to use MRPII, ERP, JIT or another control system depends on the type of business a company runs. The relationship between industry type and the different systems is shown in Figure 2.5.

Figure 2.5 Choosing the most appropriate system for the business (Vollmann *et al*, 2005: p 10)

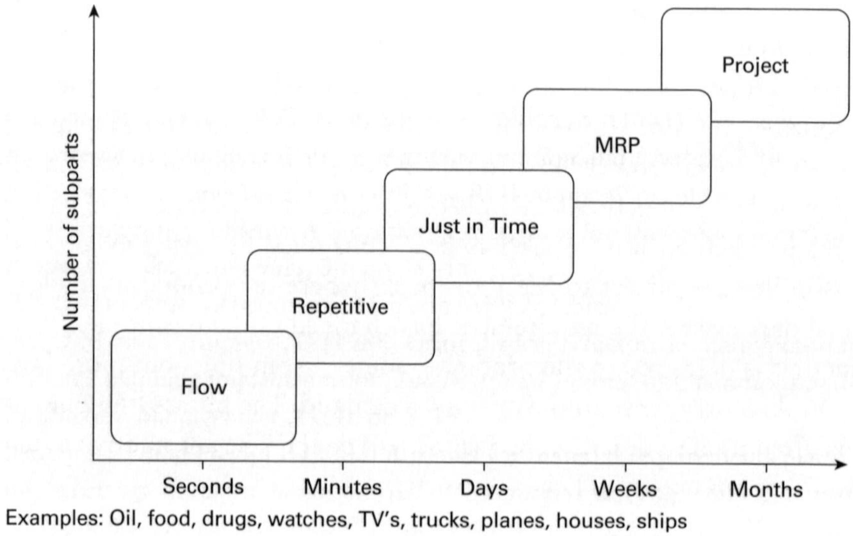

Figure 2.5 shows us clearly that:

- there is a large overlap between the systems, making it difficult to always identify what is the 'best' system;
- there is no guarantee of success by choosing well; the system must also be carefully implemented according to the needs of the business; and
- it may be appropriate for a company to implement more than one system:
  - the rate of flow and the number of subparts may well vary greatly in different parts of the business in a larger company; and
  - many batch firms run planning MRP with JIT execution systems.

The building blocks of MRPI, MRPII and ERP

The process flow: forecast, plan, execute

The process flow of forecast, plan and execute was already mentioned in Chapter 1. This will now be developed to show how the process flow informs the business systems:

- Forecasting includes quantitative or qualitative forecasting, customer order management and manufacturing planning. The objective is to decide what to do. It involves validating the customer demand before passing into the planning process.
- Planning is the second step and its objective is determining *how* to do the work and who is involved; this will look at both the manufacturing to confirm capability and supply to ensure continuity of supply.
- Execution is the third step and the objective is to carry out the plan as described by the planning step to ensure that manufacturing and purchasing are coordinated to deliver the forecast to the customer.

This is shown schematically in Figure 2.6.

Figure 2.6 Process flow from forecasting through planning to execution

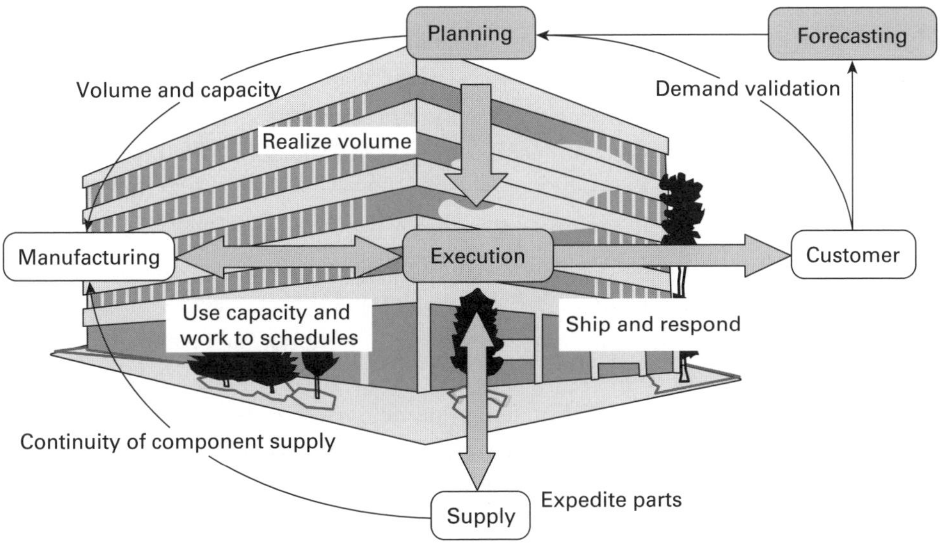

Reproduced by kind permission of Inventory Matters Ltd

These are the fundamental building blocks of MRP.

Companies, whether manufacturing or providing services, must forecast, plan and execute in a cost-effective way. To do this they must manage, efficiently and effectively, to:

- move materials through the business;
- choose and use the best people for the tasks;
- co-ordinate with suppliers; and
- serve their customers.

Material requirements planning

Material requirements planning (MRPI) works to bring the right amount of raw material and other supplies into the business to support production at the right time. MRPI includes a master production schedule (MPS) showing: what needs to be done to satisfy the expected demand; a bill of materials identifying the items required to be able to produce each product; existing stock levels of raw materials, components and finished goods; and order information for planned manufacturing and purchases from suppliers. MRPI, however, makes the false assumption that there is unlimited capacity. The MRPI basic configuration is shown in Figure 2.7.

Figure 2.7 Basic MRP (Material Requirements Planning) configuration

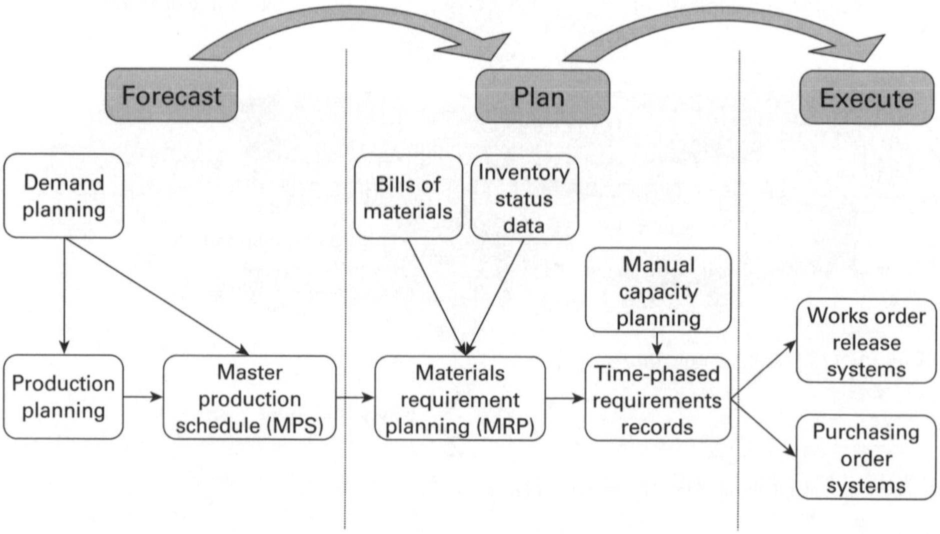

Based on Vollman *et al* (2005:8)

Manufacturing resource planning (MRPII)

Manufacturing resource planning (MRPII) was developed at least in part to satisfy the lack of capacity constraints in MRPI. In addition to the MRPI functionality, MRPII adds rough cut and detailed capacity planning, shop floor production planning and tracking, financial information, and a what-if simulation to understand the consequences of different possible production plans. MRPII plans materials, machines and people. The basic MRPII configuration is shown in Figure 2.8.

Figure 2.8 Basic MRPII (manufacturing resource planning) configuration

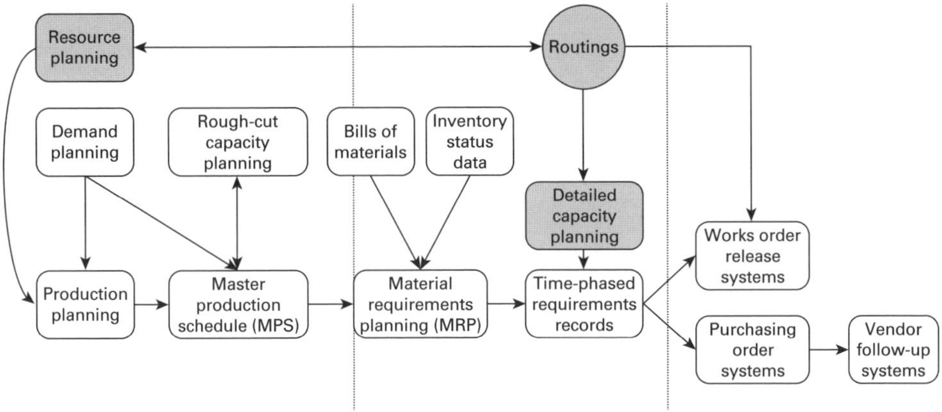

Enterprise resource planning (ERP)

Enterprise resource planning (ERP) systems integrate all functions within a company, as already shown in Figure 2.8. The planning and purchasing engine sits at the heart of the ERP system in the manufacturing industry. The large size and complexity of ERP means that it can be offered and installed as different modules. Figure 2.9 shows how the basic MRPI and MRPII has been extended to cover all the business functions, such as Finance, Quality and Engineering for an all-encompassing ERP configuration.

Forecast: the first step in the process flow

An organization needs to know or to estimate the future demand of its products or services. This information is then used to create an action plan for the work that will be needed to meet that predicted or known future demand, and in accordance with its own strategy and vision.

Figure 2.9 Basic ERP (enterprise resource planning) configuration

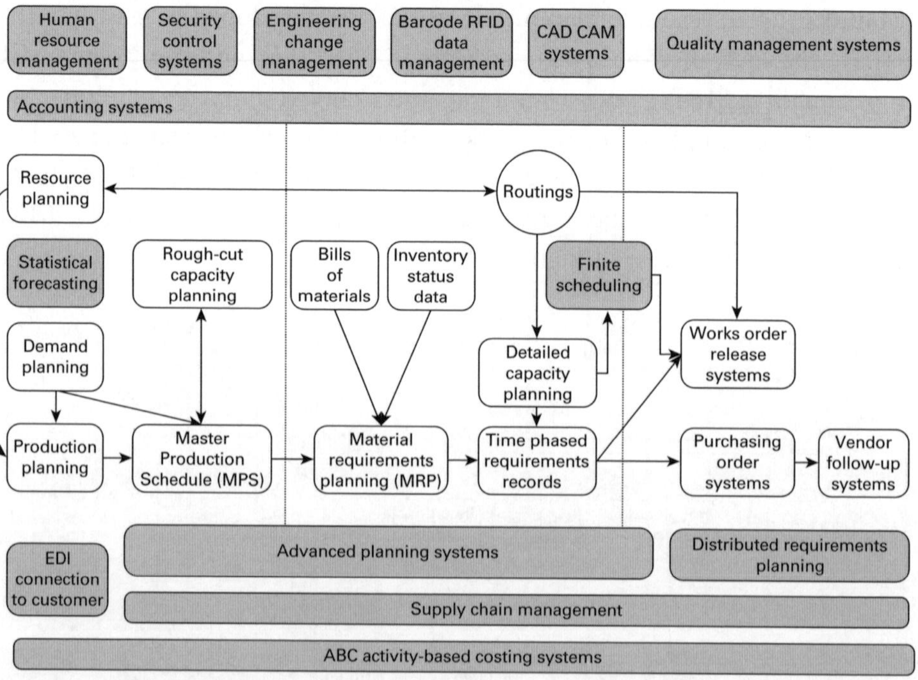

The first step in the process flow is labelled 'forecast'. In this we include all the work carried out by an organization to estimate future demand and to identify the capacity and resources needed to meet this demand.

Sales and operations planning (S&OP)

S&OP is a part of medium- to long-term planning and is carried out at a tactical level. It combines predicted sales with an understanding of the ability to achieve those sales.

APICS (APICS, 2016) defines S&OP as:

> a process to develop tactical plans that provide management the ability to strategically direct its businesses to achieve competitive advantage on a continuous basis by integrating customer-focused marketing plans for new and existing products with the management of the supply chain.

ERP assists the S&OP operation greatly because of the shared current and historical data, as well as a clear indication of the production and operational capability to achieve the future demand. The process of agreeing the predicted demand through the sales and operations planning (S&OP) review is a wide-ranging task and needs to include the following parts of an organization:

- sales and marketing;
- production;
- operations, including:
  - order processing and customer service;
  - purchasing;
  - production planning; and
  - logistics and warehousing.

Depending on the issues raised, there may need to be input from:

- finance and cash flow;
- human resources; and
- product design, engineering and R&D.

It is essential for sales and marketing to work closely together with operations and production to combine knowledge to make best use of resources and at the least operating cost. To produce the best S&OP, good communication is essential to identify:

- best estimates and plans for medium, and long, horizon sales predictions;
- understanding what level of sales are needed by the organization;
- calculating whether the existing production capacity is sufficient; and
- identifying where the skills of the current employees may need additional training or lead to new hires.

Figure 2.10 shows the linkage of the S&OP process to the company vision and the different levels of the predicted future demand, working through the strategic, tactical and operational levels and thereby across the different time scales and horizons.

Sometimes, however, predictions of future demand can be wildly incorrect. Tom Watson, while IBM chairman in 1958, is famously alleged to have said: 'I think there is a world market for about five computers.' Whether this quote is accurate or not it goes to show that there are frequently big changes in the environment, product development and the marketplace which are hard to predict. It is important to ensure that the S&OP process delivers a single agreed plan that is linked to the company vision as shown in Figure 2.10. The 'single' plan is important since MRP needs to be given a forecasted demand against which it can plan materials and orders. If the plan is too optimistic

Figure 2.10 Linking the company vision to the operational plan

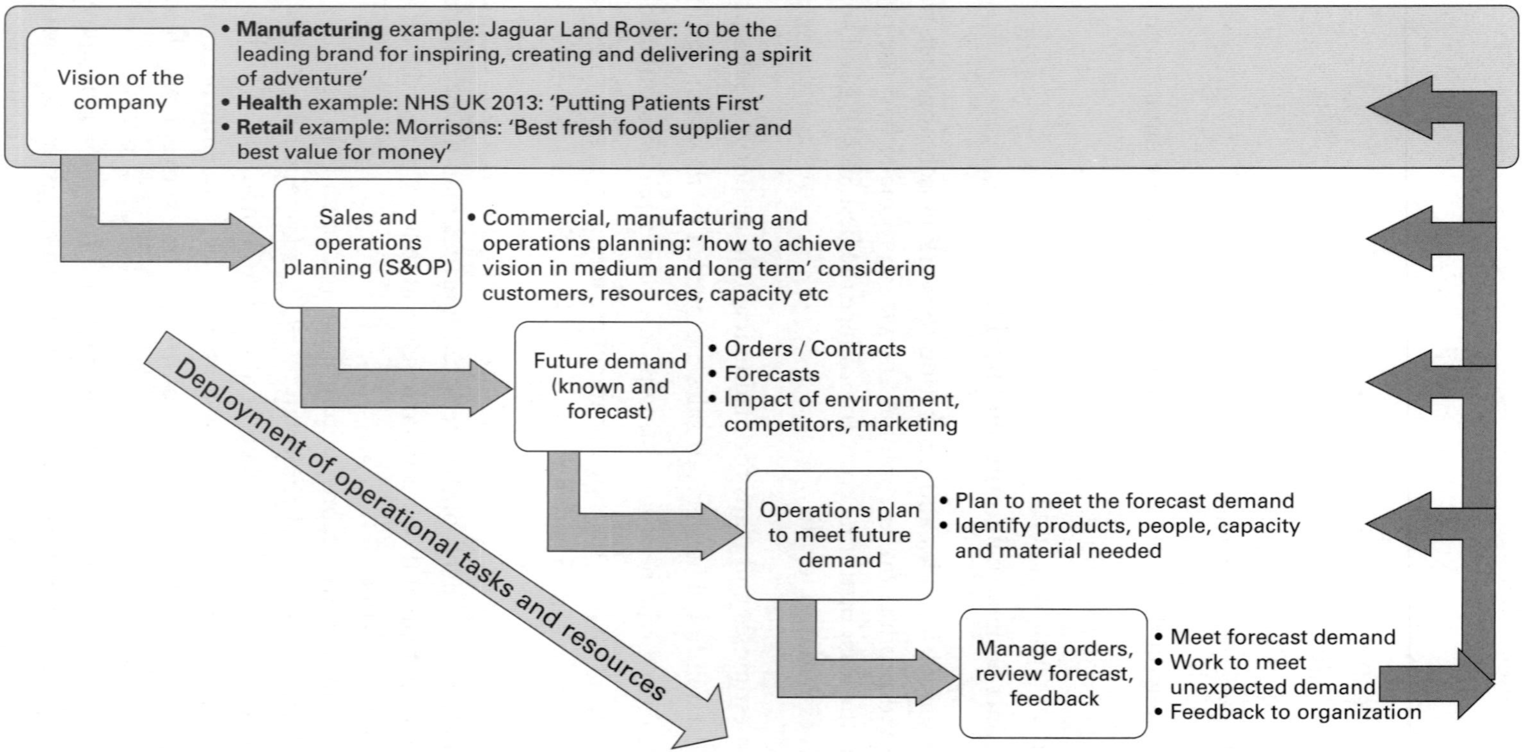

then the sales will not consume the production, and if it is too pessimistic then the production will fall short of the customer demand, leading to lost opportunities. This balance is extremely difficult to achieve and will have a significant impact on the inventory held by the business.

On a tactical level and in the medium to long term the sales and operations planning (S&OP) will identify what the likely demand levels will be and how to meet that demand. This will take into account production capacity, inventory management, outsourcing efficiencies, purchasing options etc, but not, at this stage, at a high level of detail.

In summary, S&OP brings the different demand forecasts and long-term orders together, reconciling the difference between the demand forecast and the manufacturing plan in a business planning process meeting. The MPS is the result of the S&OP process and is critical to the management of ERP/MRP systems.

Forecasting unknown future demand

For some industries there may be partly or fully known future demand. For the rest the only way of reliably predicting the future demand is to use forecasting tools. Forecasting tools assist in predicting future demand, which it recognizes is unknown. Forecasts will invariably be 'wrong' so it is important to manage the process with the correct expectations and to build in protections as well as checks and balances. This will help to minimize the effects when inevitably the forecast is not realized.

Forecasts need to consider both quantitative information (ie statistical forecast based on past sales) and qualitative information.

Quantitative forecasts:

- Single exponential smoothing is the most common method used by many business systems.
- Forecasting systems will often calculate several possible forecasts, compare them against historical sales and produce a 'best fit' forecast.
- Seasonality is included: some products sell more in summer (eg garden products, bottled water, ice cream), and others in winter (eg chocolates and turkeys around Christmas time).
- Trend is calculated: have sales increased or decreased over time?

Measuring forecast inaccuracy is essential since the amount and direction of error should be used to assist in inventory management. Common measurements include:

- Forecast error: how inaccurate is the forecast? Often used are both a rolling percentage over a number of weeks and the error of the most recent week.
- Forecast bias: is the forecast significantly above or below the actual sales over an extended period (eg 13 weeks)?
- Exception measurement: the system should alert the planners when the forecast measures go outside agreed predetermined acceptance limits.

Qualitative forecasts are not usually generated by the system since they usually relate to external influencers:

- Marketing plans: identifying and communicating marketing plans to the whole organization. It is important to understand how these marketing plans will affect demand. For example:
  - which items are to be promoted;
  - what additional advertising is planned;
  - any specific markets or prospective clients being targeted;
  - what resulting increase in demand is expected.
- Market intelligence: knowledge the organization has about external influences on the market and expected demand. This will include understanding the activity and plans of the competition.
- External environment: risks and opportunities that might arise from changes in the external environment should be considered and analysed. For example, changes in the climate/weather happening unexpectedly may cause challenges in demand and supply (eg excessive, unexpected and perhaps prolonged heat/cold; tsunami; hurricanes or tornadoes). Other problems or opportunities may be caused by legislation changes or health concerns.

Master production scheduling

The MPS is developed at a tactical level, and shows what products should be produced, in what quantity and by when. Calculating the MPS is a key activity within the S&OP process since it confirms (or otherwise) that the sales plan can be met by production. Strategically it will consider high-level production plans. A long-horizon plan will be developed for:

- production, and the people, components and materials needed to achieve that production;
- cost predictions: production costs, inventory costs, etc;

- meeting the identified future sales at minimum cost;
- an agreed length of time; and
- an aggregate level.

The MPS can be tested for validity by using Rough Cut Capacity Planning (RCCP) which will examine at an aggregate level the key capacities, ie machines and people in critical manufacturing processes.

Plan: the second step in the process flow

The first of the three steps in the process flow – forecast – has been considered. In this section we will consider the second step – planning – and look at the following:

- planning the supply/demand relationship;
- the master production schedule: using the MPS to drive the MRP planning;
- bills of materials; and
- parameters.

Planning for a balanced supply/demand relationship

There are three key supply/demand relationships, each of which results in a different inventory management process:

- Supply can follow demand variation, resulting in a need to only hold minimum inventory.
- Supply cannot match demand at peak periods (eg products with seasonal variation). This results in the need to manage inventory build-up before the peak demand starts and reduction afterwards (for example, garden products for which there is a far greater demand in the spring and early summer).
- Supply is constrained and cannot meet demand, resulting in the need to manage both demand and inventory (for example, when a highly popular new smartphone is first released).

It is essential to identify the correct inventory management processes for each type of product. A business may have all the different supply/demand relationships within a business. It is necessary to understand the forecast and orders for each item or group of items to develop a picture of the relevant inventory management process.

The first of the three key supply/demand relationships, where supply matches demand, is shown in Figure 2.11. This exists in many types of standard batch manufacture where there is little variation in supply or demand. This relationship means that it is possible to operate with minimal inventory, keeping inventory management costs to a minimum. The forecast will be stable and orders should be automated, with appropriate alerts set in case the situation changes unexpectedly.

Figure 2.11 Supply matches demand: MRP

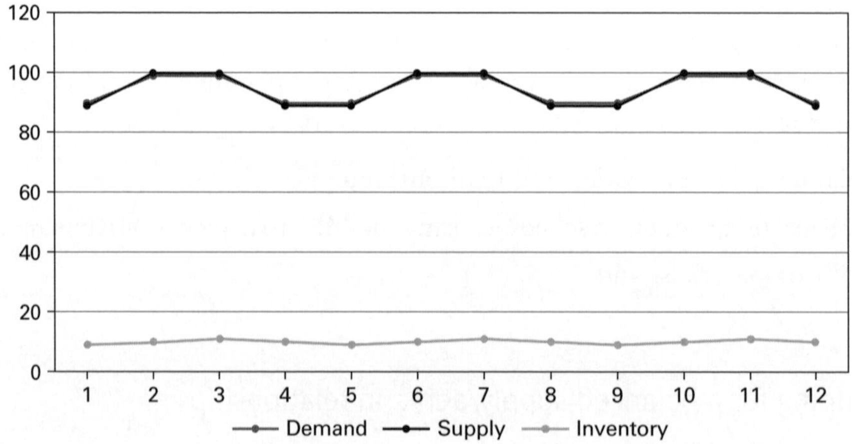

This situation can be managed well with MRP without significant consideration to capacity. The orders/forecast can be used to drive the demand within the MRP process.

The second of the three key supply/demand relationships, where demand is periodically greater than supply, is shown in Figure 2.12. This exists where there is a seasonal/cyclic element to the demand for the product. Where this exists the maximum production capacity is below that required to satisfy the peak demand. Some businesses also look to vary capacity, for example by employing additional resource at times of peak demand. The situation is most often managed by building up the inventory held before the period of peak demand. This relationship means that it is necessary to operate with more inventory, resulting in higher inventory management costs, than in Figure 2.11 where supply matches demand. The forecast will be volatile and can be affected by the weather. The management of the forecasted demand becomes critical, for example when the weather is a certain temperature above or below the seasonal average, it will need to be carefully managed. By the end of the peak demand period there needs to be a careful management of the reduction in inventory in preparation for the low season.

Figure 2.12 Demand periodically greater than supply balanced with inventory

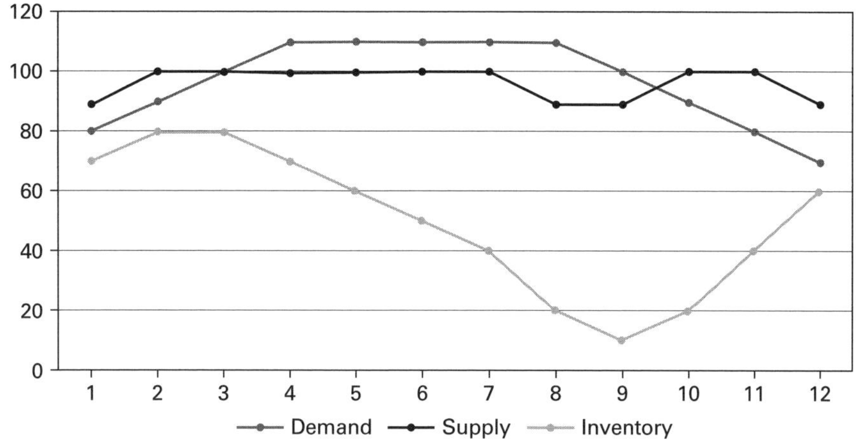

This situation needs an MPS-based inventory plan.

An example of this type of supply/demand relationship is sales of bottled water. Sales are higher in the summer and lower in the winter. Bottled water supplies are increased in the spring anticipating higher sales in the summer. When summer temperatures are hotter than usual, more water is sold, but if it is a cool summer then sales of fizzy drinks eats into the bottled water market.

The third of the three key supply/demand relationships, where supply controls demand, is shown in Figure 2.13. This exists where there is either a fixed supply which is lower than total demand (eg from a steel furnace), or where there is a much higher ongoing demand than the supply is able to meet and there is no alternative supply (eg new technology products). Production departments will ideally want to run the business on a level schedule to increase the efficiency of the manufacturing operations; there is always a risk that if this focus prevails that while the manufacturing operations are seen to be efficient, the inventory may be driven up as a consequence.

Where the product is a commodity then price can be used as a lever to dampen or stimulate demand. Price of the product to the customer may also be increased if it is a seller's market, which in turn can drive demand up further. It is common in the technology industries to use market allocation, particularly when new products are released. The MPS schedule is the key tool in helping the S&OP process determine the appropriate responses.

When forecasting these products it is important to understand if the high demand will continue or even increase as the variation of capacity is very difficult.

Figure 2.13 Supply controls demand: allocation

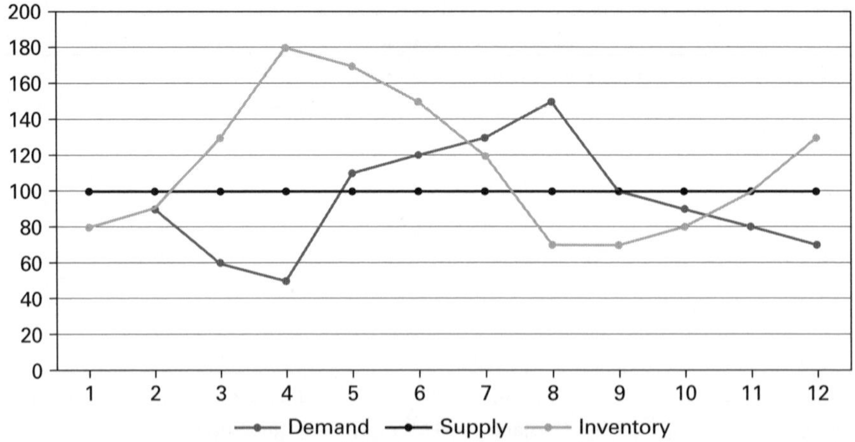

Supply/demand/inventory mechanism

When preparing for an S&OP review it is possible, given that we know our capacity, to create a supply/demand/inventory projection. The scenarios described above can be modelled to support the decision-making process. The example in Figure 2.14 is a simple supply/demand example, where there is a fixed supply situation whereby 25 units are delivered every week.

Figure 2.14 Simple supply/demand exercise

Period	1	2	3	4	5	6	7	8
Forecast demand	20	30	25	25	30	20	25	30
Supply/delivery	25							
Projected inventory Initial stock on hand = 15	20							

If supply is fixed at 25 units per period and stock on hand at the beginning of period 1 is 15 units, what is the projected inventory (PI) at the end of period 8?

The first step is to understand what is happening in period 1:

Period 1: stock on hand is 15 items at the beginning of the period. Since demand is forecast at 20 units, and there will be a delivery of 25 units, the projected closing inventory in the period will be (+15–20+25) = 20

Figure 2.15 Simple supply/demand exercise: step 2

Period	1	2	3	4	5	6	7	8
Forecast demand	20	30	25	25	30	20	25	30
Supply/delivery	25	25	25	25	25	25	25	25
Projected inventory Initial stock on hand = 15	20	15	15	15				

Following the same logic, as shown in Figure 2.15:

Period 2: projected stock on hand is 20 items at the beginning of the period. Since demand is forecast at 30 units, and there will be a delivery of 25 units, the projected closing inventory in the period will be (+20–30+25) = 15

Period 3: projected stock on hand is 15 items at the beginning of the period. Since demand is forecast at 25 units, and there will be a delivery of 25 units, the projected closing inventory in the period will be (+15–25+25) = 15

Period 4: projected stock on hand is 15 items at the beginning of the period. Since demand is forecast at 25 units, and there will be a delivery of 25 units, the projected closing inventory in the period will be (+15–25+25) = 15

Using this logic it is possible to calculate the projected inventory at the end of period 8. (Answer is given at the end of this chapter.)

This is a simple example of the calculations carried out within MRP on the thousands – often tens of thousands, sometimes hundreds of thousands – of parts planned and managed within the system. It is useful to understand the basic logic used within the system.

The master production schedule (MPS)

The MPS shows what products should be produced, in what quantity and by when. Calculating the MPS has already been considered in the discussion of the S&OP.

The MPS is translated by MRP into 'time phased net requirements and orders for each component needed to implement this schedule. MRP replans net requirements and coverage for changes in MPS, design, processing or inventory status' (Plossl, 1994).

Dependent and independent demand

Most businesses have products that have independent demand as well as components that have dependent demand. These are defined by Slack (Slack, Chambers and Johnston, 2010) as follows:

Figure 2.16 Treating demand differently with independent demand at decoupling points

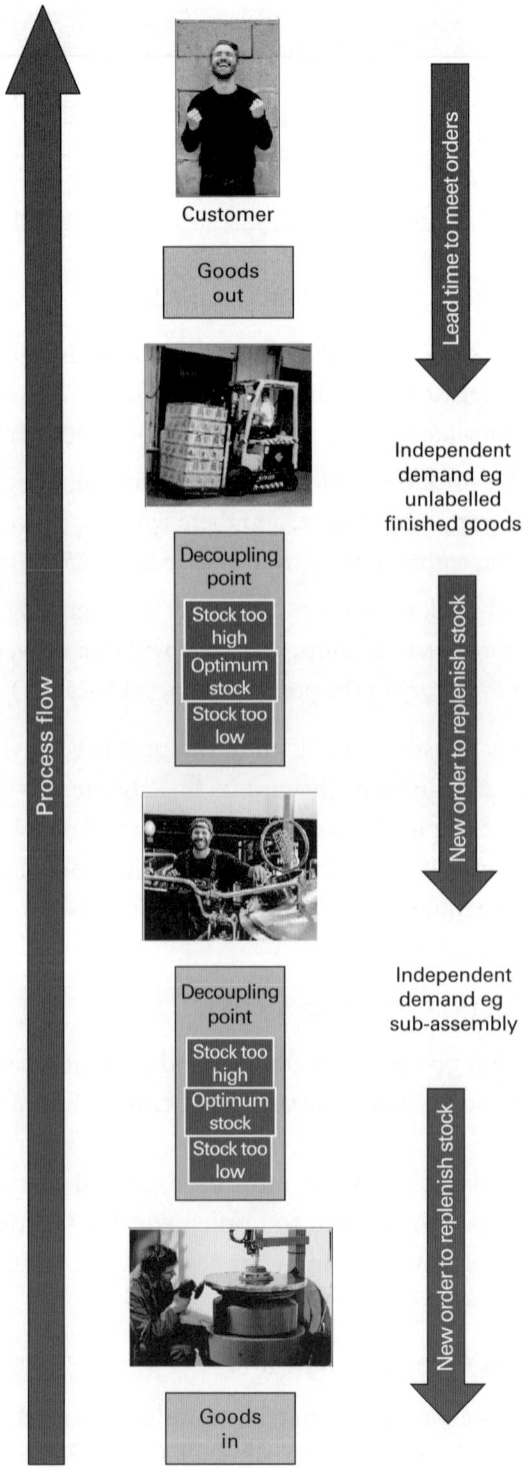

Dependent demand – demand that is relatively predictable because it is derived from some other known factor.

Independent demand – demand that is not obviously or directly dependent on demand of other products or services.

An aeroplane is an example of independent demand, and the parts that go into the building of the aircraft are mainly dependent demand. Thus it is known that for every aeroplane sold, there will be dependent demand for wings (see Figure 2.17). There will be some parts that will have both dependent and independent demand. For example, an aircraft will be assembled with one or more engines and during production these are identified as dependent demand. However, if an aeroplane is in service and a new engine needs to be fitted, at this point the demand for the engine for the aeroplane will be independent demand.

Figure 2.17 Simplistic representation of the first level of a BOM for an aeroplane

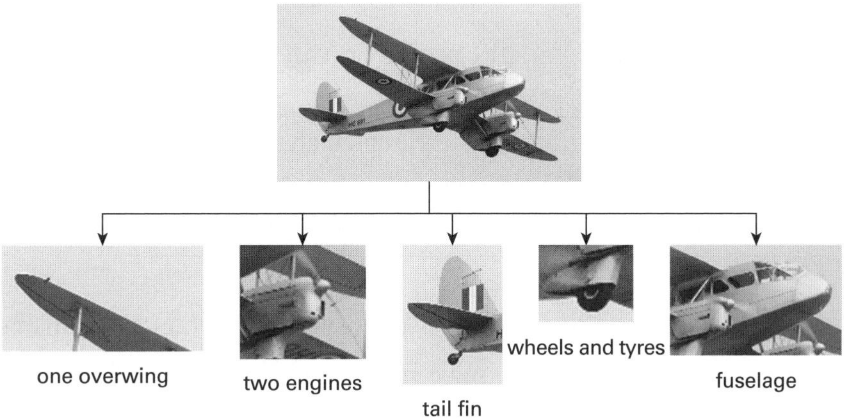

Reproduced by kind permission of Ian Young, Madhouse Designs

The management of the dependent and independent demand in MRP

The use of MRP planning systems is critically dependent on a known or forecast future demand. Customer orders and sales forecasts allow us to be able to use MRP logic to manage independent demand for these finished goods. MRP then calculates the requirements for the components and sub-assemblies needed to produce these finished goods, ie the dependent demand.

Demand-driven MRP (DDMRP) considers independent and dependent demand differently. DDMRP is a revision to traditional MRP and is discussed in the recent update of Orlicky's MRP book (originally published in 1975 and updated by Ptak and Smith (2011)). The key elements of DDMRP in Figure 2.16 show decoupling points where traditional dependent demand becomes independent demand. In a simplistic way it operates similarly to Kanban, with individual plans at intermediate levels in a simplified way, and has these steps:

- Initially forecasts are used to plan at an aggregate level.
- Decoupling points are then identified in the production process, and stock holding levels at these intermediate points calculated.
- A buffer is then built at the decoupling point, often an inventory buffer.
- Customer orders are fulfilled in a short lead time, for example from a complete-to-order stock-on-hand (eg final kitting, or labelling and packing) to shipping.
- When the stock at this part of the process falls to a specified level, demand is then passed back along the process using a Kanban style message, to replenish this stock.
- This build order then initiates production in the preceding step of the process.
- At each decoupling point the need to replenish the stock holding is treated as independent demand. One consequence of this is that the buffer gives some protection from possible forecast volatility to the earlier stages of the process.

This process builds on Eli Goldratt's 'Theory of Constraints', Lean theory and JIT, and MRP. Although the stock held at the different decoupling points is considered to have independent demand, there will be a known relationship between the various levels.

Bill of materials

The *bill of materials* (BOM) is the list of items required to manufacture or assemble a product or to deliver a service. A BOM for an aeroplane will have many levels in it – the first level of the BOM will be the major structure sub-assemblies: in Figure 2.17 these major sub-assemblies at the first BOM level are shown as a fuselage, tail fin, engines and wings. As mentioned previously, these assemblies are part of the dependent demand, with the aeroplane itself being the independent demand.

Figure 2.18 A snow shovel

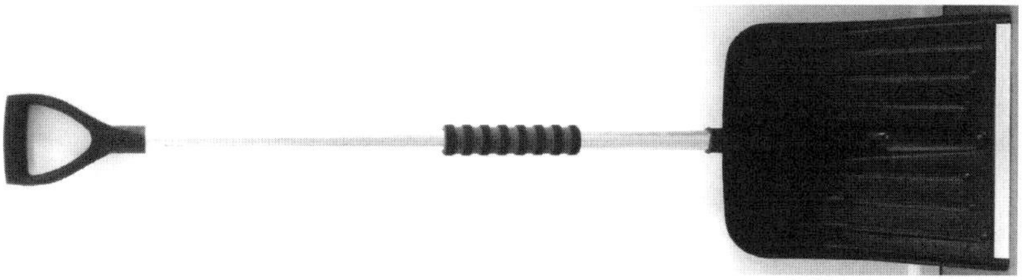

The shape or type of the BOM varies for different industries: an aircraft manufacturer has a very different type of BOM (one product, sub-assemblies, numerous components) from a company making plastic items for use in the garden (eg nozzles to go on garden hoses for watering the garden) where there are very few raw materials used but these are converted into a wide range of end products. In the petrochemical industry the BOM is sometimes referred to as a recipe: much as when baking a cake, in petro chemicals the ingredients are offered up to different heat treatment and chemical processes.

The type of BOM has an important impact on operations management, something that is frequently underestimated in organizations.

BOMs and part numbering

We will explore the BOM for a simple product – the snow shovel as shown in Figure 2.18. It has five parts at the first level down of the BOM, as clearly shown in Figure 2.19, with a further four parts at the next level down, and three at the third level.

Every separate assembly, sub-assembly, component and raw material in the bill of material must have a part number to uniquely identify it. The product may be as a result of an assembly process, ie fitting the aluminium edge to the scoop, or as a result of a manufacturing process, ie cutting a tube to length to make the shaft. Part numbering methods vary, occasionally being creatively generated by an organization, although this is generally not considered best practice. The most well-known examples are:

- GS1 – Global standards for barcodes.
- NATO Stock Numbers (NSN) Military Coding System.
- Library (ISBN) National and International Coding for Books/Maps.

Part numbers are also known as stock keeping units (SKUs), item or product or stock or article numbers. These are usually a computer generated random

Figure 2.19 Bill of materials for shovel for N123456

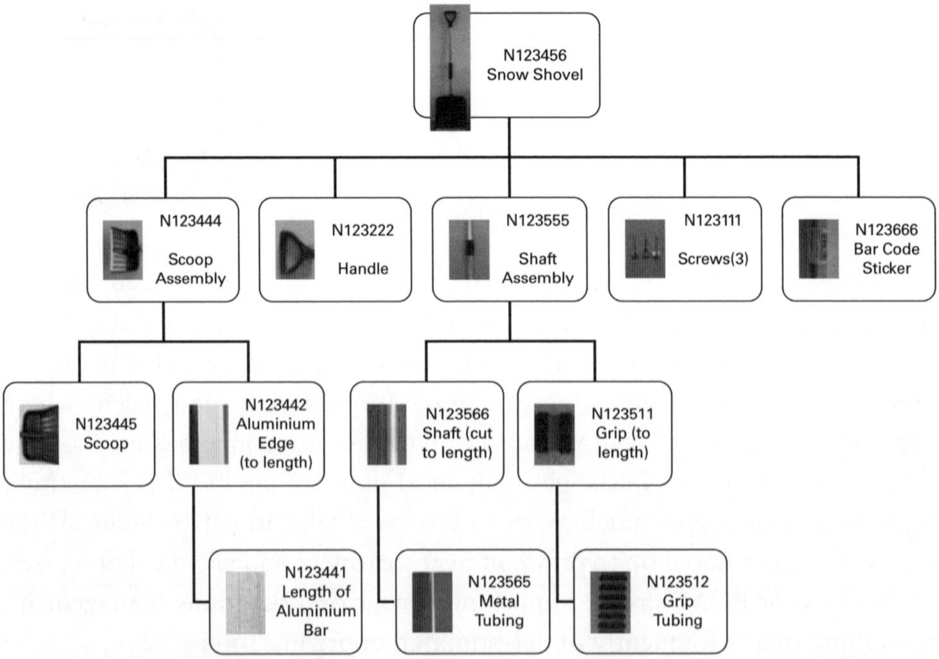

Reproduced by kind permission of WMG

or sequentially allocated number, useful in inventory management as well as being usable for bar codes and radio frequency identification (RFID) tags.

In increasingly rare cases, the part numbers contain a form of description in its number sequence, known as the British System of Component Classification.

Listing parts within the bill of materials structures

Once all parts are numbered they need to be applied to the bill of material structure. Figure 2.19 is a useful visual depiction but not so useful within an ERP planning system. The parts could be listed simply as in Table 2.2: unfortunately this wouldn't demonstrate how the product should be assembled, since there is no differentiation between the assemblies, sub-assemblies, components, etc and no clear indication of the relationship between the parts.

It is more useful to use an indented BOM, as shown in Table 2.3. Each level one is shown with one indentation, each level two with two

Table 2.2 Snow shovel BOM as a simple parts list

• N123456 Snow Shovel
• N123444 Scoop Assembly
• N123445 Scoop
• N123442 Aluminium Edge (cut to length)
• N123441 Length of Aluminium Bar
• N123222 Handle
• N123555 Shaft Assembly
• N123566 Shaft (cut to length)
• N123565 Metal Tubing
• N123511 Grip (cut to length)
• N123512 Grip Tubing
• N123111 Screws (x3)
• N123666 Bar Code Sticker

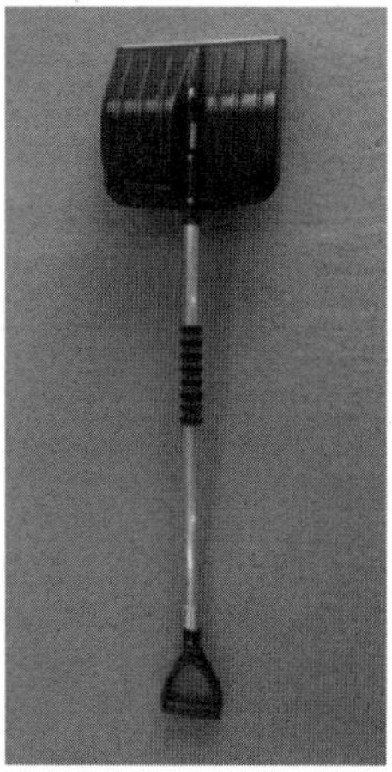

Reproduced by kind permission of WMG

indentations etc. The groupings of the parts show how the different parts gradually go together to assemble the snow shovel. The number of indentations levels demonstrates the complexity of production, and the BOM determining the material requirement.

Parameters: What they are and how they affect the way MRPII works

This sub-section will only identify the types of parameters that are used in an MRPII system: the calculations will be looked at in Chapter 4.

Figure 2.20 shows the standardized inventory saw tooth diagram. This shows a simplistic inventory plan of how stock levels vary over time. The minimum and maximum stock levels are given and the replenishment or cycle stock (ie the stock that is brought in to meet expected demand, which

Table 2.3 Indented BOM for snow shovel

- N123456 Snow Shovel
  - N123444 Scoop Assembly
    - N123445 Scoop
    - N123442 Aluminium Edge (cut to length)
      - N123441 Length of Aluminium Bar
  - N123222 Handle
  - N123555 Shaft Assembly
    - N123566 Shaft (cut to length)
      - N123565 Metal Tubing
    - M123511 Grip (cut to length)
      - N123512 Grip Tubing
  - N123111 Screws (x 3)
  - N123666 Bar Code Sticker

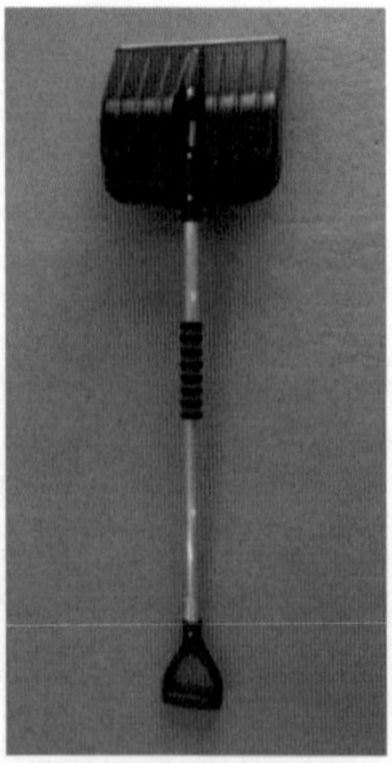

Reproduced by kind permission of WMG

is then consumed over time, until a new delivery is received to replenish the stock levels again) is planned to move between these two values. Safety stock sits underneath the minimum stock level, guarding against unexpected changes in supply or demand.

Figure 2.20 shows pictorially a number of the parameters which need to be managed to enable MRPII to calculate the correct recommendations and create an accurate transaction. The key parameters are:

- Cycle stock:
  - fixed order quantities:

    minimum order quantity (MOQ);

    multiple order quantity (Multi);

economic order quantity (EOQ);
maximum order quantity (Max);
- period order:
- order period days (OP).

- Safety stock:
  - safety quantity (SSQ);
  - safety time (ST).
- Lead time: total lead time is the sum of:
  - manufacturing lead-time (MLT);
  - purchase order lead-time (PLT);
  - order administration time (AOT);
  - inspection/good-in lead-time (GI).
- Yield: whether there is an expected reduction in acceptable product output/delivery.

Figure 2.20 The standardized inventory saw tooth diagram for MRP logic

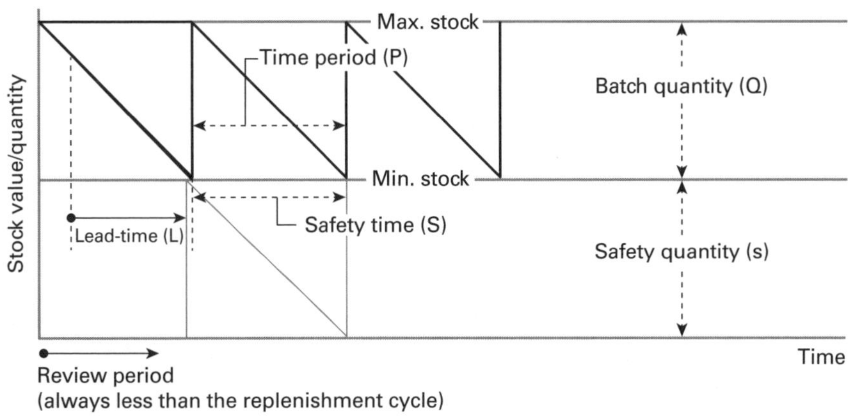

The above list shows that there are a large number of parameters to be managed for each product. Good business practices are essential for ensuring the parameters are well managed and kept up to date. Without these the system will start to 'silt-up' and the planning engine will lose its effectiveness. Although BOMs are not parameters, it is imperative that these are also carefully managed and kept up to date.

MRP management and maintenance

Measurements, system produced alerts and business reporting help instil and maintain good quality ERP operations. Measurements should include both the desired outcomes as well as the quality of the MRP process. Typically, outcome measurements would include:

- on-time delivery to customer order;
- on-time delivery from supplier orders;
- on-time delivery from works orders; and
- number of parts rejected.

The measures that are less frequently reported are those that measure the process quality, for example:

- number of short lead-time orders;
- number of orders modified by the planner/buyer (non-compliance).

The non-compliance measure is a very useful indicator of the health of the system and how well the data and parameters are being managed. If all the data in the system is correct and all the parameters are maintained, the works orders and purchase orders the system produces should be correct. If the person with responsibility for these products makes a change to the system-generated order this is referred to as *non-compliance*. Figure 2.21 shows the compliance/non-compliance process in operation.

Figure 2.21 Compliance MRP quality process

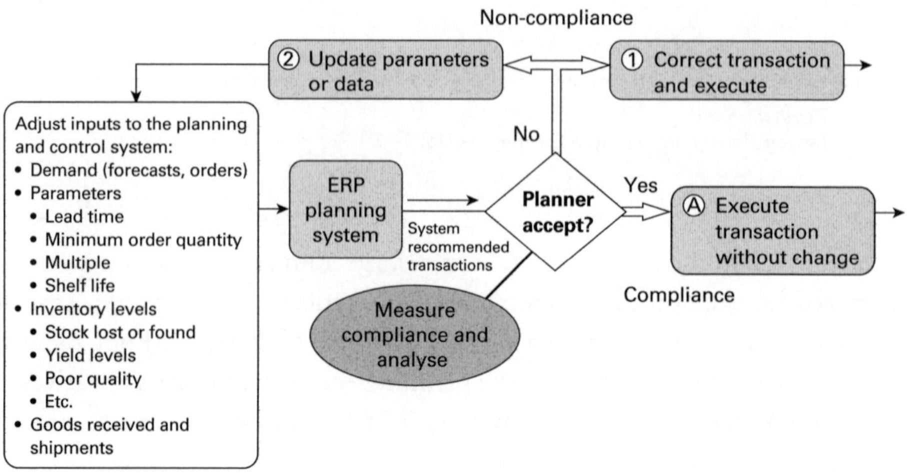

When the planner reviews a system recommended transaction, if this is acceptable then the order is released (ie the transaction is executed without change (A)). This is compliance as shown in Figure 2.21. When non-compliance happens there are two actions that are needed (as shown in Figure 2.21): the first action (1) is to correct transaction and execute; the second action (2) is to identify why the system raised an incorrect order, and correct the cause (eg change parameter settings, ensure the data inaccuracy is corrected). It is the second step that is harder to complete, especially with the pressures of daily work, but is essential nonetheless since the aim is for the system to produce the correct order the next time around. Typical causes for non-compliance include:

- unable to meet recommended date;
- bill of material errors;
- statistical group error;
- stock errors;
- order errors;
- forecast errors; and
- batch size incorrect/inappropriate.

The planner will always complete the first action to place the order, but will rarely have time to complete the second. Very few organizations measure non-compliance, but it is an excellent measure of how well the system is operating. However, today it is now more common to find ERP/MRP systems that allow the tracking of order amendments by the planner making compliance measurement easier through business intelligence management reporting data.

Execute: the third step

After the planning stage, MRP is 'run' and the next stage executed (eg manufacture, purchase, etc). The complications and examples of doing this, and trying to achieve this in as close to real time as possible are considered in the next chapter in detail.

ERP implementation and management

ERP implementations were a significant activity in business in the late 1990s and the first decades of the 21st century. There are a number of well-documented analyses of failures in ERP implementations which have identified the key critical success factors (see Table 2.4). It is helpful to learn from previous failures in implementations, and to consider where key implementation decisions later hampered the smooth working of the operations process.

Table 2.4 Analysis of critical success factors for implementing ERP

Critical Success Factor	References cited in support of CSF	
	1980–1999	2000–2014
Top management support	Anderson *et al* (1981) Wilson *et al* (1990) Callerman and Heyl (1986)	Zhang *et al* (2002) ElSayed *et al* (2013)
Business plan and vision		Somers and Nelson (2004) Nah (2003)
Re-engineering business process		Hammer and Champy (2001) Somers and Nelson (2004) Murray and Coffin (2001)
MRP requires a new way of managing	Anderson *et al* (1981) Burns and Turnipseed (1988) Wilson, Desmond and Roberts (1990) Cox and Clark (1984)	ElSayed *et al* (2013)
Effective project management and project champion	Anderson *et al* (1981) Burns and Turnispeed (1988) Cox and Clark (1984) Wilson *et al* (1990)	Zhang *et al* (2002) Somers and Nelson (2001) Remus (2006) Loh and Koh (2004) ElSayed, *et al* (2013)
Teamwork and composition		Loh and Koh (2004) Al-Mashari *et al* (2006) Remus (2006) Nah (2003)

Table 2.4 *continued*

Critical Success Factor	References cited in support of CSF	
	1980–1999	**2000–2014**
MRP requires a strong commitment to the computer resource and data accuracy	Anderson *et al* (1981) Burns and Turnipseed (1988) Cox and Clark (1984) Wilson *et al* (1990) Ang *et al* (1984)	
ERP system selection		Wei and Wang (2004) Shehab *et al* (2004) van Everdingen *et al* (2000) Sprott (2000)
User involvement		Esteves *et al* (2003) Zhang *et al* (2002)
Education and training	Callerman and Heyl (1986) Cerveny and Scott (1989) Cox and Clark (1984) Wilson, Desmond and Roberts (1990) Ang *et al* (1984)	Woo (2007) Nah *et al* (2003) Zhang *et al* (2002) ElSayed *et al* (2013)

Reproduced by kind permission of WMG

It is even more useful to know how to implement ERP correctly. To this end we will briefly consider the Oliver Wight ERP implementation and management guide.

Oliver Wight was instrumental in the development of MRPII in the 1980s. He continued to work implementing MRPII and later ERP, moving from IBM in 1969 to set up his own company Oliver Wight International Inc. He created two key approaches which are still used today:

- The implementation process guide, called: 'The Proven Path.'
- An ERP management and ongoing maintenance guide called: 'ABCD Checklist.'

'Proven Path' for ERP implementation

This is a brief summary of the 'Proven Path' described by Landvater (1997: 245–281).

Phase 1: Build the case

This phase concerns the establishment and documentation of the business case for implementation. Among other aspects, it will be key to involve and educate the executive and operating management, to have a clear vision statement which is shared with the whole organization, and to understand the time that will be needed for the implementation and what additional capabilities are needed within the enterprise.

Phase 2: Engage the company

Phase 2 is project organization. A strong, full-time project leader will be needed, together with a project team and a project plan. These changes must be driven from the top of the organization and engage employees at every level to achieve buy-in.

Figure 2.22 Simplified diagram based on Landvater proven path

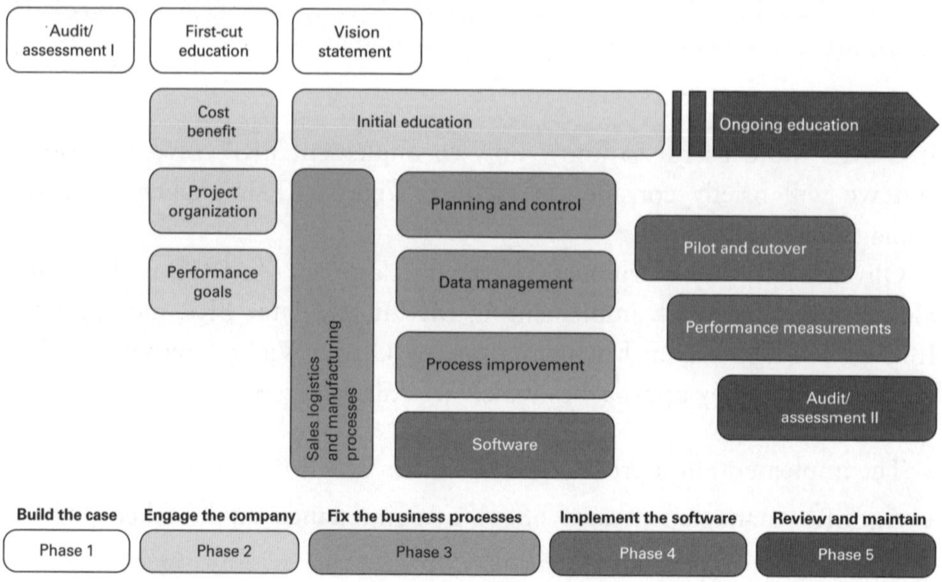

Adapted from Landvater (1997)

Phase 3: Fix the business processes

An existing company will have an existing business process, whether it is written down or not. Business process analysis of the 'as-is' (ie current process) and a clear, detailed objective of the 'to-be' business process (ie what the company feels is the best new process after the system implementation) is essential. As Wilson stated:

> Technology applied to a poor business process will only result in the automation and embedding of inefficiencies which lead to the technology trap. It is essential that processes are improved to remove non value adding activities and any process breakages before technology is applied. (Wilson, 2003)

Fixing the business process in advance of the ERP implementation is essential and has four simple steps:

- Definition of the 'as is' process.
- Development of the 'to-be' process.
- Consensus for the 'to-be' process.
- Creation of the implementation plan, including a detailed plan for the management of the data transfer/creation in the new system including both: unforgiving data (must be right), eg BOMs, routings, inventory, receipts; and forgiving data (should be right), eg forecasts, item master, parameters.

Phase 4: Implement the software

Phase 4 is the selection and implementation of the software. Once the system is selected and phases 1–3 completed, key steps involved in phase 4 include:

- Test environment, test and resolution process.
- Pilot identified for initial cut-over – there may also be a module by module phased implementation.
- Training materials identified and training carried out.
- Clearly identified implementation and process measurements, including the achievement of the original business case and vision for the new system.

Phase 5: Review and maintain

Implementing a new business process and an ERP system in larger companies can take several years. Once complete, the organization should audit the system and process to assess what has been achieved, including whether the initial business case for implementation is complete. This will identify what may still be left to do, and what has been learnt, including:

- One of the important factors is to ensure that the company and the people operating the system are in control of the system.
- A rolling education programme is needed for new employees and to refresh existing users.
- A review of the business, the system and the processes should be carried out routinely to ensure that the ERP system and the processes being carried out are still suitable for the business.
- Ongoing maintenance is essential. Processes and systems need to be maintained to prevent them from clogging up and thus losing effectiveness.
- Parameters must be kept up-to-date (eg cycle stock, safety stock, bills of materials). This should be carried out at a routine review of key parameters, process measurements and system management to ensure the system continues to operate correctly.

Key learning points of the Proven Path

ERP implementations are continuing in small, medium and large organizations. The Oliver Wight 'Proven Path' implementation process is just one method that can be followed. There is a huge amount of disruption that can be caused to a business by a bad ERP implementation although with so many examples of 'what not to do' these problems should be minimized with new implementations.

ERP management and maintenance

Once an ERP implementation is up and running, a company will begin the improvement of the system and the business processes. It is important for a company to know how well it is performing initially, and to identify what the 'best practice' is that it would like to get to (for example, in operations management), and how to get there.

'ABCD Checklist': a guide to achieving business excellence

One method of achieving business excellence, with the assistance of the newly implemented ERP system, is the use of the Oliver Wight 'ABCD Checklist'. The aim of using the checklist is to identify what level (A, B, C or D) the company is at, and how to progress to being an Class A company.

Achieving business excellence as a Class 'A' Company

One benefit of using the Oliver Wight Class A Checklist (Oliver Wight International Inc, 2010) is that it provides a clear checklist. This is intended to be used by a company to consider how well they are performing and how to progress to the next level, and their ongoing journey to excellence. Measures to be considered include the following high-level areas (as taken from the Oliver Wight Class A Checklist (Oliver Wight International Inc, 2010)):

- managing the strategic planning process;
- managing and leading people;
- driving business improvement;
- integrated business planning;
- managing products and services;
- managing internal supply; and
- managing external sourcing.

Some key areas in the checklist to help achieve best practice for operations management include:

- *Dedication*: a computer system is a tool that can assist with but not independently solve a company's problems. MRPII is simple in concept but its performance can be affected by many people in the organization (for example, the sales team will help to forecast demand, management must help determine the policy decisions, the warehouse operators are responsible for the inventory record accuracy etc). Inventory sits at the core of MRP and all functions have a responsibility to ensure their part is played. MRPII therefore requires a great amount of support and understanding throughout the company.
- *Understanding*: many people have an input to make to the system. It is essential they know the importance of their input and understand the consequences if they get it wrong. For example, during assembly a component may be found to be faulty and another one not immediately allocated. If the assembly operator takes the component required from another kit or from stores, but doesn't record this transaction on the system, the immediate problem is resolved but the computer records are now incorrect. A shortage of the component will occur in the future unless the error is rectified.
- *Realistic production/maintenance schedules*: if the available capacity in a factory is incorrectly identified (in respect to both people and machines)

the production schedule will either be impossible to achieve (resulting in high levels of work in progress and planned customer orders delivered late) or too easy to achieve (meaning that there is a danger of underutilizing capacity, and possibly spending money unnecessarily on outsourcing production that could have actually been carried out in-house).

- *Accurate bills of material*: the bill of materials sits at the centre of the planning engine. If the BOM is incorrect materials that are needed may be ignored, and material that is not needed may continue to be bought even when there are large stocks of it. BOMs are frequently subject to high levels of change (eg product specification may be changed). In many complex products, the volume of data can be enormous and difficult to maintain.
- *Accurate and timely data recording* – data accuracy is essential. The planning results and orders raised will be the result of the system calculating the needs of the business, based on the data recorded in the system. The well-known saying of 'garbage in means garbage out' applies here.

The implementation and ongoing management and improvement of an ERP system is no easy task. It is a costly undertaking which does not directly add value to the products offered to customers. However, most large companies need a system to record their data and assist with planning (where huge numbers of calculations are needed), and would not be able to operate without it. For those companies who are the leading users of ERP systems there are many benefits according to the Aberdeen Group (Jutras, 2010):

- 22 per cent reduction in inventory
- 97 per cent inventory accuracy
- 96 per cent manufacturing schedule compliance
- 98 per cent on time delivery

Additional benefits were shown in the same report, based on a survey (Jutras, 2010: 6), that best-in-class firms were:

- 111 per cent more likely to be able to quantify the business benefits [what gets measured gets done];
- best in class used to take advantage of 39 per cent more ERP functionality (use it or lose it); and
- the top 20 per cent [of best-in-class users] in terms of aggregate performance scores also enjoy an 83 per cent advantage in full visibility to their business.

Summary

This chapter has considered how inventory doesn't exist separately from a business but is integral to the whole organization. We have considered how inventory management and business systems exist within the wider context of the business itself, and how essential it is to the health of the company that they are both well implemented and well maintained. The way that the planning process works in ERP and MRP was looked at in some detail from considering the role of the S&OP process, together with the importance of parameter setting, BOMs, and the maintenance of the supply and demand relationships that will enable the systems to work efficiently and effectively. And finally, the use of non-compliance as a key measurement of the health of the system was discussed. These are intended to provide a good foundation to understand the complexities of inventory management in business systems in the following chapters.

Answer to the supply/demand balancing exercise

The answer is that there is a projected inventory of 10 items at the end of period 8.

Figure 2.23 Answer to the supply/demand balancing exercise

Period	1	2	3	4	5	6	7	8
Forecast demand	20	30	25	25	30	20	25	30
Supply/delivery	25	25	25	25	25	25	25	25
Projected inventory Initial stock on hand = 15	20	15	15	15	10	15	15	10

Period 5: projected stock on hand is 15 items at the beginning of the period. Since demand is forecast at 30 units, and there will be a delivery of 25 units, the projected closing inventory in the period will be (+15–30+25) = 10

Period 6: projected stock on hand is 10 items at the beginning of the period. Since demand is forecast at 20 units, and there will be a delivery of 25 units, the projected closing inventory in the period will be (+10–20+25) = 15

Period 7: projected stock on hand is 15 items at the beginning of the period. Since demand is forecast at 25 units, and there will be a delivery of 25 units, the projected closing inventory in the period will be (+15–25+25) = 15

Period 8: projected stock on hand is 15 items at the beginning of the period. Since demand is forecast at 30 units, and there will be a delivery of 25 units, the projected closing inventory in the period will be (+15–30+25) = 10

References

Anderson, J C, Schroder, R G, Tupy, S E and White, E M (1981) *Materials Requirements Planning: A study of implementation and practice*, APICS

Ang, J S, Sum, C C and Yang, K K (1984) MRPII company profile and implementation problems: A Singapore experience, *International Journal of Production and Economics*, **34**, pp 35–45

APICS (2016) *APICS Dictionary*, 15th edn, APICS, Chicago

Burns, O M and Turnipseed, D (1988) Critical success factors in manufacturing resource planning implementation, *International Journal of Operations and Production Management*, **11**(4), pp 5–19

Callerman, T E and Heyl, J E (2003) A model for material requirements planning implementation, *International Journal of Operations & Production Management*, **6** (5) pp. 30–37

Cerveny, R P and Scott, L W (1989) A model for Materials Requirements Planning implementation, *International Journal of Operations and Production Management* (Third Quarter), pp 31–34

Cox, J F and Clark, S J (1984) Problems in implementing and operating a manufacturing resource planning information system, *Journal of Management Information Systems*, **1**, pp 81–101

Dell (2014) Who we are. Retrieved October 2014, from Dell Technologies: http://www.dell.com/learn/us/en/uscorp1/birth-of-company?c=us&l=en&s=corp&cs=uscorp1

ElSayed, M S, Hubbard, N J and Tipi, N S (2013) Evaluating Enterprise Resource Planning (ERP) post implementation problems in Egypt: findings from case studies of Governmental, Multinational and Private Egyptian organisations, Logistics Research Network

Esteves *et al* (2003) An exploratory study of knowledge types relevance along enterprise systems implementation phases, *4th European Conference on Organizational Knowledge and Learning Capabilities*

Farfan, B (2019) Amazon Mission Statement. Retrieved May 06, 2019, from http://retailindustry.about.com/od/retailbestpractices/ig/Company-Mission-Statements/Amazon-com-Mission-Statement.htm

Hammer, M and Champy, J (2001) *Reengineering the Corporation: A manifesto for business revolution paperback*, Harper Collins, New York

Harris, F W (1913) How many parts to make at once, *Factory, The Magazine of Management*, **10**(2), 10, pp 135–36, 152

Hicks, D A and Stecke, K (1995) The ERP Maze. IIE Solutions (August), 12–16

Jurevicius, O, (2013) Dell Mission Statement. Strategic Management Insight. Retrieved May 6, 2019 from http://www.strategicmanagementinsight.com/mission-statements/dell-mission-statement.html

Jutras, C (2010) ERP in manufacturing 2010 – measuring business benefit and time to value, Aberdeen Group, Boston

Klassen, R D (2005) *Cases in Operations Management*, SAGE Publications, London

Landvater, D V (1997) *World Class Production and Inventory Management*, Wiley, New York

Murray, M and Coffin, G (2001) A Case Study Analysis of Factors for Success in ERP System Implementations, *AMCIS 2001 Proceedings*, p. 196

Ohno, T (1988) *Toyota Production System: Beyond Large-Scale Production*, Productivity Press, Portland, Oregon

Oliver Wight International Inc (2010) *The Oliver Wight Class A Checklist for Business Excellence* (6th edn), Wiley

Plossl, G W (1994) *Orlicky's Material Requirements Planning*, McGraw-Hill Inc, New York

Ptak, C A and Smith, C J (2011) *Orlicky's Material Requirements Planning* (3rd edn). McGraw-Hill, New York

Remus, R (2007) Critical success factors for implementing enterprise portals: a comparison with ERP implementations, *Business Process Management Journal*, **13** (4), pp. 538–52

Shehab, E M *et al* (2004) Enterprise resource planning: an integrative review, *Business Process Management Journal*, **10** (4) pp. 35–86

Slack, N, Chambers, S and Johnston, R (2010) *Operations Management*, Financial Times/Prentice Hall, London

Somers, T M and Nelson, K (2001) The impact of critical success factors across the stages of enterprise resource planning implementations, *Proceedings of the 34th Hawaii International Conference on System Sciences*

Sprott, D A (2000) *Statistical Inference in Science*, Springer

Strategos Inc (2019) Toyota Production System (TPS) & Lean. Retrieved May 2019 from http://www.strategosinc.com/toyota_production.htm

Toyota (2014) Toyota Global Vision. Retrieved May 2019, from http://www.toyota-global.com/company/vision_philosophy/toyota_global_vision_2020.html

van Everdingen, Y *et al* (2000) ERP Adoption by European Midsize Companies, *Communications of the ACM* **43** (4) pp. 27–31, DOI: 10.1145/332051.332064

Vollmann, T, Berry, T, Whybark, D C and Jacobs, F R (2005) *Manufacturing Planning and Control for Supply Chain Management* (5th edn), McGraw Hill, Singapore

Wei, C and Wang, M (2004) A comprehensive framework for selecting an ERP system, *International Journal of Project Management*, **22** pp 161–69

Wilson, F (2003) Walk don't run, *Manufacturing Engineer*, 2003 (June/July), pp 20–22

Wilson, F, Desmond, J and Roberts, H (1990) Success and failure of MRPII implementation, *British Journal of Management*, 5(1990), pp. 221–40

Womack, J P, Jones, D T and Roos, D (1990) *The Machine that Changed the World*, Simon & Schuster, New York

Xitek (2012) About us. Retrieved May 2019 from http://www.xitek.co.uk/company/

Zhang *et al* (2002) Critical success factors of enterprise resource planning systems implementation success in China, *Proceedings of the 36th Annual Hawaii International Conference on System Sciences, 2003*, DOI:10.1109/HICSS.2003.1174613

You do the maths

Outline brief for supply demand planning exercises

You are currently planning the Master Production Schedule (MPS) for the assembly of CB-87495-1 Control Box 4l-90 for the First Quarter beginning at week 1.

The control box final assembly department assembles all the control boxes and can achieve a maximum production rate of 50 for CB-87495-1 Control Box 4l-90 per week. However, by giving four weeks' notice (ie from week 5 onwards), the department can arrange overtime to increase the number of completed assemblies by 10 per cent up to a maximum of 55 boxes. You can also decrease production by 10 per cent to 45 boxes per week by organizing training, planned maintenance or holidays. The factory is currently working a standard Monday to Friday week.

The stock position for CB-87495-1 at the beginning of week 1 is 20 finished control boxes. The management directive is to keep a minimum stock of 10 units available, and the maximum stock should not exceed 20 units. Where possible the capacity should be kept level loaded.

- The sales team forecast a quarter-end spike so have requested that the planned quarter-end stock is set to 20 units.
- The operations management team do not want a repeat of last year's quarter-end excess stock and have requested that the maximum stock should not exceed 20 at any time for the quarter. Although the current planned maximum of 45 has been approved, this is considered a temporary measure to manage the quarter-end spike.
- Overall the forecast demand is considered volatile and it is requested that it should be refreshed every two weeks.

As the planner for CB-87495-1 Control Box 41-90 you have planned to meet the forecast demand over the quarter, as shown in Figure 2.24. Although the excess stock has been approved it is expected that it will be reduced where possible when re-planned.

Figure 2.24 Existing supply demand schedule for CB-87495-1 Control Box 41-90

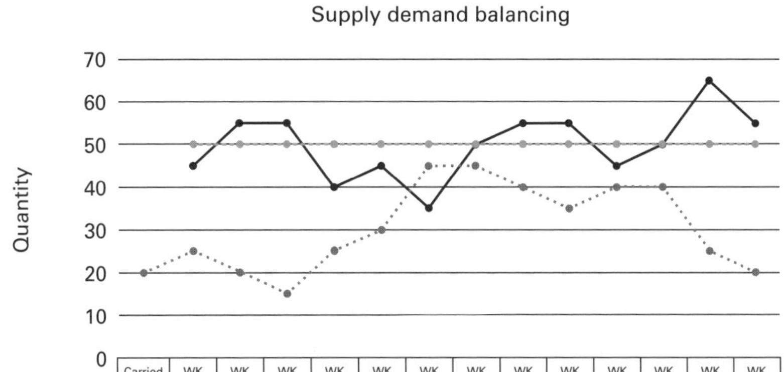

	Carried forward	WK 1	WK 2	WK 3	WK 4	WK 5	WK 6	WK 7	WK 8	WK 9	WK 10	WK 11	WK 12	WK 13
		Month 1				Month 2				Month 3				
Forecast		45	55	55	40	45	35	50	55	55	45	50	65	55
Works orders (WO)		50	50	50	50	50	50	50	50	50	50	50	50	50
Projected inventory (PI)	20	25	20	15	25	30	45	45	40	35	40	40	25	20

Exercise Part 1: supply/demand re-balancing

The forecast has now been refreshed and demand has increased by 30 units across the quarter. The new demand is shown in Table 2.5 Worksheet 1. Your task is to re-plan the works order schedule and projected inventory for the CB-87495-1 based on the changed forecast.

Table 2.5 Worksheet 1 Supply Demand Schedule for CB-87495-1 Control Box 4I-9O for wks. 1 to 13

	Carried Forward	WK 1	WK 2	WK 3	WK 4	WK 5	WK 6	WK 7	WK 8	WK 9	WK 10	WK 11	WK 12	WK 13
Base Forecast		45	55	55	40	45	35	50	55	55	45	50	65	55
Change in Forecast		5	5	–5	5	10	25	0	5	–5	10	0	–20	–5

		Month 1				Month 2				Month 3				
	Carried Forward	WK 1	WK 2	WK 3	WK 4	WK 5	WK 6	WK 7	WK 8	WK 9	WK 10	WK 11	WK 12	WK 13
Forecast		50	60	50	45	55	60	50	60	50	55	50	45	50
Assembly Capacity		50	50	50	50	50	50	50	50	50	50	50	50	50
10% Flexibility														
Works Orders (WO)														
Projected Inventory (PI)	20													

Your suggested approach is:

- First calculate quarter totals using Table 2.6:
  - demand/demand change;
  - capacity/capacity shortfalls;
  - quarter-end inventory projection of 20.
- Next determine the works order schedule:
  - how to meet the new customer demand;
  - use the flexibility of the assembly department (55 units from week 5);
  - maintain stock level of 10 minimum and 20 maximum wherever possible.

Hints:

- minimize increase in works orders;
- keep capacity level within the constraints.

Table 2.6 Template to calculate quarter totals

			Totals
A		Previous Forecast	650
B		Current Forecast	680
C	= B – A	Difference	
D		Projected Inventory (PI) C/F	20
E	= B – D + I	Projected Inventory (PI) End	
F	= B – D + E	Build to Balance Forecast & Inventory	
G		Assembly Capacity	650
H	= F – G	Additional 10% Flexibility needed	
I	= G + H	Works Orders (WO) required	

Consider: what are the critical issues in developing the new supply plan?

Exercise Part 2: supply/demand re-balancing

Time has moved on and we are now at the beginning of week 3. The forecast for CB-87495-1 has been refreshed and has reduced by five units.

Assume that the overtime for weeks 5 to 10 was approved. You can increase/decrease capacity by a maximum of 10 per cent given four weeks' notice (ie from week 7); you may wish not to continue with the overtime in weeks 7 to 10 to adjust to the new schedule. The finished goods stock for CB-87495-1 is 10 units at the end of week 3. The planned stock position at the end of the planning period which now extends to week 15 must be 20 units.

The second stage of the task is to re-calculate the new delivery plan. We now have to consider changes to the existing planned orders, ie when can the works orders for the assembly department be adjusted?

Approach:

- First calculate quarter totals for, using Table 2.8:
  - demand/demand change;
  - capacity/capacity shortfalls;
  - quarter-end inventory (week 13) projection quantity 20;
  - period-end inventory (week 15) projection quantity of 20.
- Next determine the works order schedule needed to meet:
  - the new customer demands;
  - use of the flexibility of the assembly department (55 units from week 5);
  - maintain stock level of 10 minimum and 20 maximum wherever possible.

Hints:

- Minimize increase in works orders.
- Keep capacity level within the constraints.

Table 2.7 Worksheet 2 Supply Demand Schedule for CB-87495-1 Control Box 4I-9O for wks. 3 to 15

	Carried Forward	WK 3	WK 4	WK 5	WK 6	WK 7	WK 8	WK 9	WK 10	WK 11	WK 12	WK 13	WK 14	WK 15
Previous Forecast + 2 wks		50	45	55	60	50	60	50	55	50	45	50	55	45
Change in Forecast		0	0	0	0	–5	–10	0	0	0	5	5	0	0

		Month 1				Month 2				Month 3				
	Carried Forward	WK 3	WK 4	WK 5	WK 6	WK 7	WK 8	WK 9	WK 10	WK 11	WK 12	WK 13	WK 14	WK 15
Forecast		50	45	55	60	45	50	50	55	50	50	55	55	45
Assembly Capacity		50	50	50	50	50	50	50	50	50	50	50	50	50
10% Flexibility				5	5									
Works Orders (WO)														
Projected Inventory (PI)	1													

Table 2.8 Template to calculate quarter totals

			Totals
A		Previous Forecast	670
B		Current Forecast	665
C	= B – A	Difference	
D		Projected Inventory (PI) C/F	10
E	= B – D + I	Projected Inventory (PI) End	
F	= B – D + E	Build to Balance Forecast & Inventory	
G		Assembly Capacity	650
H	= F – G	Additional 10% Flexibility needed	
I	= G + H	Works Orders (WO) required	

Consider: what are the critical issues in developing the new supply plan?

Chapter 2 exercise answers

Exercise Part 1: Rebalancing weeks 1 to 13

The calculated quarter-end totals in Table 2.9 show that 30 additional units (H) are needed to achieve the quarter end inventory target (E). These extra units can only be planned from week 5 and must be planned between week 5 and week 13, ensuring the maximum of 20 units is not exceeded.

Using Table 2.10 we can see new demand spread and that we cannot increase production until week 5. The key is to increase the supply as soon as possible, ie in week 5 and only reduce when the stock exceeds 20 units, as well as checking the quarter-end target is achieved by doing a cumulative calculation. There are only nine weeks to plan an additional supply of 30. If we plan in the first six weeks, we can see that all of the requirements are satisfied. However, planning the orders to week 11 to week 13 would not achieve the minimum stock requirement. The results of Table 2.10 are shown in Figure 2.25.

Table 2.9 Calculated quarter totals

			Totals
A		Previous Forecast	650
B		Current Forecast	680
C	= B – A	Difference	30
D		Projected Inventory (PI) C/F	20
E	= B – D + I	Projected Inventory (PI) End	20
F	= B – D + E	Build to Balance Forecast & Inventory	680
G		Assembly Capacity	650
H	= F – G	Additional 10% Flexibility needed	30
I	= G + H	Works Orders (WO) required	680

Figure 2.25 Answer 1 revised supply demand schedule for CB-87495-1 Control Box 41-90 wks. 1 to 13

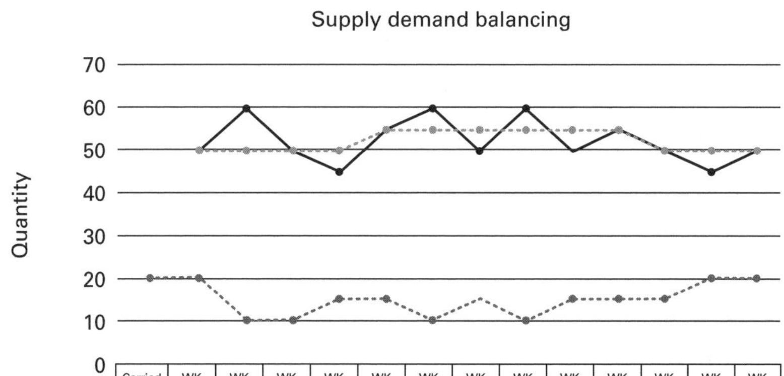

	Carried forward	WK 1	WK 2	WK 3	WK 4	WK 5	WK 6	WK 7	WK 8	WK 9	WK 10	WK 11	WK 12	WK 13
		Month 1				Month 2				Month 3				
Forecast		50	60	50	45	55	60	50	60	50	55	50	45	50
Works orders (WO)		50	50	50	50	55	55	55	55	55	55	50	50	50
Projected inventory (PI)	20	20	10	10	15	15	10	15	10	15	15	15	20	20

Table 2.10 Answer 1 Supply demand schedule for CB-87495-1 Control Box 4I-9O wks. 1 to 13

	Carried Forward	WK 1	WK 2	WK 3	WK 4	WK 5	WK 6	WK 7	WK 8	WK 9	WK 10	WK 11	WK 12	WK 13
Previous Forecast + 2 wks		45	55	55	40	45	35	50	55	55	45	50	65	55
Change in Forecast		5	5	–5	5	10	25	0	5	–5	10	0	–20	–5

		Month 1				Month 2				Month 3				
	Carried Forward	WK 1	WK 2	WK 3	WK 4	WK 5	WK 6	WK 7	WK 8	WK 9	WK 10	WK 11	WK 12	WK 13
Forecast		50	60	50	45	55	60	50	60	50	55	50	45	50
Assembly Capacity		50	50	50	50	50	50	50	50	50	50	50	50	50
10% Flexibility						5	5	5	5	5	5			
Works Orders (WO)		50	50	50	50	55	55	55	55	55	55	50	50	50
Projected Inventory (PI)	20	20	10	10	15	15	10	15	10	15	15	15	20	20

Exercise Part 2: Rebalancing weeks 3 to 15

As with the first exercise the initial step is to calculate the totals as shown in Table 2.11. Here we need to pay particular attention to the Open (C/F) and Closing (End) inventory. It is important to note that they were equal in Exercise 1. Although the overall difference in the forecast is a reduction of five units, nevertheless 25 units still need to be planned.

Table 2.11 Calculated wk. 3 to wk. 15 totals

			Totals
A		Previous Forecast	670
B		Current Forecast	665
C	= B – A	Difference	–5
D		Projected Inventory (PI) C/F	10
E	= B – D + I	Projected Inventory (PI) End	20
F	= B – D + E	Build to Balance Forecast & Inventory	675
G		Assembly Capacity	650
H	= F – G	Additional 10% Flexibility needed	25
I	= G + H	Works Orders (WO) required	675

Here the demand reduction needs to be accounted for by a matching supply reduction in weeks 8 to 10. This needs to be offset by an increase in the last two weeks to achieve the required end stock.

Learning points: supply demand balancing

If you consider this planning approach, what would make this process easier, more automatic? As it stands it relies too much on you thinking through the decision processes.

Looking at Table 2.12 we see that first we need to take account of planned additional capacity which if left would quickly cause overstock. However, it is less clear where the additional capacity should be placed as there are a range of combinations which would satisfy the planning constraints. In order to be able to plan using systems we would have to use an approach that would ensure there is only one answer.

Table 2.12 Answer 2 Supply demand schedule for CB-87495-1 Control Box 4I-9O weeks 3 to 15

	Carried Forward	WK 3	WK 4	WK 5	WK 6	WK 7	WK 8	WK 9	WK 10	WK 11	WK 12	WK 13	WK 14	WK 15
Previous Forecast + 2 wks		50	45	55	60	50	60	50	55	50	45	50	55	45
Change in Forecast		0	0	0	0	–5	–10	0	0	0	5	5	0	0

		Month 1				Month 2				Month 3				
	Carried Forward	WK 3	WK 4	WK 5	WK 6	WK 7	WK 8	WK 9	WK 10	WK 11	WK 12	WK 13	WK 14	WK 15
Forecast		50	45	55	60	45	50	50	55	50	50	55	55	45
Assembly Capacity		50	50	50	50	50	50	50	50	50	50	50	50	50
10% Flexibility				5	5	5					5	5		
Works Orders (WO)		50	50	55	55	55	50	50	50	50	55	55	50	50
Projected Inventory (PI)	10	10	15	15	10	20	20	20	15	15	20	20	15	20

In the first exercise the maximum and minimum rules are sufficient to ensure there is only one solution. However, in the second exercise several solutions are possible.

Figure 2.26 Answer 2 revised supply demand schedule for CB-87495-1 Control Box 4I-9O wks. 3 to 15

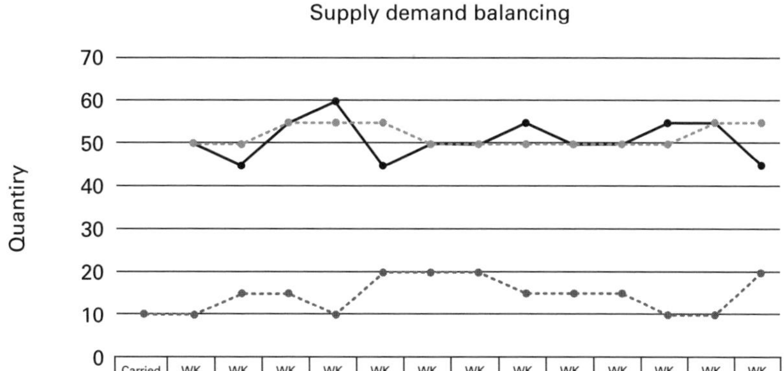

	Carried forward	WK 3	WK 4	WK 5	WK 6	WK 7	WK 8	WK 9	WK 10	WK 11	WK 12	WK 13	WK 14	WK 15
		Month 1		Month 2				Month 3					Month 4	
Forecast		50	45	55	60	45	50	50	55	50	50	55	55	45
Works orders (WO)		50	50	55	55	55	50	50	50	50	50	50	55	55
Projected inventory (PI)	10	10	15	15	10	20	20	20	15	15	15	10	10	20

The results shown in Table 2.12 are shown in graphic form in Figure 2.26.

Inventory balancing and control

03

Introduction

In this chapter we will focus on the importance of inventory **balancing** and **control**, looking at the importance of the correct business processes, appropriate organizational structure and the technology options. The chapter will examine tools and techniques for managing and improving the performance of both inventory balancing and control, including the use of Lean and JIT. Finally, the chapter will cover the effect of product variety and design on product complexity, the BOM and inventory balancing and control.

In Chapter 1 we identified that there are three key sequenced steps in a business:

Forecast → Plan → Execute

Managing inventory well is critical for all manufacturing and retail companies and is involved at all three of these stages, as shown in Figure 3.1.

Figure 3.1 Locating inventory planning, balancing and control in the three-step process

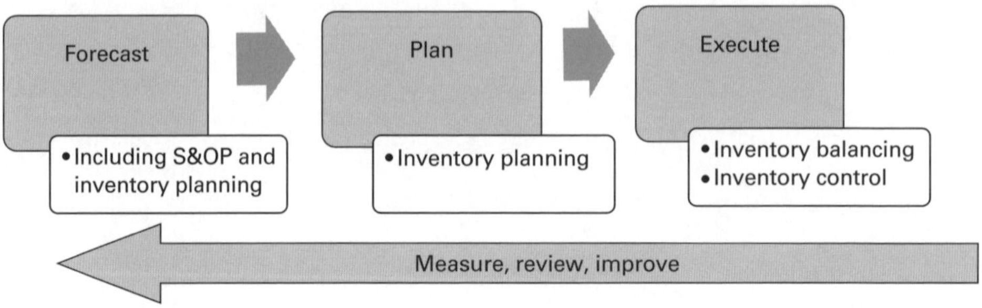

The main operational activity for inventory **balancing** and **control** is in the 'execute' step of the sequence. There is a need to focus on the importance of the processes necessary for inventory balancing and control since:

- Inventory balancing is involved in:
  - forecasting through its interaction with sales and operations planning (S&OP);
  - the routine management of the supply-demand relationship.
- Inventory control:
  - is the management of the physical inventory;
  - ensures that the physical inventory is correctly reflected in the system records;
  - will be considered in the optimization of warehouse size, location, activities, personnel, systems, automation level.

This chapter considers the process of inventory balancing and control in more detail than we have done previously. We have looked at the relationship between the three pillars of inventory management in Chapters 1 and 2, as shown in Figure 3.2. Inventory planning is considered in more detail in Chapters 4 to 7.

Key tools and techniques will be discussed to ensure a practical understanding of inventory balancing and control.

Figure 3.2 The three pillars of inventory management

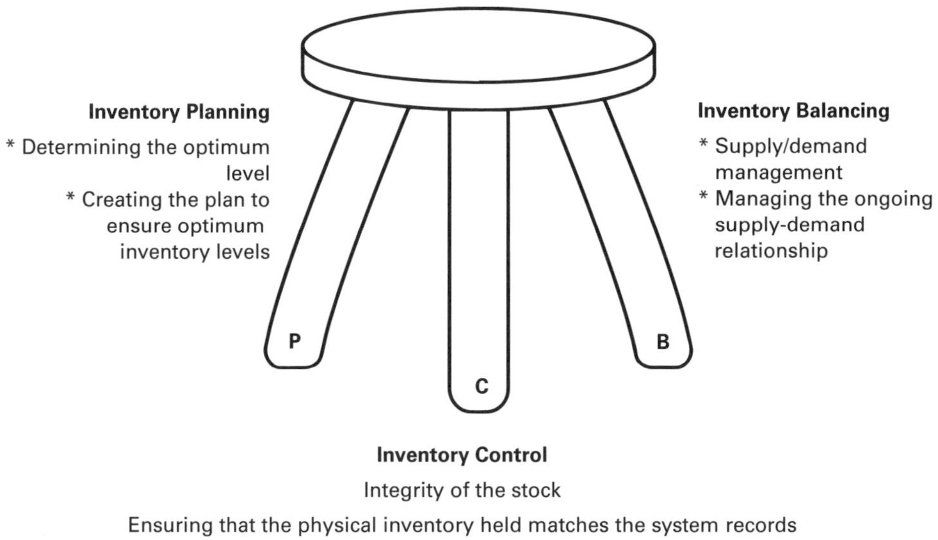

Control

The processes and concepts of inventory control (ie managing data and stock integrity) are dealt with in this chapter, together with discussions of the various types of tools and techniques used by different organizations. There are many aspects of inventory control which vary tremendously according to the individual circumstances. For example, which warehouse management system (WMS) to use, what level of automation investment should be made for handling and moving goods, what type of storage (eg shelves for tubing, container size, automated garment rails). A greater level of detail can be found elsewhere in books, journals and literature, some of which are listed at the end of the chapter. What we are predominantly concerned with here is the business approach and considerations when establishing the inventory control processes and the appropriate level of equipment, systems and technology.

Balancing

The inventory balancing processes of monitoring and returning to optimum stock levels, dealing with backlog (or 'past-due') orders, and S&OP will be discussed. The supply/demand balancing has to be constantly monitored against the plan, and optimum levels maintained despite changes in customer requirements, supplier performance, and internal process compliance. These will be discussed and links to elsewhere within this book will be highlighted where relevant.

Process, organization and technology (POT)

In Chapter 2 we discussed the reasons why a business needs to consider process, organization and technology. In Chapter 3 we will consider these for inventory balancing and control:

- Process: for example, identifying necessary tasks and the ideal sequence of activity for managing the receipt and booking in of goods.
- Organization: for example, how to ensure people are motivated in the areas responsible for inventory balancing, stock movement and holding.
- Technology: for example, the best level of automation (systems and stock handling equipment) for an individual business.

Process

It is important to understand process for many reasons including:

- A process encapsulates the sequence of actions or steps that are linked with the aim of achieving a particular outcome.
- A process is not static but changes with the business and the environment.
- The focus on the process allows us to break boundaries between different departments, so that instead of a departmental focus (eg purchasing department buying in bulk to achieve lowest unit cost) serving the customer is seen holistically (ie in terms of the total cost of product and service as delivered to the customer, for example purchasing products so that they are supplied in smaller batches more frequently).
- The focus on the process enables the removal of potentially conflicting departmental aims, eg although manufacturing can achieve lowest unit cost and greatest capacity utilization by producing large batch sizes of a single product in long runs, this may not match customer demand (which may be for small quantities of a variety of products), therefore potentially driving up inventory handling costs and late deliveries. The correct balancing for a steel producer will be very different to that of an aero engine supplier.

Inventory record accuracy is essential as always. Creating a process that helps failsafe accuracy/prevent inaccuracy is necessary to ensure that chasing accuracy does not become a fool's errand and inaccuracy levels do not prevent useful system transactions being created.

Organization

Organization is concerned with:

- People with the right abilities, approach and experiences, eg MRP knowledge and understanding, detailed and efficient attitude to goods handling and finding root causes of incorrect data.
- Product: ensuring product design is optimized and balanced for customer requirements, supplier partnership, in-company costs, planning and production.
- Culture: the values and practices of an organization and how its people interact with each other and with customers and suppliers, eg attention to detail and focus on ensuring system data and physical inventory are correct and match.

Technology

It is vital to ensure the correct business systems are installed and the right equipment is in use for effective and efficient business management. These must suit the needs and the goals of the business:

- For example, the appropriate level of warehouse management system is in use and is interfaced correctly with other enterprise-wide systems (eg ERP, engineering management, inventory planning and production control).
- In all physical areas of inventory control (receiving, holding, moving and dispatching goods) items must be handled in a satisfactory way. For example, a small corner shop and a distribution centre for a large supermarket both need to manage edible goods appropriately and ensure records are correct and up to date, but the acceptable level of automated equipment handling will be greater in the distribution centre than in a small shop.
- Stock information must be recorded accurately and up to date: systems must support this, with fail-safe checks in place where possible and the correct exception reporting.

Inventory record accuracy is essential. As Tony Wild (2011) says: 'The systems only work if the data is correct, otherwise people are making decisions based on the wrong situations or mistrust in the data entirely and doing their own thing.'

Using appropriate technology that helps ensure accuracy/prevent inaccuracy is necessary to support the processes and organization to prevent errors being introduced as transactions are created to record activity. The founding principles of Lean and Just in Time (JIT) offer excellent guidance for inventory balancing and control processes, especially in the areas of organizational design.

Lean and Just in Time (JIT)

A Lean organization focuses on those processes that add value to goods and/or services in the eyes of the customer, and for which the customer is willing to pay. Therefore, Lean organizations seek to remove Non-Value-Add (NVA) activities, whether they are working in manufacturing, production, transportation, health care, education, administration, finance or other services. Inventory control is an area where 'waste' can easily occur (for example a poorly laid out warehouse creates waste by increasing the distance travelled for putting away and picking goods). And correct levels of inventory can be maintained more easily where there are clear and visible instructions, eg using Kanban in conjunction with MRP should keep the right balancing of inventory.

Lean and JIT are subjects about which a great deal has been written. To show how they might be applied to help to achieve good inventory balancing and control we will take three well-known aspects of Lean and give examples of how they can be used. In this section we will consider:

- 5S (Gemba Kanri);
- 3-Mu;
- Seven Wastes (related to the Muda step in 3-Mu).

5S (Gemba Kanri)

5S can be used to great effect to improve the 'organization' section of POT. This is partly because it aims to improve involvement of people working for example in a warehouse. 5S helps people to feel ownership of some or all of their working environment. This is normally an excellent motivational method, helping to promote both job satisfaction for employees and benefit for the company. This applies both to the individual and to a group or team of people working together in an area.

The implementation of the tool 5S, or Gemba Kanri, can also help to create an optimum work layout. 5S focuses on effective organization of a warehouse, clear visual management and a standardization of the working practices and procedures. The primary aims of implementing 5S are:

- to introduce standard working practices to ensure that everyone understands what is expected of them and what they can expect from everyone else;
- to ensure safe, efficient and repeatable work;
- to have clear visual management, ensuring that issues are immediately obvious and not left to fester.

Figure 3.3 The five steps of the 5S process (Gemba Kanri)

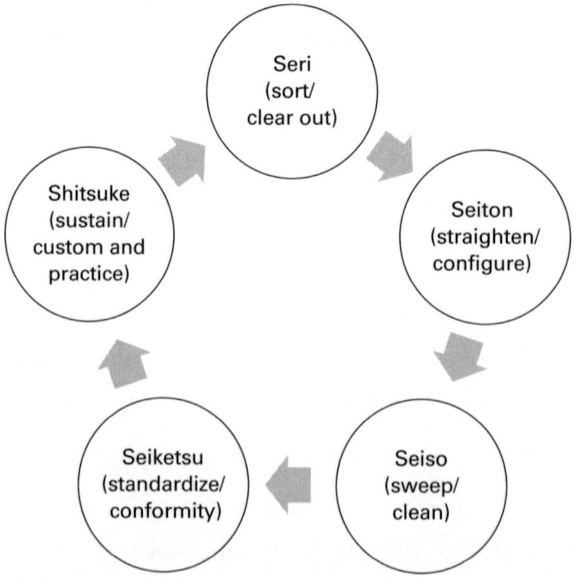

SOURCE Richards and Grinsted (2016)

The implementation of 5S needs to start with Seri (sort), proceeding in sequence through the following steps of Seiton, Seiso, Seiketsu, Shitsuke and back to Seiri, as shown in Figure 3.3. Safety is generally considered to be an underpinning condition throughout the 5S.

Implementation and routine activity examples are given for each of the steps in Table 3.1. Longer checklists and more information can be found elsewhere, for example in *The Logistics and Supply Chain Toolkit* (Richards and Grinsted, 2016).

Table 3.1 Examples of 5S implementation, routine activity and measurements

5S	Action	Performance Measures
Seri		
Implementation activity example	Identify and remove unnecessary items from work area	
Routine activity example	Identify and dispose of obsolete stock	Reduced stock holding costs; increased availability of storage areas

Table 3.1 *continued*

5S	Action	Performance Measures
Seiton		
Implementation activity example	After clutter is removed, arrange remaining items efficiently, ensuring each item has a designated place	
Routine activity example	Analysis of items by frequency of pick and arrange accordingly	Increased pick rate and decreased total pick distance
Seiso		
Implementation activity example	Create a thoroughly clean area, including tools and equipment, such that any non-conformity is obvious	
Routine activity example	Identify and remove breakages, leaks and spills	Routine visual check
Seiketsu		
Implementation activity example	Standardize the implementation activity from steps 1–3, ensuring requirements are clear and visual	
Routine activity example	Identify and segregate rejected inventory items	Time taken to remove, segregate and resolve rejects
Shitsuke		
Implementation activity example	Establish processes to maintain housekeeping, routinely audit and improve to ensure 5S becomes part of the culture of the work and management of the warehouse	
Routine activity example	Hold regular meetings within the team and with management	Number of improvements (a) made and (b) introduced

SOURCE Richards and Grinsted (2016)

3-Mu: Muda, Muri, Mura

This focuses attention on wastefulness, unreasonableness and inconsistency, usually taken as the Japanese words Muda, Muri and Mura:

- Muda (Non-Value-Add [NVA] activities): these are also known as the seven wastes of Lean – minimizing waste by eliminating unnecessary work (too early, too many or overly complex), movement (both transport and the motions of equipment or people), waiting, product, mistakes. In more recent times two additional wastes are also considered: the waste of a human being (eg a person to watch a machine), and the waste of natural resources (eg energy, water).
- Muri (unreasonableness): refers to the excessive demands on output as a result of poor quality due to the waste of defective goods.
- Mura (unevenness): the failure to achieve consistency. Eliminating unevenness or irregularities in the production process is one of the main principles of the Just-In-Time system. Key ways of identifying Mura include through the application of *Heijunka* principles and *Kanban* devices:
  - Kanban is a visual sign or signal. It is used in JIT to trigger an action, eg it authorizes the production or movement of items. Traditionally it was very tempting to react to an idle operator or machine by issuing an instruction to make more product (rather than understanding the root cause behind the situation). However, often all this instruction achieves is to push more work-in-progress into the process without any increase in sales. The additional work-in-progress would create an out-of-balancing inventory condition against the plan as well as creating more work for inventory control. A simple Kanban can be used to help prevent this (an example is shown in Figure 3.4), making less work for inventory control and forcing an acceptable inventory balancing to exist.
  - Heijunka is levelling, so that eg flow of product through production processes happens in a consistent and controlled fashion. If, for example, the snow shovel has consistent weekly demand of 1,000 units as shown in Table 3.2, then applying the Heijunka principle a level production flow would be to produce 200 a day. The demand shown could in this situation lead to a backlog occurring from the beginning of each week: to prevent this, stock-on-hand of 200 units at the beginning of each week would be necessary.

Figure 3.4 Simple Kanban to prevent build-up of WIP

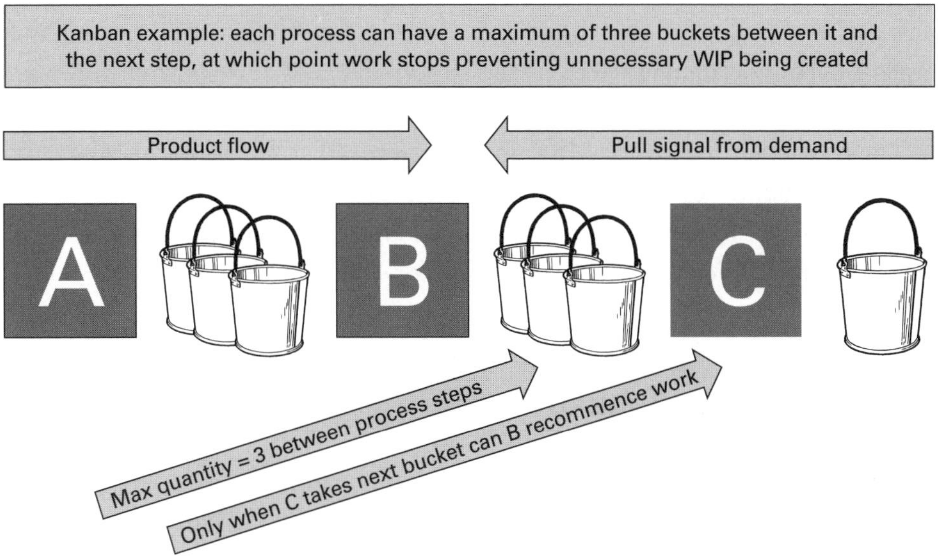

Table 3.2 Snow shovel weekly demand and level production rate

	Monday	Tuesday	Wednesday	Thursday	Friday
Demand	400	200	100	100	200
Production Level Rate	200	200	200	200	200
Backlog	–200	–200	–100	0	0

- Multi-process handling is where a person can operate more than one machine. This can also be used effectively to smooth workflow.

By focusing on these activities, optimization of the business processes can be supported. The work done on Muda, Muri and Mura can highlight key areas where process and organizational improvements can be made, as well as identify where technology may assist.

We refer to MRP and ERP frequently in this book. However, MRP is not intended to be presented as a single solution for all companies, nor as a general panacea. Many companies successfully use both Lean and MRP in various combinations, creating hybrid solutions, some similar to the examples given in Figure 3.4 and Table 3.2. Since we know that inventory balancing is the routine management of the supply-demand relationship, there are many benefits from using 3-Mu and other Lean techniques.

The relationship between MRP and 3-Mu, specifically Kanban, is discussed further in Chapter 5.

The first of the 3-Mu activities, Muda, is further broken down into the Seven Wastes, which are often considered on their own.

The Seven Wastes (Muda)

Some examples of how the seven wastes of Lean can relate to inventory control and how integration of inventory holding and movement with other value-add activities may lead to improvements are discussed below. Minimizing waste may be achieved by:

1a Eliminating work that is carried out too early or where additional items are made: the ease of measuring improvements in production efficiencies may encourage manufacturing a larger batch size (thereby reducing the 'unit cost') whilst increasing the stock holding time and activity and therefore cost. An example of this is a pharmaceutical company which in 2016 labelled items destined for the South East Asian market prematurely, but in large batches to achieve 'economies of scale': this led to a great deal of rework once the product reached the distribution centre for the intended markets, with packaging being replaced or having labels stuck on the boxes in the correct languages.

1b Eliminating work that is overly complex: goods-inwards activities may include inspecting the quality of all parts received. This is often doubling up a task that has already been carried out by the supplier prior to shipping. Where possible, goods received from trusted suppliers may be assumed to meet agreed quality targets, thus removing this step from goods-inwards processing.

2 Eliminating unnecessary transportation: cross-docking is a good example here – goods are moved from goods inwards direct to goods outwards, with recombining of loads as required, without the need to move items onto warehouse shelves in between.

3 Eliminating unnecessary motions of equipment or people: ergonomically it is better for a person picking an item in a warehouse to lift it from a shelf at waist height and place it into a basket at a similar height with minimum rotation, than to have to constantly bend, rotate and stretch. Thus, shelving height is important. Therefore, for each item, by combining shelf height and location with pick frequency information, items picked most often can be best positioned.

4 Eliminating unnecessary waiting: the longer inventory stays in an organization, the higher the inventory holding cost. For example, an efficient goods-inwards section ensures items are received and moved to where they are needed or put away as quickly as possible. Automatic identification tools and techniques, effective processes, good planning and communication, and excellent visibility can all assist here.

5 Eliminating unnecessary product: one example is the elimination of unnecessary packaging by reducing the use of branded external cartons.

CASE STUDY

Lego Group example for eliminating unnecessary product

In 2003 the Lego Group were in financial trouble and needed to make some major changes. Lego were able to eliminate unnecessary product largely through the move to a complete-to-order production pull process: prior to this the company was holding and managing a high volume of finished products, whereas subsequently inventory was held at the pre-kitting stages, and stock levels were driven down (Lego Group, 2014). Jorgen Knudstorp (Lego CEO since 2004) said that part of the problems of the Lego group in 2003 was that 'We had too much capacity, too much stock... sitting in the wrong countries' (Ashcroft, 2014). By moving to a complete-to-order process Lego were able to eliminate the unnecessary holding of excessive finished goods. Through this change and several others, Lego went from near bankruptcy in 2003 to become the largest global toy company in 2016.

6 Eliminating unnecessary mistakes: it is well known that mistakes add costs to goods and services. Unnecessary mistakes can be reduced or prevented altogether by creating fail-safe or fool-proof processes. Also known as poke yoke or mistake proofing, errors are prevented by a process designed to prevent them happening, or to easily identify when a flaw or error occurs. An example is one inventory control system which assumes idiot-proofing is the use of pick-by-light, put-by-light, pack-by-light warehouse systems.

Using pick-by-light, put-by-light and pack-by-light systems to eliminate unnecessary mistakes

Pick-by-light, put-by-light and pack-by-light systems use lights to direct a warehouse operator to select or place items correctly.

A basic system will have lights above or below racks or bins from where items will be picked or placed. The operator will identify warehouse or customer requirements, eg by scanning a bar code on a container, then correctly place the item(s). To confirm the pick or put, the operator will press the light. The pick or put will be complete when all illuminated lights turn off.

An alternative pick/put/pack-by light system uses augmented reality (AR). Instead of having light systems installed on shelving or bins, the operator will wear a headset or glasses. Information is displayed virtually and superimposed onto the real environment, ie the operator sees both the information and their surroundings. The information displayed directs the operator to select and place items according to the pick/put/pack situation.

Errors in a manual system which cause unnecessary mistakes include picking the wrong item, the wrong quantity, or omitting the item altogether. Manual systems that use paper orders are also slower. Companies who require accurate and fast picking, whilst retaining the flexibility of human operators, often find pick-by-light systems effective and efficient, whilst concurrently helping to eliminate unnecessary mistakes.

7a Eliminating unnecessary time of human being: this includes employing a person to watch a machine, manual entry of data rather than the use of RFID or barcodes, and carrying items (in person or with a forklift truck etc) where it would be possible to move items automatically via roller tracks.

7b And finally, minimizing waste by eliminating unnecessary use of natural resources (eg energy, water) – see warehouses of the future.

Inventory balancing

Inventory balancing requires monitoring stock levels throughout an organization and ensuring corrective actions are initiated where we need to return to optimum stock levels. This is of fundamental importance, as shown in Figure 3.5, since inventory levels will have been planned to get the balancing

Figure 3.5 Inventory balancing – getting the inventory just right

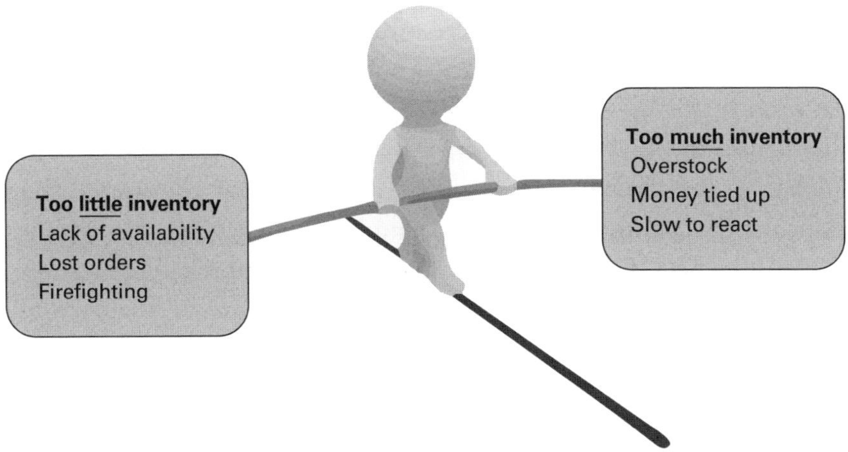

Reproduced by kind permission of Inventory Matters Ltd

between too much and too little inventory just right. Unless inventory balancing is being carried out correctly, stock levels can vary outside the optimum limits: without remedying product levels we can veer into a zone where production may be halted, sales may be lost, or the carrying cost and incorrect location of the inventory can jeopardize the business, as it did with Lego in 2003. In addition, if the inventory levels require significant and frequent rebalancing, the business may have a larger problem, for example: is the inventory plan correct, or are there issues with the product or packaging?

In this section we will cover:

- Sales and operations planning (S&OP): this identifies the expected demand over a medium- to long-term period and how the business can organize resources to meet it.
- Returning to optimum (keeping inventory in balancing): knowing when the inventory is in overage, underage and shortage, and how to return to acceptable quantities.
- Backlog: if orders are in arrears, why has this happened, what is the impact on the business and what steps need to be taken to rectify the situation?

Sales and operations planning (S&OP)

The sales and operations plan (S&OP) is a planning and communication process necessary for balancing supply and demand at strategic, tactical and operational levels within an organization. S&OP identifies the expected demand over a medium- to long-term period and calculates how the business will meet the demand to ensure there are there sufficient people, equipment and machinery, and if the necessary raw materials and other supplies are available and affordable. This high-level plan drives the inventory plan which in turn drives the inventory balancing activity. It is relevant in inventory balancing at the operational level to identify how the supply/demand relationship is working and to look for improvements, which in turn must be fed back to the S&OP. Thus S&OP must also relate to the short-term period through inventory balancing.

The sales and operations plan brings together the three aspects of supply and demand, ie a business:

- must identify an expected level of demand for its goods and services;
- orders from its suppliers who then deliver raw materials and components;
- must calculate, as a result of company policies and of the first two steps, the inventory it will need to hold to ensure customer orders are met.

A sales and operations plan needs to make allowance for:

- Variations in demand, eg unexpected spikes in buying patterns, seasonality, customer requirements for changes, etc. Some of the factors (eg seasonality) can be built into the plan, others require an understanding of the likely degree of variation.
- Variation in supply, eg an external supplier may need time to process a request to increase or decrease an order size, an internal supplier (eg a manufacturing process) may have its priorities changed and be unable to deliver to a promise date.
- Variation in inventory levels: if the supply-demand relationship were perfect and in perfect harmony, always, inventory would not be needed. If inventory data (and BOMs) were always 100 per cent accurate, if yields were always 100 per cent, if stock was never damaged or deteriorated, then inventory levels would be easy to calculate and manage. However, there are always variations in these areas, some companies experiencing greater demand volatility than others. Hence the need to ensure good exception reporting and inventory balancing techniques are available.
- Flexibility: ensuring that the process has sufficient capability and flexibility to be able to respond cost-effectively to the changes in the demand. Lean techniques are one way to consider increasing the process flexibility.

Returning to optimum inventory

Returning to optimum (keeping inventory in balancing) is knowing when the inventory is in overage, underage and shortage, and how to return to acceptable quantities. In Chapter 2 the standardized inventory saw tooth concept was introduced, including in Figure 2.20, where key parameters were shown, all of which need to be managed to enable MRP to calculate the correct recommendations and create accurate transactions.

Inventory moves into 'underage' when levels fall below the minimum stock, where safety stock consumption will take place. If this happens too rapidly and before a delivery is received, then a part may move into shortage. The solution of course revolves around obtaining more product within an optimum timescale.

Companies tend to have greatest focus on inventory shortages because they understand the cost of losing sales or stopping production because stock is unavailable.

Figure 3.6 When a part is in overage

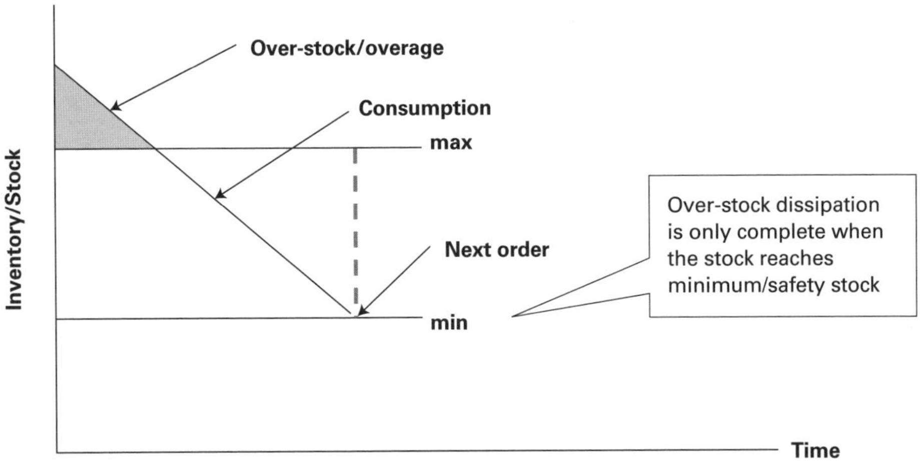

SOURCE Relph and Barrar (2001)

The cost of holding excess stock, ie when the stock is in overage, is less well understood. Overage happens where stock levels rise above the maximum set, as shown in Figure 3.6. Where products are in overage steps must be taken to recover, ie to return to the optimum range, since outside this range additional inventory holding costs will be incurred, additional working capital will be tied up and there is a greater risk that the parts may become obsolete.

Moving back from overage into the optimum range must be formally planned and managed properly. Companies often hold far too many products in overage, tying up a significant investment, as Relph and Barrar (2001) show. This is dealt with in more detail in Chapter 6 and Figures 6.13 to 6.16.

Inventory balancing is concerned with returning products that are in overage or underage back to the optimum range. The term 'overage dissipation' is used to manage a product from over-stock back to the minimum stock level, as shown in Figure 3.6.

It is not, however, always easy to resolve overage, which often happens when there is a change in the expected supply or demand. For example, the weather in the UK is very changeable and it is very hard to predict when there will be snow. When it snows, demand for snow shovels and for salt skyrocket. A company selling snow shovels needs to calculate how many snow shovels to stock in the winter. The number will certainly be more than in the summer, but more in a snowy winter than in a normal winter. Since demand will be so weather dependent, it is almost impossible to predict correctly.

Other products that have a more stable and less volatile demand pattern, eg cans of dog meat or baked beans, are more likely to be managed into the optimum range.

Figure 3.7 Overage dissipation of a number of products

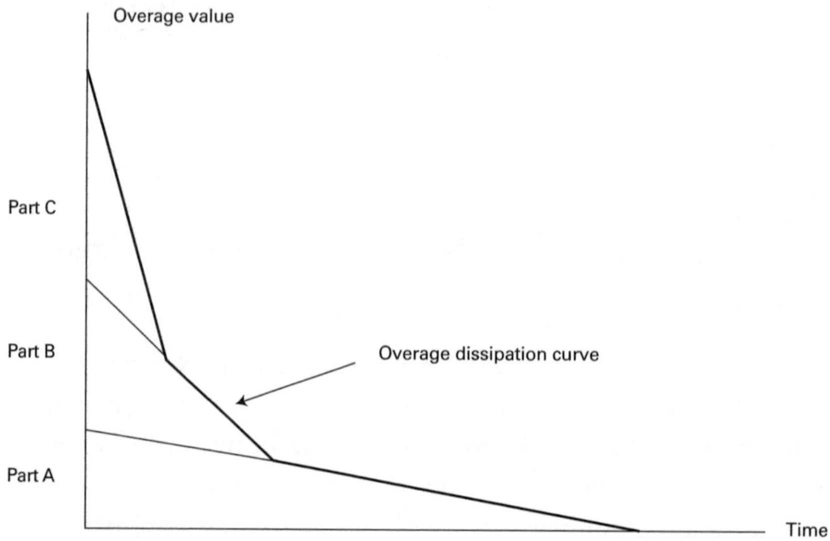

SOURCE Relph and Barrar (2001)

Dissipation of inventory from overage should be considered both on an individual and an aggregate level: only by considering the aggregate level can the true cost of overage be understood. Figure 3.7 shows a dissipation curve, which is produced for a group of parts. High-value parts in overage are likely to be managed back to the optimum as quickly as possible (eg part C in Figure 3.7), because of the high cost to the business; other parts are low in value (eg part A) and may remain in overage for a long time. Overage dissipation is an important management tool and is discussed in more detail in Chapter 6.

Unexpected variations in supply and demand are well-known causes of overage, underage and shortage. In addition, incorrect system parameters and/or data may be the underlying cause. These are usually the most correctable mistakes, both to change the parameters or data as well as identifying improvement steps needed to the system or the process to prevent the problems recurring.

Backlog

Backlog happens when work has not been completed by its due date or a delivery is not received when expected. If demand is not met on time and in full then backlog is created and must be reviewed:

- Is it still required?
- Are we able to recover the situation?
- What needs to be done?
- What are the priorities?

If the work or delivery is still required, then recovering backlog obviously puts an additional load onto a business. The planning system, eg MRP, will have already planned new work based on predicted available resources and on the assumption that previously allocated work will have been completed:

- Is there sufficient capacity to complete the backlog in addition to the new work?
- Does the new work rely on the completion of the backlog (eg supply of items into final assembly)?
- Are the BOMs correct? And have all the tasks to make the component parts of the BOM been rescheduled?

- Is the priority to recover the backlog or start on the new planned work?
- When can the supplier deliver the order?

Decisions will need to be made. If the planning system is not adjusted, it will assume all is well and drive the inventory into the business on the assumption that the orders are still required, the backlog will be recovered or that the critical supplier will deliver on time respectively.

The results of the failure to adjust the plan/system correctly include:

- unbalanced inventory sitting in the business;
- there are no longer customers wanting the product;
- there is no capacity in manufacturing to make the products;
- without the critical component the production process cannot proceed any further.

Inventory balancing is a reaction to circumstances and an attempt to return to inventory levels as set by the inventory plan. Backlog may be caused by a lack of material, people or equipment, or failure of a supplier to deliver. The rebalancing of the inventory therefore cannot always be based on a predetermined calculation since there may be unknown conditions and assumptions.

How can a business recover when backlog happens?

Recovering from serious backlog include options such as:

- reducing the manufacturing output to respond to a customer's cancelled order;
- resetting the MPS to reflect that the arrears will not be recovered;
- delaying a customer order because of a known issue with a critical supplier.

Inventory control

As already stated, inventory control is concerned with:

- the activities of receiving, holding, moving and dispatching goods;
- the recording of inventory movement throughout the business;
- the management of the physical inventory; and

- ensuring that the physical inventory is correctly reflected in the system records.

Physical inventory within an organization is on a journey from when it is initially received (goods inwards) through to when it is dispatched (goods-outwards) and received by the next customer in the supply chain. Figure 3.8 shows a brief outline of this journey.

Figure 3.8 Three stages in inventory control from goods inwards to customer delivery

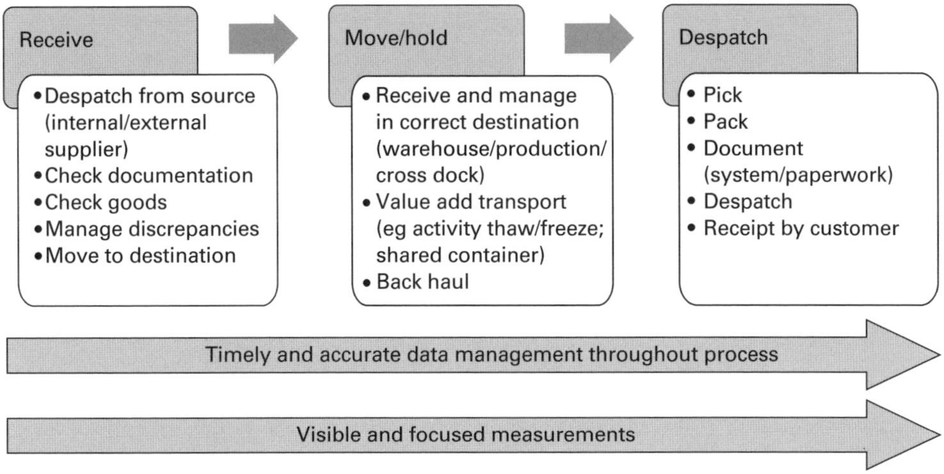

During the journey from goods-inwards to customer delivery the inventory is either:

- in a process where activity is being performed on it, ie it is moving or flowing: activities include collection, delivery and production tasks;
- being held awaiting the next process to be performed, ie it is stopped: reasons for holding inventory include finished goods stock awaiting customer orders, supplier minimum order quantity is greater than production batch sizes, and uncertainty of supply of raw materials and components.

As it moves along this journey the physical inventory and the electronic records on the business system must match each other. An example of some of the main steps in this journey is shown in Figure 3.9.

In this section we will consider inventory control in terms of:

- the steps of the physical inventory: receive, hold, move, dispatch;
- process, organization and technology:

Figure 3.9 Control of physical inventory must match electronic records

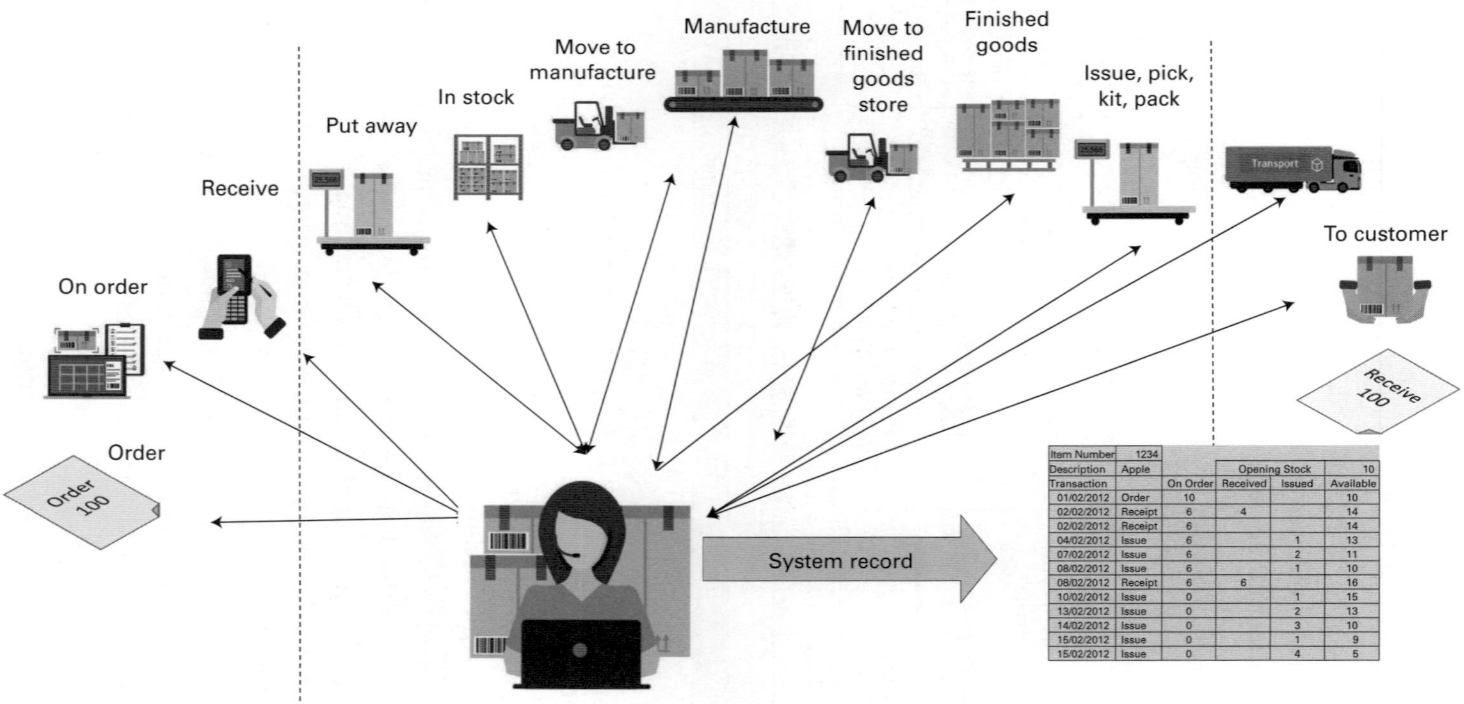

Item Number	1234				
Description	Apple		Opening Stock		10
Transaction		On Order	Received	Issued	Available
01/02/2012	Order	10			10
02/02/2012	Receipt	6	4		14
02/02/2012	Receipt	6			14
04/02/2012	Issue	6		1	13
07/02/2012	Issue	6		2	11
08/02/2012	Issue	6		1	10
08/02/2012	Receipt	6	6		16
10/02/2012	Issue	0		1	15
13/02/2012	Issue	0		2	13
14/02/2012	Issue	0		3	10
15/02/2012	Issue	0		1	9
15/02/2012	Issue	0		4	5

- process: for example, to identify necessary tasks and the ideal sequence of activity for managing the receipt and booking in of goods;
- organization: for example, how to ensure people are motivated in the areas responsible for stock movement and holding;
- technology: for example:

  the best level of automation for an individual business;

  where manufacturing can achieve lowest unit cost and greatest capacity utilization by producing large batch sizes of a single product in long runs. This may not match the flow of customer demand (which may be for small quantities of a variety of products), therefore potentially driving up inventory handling costs and late deliveries.

Goods inwards: receiving

In this section we will consider the process as shown in Figure 3.10, organization, and briefly review some of the relevant technology.

Goods inwards, also known as goods receipt, is a critical process and starts with dispatch from source (internal/external supplier) and ensuring that the supplier will be packaging the goods in the way specified by the customer (eg correctly sized cartons and pallets, bar codes or RFID tags).

Goods inwards broadly includes:

- arrival of goods;
- check documentation;
- check goods;
- manage discrepancies;
- move to destination.

Process

The goods-inwards process needs to ensure that the right products have been delivered, at the right time and place, to the right quantity and quality. However, there are different ways of achieving this and the daily activity at goods inwards, as shown in Figure 3.10, may not need to include all these tasks every time. By establishing a good relationship with their suppliers, many companies trust their suppliers to have delivered the right product, quantity and quality; the supplier will have checked the goods are correct

Figure 3.10 Process flow in goods receiving: reducing number of necessary steps increases receipt rate

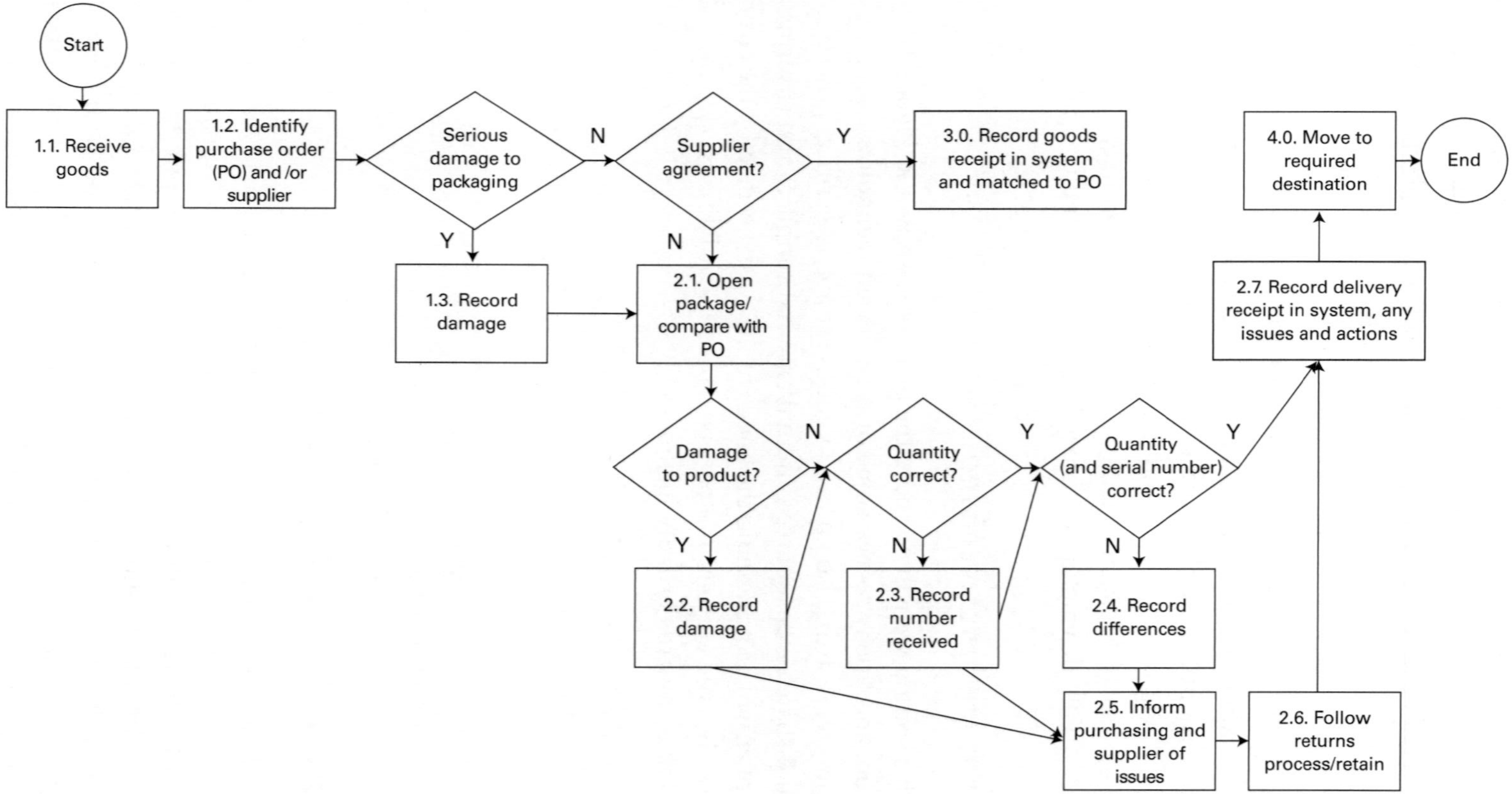

prior to dispatch, so why should the receiving company check exactly the same details again? By establishing this trust, the goods-inwards process is streamlined and the capacity to handle goods receipt is increased (Evans, 2015).

Figure 3.10 shows that a key task, 'serious damage to packaging?' remains even where there is a supplier partnership established. Serious packaging damage may have been caused in transit by a third party, and the integrity of the product(s) inside the packaging must therefore be checked.

Organization

The goods-inwards environment is improved when people can work effectively. This helps when deliveries are staggered and there is a clear visibility of the planned receipts. For example, it is easy to see what deliveries are expected, what has been received and needs processing, what has already been processed, and what the planned targets are for the day. The use of basic manual white boards is often extremely effective, or electronic screens with automatic updates, especially when combined with short start-of-shift team meetings. Business are known sometimes to race to embrace technology, without sufficient attention to the way people are organized and motivated (as shown earlier in 5S (Gemba Kanri)).

Technology

The use of technology at goods inwards includes tools and techniques such as:

- Automated item identification and data capture: use of 2D and 3D (or QR) bar codes and RFID tags to aid in processing and handling goods at all stages of holding and movement will help to decrease the time needed:
  - Bar codes:

    (1D): a rectangle containing a series of numbers and most commonly a pattern of parallel white and black bars of different thicknesses used to aid with the automatic identification of items.

    (2D): a square or rectangle containing many bars or dots of different thicknesses used to aid with the automatic identification of items. 2D barcodes include QR codes, DataMatrix and PDF417 (Portable Data Format) and hold significantly more information than a 1D bar code.

    (3D): most commonly similar to a 2D bar code with the lines and dots at different physical depths or in different colours.

- Radio Frequency Identification (RFID): tags which hold electronically stored information, eliminating the need for manual entry of data and significantly reducing the error rates for data entry. Some examples are shown in Figure 3.11. RFID tags are read through the use of electromagnetic fields and do not have to be physically visible. This is an important consideration, since items can remain inside packaging and still be readable. Tags are either active (which have their own power source) or passive (which do not). Some tags, most commonly the active tags, are re-used.
- Quick response (QR) codes: a matrix bar code used to aid with the automatic identification of items, first designed in 1994.

Figure 3.11 Examples of passive RFID and barcoding labels

- Handling equipment: there are various types of handling equipment. Some of the most common are:
  - Forklift trucks: counterbalanced forklift trucks are frequently used in the loading and unloading of vehicles as well as moving and lifting goods in the warehouse, unless storage is higher than a forklift truck can reach, in which case a reach truck is used. Articulated trucks combine the flexibility of the counterbalanced forklift with the ability of the reach truck to move goods to and from high shelving (Richards, 2011).
  - Automated case loading/unloading systems: where cases arrive without accompanying pallets (eg to save space in a shipping container), alternatives to manual handing are machines that can use clamps or suction

to extract cartons from the truck or container (Rushton, Croucher amd Baker, 2017). These machines have to be carefully calibrated to be able to grab a carton without damaging the goods inside.

- Warehouse Management System (WMS): WMSs or modules are designed for managing the warehouse. They can be integral to ERP or a separate system interfaced with it. Separate specialist WMS modules are frequently found in retail companies; where separate ERP and WMS modules are implemented there is a need to ensure good integration between the business systems (eg for information such as orders placed on suppliers or received from customers). A WMS module will carry out many activities, including in goods-inwards yard planning and management, and workload planning.

Handling returned goods is a big issue, especially for companies with a large volume of e-commerce sales, and specific processes will be required to deal with this. At goods inwards, the packaging of the returned items will be inspected to ensure that it is sufficient. Amazon deal with a significant number of small-value sales by refunding the customer but not requiring the item to be returned, thus saving handling costs.

Holding and moving goods

Warehouses, as for the rest of an organization, need to manage process, organization and technology when considering their effectiveness and their efficiency:

- Process: good processes ensure that a warehouse will operate as effectively as possible. For example, cross docking is where goods are moved from goods inwards directly to goods outwards without being put away. At goods outwards they may be shipped directly or unpacked and redistributed to create several new loads, often where the parts are consolidated with others. By removing the need to put parts away in the warehouse the workload is reduced.
- Organization: the culture of a business is an important factor in creating the work environment and motivating people. Some methods to assist with good organization are: encouraging input and ideas from staff; erecting clearly visible information boards; regular short, formal meetings help ensure good and up-to-date communication; clear positive leadership.
- Technology: systems, automatic reading and identification techniques, equipment and automation are all important considerations here. For

example, the use of RFID tags enables a business to track parts from goods inwards onwards without the need for line of sight. The need for manual data entry is removed, thereby increasing data accuracy in the system. Businesses should embrace technology, but at the level which is best for them, and always with proper consideration for people and process.

In this section all three of these are considered.

The primary purpose of a warehouse is to hold, move and manage raw materials, components, WIP and finished goods on their journey between supply and demand. The items should be in transit, and although some parts move more quickly than others, they will all move eventually. Traditionally 'warehouses' were thought of as somewhere to hold goods for a host company, and later 'distribution centres' were introduced as a bridge between customer and supplier where goods move quickly, offering product mixing, order fulfilment, cross docking, etc. In this book we do not make a distinction between them and use the term 'warehouse' generically.

Goods are also held in production: for smaller raw materials and components, quantities of items are often held on the shop floor close to where they will be required; WIP of partially completed products will also be held on the shop floor. These are illustrated in Figure 3.12. Once work is released to the shop floor it requires close control. It is important to minimize the number of journeys made by sub-assemblies to return to the store as well as the number of bookings. The use of phantom BOMs helps here.

Figure 3.12 Key stages of work-in-progress (WIP) as items travel along the production journey

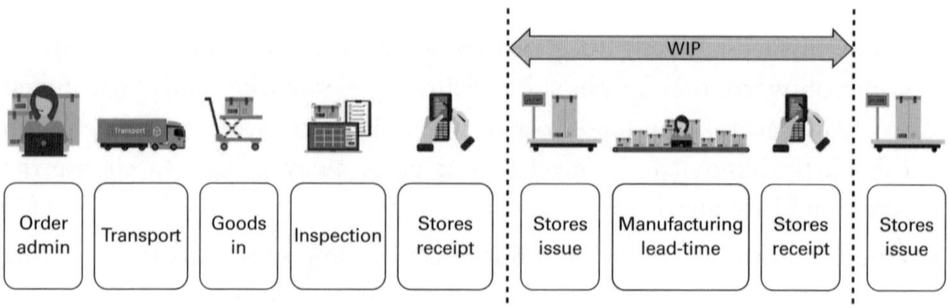

Warehouses perform many activities, as well as the receiving discussed in the previous section, including:

- handling: put-away, order picking, kitting, packaging, loading;

- moving: transporting between stages in the process and locations;
- managing: organizing people, equipment, shelving.

Other value-adding activities carried out in warehouses may include labelling, testing, packing, shrink wrapping, sub-assembly, rectifying products to meet an engineering change, gift wrapping, sending out samples (eg fabrics), bottling (eg wine).

Holding inventory

Storing

The physical storage of items in a warehouse will be on fixed or moving shelving, garment rails, in containers, on pallets etc (Richards and Grinsted, 2016). Both the vertical and horizontal layout are important. The Ocado warehouse, where robots move horizontally and pick from multi-layered vertical containers, is unusual in layout and demonstrates the importance of the use of the two dimensions. One example of warehouse automation is shown in Figure 3.13.

Figure 3.13 Automated warehouse system 2018

SOURCE Shutterstock

In addition to considering the physical layout of the warehouse, there are also many methods for stock replenishment, including:

- Two-bin system: a simple visual system in which items are re-ordered when the first bin is emptied. Whilst the new order is being waited for, items from the second bin are used. Similarly, there are also three-bin systems used, with the third bin being considered safety stock.
- Consignment stock: inventory is held on an organization's premises and is managed by the customer. Levels of service are agreed, and stock remains the property of the supplier until used.
- Vendor-managed inventory (VMI): inventory is held on an organization's premises and is managed and controlled by a supplier:
  - Minimum and maximum levels of inventory are agreed.
  - Stock remains the property of the supplier until used.
  - The use of a two-bin system is a frequently used process in VMI.
  - The difference between VMI and consignment stock is that, although the product sits on the customer's premises and is owned by the supplier in both instances, for consignment stock the stock is being managed by the customer and for VMI the stock is being managed by the supplier.
  - VMI is commonly used in many types of industry from BAE Systems to retail.
- Outsourcing/4PL, where a third party owns and manages the warehouse and the entire operation.

Layout

The location of items in the warehouse is of great importance. If the most frequently handled items are located near to the picking and packing bays, the distance travelled and time taken to move items will be minimized. Pareto by frequency of issue can be used to identify location of part in warehouse. The Pareto technique is explained in more detail in Chapter 6.

The warehouse layout will need to be based on the business strategy. For example, for handling very high volumes of items (eg Amazon or Ocado distribution centres) businesses will tend to invest heavily in automation. Where volumes are low, there will tend to be a lower investment in automation. Strategically, organizations will need to consider the following:

- Layout optimized for lower volume of items being handled, where people move to different locations to collect items.

- In warehouses that have a great degree of automation the arrangement is often fundamentally different. Containers are brought to people (or, less frequently, robots) who are in a single location and perform the packing.
- Completely automated warehouses or parts of warehouses – no lights, limited heating, environment ideal for the parts, not for people.

Stock counting

- Many organizations use perpetual stock counting, ie stock is counted on an ongoing basis.
- A tool used to identify frequency of stock, counting each part, is Pareto, based on total inventory value of item:
  - A-Class items: counted eg weekly. These will be approximately 20 per cent of items, making up approximately 80 per cent of the total value of the items held.
  - B-Class items: counted eg monthly. These will be approximately the next 30 per cent of items, making up approximately the next 15 per cent of the total value of the items held.
  - C-Class items: counted eg six-monthly. These will be approximately the final 50 per cent of items, making up approximately 5 per cent of the total value of the items held.
- An alternative is to calculate by number of total transactions for each item:
  - This is used less frequently.
  - The traditional ratios remain the same as above.
- Annual stock count: this is a legal requirement in many countries since the book value of the inventory held in the business is part of the reported total value of the business:
  - Annual stock counts are less problematic where a business has a higher frequency stock count organized as detailed above.

Managing

Warehouse management includes organizing the work through people, equipment, shelving, etc. This is often assisted through the use of a warehouse management system (WMS). As discussed earlier in this chapter, these are systems for managing the warehouse, and benefit from good integration with other business systems (eg integral to ERP or interfaced with it). A WMS module is often available as part of ERP packages sold by software companies. WMS modules specifically focus on the management of movement within the warehouse. They can be used for managing workload, directing the warehouse staff to the stock location for both putting away and collecting, managing FIFO, and planning and requesting stock counting.

Goods outwards

Goods outwards dispatches goods to their required destinations in a timely manner. It has to be managed closely with the pick-and-pack activities in the warehouse, and with goods inwards for cross-docking activity. Goods-handling equipment will be similar to that used at goods inwards.

Goods outwards must co-ordinate closely with onward transportation times and activities. Transportation may be managed by the business, or very often by a 3PL or 4PL provider.

Additional strategic considerations for the movement of goods onwards from the business include:

- Value-add transport: is it possible to use the transport time to perform a value-add task? Examples include thawing frozen bread, and factory ships travelling from South East Asia to Europe.
- Shared container or transport: a communal approach between several businesses can bring a benefit in sharing containers or transport.
- Backhaul: after making a delivery, a truck, train, ship, etc may need to make a return journey. The backhaul refers to goods that are made on the return journey, and this is usually a less expensive transport cost than the initial outward journey.

Warehouse location

The location of a warehouse is important and will consider many factors, including:

- What is the primary purpose of the warehouse?
- Where are the primary markets?
- What infrastructure is available (road, rail, water, etc) and how efficient is it (eg roads in poor conditions, overcrowded roads and rail)?
- Where are the manufacturing centres?

There are optimization models (as discussed for example in Chopra and Meindl, 2016) and linear programming approaches which can be used to identify the best location for warehouses, although a great deal of decision making and preparation of data tends to precede their use.

CASE STUDY

Inventory management in humanitarian aid: Operation RUMAN

Inventory planning, balance and control must be strategically aligned with the goal of the organization. Inventory management is traditionally thought of as the preserve of manufacturing and retail, where the profit motive drives much of the thinking. However, good practice applies to all cases where inventory needs managing. This example from the disaster relief sector illustrates that good practice is even more important in a crisis.

Good inventory management in humanitarian relief situations is essential. Offering aid is a combination of coordinating personnel and equipment and ensuring the right supplies reach the right areas as quickly as possible, following natural and man-made disasters.

Severe hurricanes hit the British Overseas Territories in the Caribbean in September 2017. Operation RUMAN was a Joint Service UK military response to the problems caused initially by Hurricane Irma and that then continued during the onslaught of Hurricanes Jose and Maria. Humanitarian aid and assistance was given to a critical situation where lives were at risk and stabilization of the area was essential.

Speed of the response was an imperative. The UK military deployed only 24 hours after the first hurricane, Irma, had struck the Caribbean. Barbados was chosen as the hub of operations, and the first flight was dispatched with supplies to the area of devastation within two hours of arrival, using A400M military transport as shown in Figure 3.14. Within the first 36 hours, items for humanitarian aid, vehicles and personnel were organized and dispatched. Working in a disaster-stricken region, where infrastructure was badly damaged and in extremes of climate, both tropical storm and baking heat, the military continued to offer aid and support over the next 30 days.

In one month, the Operation RUMAN team planned, assisted with, and delivered over 2,000 tonnes of humanitarian aid, including water, food, shelter kits, building supplies (tools, paint, paint brushes, tiles, grout, sand, plasterboard, timber etc), medical supplies, hygiene kits, first aid kits, water purification tablets, disposable aprons, buckets, baby products, toys, sheets, blankets, toiletries and wellington boots.

The Defence Logistics Directorate, alongside the Department for International Development and the Foreign and Commonwealth Office, coordinated and led the humanitarian aid given in Operation RUMAN. Their motto is: 'prepared, responsive, precise'. The three challenges of good inventory management were clearly evident in Operation RUMAN:

- **Planning:** identifying supplies most likely to be needed in humanitarian relief situations, purchasing some items in readiness and knowing where to obtain others at a moment's notice; identifying skills needed and readying personnel; identifying transport options. All these are needed in order to be *prepared* and *responsive*.

- **Balancing:** the 'S&OP' of matching demand and supply will be a constantly updating activity. Monitoring 'backlog' is essential in this quickly changing environment, ie are supplies reaching their intended destination On Time In Full (OTIF)? If not, correct this and identify the reasons causing discrepancies. Are supplies in overage, where too much has been delivered or in shortage, where supplies are still insufficient? Optimum inventory levels need to be identified, adjusted to suit the ground conditions and rectified, even though these levels will be changing quickly. All this is needed in order to be *prepared, responsive, precise*.
- **Control:** managing the physical integrity of the supplies is challenging but nonetheless essential in humanitarian relief. The aim must be to assert realistic control of the physical inventory even when working in difficult situations, potentially with extremes of heat and cold, concern over basic safety, as well as likely damage to infrastructure. Managing the data is essential: recording what supplies are being dispatched, when and to where; recording what inventory is due to arrive; recording inventory arrival. All this control is necessary (use of barcoding and RFID might be possible, but automated handling equipment will be very limited to non-existent) to ensure items can be used with greatest impact. All this care and precision is needed in order to be *prepared* and *responsive*.

Figure 3.14 A400M Atlas preparing for flight to Barbados on Operation RUMAN

SOURCE Group Captain Neil Jones

As we can see in Operation RUMAN, good inventory planning, balancing and control in fast-response and fast-changing humanitarian relief situations is essential to ensure the greatest value impact and the most effective use of resources. This case study strives to show that the value of good inventory management is relevant to any occasion where inventory is concerned:

> Overall, the deployment of the UK military on Op RUMAN was a resounding success. Though logistically challenging, with the issues of range, reach, speed and mass at the forefront, sound planning, excellent integration, a drive to succeed and a will to do the right thing won through. (Group Captain Neil Jones)

Group Captain Neil Jones, MSc(Linc) FCILT RAF, Deputy Chief of Staff, Operation RUMAN.

Warehouses of the future

A consideration of warehouses of the future needs to include:

- What improvements will happen to the warehousing structure and operations?
- What external trends will influence how we view warehouses?

Improvements to warehousing structure and operations will continue to be driven by environmental, cost, corporate social responsibility and legal considerations, for example:

- Savings in energy usage and carbon emissions can be achieved in the key areas of lighting and heating for warehouses. As much as 70 per cent of total energy costs are caused by lighting in non-automated warehouses (Richards, 2011). Renewable energy (eg solar panels in the roofs or a warehouse) has been introduced by many companies as well as using natural heating and ventilation wherever possible, both to decrease costs and the environmental impact, as well as to comply with legislation. A drive for fast-turnover businesses is to achieve 'light out warehousing' using AI and robotics for highly automated warehouses.
- Waste management is crucial. Product packaging is a critical aspect for warehouse management. This includes primary (sales packaging, eg bottles, tins), secondary (grouped, eg outer carton, shrink wrap) and tertiary (handling for transport, eg pallets, metal cages). Designing packaging for re-use wherever possible benefits the environment and can also decrease costs, by carefully segregating its waste into cardboard

boxes, plastics and general waste, one food contract packaging company reduced its waste removal costs by 45 per cent and is now recovering approximately 30 per cent of its packaging (Richards, 2011).

Some of the many external trends which will influence how we view warehouses include:

- Environmental considerations: reducing availability of raw materials and the awareness of the damage caused by a throw-away society will drive down demand and therefore production, thereby reducing the work of and requirement for warehouses. One example is the re-purposing of clothes and fabrics in Hong Kong (see case study).
- Changing global economics: the deluge of items from China to Western Europe and North America will continue to reduce.
- Greater use of existing technology: for example, 3D printing will reduce the production of spare parts held just in case where they can be created at or near location when required, thus reducing the numbers of items being held.
- Servitization: an example of servitization is Rolls Royce, who moved away from selling aero engines and into selling power-by-the hour for aeroplanes. For Rolls Royce to be more profitable from this business model, this drives product design and production towards ever longer life with fewer breakdowns (Harrison, 2014).

CASE STUDY

One environmental trend that will impact warehousing

Scarcity of raw materials and a move away from the throw-away society will support the production of products to last, decreasing levels of individual ownership and increasing servitization and communal ownership. The resulting decrease in the volume of goods being produced and delivered to customers is likely to repurpose and decrease the number of warehouses. A Hong Kong initiative illustrates an example in the fast-fashion industry: 'Global consumers purchased 60 per cent more clothing in 2016 than in 2000 and only kept each item half as long, a report by McKinsey consultancy found' (AFP, 2018).

In Hong Kong, landfill sites receive 343 tonnes of textiles daily. In addition, Greenpeace reported in 2016 that 17 per cent of clothes bought by residents were seldom or never worn.

Hong Kong designers Kay Wong and Toby Crispy founded 'Fashion Clinic' in response to this. They created pop-up stalls at clothing stores, popularizing repair services, offering repurposing advice and teaching people how to mend their own garments.

Inventory exchange curve

It is widely accepted that more frequent deliveries of smaller batches decreases the total inventory held in a business, as proven by Relph and Barrar (2001) and often repeated, for example in the book *Fashion Logistics* (Fernie, 2015).

To illustrate this, Figure 3.15 shows that for a given total quantity required of a part, supply can be achieved either with fewer deliveries of a higher quantity or more deliveries of smaller quantities. However, inventory holding costs (as discussed in Chapter 2) are greater with fewer deliveries of a higher quantity, and inventory holding costs are lower with more deliveries of smaller quantities. It is also true that with more deliveries of smaller quantities the business will have to be more capable, for example:

- The ordering process will need to be able to place orders more frequently (eg blanket orders with regular call-offs, JIT agreement with suppliers, VMI, etc).
- In goods inwards there will be greater handling of more frequent deliveries.
- To manufacture smaller batches more frequently, change-over time between producing different products must be driven down.
- Suppliers will need to improve their ability to produce and deliver smaller batches more frequently, or if they opt to continue to produce larger batches, they will increase their inventory holding costs.

Companies are normally aware of the cost to them of holding inventory, often seeking to reduce the amount of inventory and the related investment tied up in it. The exchange curve which is based on Figure 3.15 can assist greatly with this and is illustrated in Figure 3.16.

The exchange curve principle is based on the following:

- The amount of inventory an organization needs to hold to meet demand depends greatly on the ability of the organization to perform the necessary tasks.
- One of the primary ways of reducing inventory is by reducing batch size which increases the delivery frequency.
- To be able to increase the delivery frequency the associated processes need to speed up (eg manufacturing, ordering and goods-handling processes).
- To be able to increase the frequency and therefore the process speed the organization will eventually need to increase its capability.

Figure 3.15 Relationship between batch size and number of deliveries for a given total quantity

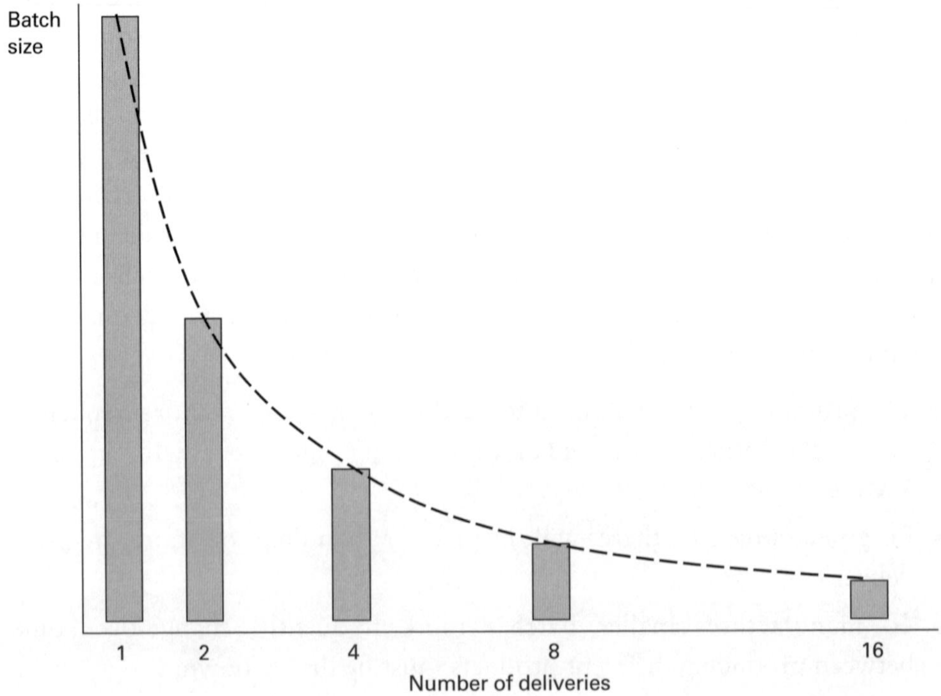

The example of goods inwards or receipt, as shown in Figure 3.10 and discussed earlier, can be used to illustrate the exchange curve:

- Process: improving the process can reduce the number of tasks needed to receive the deliveries at goods inwards. Figure 3.10 shows that by establishing supplier agreements (eg through a contract) with suppliers, deliveries need not always be checked at receipt, since if we are confident that the supplier has delivered to the right quantity and quality, and according to the purchase order on our system, then there are fewer tasks to be performed at this stage. Thus, capacity may be increased.
- Organization: productivity is enhanced when an environment is created where it is easy to see what is required and progress against targets (eg white boards or electronic screens at goods inwards, showing what deliveries have been expected, what has been received, and what percentage have been progressed to the following task). Although a business should embrace relevant technology, the way people are organized and motivated (as shown earlier in 5S (Gemba Kanri)) impacts hugely on how well a process is performed (Proctor, 2017).

Figure 3.16 Inventory exchange curve showing relationship between inventory value and capability

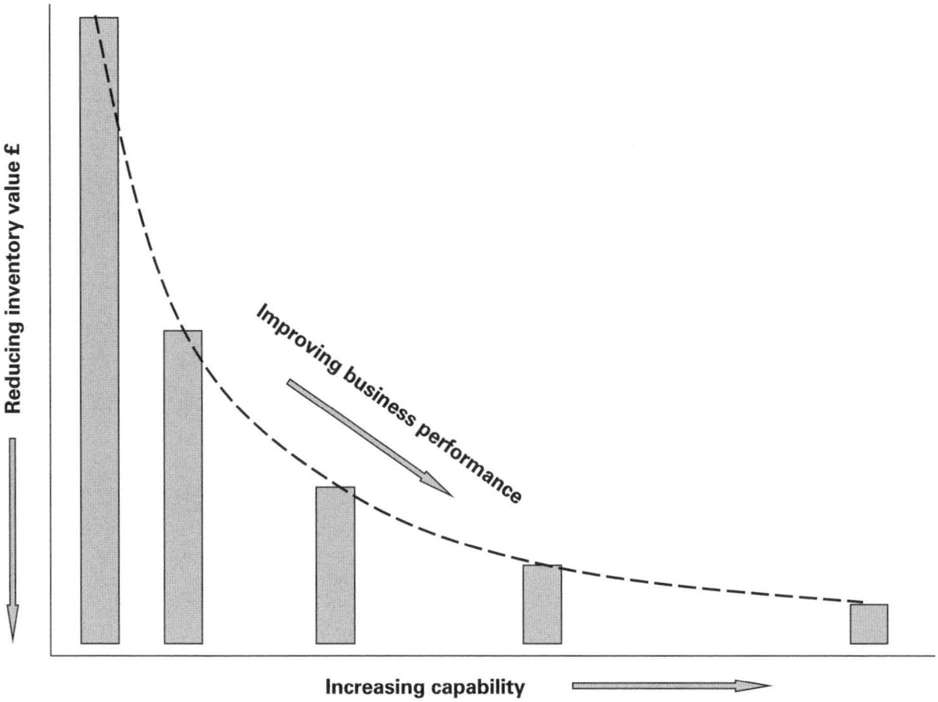

- Technology: the use of technology at goods inwards includes many of the tools and techniques discussed earlier in this section, including automatic reading of labels (barcodes, RFID, etc), handling equipment and a good system (eg WMS).

Extending beyond your company

Inventory balancing and control is primarily about the inventory that exists within the business itself. In addition, there are considerations possible outside the company, both with suppliers and with customers.

Suppliers

A business benefits when it is able to help to maximize the capabilities of suppliers, both first tier and possibly second tier and beyond. This can be achieved by understanding and agreeing the fixed or frozen planning horizons, the percentage of quantities and dates to short-timescale changes, and having clear lead times agreed. These can all impact the way a business carries out inventory balancing.

Figure 3.17 Comparison of pipeline stocks for local and global supply chain (Harrison, 2014: 149)

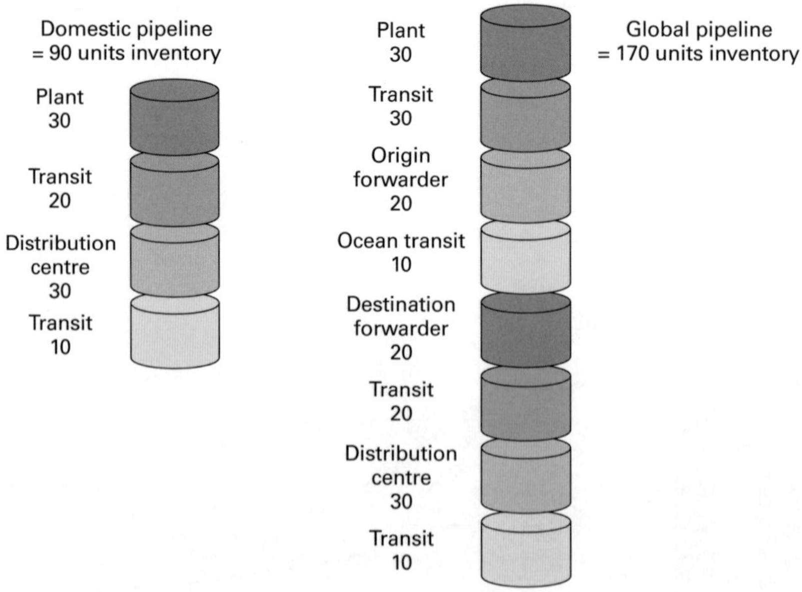

Where products are purchased from global suppliers the inventory pipeline is naturally much longer than for local suppliers, potentially tying up capital investment for much longer (Figure 3.17). Inventory control may therefore have to extend much further, and inventory rebalancing is likely to take much longer.

Customers

A business benefits from having a good understanding of what its customer wants, both in terms of the product requirements and the accompanying service (eg time to deliver an order).

Companies use customer relationship management (CRM) systems for managing the relationship with the customer (eg customer data, customer communication and interaction, marketing, sales automation), which benefits from good integration with other business systems such as ERP.

In addition to a business understanding its customer requirements in a relationship, some companies extend that to understanding the buying activity of their customers' customers, for example Nestlé (see case study and Figure 3.18) who monitor real-time sales on certain of their customers' shelves. This visibility offers them a much greater reach and understanding when carrying out inventory balancing.

CASE STUDY
Nestlé

Nestlé is the world's largest food and beverage company, with sales of CHF 89.8 billion, over 2000 brands, present in 189 countries, and employing 323,000 people around the world (Nestlé Annual Report 2017, 2018). Part of the supply chain team in Nestlé UK & Ireland is responsible for their major supplier-customer relationships, focusing on building strong, collaborative partnerships, and has been recognized as best in class in the eyes of their customers in an annual industry survey for two consecutive years. Nestlé have consciously evolved from the traditional supplier-customer relationship where responsibility for product integrity, inventory and availability shifts to the retailer once it has been goods receipted, to a more shared approach where the manufacturer is focused on product availability at the point of purchase. An example of this collaboration in action is the monitoring of real-time sales of Nestlé products on certain retailer shelves. This allows the manufacturer to track sales, as well as store-level inventory and forward forecasts, in order to make amendments where required to increase availability. Nestlé will also use their field team to target stores, and specific product lines within those stores, where additional attention is needed. They can feed data back to the business and any availability challenges can be addressed through root-cause analysis. Therefore, the manufacturer has extended the domain in which they can observe and improve their inventory balance, and by measuring and reporting movement of inventory levels on the shelves of their customers on a daily basis, difficulties can be identified and rectified early, increasing availability and consequently sales at the retailer.

Paul Daniel, Customer Supply & OSA Manager; Liz Cawthorn, OSA Co-ordinator, Nestlé UK & I Ltd; Daniel (2018); (Nestlé Annual Report 2017, 2018).

Figure 3.18 Nestlé delivering product

SOURCE Liz Cawthorn, Nestlé

The effects of product design and variety on inventory balancing and control

Figure 3.19 Where are the true costs in offering customer choice?

Mini Cooper S 3-door classic with manual gearbox

Pepper White £20,920

Lapisluxury Blue £21,670

Image and prices from: www.mini.co.uk, correct at 15 Dec 2018

Product variety

In the markets today 'customer choice' is often said to be a necessary evil to attract customers. Inventory management is harder, and therefore potentially more expensive, as greater customer choice is introduced.

An example of how two companies adopt different strategies in their approach to product variety and customer choice can be seen by comparing two of Britain's supermarkets, Aldi and Tesco. Aldi are able to significantly reduce costs by limiting the ranges offered, whilst Tesco believe that offering greater choice creates greater demand (Evans, 2015).

Figure 3.19 shows a car, the Mini Cooper S 3-door classic, and the cost of buying it in two different colours, the standard colour (Pepper White) and a Lapisluxury Blue. The car is identical apart from the external colour, but the cost of the car is £750 less when the standard colour is chosen. This is partly because of the additional cost to a business of offering variety, and in 2018 this model offered a total of 12 colour choices, all of which cost more than the Pepper White. By offering an acceptable colour as the standard option and 'at no extra cost' the company effectively drives sales to be highest in this colour, thereby making product variety and customer choice a little more manageable.

CASE STUDY

Simplified inventory processes at Aldi

The first Aldi supermarket opened in the UK in 1990. Aldi, a German company, takes its name from the first two letters of the founding family name – Albrecht – and the word for discount, thus AL + DI became Aldi. Aldi call themselves a 'limited line discount retailer'. Their current UK advertising slogan is 'Everyday amazing', changed from a previous statement of 'Spend a Little. Live a Lot'. This move appears to be to focus customer perception more on 'amazing' and less on 'low price'. Aldi won the Grocer of the Year Award in 2018 for the fourth time in six years. The award recognized the supermarket, amongst other aspects, for its investment in quality, range extensions in fresh food, beers, wines and spirits (BWS), and non-food, as well as for having the best-paid shop floor staff in the industry.

Unarguably, Aldi offers a more limited number of choices of each item than the top four UK supermarkets (Tesco, Sainsbury, Asda and Morrisons). Online research in December 2018 for tomatoes in tins and cartons offered by UK supermarkets, showed that Aldi offers four types (chopped and whole, Aldi everyday essential and Aldi own-brand Sweet Harvest), and Tesco lists 28 options, including different brands and pack sizes.

One reason why there are fewer purchasing options for Aldi tomatoes in tins and cartons is that Aldi offers few branded products for sale, preferring to have their own-brand items over which they have greater control, for both quality and price.

Aldi sell mainly their own-brand items – Heinz products are rarely if ever available, for example – although they do stock some shoppers' favourites like Nescafé, a range of Cadbury's chocolate products and Marmite. The online price for Marmite Yeast Extract 250g is the same at Aldi, Tesco and Ocado (£2.40 on 10 Dec 2018): whilst Aldi offered one option for Marmite spread, seven options were offered online by Ocado and five by Tesco. This demonstrates that Aldi have less price-setting control for well-known brand items such as Marmite, preventing them from offering a low-cost benefit to their shoppers on these products. In the same way, Heinz product prices are determined to a large extent by Heinz. Thus, by offering only a few branded items alongside their own-brand products, Aldi are able to offer lower-price items overall.

Aldi's strategy is to offer a more limited range. A store has around 2,000 items for sale at any time, increasing to 2,500 at peak times like Christmas, and includes a core of 1,400 lines such as milk and butter. This compares to their competitors holding around 25,000–30,000 core items, and means that inventory planning, balancing and control is simpler for Aldi than for other supermarkets.

Shelf-ready packaging has been used by Aldi as well as most other supermarkets for many years now. Product is delivered to Aldi in packaging suitable for efficient and effective shelf stacking in the store, both from the retailer and the customer perspective, and ensures minimum handling of products when they reach the stores. This has reduced the number of tasks necessary between items being delivered to a store and being displayed on the supermarket shelf.

The Aldi approach to bar codes is different from other supermarkets, as shown on the tins of Aldi tomatoes in Figure 3.20. Their products have longer or more bar codes (items with up to five bar codes were identified) than other supermarkets, allowing faster scanning at the till, reducing customer wait time and increasing customer satisfaction. By increasing the check-out efficiency, Aldi is also improving its selling rate. This inventory handling benefit is at the shelf-to-check-out-to-customer-basket part of the process.

Figure 3.20 Aldi bar code example

SOURCES aldisuppliers.co.uk; www.telegraph.co.uk; www.aldi.co.uk; www.thegrocer.co.uk; Jenkins and Williamson (2015).

As a result of all these approaches, inventory management at Aldi is simplified, and the all-important margin is managed through achieving lower operating costs, many of which can be passed on to customers as low prices. Aldi suppliers, warehouses and delivery logistics are closely managed and monitored, and item locations in store are carefully organized. Benefits of inventory management include:

- Inventory balancing: where there is a smaller range of goods to plan and keep track of – in the S&OP activity, maintaining the correct levels of stock, and managing backlog – the inventory balancing is greatly simplified.
- Inventory control: the vastly smaller product range, shelf-ready packaging, and multiple bar codes all help to simplify the inventory handling and control process; the smaller product range also reduces the number of SKUs for which data parameters have to be managed on the systems.

Aldi has targeted its offering to the marketplace as 'amazing, everyday' and implicit in its reputation is good value and low cost. It has been very successful in many countries, including its heartland of Germany and in the UK. The more limited choice offered to shoppers in Aldi stores, which we would postulate is based on the fact that if customers want a tin of tomatoes or a jar of Marmite, they want product availability, not necessarily a huge choice, would appear to be successful: in the UK, Aldi overtook the Co-op as the fifth-largest supermarket in 2017.

Product variety and design using the snow shovel as an example

A snow shovel was used in Chapter 2 to illustrate the discussion on bills of materials, where a single type shovel variety was introduced. In this chapter we will expand the range of snow shovels to illustrate the impact of product variety on inventory management.

The company producing the snow shovel has decided to expand their range. A key customer is a retailer whose brand colour is red. The retailer wishes to buy snow shovels with red scoops, since they have a concern that the black scoop could be confused with a competitor's brand. The retailer would also like to offer a budget version for the south of England where snow is rare, whereas in Scotland, where snow is more common, they believe people are prepared to pay more for a robust, longer-lasting snow shovel.

The producer believes that the greater range will create a much higher demand and has agreed to sell the new red snow shovels. In addition, the company has decided to offer the black snow shovel in both the original and in the cheaper version. The new product range is shown in Figure 3.21, namely:

- Initial model: black scoop with aluminium strengthening strip along the edge.
- Second model: cheaper black scoop without strengthening strip.
- Third model: retailer-requested red scoop with aluminium strengthening strip along the edge.
- Fourth model: retailer-requested cheaper red scoop without strengthening strip.

Figure 3.21 Development of snow shovel product range

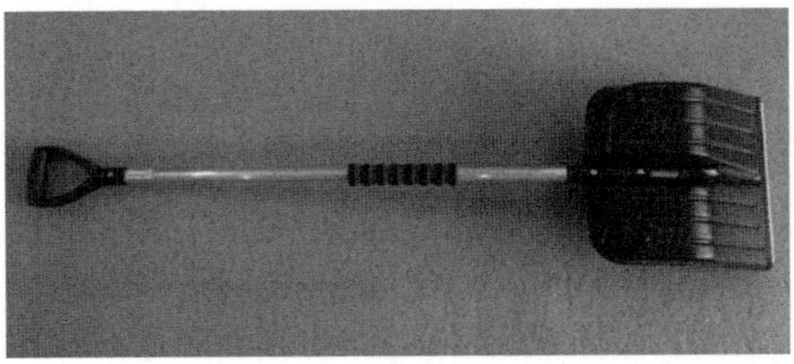

Inventory planning for product ranges

Product variety introduces complexity into inventory management and production planning. In the new range of snow shovels there are:

- four different finished products;
- four scoop options:
  - black with the aluminium strip;
  - black without the aluminium strip;
  - red with the aluminium strip;
  - red without the aluminium strip.
- all products use the same handle, shaft assembly and screws;
- four different bar code stickers.

Figure 3.22 Snow shovel second colour choice impact on BOM

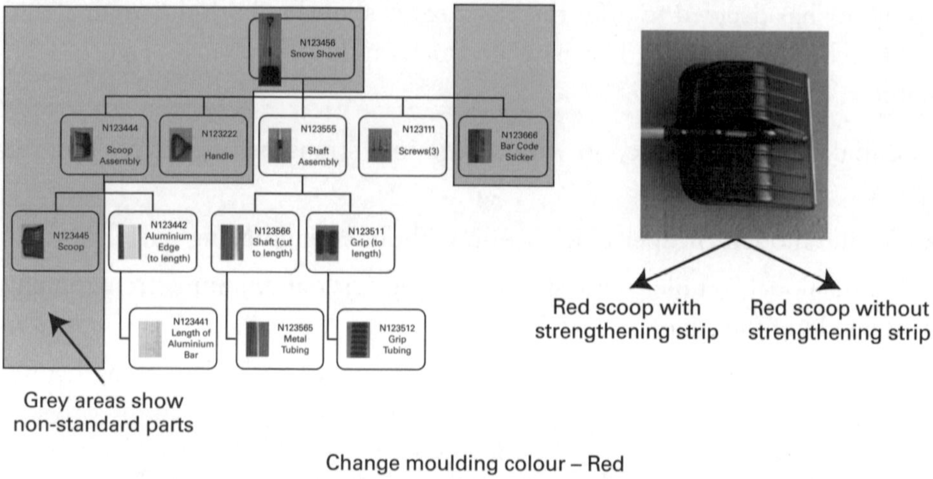

There will also be four packaging options, which we will not deal with here for the sake of simplicity.

Standardization wherever possible in the design of the four varieties is crucial to allow easier planning and production. Standard and non-standard parts of the BOM are shown in Figure 3.22. For example:

- retaining the same handle, screws and shaft on all four models;
- ensuring the shapes of the red and black scoops are the same allows:
  - the same moulds to be used for both, with different-coloured ingredients;

  - the fitting of the red scoop to the shaft to be identical to fitting the black scoop to the shaft;
  - fitting of the aluminium strengthening strip to the scoop to be identical for both colours.
- Planning the fixing of the aluminium strengthening strip to the scoop and the attachment of the bar code stickers as final tasks allows late customization, potentially once customer demand is known, depending on:
  - volume of demand;
  - cost of production process options.

Where the above is feasible and cost-effective, this can reduce the need for interim stock, eg the common handles and shafts can be held pending orders, but not the assembled final products. The simple snow shovel is used to illustrate inventory management issues, including the relationship between inventory, production and design. This shows that there are key considerations which will significantly reduce complexity and allow easier planning.

BOM complexity

As the product range is developed the basic BOM is affected and as a result new product codes have to be introduced. Figure 3.22 shows that different parts of the BOM are affected and thus complexity is added to the MRP processing. To simplify the task a matrix BOM can be used, as shown in Table 3.3.

To reduce the planning complexity MPS planning can be introduced at the level of the BOM matrix. By creating the MPS at this level rather than at the finished product level the planning task is simplified, as can be seen when comparing Figure 3.22 with Table 3.3.

Forecasting therefore can be considered at this more aggregate level (ie the requirements for all snow shovels rather than for each variety separately). The need to forecast is significantly reduced, and from this aggregate forecast a ratio of black vs red and standard vs budget can be calculated.

Engineering change

During the life of a product there will often be changes in design. This may affect the inventory held: if there is existing inventory of the product in the 'current' design, will this require re-work to meet the new design, or will the

Table 3.3 Matrix BOM for planning snow shovel

Snow Shovel Matrix			Black		Red	
Part	**Description**	**Category**	**with metal edge**	**without metal edge**	**with metal edge**	**without metal edge**
N123456	Snow Shovel (black, premium)	Top Assy	X			
N234567	Snow Shovel (black, economy)	Top Assy		X		
N345678	Snow Shovel (red, premium)	Top Assy			X	
N456789	Snow Shovel (black, economy)	Top Assy				X
N123444	Scoop Assembly, black	Option	X			
N123455	Scoop Assembly, red	Option			X	
N123445	Scoop, black	Option		X		
N123449	Scoop, red	Option				X
N123442	Aluminium Edge (cut to length)	Option	X		X	
N123222	Handle	Common	X	X	X	X
N123555	Shaft Assembly	Common	X	X	X	X
N123111	Screws (x3)	Common	X	X	X	X
N123666	Bar Code Sticker	Option	X			
N129001	Bar Code Sticker	Option		X		
N129002	Bar Code Sticker	Option			X	
N129003	Bar Code Sticker	Option				X

© Inventory Matters Ltd

change to the new design be planned for a later date when the existing stock has been used?

An engineering change for the snow shovel could be replacing screws with glue: a decision might be taken that production costs can be reduced by gluing the shaft to the handle rather than attaching them using screws. This would be a significant engineering change involving many departments, as shown in Figure 3.23.

Figure 3.23 The snow shovel and the engineering change notification (ECN)

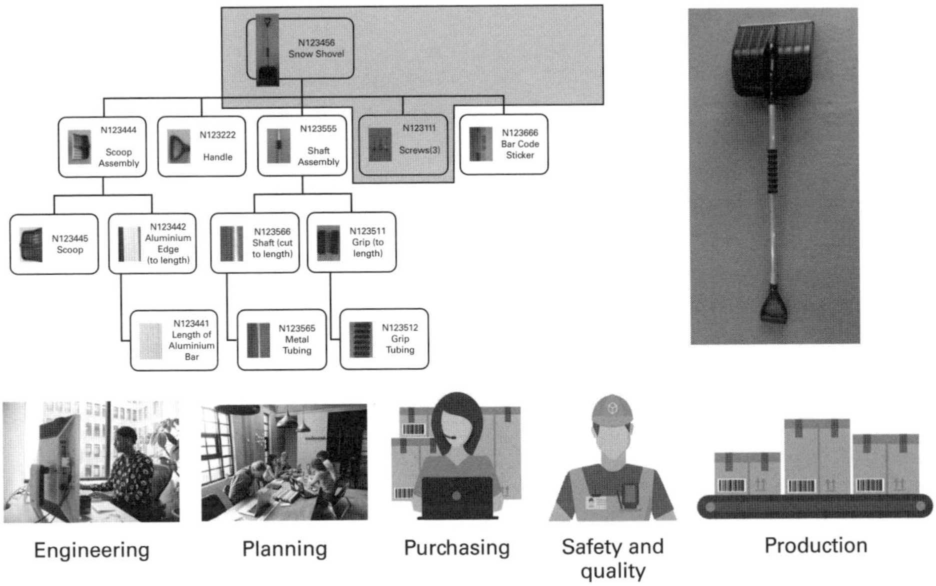

Photo of snow shovel authors' own

Engineering Change Management is of critical importance to the successful running of MRP systems. There are three elements, which involve every department within the organization:

- Part number control and engineering change level: the rule is that 'if FORM-FIT-FUNCTION are affected, change the part number:
  - Form: characteristics such as weight, dimensions, visual appearance.
  - Fit: how a part connects with another feature or part.
  - Function: performance specifications.
- Break-in point:
  - Implementation needs to be coordinated to ensure all the new EC level parts arrive on time.

- Priority or disposition: the urgency of the change needs to be agreed. This is known as disposition, and there are typically four categories:
  - Safety – all stock scrap – stop shipment of finished goods.
  - Critical – all stock scrap – work in process only.
  - Dated – only agreed scrap – implemented by a fixed date.
  - Non-critical – use up stock – no priority.

The combined effect of the three elements creates an organizational problem of major proportions and is a subject in its own right.

Summary

In this chapter we have looked at two of the three legs – balancing and control – of inventory management in a little more detail.

Balancing is about reactiveness, which means that it is hard to remove the manual element from these processes. The key tool in balancing is communication through processes such as:

- Sales and operations planning (S&OP) ensuring that all parties from sales, manufacturing and suppliers are informed and scheduling is kept in line.
- Overage/optimum/stock out, use of KPI that allows the identification of out-of-line products.
- Building product structures that make the process of balancing easier and optimize choice whilst minimizing complexity using tools like Matrix BOM and Module-Level MRP.
- At the stage where the plan is executed, MRP recommendations must be adhered to, or if changes are necessary the causes must be corrected in the planning. The importance of reporting compliance and non-compliance is critical to ensure the system is working well.

The key to good inventory control is:

- Reduction of errors: modern systems will continue to increase the automation of sharing of data (eg Internet of Things, Industrie 4.0). This increasing interconnectedness, where calculations and decisions of more pervasive systems will be based on more and more remote data, means the dependency on accuracy will be ever more critical.

- The first stage for accuracy is housekeeping. This chapter has looked at common 'lean' principle tools: these focus on the physical environment as well as principles of design.
- Accuracy will increase with the greater use of technology to reduce errors (automatic identification, exception reporting, etc). Where there are decreasing costs of technology it will become more widely used. The cost-benefit analysis for this will vary between companies, but the importance of basic data accuracy cannot be underestimated.
- Accuracy assists the effectiveness of processes to manage throughput.
- Control can be more difficult as the movement of product through warehouses is increasingly merged with production processing.
- It is essential to manage the physical inventory well. People are crucial in this and are likely so to remain. Establishing effective processes is essential: these must be right for the business goals and strategies, as well as allowing for flexibility to be able to react to external changes. Technology must be embraced, both with systems and automation, but this must suit the business needs and culture: one size doesn't fit all.

And finally:

- The strategy of the business must always drive inventory management.
- Inventory planning will drive balancing in particular and, to a slightly lesser extent, control.
- The external environment will continue to change and will always influence the way a business has to perform to best achieve its goals. Therefore, inventory management has to include a degree of flexibility and have excellent people to be able to react to changes in the bigger picture.
- Good management of process, organization and technology are essential to enable a business to be effective and efficient when carrying out inventory balancing and control activities.

Tools and techniques discussed in this chapter

- 3-Mu
- 5S (also called Gemba Kanri)
- Seven wastes of Lean

- Bar codes (1D, 2D, 3D)
- Consignment stock
- Cross docking
- Customer relationship management (CRM) systems
- Pareto by frequency of issue, by inventory
- Poke Yoke
- Quick response (QR) codes
- Radio frequency identification (RFID)
- Sales and operations plan (S&OP)
- Two bin system, three bin system
- Vendor managed inventory (VMI)
- Warehouse management systems (WMS)

A complete list of all the tools and techniques used in this book is given in Appendix C. More information on each one can also be found through the index.

References

AFP (2018, September 30) Hong Kong's new fight against fast fashion, *Bangkok Post*. Retrieved April 2019 from https://www.bangkokpost.com/news/world/1549418/hong-kongs-new-fight-against-fast-fashion

Ashcroft, J (2014) *The Lego Case Study 2014*, John Ashcroft and Company.

Chopra, S and Meindl, P (2016). *Supply Chain Management: Strategy, planning and operation*, Pearson, Harlow, UK

Daniel, P (2018, November 12) Building Collaborative Supplier and Retailer Relationships, Presentation at Warwick University

Evans, B M (2015) *The Lean Supply Chain: Managing the challenge at Tesco*, Kogan Page, London

Fernie, J G (2015) *Fashion Logistics*, Kogan Page, London

Harrison, A V (2014) *Logistics Management and Strategy: Competing through the supply chain*, Pearson, Harlow, UK

Jenkins, W and Williamson, D (2015) *Strategic Management and Business Analysis*, Routledge

Lego Group (2014) Conference: Plan and Take Control, IOM Annual Conference, Stratford Upton Avon, UK

Nestlé Annual Report 2017 (2018, November 22) [online] www.nestle.com/asset-library/documents/library/documents/annual_reports/2017-annual-review-en.pdf [accessed 2019]

Proctor, R (2017) Putting a Zebra on the Moon, conference presentation, Warwick, Warwickshire, UK

Relph, G and Barrar, P (2001) Overage inventory – how does it occur and why it is important? *International Journal of Production Economics*, ISIR Proceedings (81–82), pp. 163–71

Richards, G (2011) *Warehouse Management*, Kogan Page, London

Richards, G and Grinsted, S (2016) *The Logistics and Supply Chain Toolkit*, Kogan Page, London

Rushton, A, Croucher, P and Baker, P (2017) *The Handbook of Logistics and Distribution Management*, (6th edn) Kogan Page, London

Wild, T (2011) *Improving Inventory Record Accuracy: Getting your stock information right*, Routledge

You do the maths

Outline brief BOM product planning and backlog planning exercises

You are currently the product planner for the Control Box range CB-874xx-x Control Box xl-xO. You have consolidated the four indented manufacturing BOMs (from Appendix A) into a single Matrix BOM shown in Table 3.4 which shows all the common parts as well as the options. In Appendix A you can view the individual BOMs for all four varieties of control boxes.

Table 3.4 Consolidated modular BOM for CB-874xx-x Control Box xl-xO from Appendix A

Matrix BOM CB-874xx-1 Control Box xl-xO		2l		4l	
		5O	9O	5O	9O
Part Number	Description				
CB-87483-1	Control Box 2l-5O	1			
CB-87484-1	Control Box 2l-90		1		
CB-87496-1	Control Box 4l-5O			1	
CB-87495-1	Control Box 4l-9O				1
.BC-24919-6	Base Casting Common	1	1	1	1
.TC-57843-4	Top Cover	1	1	1	1
.LC-87650-4	Logic Card	1	1	1	1
..RC-67896-8	Raw Card	1	1	1	1
..LD-25376-2	Logic Device	2	2	2	2
..RV-23458-7	Resistor 1Meg	8	8	8	8

Table 3.4 *continued*

Matrix BOM CB-874xx-1 Control Box xI-xO		2I		4I	
		5O	9O	5O	9O
..WR-14259-2R	Wire – Red	6	6	6	6
.IP-4682-A2I	Input Panel Assy 2I	1	1		
.IP-4682-A4I	Input Panel Assy 4I			1	1
..IP-23572-2I	Input Panel 2I	1	1		
..IP-23572-4I	Input Panel 4I			1	1
...IC-25376-1	Input Panel Casting	1	1	1	1
..IP-3654-A2R	Input Socket – Red Assy	2	2	4	4
...CB-47898-7	Connector – Common	2	2	4	4
...IP-35367-2R	Input Socket – Red	2	2	4	4
...FS-56124-1	Fixing Screw	4	4	8	8
..GT-25834-1	Gasket 2I	1	1	1	1
...GP-42317-4	Gasket Paper (2" Strip)	4	4	4	4
..FS-56124-1	Fixing Screw	4	4	4	4
.OP-67236-A5O	Output Panel Assy 5O	1		1	
.OP-67236-A9O	Output Panel Assy 9O		1		1
..OP-89712-5O	Output Panel 5O	1		1	
..OP-89712-9O	Output Panel 9O		1		1
...IC-26345-1	Output Panel Casting	1	1	1	1
..OL-26877-15O	Output Lead Assy 5O	1		1	
..OL-26877-19O	Output Lead Assy 9O		1		1
...OC-25369-1R	Output Connector – Red	2	4	2	4
...OC-25679-1B	Output Connector – Black	2	4	2	4
...OC-25754-2G	Output Connector – Green	1	1	1	1
...WR-14259-2R	Wire – Red	2	4	2	4
...WB-14625-5B	Wire – Black	2	4	2	4
...WG-14765-5G	Wire – Green	1	1	1	1
...SS-32992-2	Shrink Sleeve	3	3	3	3
...FS-56124-1	Fixing Screw	10	18	10	18
..GT-46574-2	Gasket 5O	1		1	
..GT-46573-2	Gasket 9O		1		1
...GP-42317-4	Gasket Paper (2" Strip)	4	4	4	4
..FS-56124-1	Fixing Screw	4	4	4	4
.FS-56124-1	Fixing Screw	4	4	4	4

Exercise 1 Part 1: BOM common parts

Production planning have requested that the following common parts are to be bulk-issued to each section of the assembly shop:

- WR-14259-2R Wire – Red
- WB-14625-5B Wire – Black
- WG-14765-5G Wire – Green
- SS-32992-2 Shrink Sleeve
- FS-56124-1 Fixing Screw

Your task in Exercise 1 is to calculate the total requirements for each of the common parts. Using Table 3.5, draw up a table showing the common and option usages for these parts.

Table 3.5 Matrix BOM showing the usage for Fixing Screws and Wire

Consolidated List of Bulk Issue Fixing and Wire		2I		4I	
		50	90	50	90
Part Number	Description				
CB-87483-1	Control Box 2I-50	1			
CB-87484-1	Control Box 2I-90		1		
CB-87496-1	Control Box 4I-50			1	
CB-87495-1	Control Box 4I-90				1
..WR-14259-2R	Wire – Red				
...WR-14259-2R	Wire – Red				
...WB-14625-5B	Wire – Black				
...WG-14765-5G	Wire – Green				
...SS-32992-2	Shrink Sleeve				
...FS-56124-1	Fixing Screw				
..FS-56124-1	Fixing Screw				
...FS-56124-1	Fixing Screw				
..FS-56124-1	Fixing Screw				
.FS-56124-1	Fixing Screw				

Exercise 1 Part 2: BOM common parts

The total demand for the second quarter is planned as follows:

- CB-87483-1 Control Box 2I-50 — 650 units are planned at 50 units a week + overtime if needed.
- CB-87484-1 Control Box 2I-90 — 530 units are planned at 40 units a week + overtime if needed.
- CB-87496-1 Control Box 4I-50 — 720 units are planned at 55 units a week + overtime if needed.
- CB-87495-1 Control Box 4I-90 — 675 units are planned at 50 units a week + overtime if needed.

Using Table 3.6, calculate for the FS-56124-1 Fixing Screw the overall demand for the quarter, and assuming level production, the average weekly requirement.

Marketing have asked sales order entry staff to ensure that all promotions and all new demand go to CB-87495-1 control box 4I-90.

Following the marketing promotion, the demand for CB-87483-1 Control Box 2I-50, CB-87484-1 Control Box 2I-90, CB-87496-1 Control Box 4I-50 is to cease and only CB-87495-1 Control Box 4I-90 is to be manufactured. The quarter demand for CB-87495-1 Control Box 4I-90 is planned at 2,575 units, based on manufacturing capacity of 198 units a week + overtime if needed.

Table 3.6 Worksheet for the calculation of current second quarter demand for FS-56124-1 Fixing Screw

Current 2nd Quarter Demand

		2I		4I		Total
		50	90	50	90	Boxes
Part Number	Description					
CB-87483-1	Control Box 2I-50					
CB-87484-1	Control Box 2I-90					
CB-87496-1	Control Box 4I-50					
CB-87495-1	Control Box 4I-90					
	Totals					
FS-56124-1	Fixing Screw					
	Total Quarter requirement					
	Average Weekly requirement (13 weeks)					

Unfortunately, the promotion was not communicated to the planning departments in time. Now it is the beginning of the quarter and the supplier has indicated that there is a critical supply issue for the retaining screws, which can only be delivered in the quantities as previously ordered.

Using Table 3.7 to help you, calculate for the FS-56124-1 Fixing Screw the increase in the overall demand for the quarter and, assuming level production, the average weekly requirement.

Table 3.7 Worksheet for the calculation of proposed second quarter demand for FS-56124-1 Fixing Screw

Proposed 2nd Quarter Demand

		2I		4I		Total
		50	90	50	90	Boxes
Part Number	Description					
CB-87483-1	Control Box 2I-50					
CB-87484-1	Control Box 2I-90					
CB-87496-1	Control Box 4I-50					
CB-87495-1	Control Box 4I-90					
	Totals					
FS-56124-1	Fixing Screw					
	Total Quarter requirement					
	Average Weekly requirement (13 weeks)					

	Total	%age
Quarterly increase		
Weekly increase		

Exercise 2: Backlog management

The supplier has been able to source additional Fixing Screws and can air-freight from China; however, they will only be available in four weeks.

Production have agreed that given the additional Fixing Screws they can increase production by 15 units per week.

Using Table 3.12, what would you propose as the maximum units that can be made available for sale by the end of the quarter?

For planning purposes:

- you can assume level production;
- the supply of additional fixing screws will be available at the beginning of week 5.

Chapter 3 exercise answers

Answer Exercise 1 Part 1: Common parts from Matrix BOM

Table 3.8 Answer for Table 3.5 Modular BOM showing the common and option usage for FS-56124-1

Consolidated List of Bulk Issue Fixing and Wire		2I		4I	
		50	90	50	90
Part Number	Description				
CB-87483-1	Control Box 2I-50	1			
CB-87484-1	Control Box 2I-90		1		
CB-87496-1	Control Box 4I-50			1	
CB-87495-1	Control Box 4I-90				1
..WR-14259-2R	Wire - Red	6	6	6	6
...WR-14259-2R	Wire - Red	2	4	2	4
		8	10	8	10
...WB-14625-5B	Wire - Black	2	4	2	4
		2	4	2	4
...WG-14765-5G	Wire - Green	1	1	1	1
		1	1	1	1
...SS-32992-2	Shrink Sleeve	3	3	3	3
		3	3	3	3
...FS-56124-1	Fixing Screw	4	4	8	8
..FS-56124-1	Fixing Screw	4	4	4	4
...FS-56124-1	Fixing Screw	10	18	10	18
..FS-56124-1	Fixing Screw	4	4	4	4
.FS-56124-1	Fixing Screw	4	4	4	4
		26	34	30	38

Table 3.9 Answer for Table 3.6 the calculation of current 2nd quarter demand for FS-56124-1 Fixing Screw

Current 2nd Quarter Demand		2I		4I		Total
		50	90	50	90	Boxes
Part Number	Description					
CB-87483-1	Control Box 2I-50	650				
CB-87484-1	Control Box 2I-90		530			
CB-87496-1	Control Box 4I-50			720		
CB-87495-1	Control Box 4I-90				675	
		650	530	720	675	2,575
FS-56124-1	Fixing Screw	26	34	30	38	
	Total Quarter requirement	16,900	18,020	21,600	25,650	82,170
	Average Weekly requirement (13 weeks)	1,300	1,386	1,662	1,973	6,321

Learning points bulk issue/common parts

Many manufacturing companies use common parts for a wide variety of final goods/final assemblies. The pegging functionality in MRP allows companies to identify all components, sub-assemblies and final goods where there is a common part, such as a fixing screw, wire and common usage parts.

Many companies will arrange for a local supplier to supply these parts direct to line and possible manage the stocking of these parts, with agreed limits. This may remove the need to manage within the MRP systems.

What companies can you think of where this is occurs? What common parts will be used in their products?

Answer Exercise 1 Part 2: Common parts – demand change

Table 3.10 Answer for Table 3.7 the calculation of current second quarter demand for FS-56124-1 Fixing Screw

Proposed 2nd Quarter Demand		2I		4I		Total
		50	90	50	90	Boxes
Part Number	Description					
CB-87483-1	Control Box 2I-50	0				
CB-87484-1	Control Box 2I-90		0			
CB-87496-1	Control Box 4I-50			0		
CB-87495-1	Control Box 4I-90				2,575	
		0	0	0	2,575	2,575

Table 3.10 *continued*

Proposed 2nd Quarter Demand

		21		41		Total
		50	90	50	90	Boxes
Part Number	Description					
FS-56124-1	Fixing Screw	26	34	30	38	
	Total Quarter requirement	0	0	0	97,850	97,850
	Average Weekly requirement (13 weeks)	0	0	0	7,527	7,527

	Total	%age
Quarterly increase	15,680	19%
Weekly increase	7,527	

Once the new MPS for the quarter's demand is known, using a simple summary as shown in Table 3.9 can be a useful check on the base requirement. It becomes particularly useful if there is an urgent need to calculate a change in requirement that may not yet be reflected in MRP. In this exercise the demand changes significantly affect the demand for the screw but also as seen in Table 3.10.

Table 3.11 Estimate of the production shortfall

	Usage for 41 90	Total Requirement	Weekly Total	Production per week
Production Based on Proposed Demand	38	97,850	2,575	198
Production Based on Available Supply	38	82,170	2,162	166
		Shortfall		32
		Quarter shortfall		413

If it is not possible to resolve the supply issue, the next question will be to determine the impact on production. This can be done by calculating the maximum possible production from the agreed supply as shown in Table 3.11. A quick look at the total shows that there would be a two-week backlog by the end of the quarter.

Although the quantity represents a two-week backlog, once the problem with supplying the parts is rectified, any recovery programme is based on the ability of production to increase the quantity manufactured.

Table 3.12 Worksheet to calculate maximum backlog recovery

	Month 4				Month 5				Month 6				
	WK 14	WK 15	WK 16	WK 17	WK 18	WK 19	WK 20	WK 21	WK 22	WK 23	WK 24	WK 25	WK 26
Cumulative Production													
Cumulative Constrained Production													
Cumulative Backlog													
Cumulative Overtime													
Revised Production													
Revised Cumulative Schedule													
												Total Production + Overtime	
												Remaining Shortfall	

Answer Exercise 2: Backlog scheduling

The best approach is always to create a cumulative schedule to identify the total extent of the problem. Thinking that you are only 32 units short could allow you to think that it would be easily recoverable. The schedule in Table 3.13 shows that once the supply has been recovered production can be increased, but only by the agreed overtime limit. The shortfall for the end of the quarter would be 278 units, which is less than the initial 413 based on the shortfall in supply. It would be important to adjust the schedules to the 'achievable' plan which should be agreed during the S&OP meetings that would inevitably have resulted when the supply problem surfaced. Simply telling manufacturing and operations to work to the original plan in the hope a solution may be found would only store up problems for later.

Learning points: Backlog scheduling

It is essential for companies to ensure that all functions work in a coordinated way. Good communication between functions, for example through a formal sales and operations planning (S&OP) process, is necessary to ensure effective use of resources and company focus.

In reality a backlog caused by insufficient numbers of retaining screws being supplied would have created additional problems:

What other problems could have happened?

What would the retaining screw position be if the marketing department had decided, again with insufficient communication, to promote CB-87483-1 Control Box 21-50 instead?

Table 3.13 Revised schedule showing overtime and revised production schedule

	Month 4				Month 5				Month 6				
	WK 14	**WK 15**	**WK 16**	**WK 17**	**WK 18**	**WK 19**	**WK 20**	**WK 21**	**WK 22**	**WK 23**	**WK 24**	**WK 25**	**WK 26**
Cumulative Production	198	396	594	792	990	1,188	1,387	1,585	1,783	1,981	2,179	2,377	2,575
Cumulative Constrained Production	166	333	499	665	832	998	1,164	1,331	1,497	1,663	1,830	1,996	2,162
Cumulative Backlog	32	63	95	127	159	190	222	254	286	317	349	381	413
Cumulative Overtime					15	30	45	60	75	90	105	120	135
Revised Production	166	166	166	166	181	181	181	181	181	181	181	181	181
Revised Cumulative Schedule	166	333	499	665	847	1,028	1,209	1,391	1,572	1,753	1,935	2,116	2,297
												Total Production + Overtime	2,297
												Remaining Shortfall	278

The complexity of inventory management within business systems

04

Introduction

Business systems, no matter how good, only manage inventory for a business according to the instructions given to them by people. The instructions given to the systems are based on the decisions of those managing the organization.

This chapter looks at:

- complexity: how businesses regularly have to deal with hundreds of thousands of decisions to manage their inventory;
- results-driven inventory management;
- volumes of data to manage;
- how MRP calculates and executes this data;
- parameter management;
- KPIs, including compliance/non-compliance and exception management; and
- the cost of control.

We will start by looking at inventory planning at its simplest.

Inventory planning at its simplest

At its simplest, inventory planning has four straightforward steps:

- Understand the current inventory position: how much stock do I have on hand?
- Identify the business targets for inventory: what inventory do I need?
- Create an inventory plan: what do I have to do to achieve the business targets and how difficult will it be?
- Implement the plan: what actions must I take to achieve the plan?

The simple stock record that Brown (1982) used to demonstrate the re-order process shown in Figure 4.1 is still in use in small businesses today, and forms the basis of simple accounting-based stock control systems. It starts from the same position as the four straightforward steps for inventory management: how much inventory do I have on hand? Figure 4.2 shows the flow of these four steps from this initial position.

Inventory management can be very straightforward in simple and usually very small organizations. And indeed when a simple inventory management approach works, there is no need to overcomplicate the situation. However,

Figure 4.1 Simple stock record (Brown, 1982)

Transaction log

Source	Cost	Unit	Package
J.B. BIGLEY 930 THIRD AVE. NYC 10020	3.07	EACH	200
	Order up to: 2800		Reorder point: 2000

Date	To/from reference	Compl date	Due date	Quantity IN	Quantity OUT	On Hand	Available stock
DEC 30,78	Physical Inventory	12/30/78				2675	2675
JAN 3,79	S-11279 JONES	1/3/79			600	2075	2075
JAN 4,79	S-11283 SMITH	1/4/79			319	1756	1756
JAN 5,79	P-88357 BIGLEY	3/8/79	MAR	1000		1756	2756
FEB 11,79	S-11306 HARRIS	2/11/79			350	1806	2406
FEB 18,79	S-11511 JONES	2/18/79			350	1056	2056
MAR 8,79	P-88357	3/8/79		1000		2056	2056
MAR 9,79	S-11382 JACKSON	3/9/79			800	1656	1656
MAR 10,79	P-88402 BIGLEY		MAY	1200		1656	2856
MAR 17,79	S-11497 SMITH	3/17/79			373	1283	2483

Part No	Description	Buyer	Class
J0061	WIDGET SPROCKETS	20	A

Figure 4.2 Inventory management at its simplest

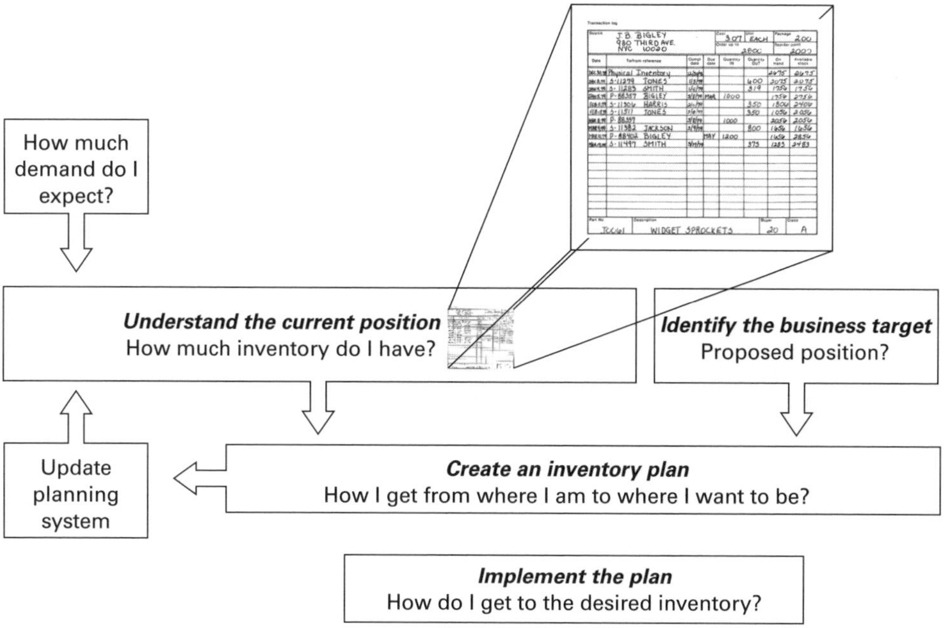

in many organizations, and in the vast majority of manufacturing organizations, inventory will need careful management.

What is complexity?

Inventory decisions at strategic, tactical and operational levels

In Chapter 2 we looked at how organizations need to manage long-, medium- and short-term objectives and needs by operating at strategic, tactical and operational levels. Figure 4.3 gives a brief overview of factors that affect inventory management at these different levels.

Strategic decisions include:

- the number of production units required and where they should be located;
- high level product volumes to be produced by country and by factory;
- product strategy and portfolio;
- investment needed in production units, warehouses, large equipment, people (recruitment, skills, reduction);
- the correct production process for the product/market, for example:
  - whether to make to order, assemble to order, or make to stock;

Figure 4.3 Inventory management at strategic, tactical and operational levels in the organization

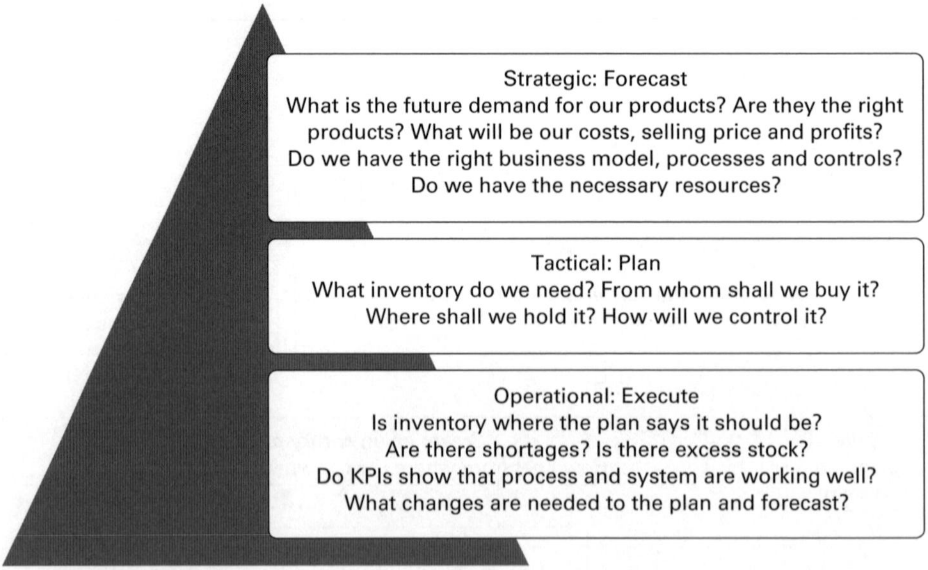

– how to include product customization as late as possible in the process.

Tactical decisions will be viewed on a shorter timeframe and may be made for a single production unit (or small number of units) or warehouse. They occur at the level of the MPS and are likely to include:

- production volumes at a more detailed level (eg how to make best use of production capacity where there is uneven demand);
- deployment of people (holiday plans, flexibility and skills, suitability, training and development);
- supplier relationships;
- investment of capital for projects; eg new or replacement equipment, automation of existing processes; and
- protection against unexpected changes in demand and in supply (eg safety stock decisions).

Operational decisions are made at a detailed level in a short timeframe. In manufacturing this deals with shop floor scheduling and control, to direct and track production in as near to real time as possible. Decisions include:

- production schedules for the day, week and/or month;
- material availability information – shortages, overstock, supplier performance;
- production status – schedule performance, backlog, machinery performance and breakdown; and
- staff status – availability, holiday cover.

A simple financial decision driving a complex operational process

In Chapter 1, we also looked at how the decisions made by senior management at a strategic level are made in financial terms (eg reduce inventory by 25 per cent, or reduce by a financial amount). These then need to be translated into product information at a tactical level before the effect of the impact to the business (eg availability of products for production or to customers) can be understood. This is shown in Figure 4.4.

Figure 4.4 Translating financial saving to detailed items in the inventory management pyramid

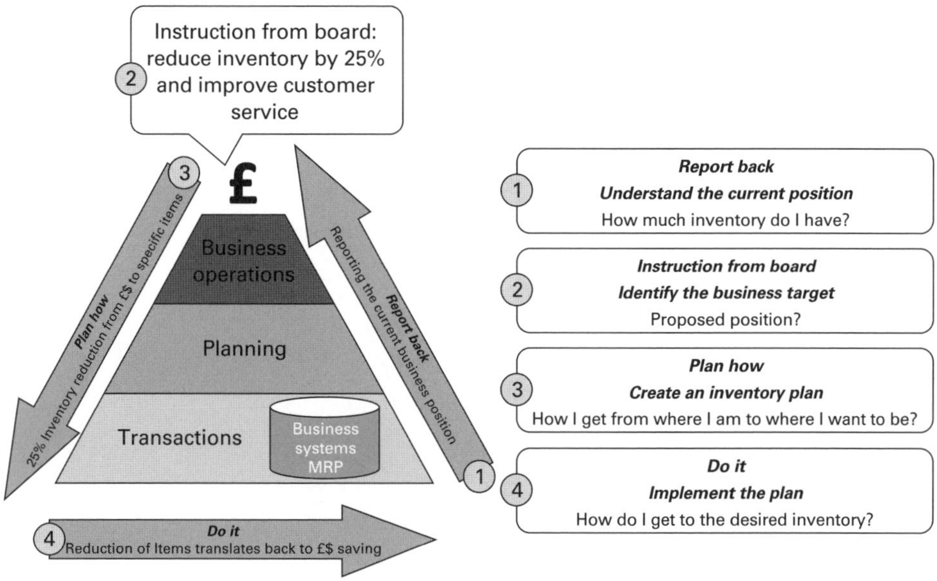

In most MRP systems, whether MRPI or MRPII, it can be a lengthy process to test out how and where to reduce inventory in order to meet a business directive to cut costs. This is because what MRP asks the planner to do is to

make many decisions in an attempt to achieve the desired outcome (ie in this case to reduce the inventory), for example:

- Which products will be changed and which ones will be left unchanged?
- Will batch sizes be reduced? If so, is there the capability in the business to manage the additional number of batches?
  - If we decrease the batch sizes in production this might increase the number of product changeovers, reducing capacity utilization and increasing unit costs.
  - If we decrease the batch sizes in purchase orders, do we have the capacity to process the increased number of deliveries received? What is the cost implication?
- If products are to be moved between different inventory management categories, which ones are to be moved or how will we move the boundaries?
- Do we know our true inventory management costs? Can we reduce them? Can we change our processes?

Once a planner has made many decisions and made the necessary changes to the relevant parameters for the chosen products in MRP, then MRP will process these decisions (preferably in a what-if planning environment).

Figure 4.5 Inventory complexity: the operations view of inventory in MRP

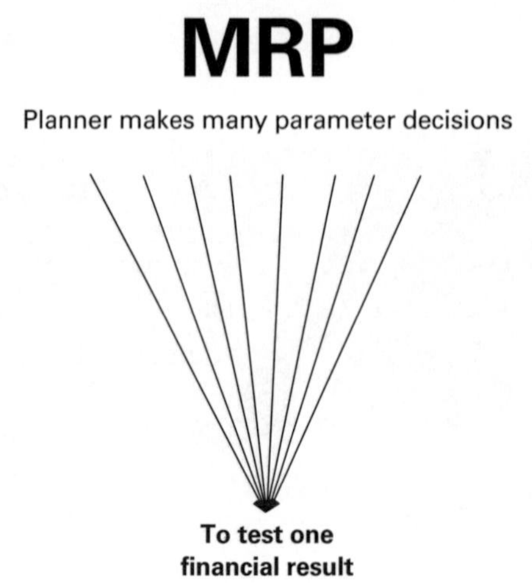

The result from MRP then needs to be tested to see if it meets the business objective of a reduction in costs. It may then be necessary to change the decisions

made, change different parameters or different products, run MRP again, test against the desired result, and repeat until the desired answer is found, as shown in Figure 4.5.

In this situation the planner has to rely on experience and to be able to make many changes as well as to run many what-if scenarios. This starts to explain one reason why inventory is complicated to manage within the wider context of the business.

Businesses obviously vary tremendously, with the number of parts varying greatly too. As can be seen from the examples in Figure 4.6, the number of parts being handled in a business can easily run into the tens of thousands and even the hundreds of thousands.

The operations view of inventory in MRP is one that considers what parts are needed to meet demand, and all the items that need to be planned and managed as a result. Whether this is considering the parts at aggregate level (ie by group) or individually, ultimately the decisions will always have to be made at the individual level, part by part.

This is a different view point from the financial view which is looking to make one financial decision, and using that to drive the many parameter decisions, whether these changes are made to many hundreds or many thousands of parts, as shown in Figure 4.7.

Simplifying the operational process

Financial management may give a single constraint or target for the cost of inventory management or a reduction in inventory costs. This then needs to drive the number of decisions made, allowing you to then verify the decisions and remain in control. In Chapter 5 we look at this problem again and show how to drive the changes in MRP through making a small number of decisions and greatly simplifying the decision-making process that needs to be made in operations.

Volumes of data to manage

The volumes of data that need managing in the planning system tend to be either large or very large. We considered the different parameters that need to be managed for each part in Chapter 2. Table 4.1 gives an indication of the size of the data control challenge in inventory management, and shows how, in many typical organizations, what for the financial controller looks like a simple decision to reduce inventory presents a massive challenge to the planner to determine the appropriate actions.

Figure 4.6 How many parts on a product?

- Number of parts on an aircraft: the Airbus A380 has approximately 4 million individual components with 2.5 million part numbers (Airbus, 2019)
- Number of parts on a car: Toyota estimate there are around 30,000 parts on a car, including every part down to the nuts and bolts (Toyota, nd)
- The number of parts stocked in a supermarket can be huge – a large retail grocery store will have around 30,000 products on the shelves in a supermarket at any one time – although approximately half the sales revenue will come from the thousand top selling products (Sharp, 2012)
- Number of parts on a mobile phone: even a mobile phone has many parts, including: the top and bottom halves of the case, a circuit board (which has many parts soldered on it, eg semiconductors, connectors, sim-card holder, memory, radio frequency converters), antenna, a liquid crystal display (LCD), a keyboard, a microphone, a speaker, and a battery (Brain, nd)

Number of parts to make a single snow shovel: 15 plus packaging

Figure 4.7 Inventory complexity driven by a simple financial view of inventory

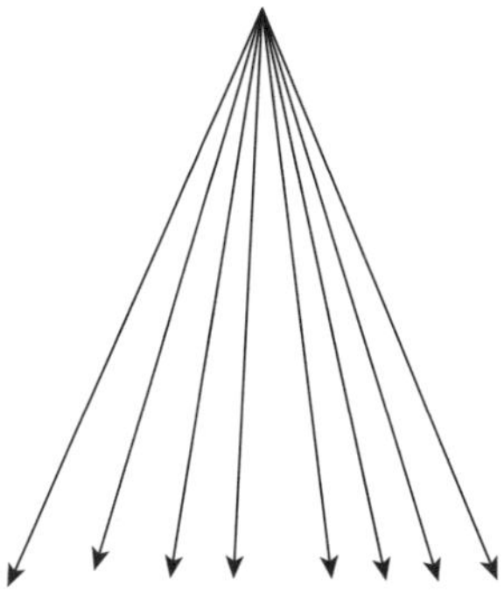

Table 4.1 The number of parameters that typically need to be managed in a business

Example	Commercial retailer with a central warehouse and 60 branch outlets
Finance controller's view	Only two inventory values to manage • Central Warehouse Stock = £20m • Branch Stock = £2.5m • Total Inventory = £22.5m
Planner's view	Planner needs to manage for each SKU up to 10 parameters to control/adjust inventory level in MRP
# parts/#SKUs	• The central warehouse manages total range of 25,000 SKUs • Each branch outlets manages a range of 3,000 locally stocked SKUs • Thus SKUs to be managed = 25,000 + 60 x 3,000 = 205,000
# parameters	There are a minimum of 10 parameters that define/control each SKU
# parameters decisions	Parameters to managed by planner • Central warehouse = 25,000 x 10 = 250,000 • Branch parameters = 3,000 x 60 x 10 = 1,800,000 • Total parameters = 250,000 + 1,800,000 = 2,050,000

It would be inefficient in most businesses to set all parameters individually by SKU – in the case illustrated in Table 4.1 over two million parameters would need to be analysed and set, and in most cases this would not make good business sense.

It's good inventory management practice to group parts by similar inventory characteristics (for example, frequency of demand: for more details of this grouping by inventory characteristic please see Chapter 6) and to then create rules that can be applied to the different groups (ie specify the parameters that will apply across the parts in that group, for example one group might have purchase orders raised to cover demand for the next five days).

It is essential to complete parameter information for all parts (for example, lead time, purchasing batch sizes, manufacturing batch sizes, safety stock, etc). Once the parameters are filled in and demand predicted, it will be possible to automate planning decisions in MRP. MRP is then able to calculate the decisions resulting from the parameter information, the bills of materials (discussed in Chapter 2) and the predicted demand, and tells the planner:

- purchase order receipts;
- works order receipts; and
- order changes – moving orders closer or pushing them out, or cancelling orders.

Inventory management still has the four basic steps as was shown in Figure 4.2. These simple steps are still true but can now be considered in the context where many thousands of parts need to be managed by a business system.

- Understand the current inventory position: how much stock have I currently got?
  - What stock is there and what stock will result from current orders? What is the status of the current stock – are we overstocked? Are there shortages?
- Identify the business targets for inventory: what do I have to achieve?
  - What are the inventory management targets set by the business? How do I achieve these while satisfying the production and sales requirements?
- Create an inventory plan: what do I have to do to achieve the business targets and how difficult will it be?
  - What is the proposed position from my analysis rules? Is my current analysis working?

- Implement the plan: what actions must I take to achieve the plan?
  - Is the plan working? Is demand being met?
  - What problems are there? Have the necessary corrections been made?

Figure 4.8 shows a more detailed flow around these four steps.

Figure 4.8 Inventory planning within the business system

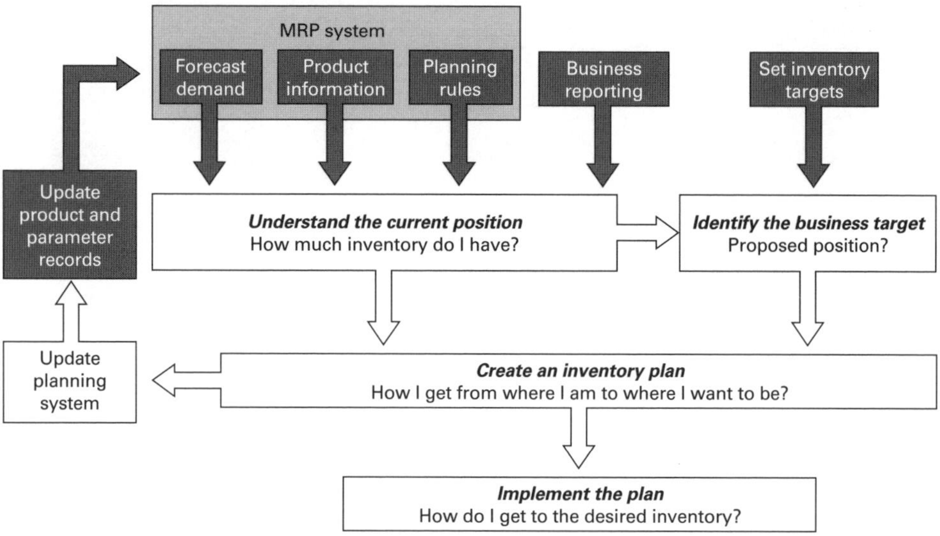

CASE STUDY

Airbus inventory management challenges in a complex business

Airbus, one of the world's leading aircraft manufacturers, is a global company with manufacturing and design facilities in France, the UK, Germany, and Spain, and subsidiaries in China, the US, Japan, and the Middle East. Their largest passenger aircraft is the A380, which can fit as many as 853 passengers

Airbus press centre information shows the size of the inventory management challenge:

> An A380 consists of around 4 million individual components with 2.5 million part numbers produced by 1,500 companies from 30 countries around the world. It takes 13,000 rivets to join the 3 sections of the fuselage and 4,000 rivets are used for the junction of the wings and the fuselage.

Final European assembly of the A380 takes place in Toulouse, France, as shown in Figure 4.9. Figure 4.10 shows where the production of the major structures takes place.

Figure 4.9 Airbus A380 assembly in Toulouse, France (© Airbus permission granted)

Figure 4.10 Airbus A380 major structure assembly locations in Europe (© Airbus permission granted)

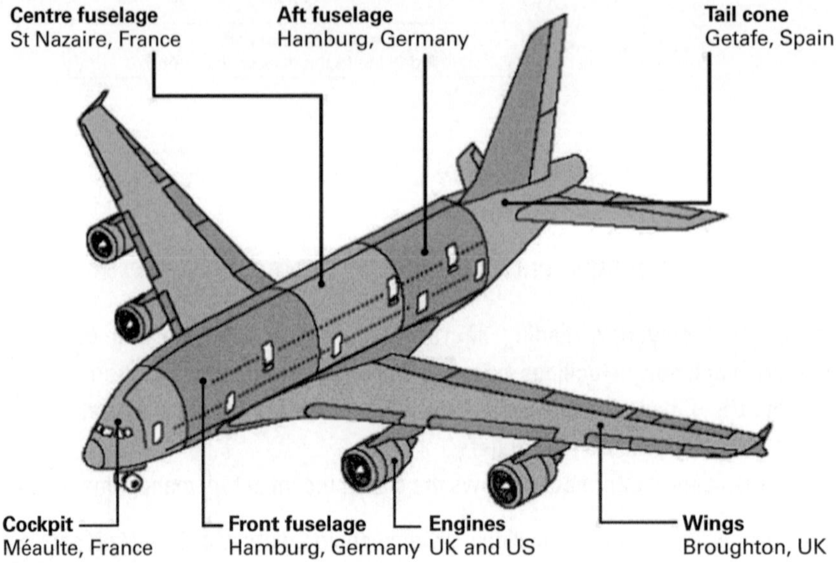

SOURCE Airbus A380

The wings are assembled in Broughton in the UK, as shown in Figure 4.11. Each wing is built of around 32,000 major parts, plus 750,000 bolts and rivets. The origin of every part and fastener is recorded: the supplier of each is documented along with the batch of base metal and the time and date of manufacture.

Figure 4.11 Airbus A380 wing assembly locations in the UK (©Airbus permission granted)

In addition to the major structure assembly locations, there are many suppliers of components and key parts, 800 of whom are in the United States. The largest four suppliers are Rolls Royce, Safran, United Technologies and General Electric.

Airbus uses the SAP ERP system throughout its design and manufacturing locations in Europe. Production planning, including inventory and capacity management, is handled within its SAP system.

(Airbus, 2019) Edemariam, 2006; HP, 2009

Complexity in managing inventory in MRPI *and* MRPII

Calculations within the MRP system

Master Production Schedule

The creation of the production plan is the first major planning task. This is the Master Production Schedule (MPS) and has a large input from the sales and operations plan (S&OP), as shown in Figure 4.12. It works at the finished goods level and records demand and production, ie wherever there is independent demand. This will take into account any policy decisions, forecasts of demand, known customer orders and finished goods stock on hand.

Figure 4.12 Creation of the Master Production Schedule (MPS) for independent demand (simplified from Vollmann *et al*, 2005, p 8)

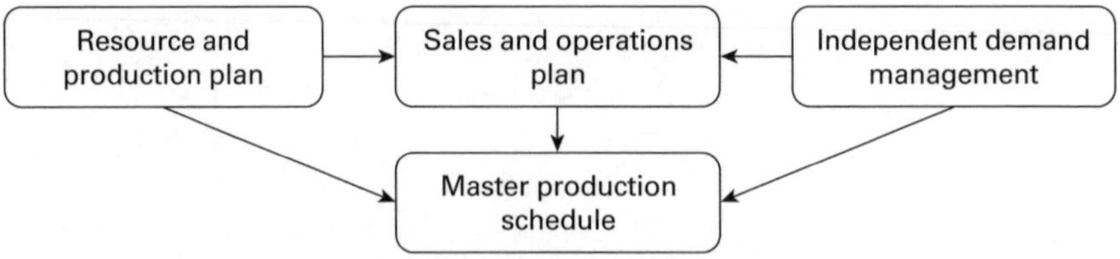

The MPS may smooth the production plan, as shown in Table 4.2. This will relate to the calculation of batch size information; for example, there may exist a maximum capacity of 20 units and a production minimum of 10 units with a multiple of 10 units. Table 4.2 shows the logical MPS that would be created to meet demand within the rules.

Table 4.2 The MPS determines production of finished good stock (FGS) for which there is independent demand

	Week 1	Week 2	Week 3	Week 4	Week 5	Week 6
Forecast demand	5	10	15	15	25	15
MPS	10	10	20	20	20	10

The MPS will also consider minimum stock or safety stock requirements and the current and predicted inventory/stock on hand (SOH). In Table 4.3 these factors now show why the MPS has planned additional production in weeks 3, 4 and 5.

Table 4.3 MPS considers predicted stock on hand (SOH) for each time period and safety stock

	Week 1	Week 2	Week 3	Week 4	Week 5	Week 6
Opening (Stock on Hand) SOH	5	10	10	15	10	15
Forecast demand	5	10	15	15	25	15
MPS	10	10	20	20	20	10
Closing finish good SOH	10	10	15	20	15	10
Safety Stock	10	10	10	10	10	10

The master production schedule then drives the manufacturing resource planning.

Executing the manufacturing resource planning

Figure 4.13 shows how MRP is fed by the master production schedule (MPS).

Figure 4.13 MRP is fed by the MPS to enable it to consider material and capacity in its creation of detailed production plans (simplified from Vollmann *et al*, 2005, p 8)

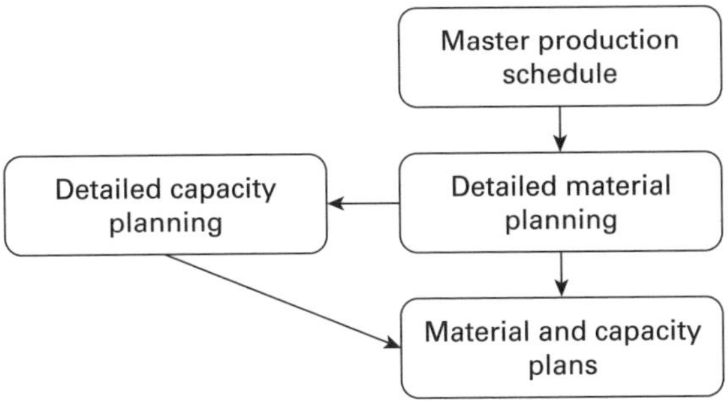

If we now consider the snow shovel which we looked at in Chapter 2, we can look at some MRP calculations that would result from the above MPS. Figure 4.14 shows that one of the sub-assemblies needed to produce the snow shovel is the scoop assembly.

Figure 4.14 Bill of materials for the snow shovel

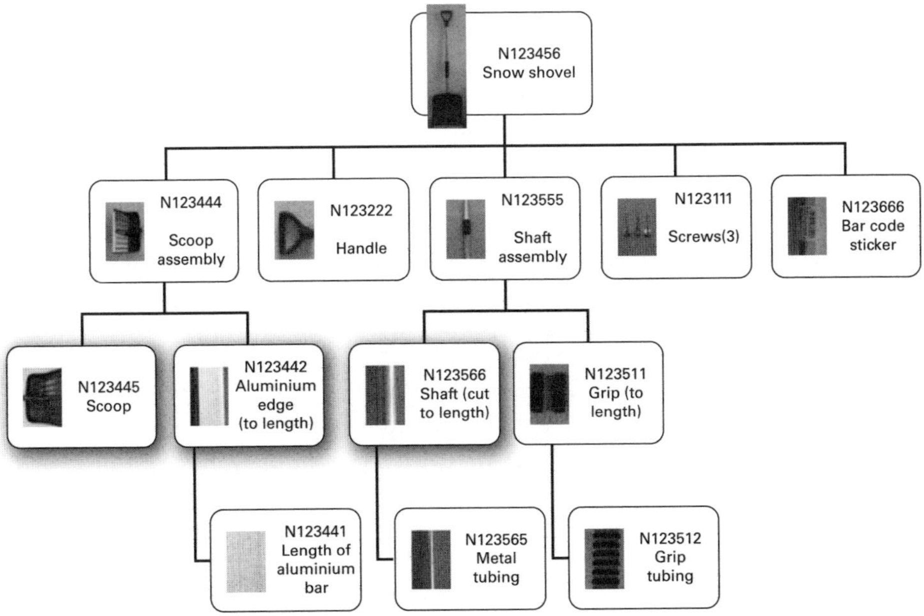

Reproduced by kind permission of WMG

MRP (explosion) process

When the planning processes are all run in the system and all the changes and new orders created, this is sometimes described as an MRP explosion. This process is described either as a regenerative or net change process.

Regenerative and net change processing

Businesses expect and in many cases need to operate with data that is as up to date as possible. MRP systems originally were unable to achieve this because the computer power needed to regenerate all computer records was unavailable while the business was operating. This processing of all part records in a single computer run meant that there was a regeneration of the records overnight (or perhaps only at the weekend). The regenerative process would completely recalculate the whole MRP: it calculated the existing and new orders and changes to existing orders for every item for every order from the top level. Later net change processing became possible where only those records affected by new or changed information were reconstructed.

In large companies even today it may be that not all data is able to be accurate with up-to-the-minute changes because of the amount of processing that has to be carried out. There are advantages to both regenerative and net change processing, and both are still in use.

Parameters

In Chapter 2 we introduced the importance of parameters. If parameters are not well managed then the results from the planning system will need many changes. Here we will consider the importance of a few of those: lead time, cycle stock and safety stock parameters.

Lead time If the lead time in MRP to produce the scoop assembly is one week, then the scoop assembly must be available one week before the final assembly of the snow shovel. MRP must therefore raise the works order for the assembly of the works order one week earlier than the week the finished snow shovel is to be assembled, as shown in Table 4.4.

Once the time-phased MRP calculations are complete for all the dependent demand of all products the instructions (eg works orders, purchase orders) are then executed.

Table 4.4 MRP scheduling of scoop assembly production with one week lead time to meet independent demand for the snow shovel

	Week 1	Week 2	Week 3	Week 4	Week 5	Week 6
MPS for the snow shovel	10	10	20	20	20	10
Opening SOH scoop assembly	10	10	30			
Assemble scoop works order	10	20	20	20	10	10
Closing SOH scoop assembly	10	30				
Min / safety stock	10	10	10	10	10	10

MRP needs to record both forecast orders and actual orders placed by customers, and to be able to differentiate between them. If there is then a conflict in resource utilization, operations can give priority to the customer order.

This can be relevant where there is late customization of products (for example in the automotive industry). In these industries sub-assemblies are often built as modules, which may be fitted on any final product. An example would be that all cars are built with seats in them, but only some of them will have seat heaters; the seats are likely to be interchangeable and can be fitted near the end of the build depending on actual customer orders.

Management of product lead time is essential in all planning systems. There will always be a lead time within which changes cannot, or perhaps should not, be made, often known as the frozen planning horizon. Within a defined 'frozen planning horizon' production planning systems will not make changes to the production plan automatically. The benefits of techniques like late customization can help here as they in effect reduce the overall lead time and reduce the effect of late changes demand. Outside of the lead time the system can continue to adjust the production plans, according to the parameters that it has been given to work with.

Planning systems for purchasing similarly will work to a lead time, within which the system cannot automatically make changes (for example to the purchase orders and the scheduled deliveries), but outside the lead time the system will be able to continue to make changes.

Table 4.5 Snow shovel net demand calculations inside the frozen planning horizon, within lead-time and outside lead-time

	Week 1	Week 2	Week 3	Week 4	Week 5	Week 6	Week 7	Week 8
	Within lead-time			Outside lead-time				
Forecast	1,000	1,000	1,000	1,000	1,000	1,000	1,000	1,000
Orders (start with backlog of 200)	950	980	1050	750	400	20	0	0
Net Demand	1,150	980	1,050	1,000	1,000	1,000	1,000	1,000
MPS	1,000	1,000	1,000	1,000	1,000	1,000	1,000	1,000
FGS closing stock (starting SOH = 300)	150	170	120	120	120	120	120	120

A typical schedule for the net demand of the snow shovel is shown in Table 4.5.

In simple terms the calculations are as follows:

- Net demand inside the lead-time is the orders plus any backlog. In week 1, net demand is: Orders + Backlog = 950 + 200 = 1,150, which is higher than the original forecast of 1,000.
- Net demand inside the lead-time is generally the higher of the forecast or orders, so for week 4, net demand is 1,000, thus the order book would be described as 75 per cent complete.
- Predicted closing stock (SOH) in week 1 is: Opening SOH – net demand + planned production (MPS) = 300 – 1,150 + 1,000 = 150.
- Predicted closing stock (SOH) in week 2 is: Opening SOH – net demand + planned production (MPS) = 150 – 980 + 1,000 = 170.

Figure 4.15 Material and capacity plans drive the shop floor and purchasing systems (simplified from (Vollmann *et al*, 2005))

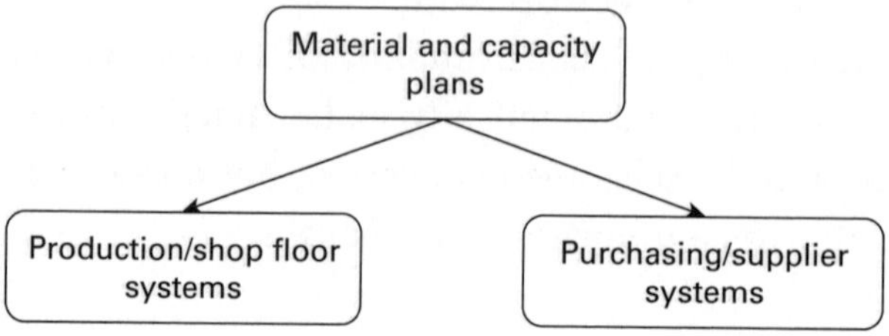

Managing cycle stock and safety stock Cycle stock is the stock that is replenished for routine use or sale, and was included in Chapter 2 when the standardized saw tooth diagram was considered. One of the decisions that needs to be made when implementing an MRP system is whether cycle stock should be replenished by a fixed quantity or at a fixed interval.

Fixed quantity ordering is when the system is set to reorder a fixed quantity each time an order is placed, which means that the frequency of ordering may vary, as shown in Figure 4.16.

Figure 4.16 Fixed quantity ordering

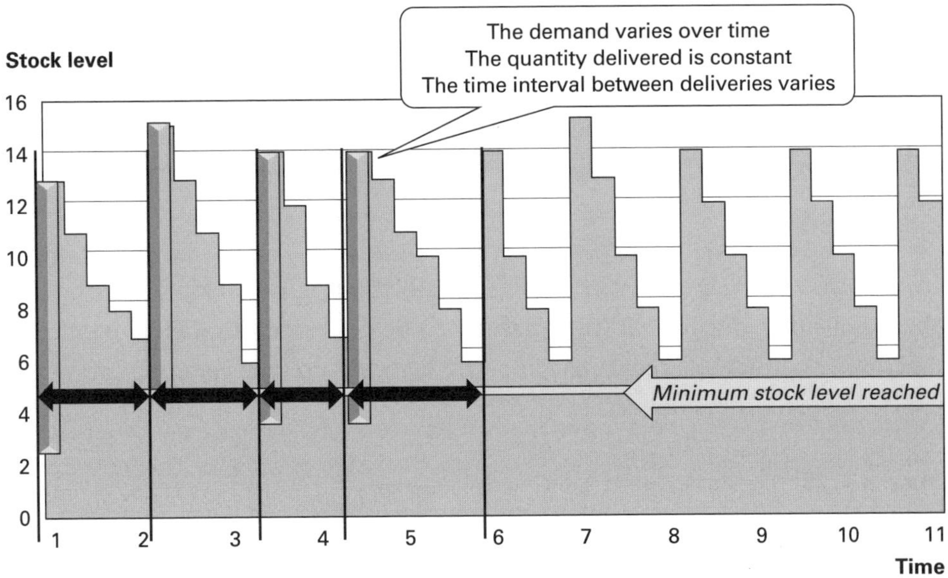

The opposite of fixed quantity ordering is fixed interval ordering. This is where we keep the time between ordering the same and vary the quantity ordered. For example, a supplier gets an order every Monday but the quantity ordered varies slightly, as shown in Figure 4.17.

The benefit of fixed interval ordering isn't necessarily immediately obvious. Figure 4.18 shows a product where demand has reduced significantly over time. If fixed quantity ordering were being used then the MRP system would continue, until told otherwise, to place an order for the same number of items every time an order were placed, although the frequency of the order would be less often. The inventory would then take longer and longer to be consumed, tying money up in unnecessary inventory.

Figure 4.17 Fixed interval ordering

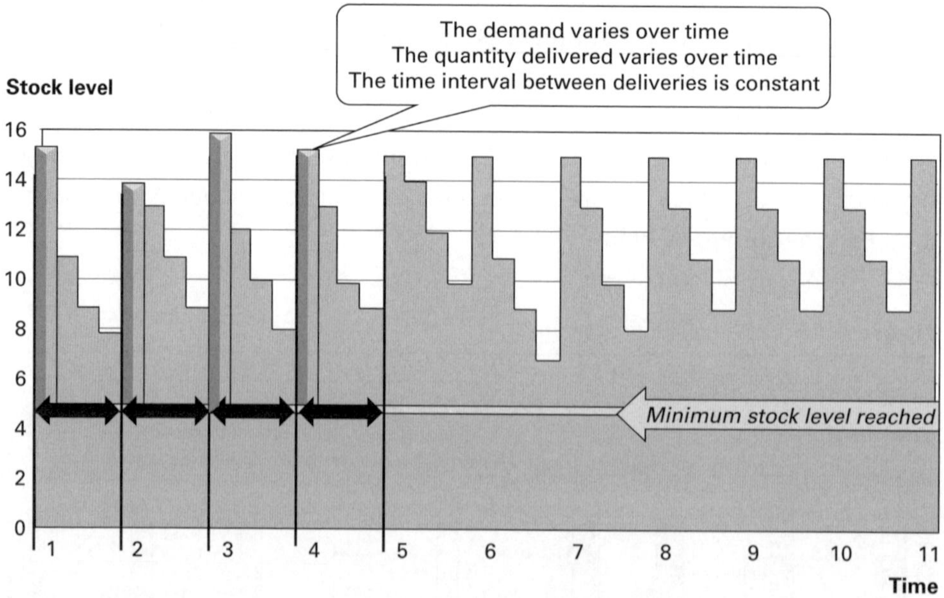

In this case the demand variation is small, there is no obvious trend, and there is a small variation in the quantity to be delivered. Replenishment considerations, either the fixed period is the lead time or the fixed period is the time between orders/deliveries.

Figure 4.18 The advantage of fixed interval ordering

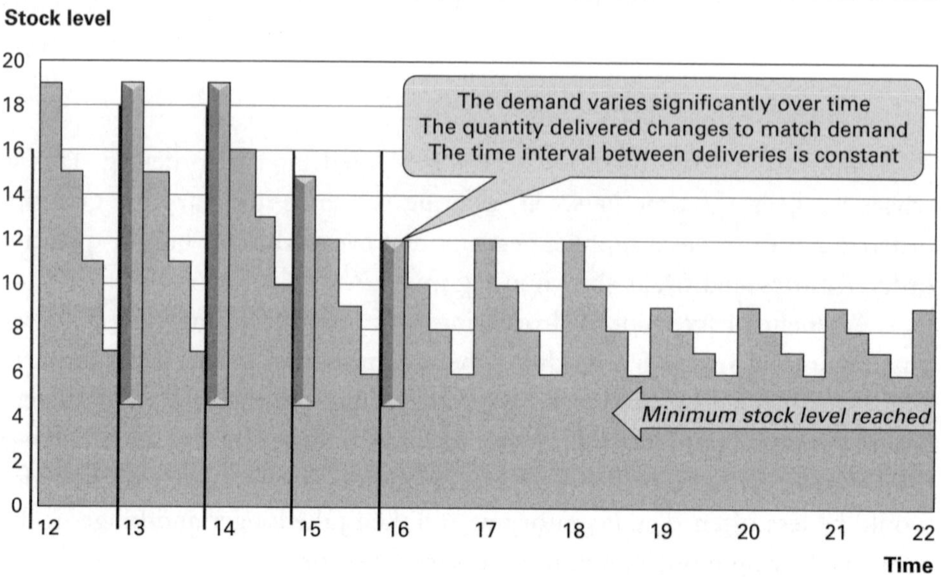

In this example the key point is that the demand is changing significantly and as a result the advantage of using time-based parameters which match demand patterns, rather than quantity-based parameters (which need to be adjusted if they are to match demand) is that they self-adjust to the demand variation replenishment considerations.

MRP can respond to this problem, without any intervention, if fixed interval ordering is used. When the product demand varies significantly over time, the time interval between deliveries remains constant, and the quantity delivered automatically changes to match demand, as shown in Figure 4.18. Because the system is set up to order the quantity needed to meet demand in the next time period (which has been specified), the quantity ordered adjusts automatically.

Businesses that have many thousands of parts can prevent excess inventory building up by choosing to have cycle stock replenishment rules set to fixed interval ordering, as well as it taking less maintenance and input from the planner.

There are other ways of managing cycle stock that should be considered for some products. For example, vendor managed inventory (VMI) is used to good effect in many industries for replenishment of low value, high volume products such as nuts and bolts.

Safety stock settings may also be set to safety time or safety quantity replenishment in MRP and planning systems. Safety time should be chosen for the same reasons as for cycle stock. However, as we shall see in Chapter 8, there are other considerations when safety stock rules are created for products (for example if a product has volatile and low demand then a minimum stock or hybrid rule may be implemented).

Managing inventory control data

Inventory: parts, audit trail and value

Parts are recorded and tracked together with their inventory management data through the planning system. Current information on part number, item description, location and cost are all needed. The cost of an item increases through the process as it moves from raw material, via work in progress and on to final product. This is a useful piece of information, and needs to be updated through the process so that people from the whole organization can access valid information, whether they are from sales, finance, purchasing or production.

Many organizations also need to retain quality information and records to ensure that there is an audit trail that can be followed. The Airbus case study earlier in this chapter is a good example of this. It is clear that the quality of the parts and assemblies is critical to the product; this has seen the rise of six sigma as a quality philosophy. What is less obvious is that data accuracy within MRP systems is equally important and vital to the efficiency of the business.

Consider the question: is 99 per cent accuracy acceptable for MRP data?

MRP will make many thousands of decisions based on the data that is in its databases. If, for example, our stock information was 99 per cent accurate, we had 10,000 parts in which MRP needs to plan for a planning period of 104 weeks (two years). Based on the above there would be in the order of 1% × 10,000 × 104 = 104,000 time-phased demand records that were potentially incorrect. This type of failure rate would not be accepted in the build of an aircraft or a car, and should not be accepted in the data. ***Data accuracy is vital to the effectiveness of MRP systems.***

We started this chapter talking about the four easy steps to inventory planning, which become more challenging as the complexity of the business increases. The four steps are still valid, and Figure 4.19 expands the earlier

Figure 4.19 Inventory planning within the business system and focused on business needs

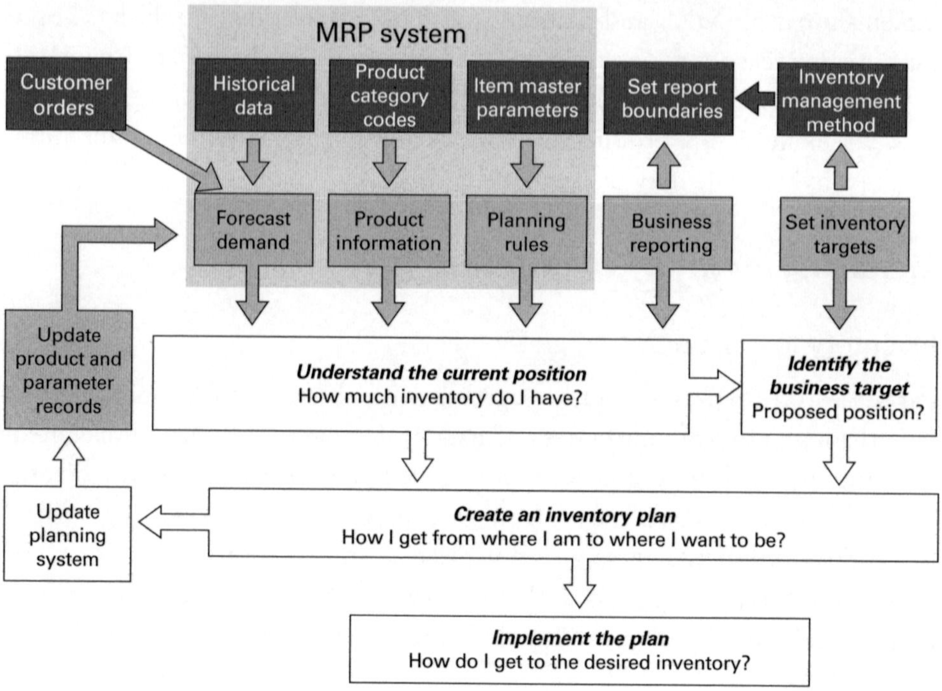

Figure 4.8 by adding the top line of data, targets, parameters and inventory management methods. This then allows the inventory planning process to work within the system as well as being focused on the business needs.

Measuring success

Key performance indicators (KPIs)

There's an old saying: 'what gets measured gets done'. It is also true that if different parts of an organization are being judged on measures that conflict with those elsewhere in the business then they are likely to be pulling against each other.

KPIs are essential for an organization and ERP systems give businesses a great deal of data to choose to report from. Measurements are very important but should be not be contradictory or overly onerous to produce.

Table 4.6 shows some typical KPIs used for operations and inventory management; it is important that the KPIs should tie into the critical success factors (CSFs) in an organization, which should be set to tie into the business's strategy.

Compliance/non-compliance

Non-compliance is a key measure of how well a planning system is working. It is one that many companies overlook, and as a consequence it is hard for them to judge how well their system is being managed and how effective it is.

Non-compliance measures the number of system-generated transactions (eg works and purchase orders) that have to be changed by a person. Conversely, compliance is the number of system-generated transactions that do not need to be changed.

When a new system is first implemented it is likely that there will be a high level of non-compliance. Figure 4.20 shows how, when a non-compliance to a system transaction is necessary, there are two actions that need to be taken:

1. The transaction needs to be corrected and executed. This is the first step and this corrective action is almost always taken.
2. The underlying reason why the transaction was incorrect needs to be corrected if at all possible. This is the second step, and if it is not taken and the root cause corrected then incorrect transactions are likely to continue to be generated.

Table 4.6 Some typical inventory management KPIs

Measure	Description	Reason
Inventory turns/stock turn	The number of times the inventory in a business turns or is consumed in a year	Gives a comparison between similar businesses and helps external benchmarking. Also monitors inventory holding costs
On time delivery in full (OTIF)	The percentage of times customer orders were completed and delivered complete and on time	Monitors customer service and delivery performance
Finished goods stock (FGS) in inventory	Amount of FGS held in days, quantity and cost	Inventory holding costs, over stock indicators, inventory control implications
Raw material/component inventory	Amount of non-FGS held in days, quantity and cost	Inventory holding costs, over stock indicators, inventory control implications
Total work in progress (WIP)	Amount of WIP held in days, quantity and cost	Inventory balancing and control
Total lead time/cycle time	Total time for an order to be processed/time taken from start to end of process	Monitors efficiency and WIP increases or decreases accordingly
Non-compliance	The number of system generated transactions (eg works and purchase orders) that have to be changed by a person	Measures the effectiveness of the system. The more changes that are necessary the less effectively the system is working

Figure 4.20 Non-compliance is a key measure of how well the planning system is working

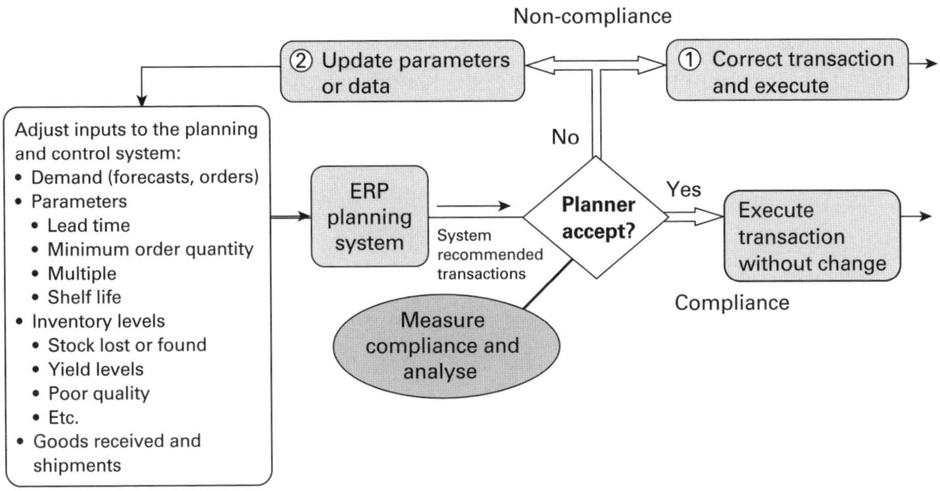

This starts to show the importance of measuring non-compliance. It will focus on parameter management and encourage people to make the system as effective and efficient as possible. It is a good indicator of how well the system is being managed and how well it is able to calculate information so that it is able to create the correct transactions.

Exception management

We have looked at the magnitude of the inventory planning challenge in some businesses in this chapter. Realistically, it is not possible to manage all parts equally. In Chapter 6 we look at some traditional ways of analysing parts so that the ones that should have the most attention can be given it. However, one aspect of ERP and planning systems is that exception management reports can be produced and put to great use.

For example, overstock of high value items, unless of exceptional strategic importance, is more important in inventory management than overstock of nuts and bolts.

Traditionally decisions were made individually, and were normally left to the planners to make them. Exception reporting can be generated from some simple rules-based systems, and a much better overview achieved of the individual parts as well as the whole business.

Is the cost of control too high?

The benefit of business systems is the increased planning and control over what happens within the organization and the improved business insight provided. These benefits come at a cost, however, and the trade-off between the cost and the value of the increased control needs to be understood.

A company does not have to be very complex before it can benefit from an effective planning and control system to help manage the delivery of good service to its customers. The mantra is well-known: right product, right place, right quality, right time and right cost.

The planning and control system itself, though, does not add to the value of the product in the eyes of the customer. So what is its value to the company itself? And does this outweigh the cost?

The costs of the system itself come from several sources, including:

- the initial implementation, for example: company disruption, planning and control system costs (eg licence), implementation services (eg integration, data migration, training), hardware and infrastructure;
- the ongoing management and maintenance of the system (eg maintenance and support fees, updates and retraining);
- adapting to changes that may be required to meet the changing needs of the business without being a drain on valuable resources; and
- the capability to manage the transactions required to make the system work and the frustrations that these may not be seen as optimal by the people who have to interact with the system routinely.

There are, however, costs of not having an ERP system. An estimation of the cost of losing control is not easy to estimate. Many factors would need to be taken into account, including:

- the cost of poor service and late delivery: contracts often carry penalty clauses, lack of availability can cause customers to take their business elsewhere, poor performance may well lose business and create a bad reputation;
- a greater manual effort in planning the business – what purchase orders need to be placed and when (unit price, amount of stock on hand predicted at the point in the future when the order will be delivered, quantity, delivery date), scheduling and placing production orders to meet future needs, etc;
- many islands of un-joined-up and possibly conflicting data;

- lack of efficiency increasing costs and threatening competitiveness; and
- lack of business insight.

This book is not about whether or not a company should implement an ERP system. It is about the management of a company's inventory within a planning and control system such as ERP. However, it is our experience with companies that often there can be a tangible level of frustration with the system and the way it works. Some of this may be due to a lack of understanding about the system or a lack of training, or it may be that the business has developed over the years since implementation and the system is unable to accommodate some of the changes, or it may be that the level of customization or integration with legacy systems has been more costly or difficult to manage than anticipated. Whatever the frustrations or problems with an existing system it is always important to understand the costs to the business of being completely without a planning and control system (eg ERP). The frustrations and problems can then be managed within whatever 'big picture solution' is right for the business.

Summary

The four simple steps to inventory planning are clear:

- Understand current position.
- Identify the business target.
- Create an inventory plan.
- Implement the plan.

Also, the levels of organizational planning are well recognized:

- Strategic – long term – 3–5 years.
- Tactical – medium term – 1–3 years.
- Operational – short term – weeks–12 months

We have looked at how, although simple, when the MRP logic is applied even to a simple product, there is a rapid increase in complexity. Today, MRP as part of more functionally rich ERP systems is now, in effect, the de facto tool for planning for the vast majority of batch manufacturing. It is important to understand how to manage this complexity when managing MRP systems, from the simple products like the shovel to the hugely complex automotive and aerospace products. By considering the way that MRP calculates requirements at all the different levels of the bills of materials, this chapter has shown how accurate data and well-managed parameters are key to an effective and efficient operation of MRP within the wider ERP planning systems. KPIs are an essential tool for the correct focusing of operational teams and it is important to consider performance measurements such as inventory value as well as process measurements like non-compliance. Compliance/non-compliance is a powerful tool for showing how well the MRP system is being used and where to focus to improve the effectiveness of these systems.

In the following chapters we will look in more detail at the different tools and techniques for the analysis and planning of inventory that can help a business to improve inventory performance.

Tools and techniques discussed in this chapter

- Materials requirements planning (MRP)
- Key performance indicators (KPIs)
- Compliance/non-compliance

References

Airbus (2019) https://www.airbus.com/aircraft/how-is-an-aircraft-built/production.html [accessed 2019]

Brain, M (nd) http://electronics.howstuffworks.com/inside-cell-phone.htm. Retrieved 2 November 2014

Brown, R (1982) *Advanced Service Inventory Parts Control* (2nd edn), Material Management Science Inc, Norwich

Edemariam, A (2006) Wings of desire. Retrieved Nov 2014, from http://www.theguardian.com/business/2006/feb/23/theairlineindustry.travelnews

HP (2014) HP Boosts High Performance Computing for Airbus. Retrieved from https://www8.hp.com/uk/en/hp-news/press-release.html?id=1719956

Sainsburys (2016) Annual Report and Finincial Statements. Retrieved April 2019, from https://www.about.sainsburys.co.uk/~/media/Files/S/Sainsburys/documents/reports-and-presentations/annual-reports/annual-report-2016.pdf

Sharp, B (2012) Why stores stock many items that hardly sell. Retrieved April 2019, from https://byronsharp.wordpress.com/2012/08/16/shopping_long_tail/

Toyota (2014) Childrens Question Room. Retrieved November 2019 from https://www.toyota.co.jp/en/kids/faq/d/01/04/

Vollmann, B W *et al* (2005) *Manufacturing Planning and Control Systems*, Irwin McGraw-Hill, New York

You do the maths

Outline brief for materials requirements planning exercises

The MPS for the four products has been re-calculated for the third Quarter. The following exercises require an explosion of the dependent demand for WR-14259-2R Wire-Red and examines the difference between planned order release and off-set requirements planning, only applying batching rules at the purchased component level.

Exercise 1: Component requirement calculation using batching rules

RS Components supplies WR-14259-2R Wire-Red to Control Box UK PLC. There is currently an industry-wide shortage of this particular type of wire. RS components have urgently requested an update to the requirement for this wire. The WR-14259-2R Wire-Red is used in two different components, as shown in the extract from the Matrix BOM in Table 4.7.

Table 4.7 Extract from Matrix BOM showing usage of WR-14559-2R Wire-Red

		21		41	
		50	90	50	90
Part Number	Description				
..RC-67896-8	Raw Card	1	1	1	1
..WR-14259-2R	Wire – Red	6	6	6	6
..OL-26877-150	Output Lead Assy 50	1		1	
..OL-26877-190	Output Lead Assy 90		1		1
...WR-14259-2R	Wire – Red	2	4	2	4

Use the MRP logic explained in Chapter 4 to calculate the projected on hand and net requirements for following components:

1 RC-67896-8 Raw Card
2 OL-26877-150 Output Lead Assy 50
3 OL-26877-190 Output Lead Assy 90

Worked example of projected on hand, net requirement and planned order release steps

1 Projected on hand:
   a opening projected on hand;
   b plus scheduled receipts;
   c less gross requirements;
   d equals new projected on hand;
   e if positive, repeat until projected on hand becomes negative.
2 Using the calculated projected on hand for week 33:
   a Week 33 projected on hand = –45
3 Add planned order quantity = 90.
4 New projected on hand = –45 + 90 = 45:
   a net requirements is the shortfall of the projected on hand for the first week ie week 33;
   b thereafter it is equal to the gross requirement.
5 Planned order release is the planned order receipt offset by the stated lead time, ie six weeks from week 33 back to week 27. That is, to ensure the order to arrives in week 33 it must be ordered in week 27.

Using worksheet provided (Table 4.9) calculate the projected on hand and net requirements for the three assemblies; RC-67896-8 Raw Card projected on hand and net requirements have been calculated as a worked example in Table 4.8 as a reference.

Table 4.7 shows that the three parts are the only ones using by WR14259-2R; use Table 4.9 to calculate the projected on hand, net requirements and the planned order release.

Exercise 2: Calculation of component requirement using planned order release

Having calculated the planned order release for the WR-14259-2R, Wire-Red is used in three different components:

1 RC-67896-8 Raw Card
2 OL-26877-150 Output Lead Assy 50
3 OL-26877-190 Output Lead Assy 90

Based on the planned order release schedules for the three above components, use Figure 4.10 to calculate demand for WR-14259-2R Wire Red using the planned order approach.

Table 4.8 Exercise 1 worked example showing Planned Order Logic

		Month 7				Month 8				Month 9				
RC-67896-8	Week No	WK 27	WK 28	WK 29	WK 30	WK 31	WK 32	WK 33	WK 34	WK 35	WK 36	WK 37	WK 38	WK 39
Gross Requirements		(c) 10	25	20	30	15	45	50	10	20	30	25	35	20
Scheduled Receipts		(b)			90									
Projected on Hand	(a) 60	(d) 50	25	5	65	50	5	(2) 45	35	15	75	50	15	85
Net Requirements		0	0	0	0	0	0	(4) 45	10	20	30	25	35	20
Planned Order Receipts	Qty 90							(3) 90			90			90
Planned Order Releases	6 weeks	(5) 90	0	0	90	0	0	90	0	0	0	90	0	0

Table 4.9 Assembly requirements for the three components using WR-14259-2R Wire-Red

Exercise 1 – Worked Example

		Month 7				Month 8				Month 9				
RC-67896-8	Week No	WK 27	WK 28	WK 29	WK 30	WK 31	WK 32	WK 33	WK 34	WK 35	WK 36	WK 37	WK 38	WK 39
Gross Requirements		10	25	20	30	15	45	50	10	20	30	25	35	20
Scheduled Receipts					90									
Projected on Hand	60													
Net Requirements														
Planned Order Receipts	Qty 90													
Planned Order Releases	6 weeks													

Exercise 2 – Calculated projected on hand and net requirement

		Month 7				Month 8				Month 9				
OL-26877-15O	Week No	WK 27	WK 28	WK 29	WK 30	WK 31	WK 32	WK 33	WK 34	WK 35	WK 36	WK 37	WK 38	WK 39
Gross Requirements		3	8	7	10	5	15	17	3	7	10	8	12	7
Scheduled Receipts					35									
Projected on Hand	30													
Net Requirements														
Planned Order Receipts	Qty 35													
Planned Order Releases	1 week													

		Month 7				Month 8				Month 9				
OL-26877-19O	Week No	WK 27	WK 28	WK 29	WK 30	WK 31	WK 32	WK 33	WK 34	WK 35	WK 36	WK 37	WK 38	WK 39
Gross Requirements		7	17	13	20	10	30	33	7	13	20	17	23	13
Scheduled Receipts				40										
Projected on Hand	25													
Net Requirements														
Planned Order Receipts	Qty 40													
Planned Order Releases	1 week													

Table 4.10 INet requirement planning for WR-14259-2R based on planned order release

Exercise 3 – Calculated gross requirement, projected on hand and net requirement

Case 1 – Requirements based on Planned Order Release

		Month 7				Month 8				Month 9				
Planned Order Release	Week No	WK 27	WK 28	WK 29	WK 30	WK 31	WK 32	WK 33	WK 34	WK 35	WK 36	WK 37	WK 38	WK 39
RC-67896-8		90	0	0	90	0	0	90	0	0	0	90	0	0
OL-26877-15O														
OL-26877-19O														

		Month 7				Month 8				Month 9				
Gross Requirement	BOM Usage	WK 27	WK 28	WK 29	WK 30	WK 31	WK 32	WK 33	WK 34	WK 35	WK 36	WK 37	WK 38	WK 39
RC-67896-8	6	540	0	0	540	0	0	540	0	0	0	540	0	0
OL-26877-15O	2													
OL-26877-19O	4													
Total Gross Requirement														

		Month 7				Month 8				Month 9				
WR-14259-2R	Week No	WK 27	WK 28	WK 29	WK 30	WK 31	WK 32	WK 33	WK 34	WK 35	WK 36	WK 37	WK 38	WK 39
Gross Requirements		540	0	0	700	0	160	610	160	0	160	610	0	160
Scheduled Receipts					900									
Projected on Hand	900													
Net Requirements														
Planned Order Receipts	Qty 900													
Planned Order Releases	1 week													

Exercise 3: Calculation of component requirement using offset net requirements

What is the effect if the *offset net requirements* are used rather than the planned order release to create the gross requirement? Use Table 4.11 to calculate this.

Offset net requirements can be used in place of defining a planned order size (Minimum Order Quantity/MOQ); it is possible if the order size (MOQ) is set to 1 or Lot-for-Lot of the lot size is one.

In this case you will simply offset the net requirements by the lead time as shown for RC-678796-8.

Note offset net requirements not calculated in Exercise 2 are shown where appropriate.

Table 4.11 Net requirement planning for WR-14259-2R based on offset logic

Exercise 4 – Calculated gross requirement, projected on hand and net requirement

		Month 7				Month 8				Month 9				
		WK 27	WK 28	WK 29	WK 30	WK 31	WK 32	WK 33	WK 34	WK 35	WK 36	WK 37	WK 38	WK 39
RC-67896-8	6 weeks	45	10	20	30	25	35	20	10	45	20	20	15	40
OL-26877-15O	1 week													3
OL-26877-19O	1 week													7

		Month 7				Month 8				Month 9				
Gross Requirement	BOM Usage	WK 27	WK 28	WK 29	WK 30	WK 31	WK 32	WK 33	WK 34	WK 35	WK 36	WK 37	WK 38	WK 39
RC-67896-8	6	270	60	120	180	150	210	120	60	270	120	120	90	240
OL-26877-15O	2													
OL-26877-19O	4													
Total Gross Requirement														

		Month 7				Month 8				Month 9				
WR-14259-2R		WK 27	WK 28	WK 29	WK 30	WK 31	WK 32	WK 33	WK 34	WK 35	WK 36	WK 37	WK 38	WK 39
Gross Requirements		270	60	120	188	270	342	154	126	370	204	236	156	274
Scheduled Receipts					900									
Projected on Hand	900													
Net Requirements														
Planned Order Receipts	Qty 900													
Planned Order Releases	1 week													

Chapter 4 exercise answers

Answer Exercise 1: Component requirement calculation using batching rules

Table 4.12 Answer 1 Assembly requirements for parts using WR-14259-2R

Exercise 1 – Worked Example

		Month 7				Month 8				Month 9				
RC-67896-8	Week No	WK 27	WK 28	WK 29	WK 30	WK 31	WK 32	WK 33	WK 34	WK 35	WK 36	WK 37	WK 38	WK 39
Gross Requirements		10	25	20	30	15	45	50	10	20	30	25	35	20
Scheduled Receipts					90									
Projected on Hand	60	50	25	5	65	50	5	45	35	15	75	50	15	85
Net Requirements		0	0	0	0	0	0	45	10	20	30	25	35	20
Planned Order Receipts	Qty 90							90			90			90
Planned Order Releases	6 weeks	90	0	0	90	0	0	90	0	0	0	90	0	0

Exercise 2 – Calculated projected on hand and net requirement

		Month 7				Month 8				Month 9				
OL-26877-15O	Week No	WK 27	WK 28	WK 29	WK 30	WK 31	WK 32	WK 33	WK 34	WK 35	WK 36	WK 37	WK 38	WK 39
Gross Requirements		3	8	7	10	5	15	17	3	7	10	8	12	7
Scheduled Receipts					35									
Projected on Hand	30	27	19	12	37	32	17	0	32	25	15	7	30	23
Net Requirements		0	0	0	0	0	0	0	3	7	10	8	12	7
Planned Order Receipts	Qty 35								35				35	
Planned Order Releases	1 week	0	0	0	0	0	0	35	0	0	0	35	0	0

		Month 7				Month 8				Month 9				
OL-26877-19O	Week No	WK 27	WK 28	WK 29	WK 30	WK 31	WK 32	WK 33	WK 34	WK 35	WK 36	WK 37	WK 38	WK 39
Gross Requirements		7	17	13	20	10	30	33	7	13	20	17	23	13
Scheduled Receipts				40										
Projected on Hand	25	18	1	28	8	38	8	15	8	35	15	38	15	2
Net Requirements		0	0	0	0	2	30	33	7	13	20	17	23	13
Planned Order Receipts	Qty 40					40		40		40		40		
Planned Order Releases	1 week	0	0	0	40	0	40	0	40	0	40	0	0	40

Answer Exercise 2: Component requirement calculation using planned order release

Table 4.13 Answer 2 Total requirements for WR-14259-2R Planned Order Release logic

Exercise 1 – Worked Example

		Month 7				Month 8				Month 9				
RC-67896-8	Week No	WK 27	WK 28	WK 29	WK 30	WK 31	WK 32	WK 33	WK 34	WK 35	WK 36	WK 37	WK 38	WK 39
Gross Requirements		10	25	20	30	15	45	50	10	20	30	25	35	20
Scheduled Receipts					90									
Projected on Hand	60	50	25	5	65	50	5	45	35	15	75	50	15	85
Net Requirements		0	0	0	0	0	0	45	10	20	30	25	35	20
Planned Order Receipts	Qty 90							90			90			90
Planned Order Releases	6 weeks	90	0	0	90	0	0	90	0	0	0	90	0	0

Table 4.13 *continued*

Exercise 2 – Calculated projected on hand and net requirement

		Month 7				Month 8				Month 9				
OL-26877-15O	Week No	WK 27	WK 28	WK 29	WK 30	WK 31	WK 32	WK 33	WK 34	WK 35	WK 36	WK 37	WK 38	WK 39
Gross Requirements		3	8	7	10	5	15	17	3	7	10	8	12	7
Scheduled Receipts					35									
Projected on Hand	30	27	19	12	37	32	17	0	32	25	15	7	30	23
Net Requirements		0	0	0	0	0	0	0	3	7	10	8	12	7
Planned Order Receipts	Qty 35								35				35	
Planned Order Releases	1 week	0	0	0	0	0	0	35	0	0	0	35	0	0

		Month 7				Month 8				Month 9				
OL-26877-19O	Week No	WK 27	WK 28	WK 29	WK 30	WK 31	WK 32	WK 33	WK 34	WK 35	WK 36	WK 37	WK 38	WK 39
Gross Requirements		7	17	13	20	10	30	33	7	13	20	17	23	13
Scheduled Receipts				40										
Projected on Hand	25	18	1	28	8	38	8	15	8	35	15	38	15	2
Net Requirements		0	0	0	0	2	30	33	7	13	20	17	23	13
Planned Order Receipts	Qty 40					40		40		40		40		
Planned Order Releases	1 week	0	0	0	40	0	40	0	40	0	40	0	0	40

Answer Exercise 3: Component requirement calculation using offset net requirements

Table 4.14 Answer 3 Total requirements for WR-14259-2R offset requirements logic

Exercise 4 – Calculated gross requirement, projected on hand and net requirement
Case 2 – Requirements based on Offset Net Requirements

		Month 7				Month 8				Month 9				
Offset Net Requirement	Offset	WK 27	WK 28	WK 29	WK 30	WK 31	WK 32	WK 33	WK 34	WK 35	WK 36	WK 37	WK 38	WK 39
RC-67896-8	6 weeks	45	10	20	30	25	35	20	10	45	20	20	15	40
OL-26877-15O	1 week	0	0	0	0	0	0	3	7	10	8	12	7	3
OL-26877-19O	1 week	0	0	0	2	30	33	7	13	20	17	23	13	7

		Month 7				Month 8				Month 9				
Gross Requirement	BOM Usage	WK 27	WK 28	WK 29	WK 30	WK 31	WK 32	WK 33	WK 34	WK 35	WK 36	WK 37	WK 38	WK 39
RC-67896-8	6	270	60	120	180	150	210	120	60	270	120	120	90	240
OL-26877-15O	2	0	0	0	0	0	0	6	14	20	16	24	14	6
OL-26877-19O	4	0	0	0	8	120	132	28	52	80	68	92	52	28
Total Gross Requirement		270	60	120	188	270	342	154	126	370	204	236	156	274

		Month 7				Month 8				Month 9				
WR-14259-2R		WK 27	WK 28	WK 29	WK 30	WK 31	WK 32	WK 33	WK 34	WK 35	WK 36	WK 37	WK 38	WK 39
Gross Requirements		270	60	120	188	270	342	154	126	370	204	236	156	274
Scheduled Receipts					900									
Projected on Hand	900	630	570	450	1162	892	550	396	270	800	596	360	204	830
Net Requirements		0	0	0	0	0	0	0	0	100	204	236	156	274
Planned Order Receipts	Qty 900									900				900
Planned Order Releases	1 week	0	0	0	0	0	0	0	900	0	0	0	900	0

Key learning point for MRP

Looking at the gross requirements in Tables 4.13 and 4.14 we can see that:

1 The use of any batching rules brings forward the demand in time to earlier weeks.

2 It also increases the lumpiness of the demand: look at weeks 28 & 29 and 31 & 32 in Table 4.13 case 1 – they are 0. The variation in the demand in Table 4.13 case 1 is 540 (requirements of 700 to 160), whereas in Table 14.8 case 2 the variation in the demand is 210 (270 to 60), which is considerably smaller.

The selection of the batch size is critical to the stability and ease of management of the recommended orders. It is also a tempting as a planner to use a batch size of 1 and apply the batching rules at the time as placing the planned order. This can be a false economy, as often batch rules exist, typically from suppliers, which will dictate the result and only result in unnecessary work for the planner.

Stack and flow inventories 05

Introduction

This chapter will look at the different ways we focus on inventory at a specific product level to identify where inventory is held, or at a business level either strategically, tactically or operationally. In simplistic terms, inventory is either being stored (stacked) or is being processed (flowing). If we consider this premise in more detail, in a manufacturing operation or a supply chain, inventory is either stored (stacked) in a secure store/warehouse where it is kept until it is needed for manufacturing or to fulfil a customer requirement (demand), or the inventory is 'work in process' (flowing) which means that it is being processed to add value to the item, ie items issued to manufacturing for assembly.

In the example in Figure 5.1 we can see the stock in the raw material stores (stacked) which is then moved through various manufacturing stages (flow) to the finished goods store. What we see is that inventory flow takes from one inventory stack to the next. This flow is either:

- inside the manufacturing unit;
- being received into a warehouse;
- being dispatched from a warehouse;
- moving between manufacturing operations or warehouses;
- through a manufacturing operation including inspection, packing;
- being placed in another stack for storage whilst waiting for the next process;
- moving to another geographical location.

This chapter will look at aggregate planning for a group of items and different ways and time frames for planning.

Figure 5.1 Example of a manufacturing operation showing the stack and flow

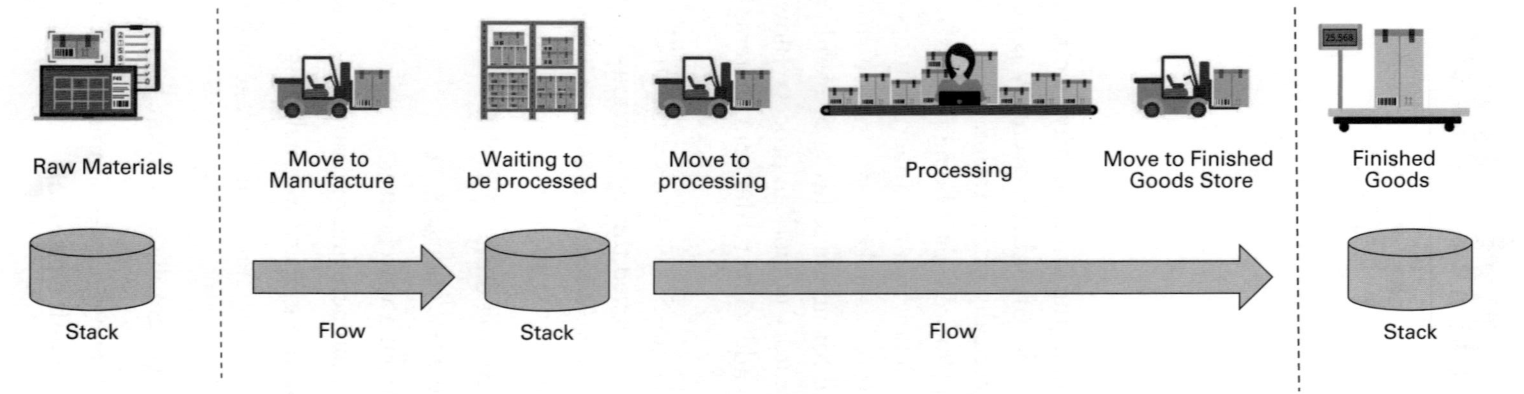

Optimization of stack and flow inventories

The aim should be to optimize the inventory when it is stationary as it may not be adding value. When it is moving, we need to maximize the speed of flow and ensure there are a minimum of non-value-add process steps. There are many techniques available that are designed to help us control the movement of inventory and examine the process flow. For example:

- Kanban controls the movement based on consumption;
- VA/NVA (value add/non-value add) identifies where waste exists in the process;
- process analysis looks at the overall process flow.

These techniques focus on movement and waste but not necessarily whether the inventory value is correctly placed.

Each of the stack and flow inventory categories have specific purposes and optimum values are determined differently in each case. The result is that there is a risk that a planner or manager can get confused by this wide range of techniques and strategies. Different process approaches and systems will use different terms to describe inventory.

Inventory stack

First, we will consider the inventory stacks at a high level. Inventory stacks will be raw materials and components from suppliers in stock ready for the manufacturing process, or sub-assemblies, work in progress (WIP) on the shop floor waiting to be moved or processed. There are several types of inventory stacks.

Cycle/batch stock

The size of the batch being processed will determine the inventory level. The ideal minimum is to achieve one-piece flow; it is important to note that in any process these temporary stacks are formed when the process batch size is greater than one between processes steps. The determination of optimum cycle stock will be examined in more detail in the next chapter.

Safety stock, buffer stock

Safety stock is an inventory stack used to compensate for the volatility of the supply/demand. The degree of variability will have a big impact on the level of safety stock. The quality of the supply/demand is a reflection of the flow processes that join the stacks. In Chapter 4 we looked at simple supply/demand planning for an item and the importance of the BOM to MRP processes. Safety stock protects for failures in both the physical and system processes. The determination of optimum safety stock will be examined in more detail in the next chapter.

Kanban

Kanban inventory is automatically connected to a flow process such that if the demand stops it will automatically stop the supply. This is known as 'pull' processing, unlike MRP systems which will assume the planned demand will happen and will continue to bring in further supplies until the MRP demand is changed: this is known as 'push' processing. There are significant advantages to using 'pull' processing over 'push'. However, its principal weakness is that it cannot manage product variety and complexity, which has given rise to the development of hybrid MRP systems that have 'pull' processes incorporated in the MRP logic. This has been made possible with the increased ability to offer real-time MRP systems. The calculation of the amount of stock held in a Kanban has a lot of similarities with other common batch and safety stock calculations. The example quoted by (Richards and Grinsted, 2016) is shown in Table 5.1, which also shows the relation to the standardized saw tooth diagram in Figure 2.20. The similarity to other methods of batch sizing and safety stock will be clearer as these methods are explored in more depth in the next chapter. Suffice to say that the net effect of the calculation is to determine the size and value of a self-managing stack of inventory to be held in the process.

Capacity or anticipation

In Chapter 2 Figure 2.12 we discussed the problem where demand periodically exceeds supply and that typically the business will plan ahead and build up stock in 'anticipation' of the higher demand. This is most used where a product or business has a degree of seasonality. Examples of seasonal stock would be the high demand for gardening watering equipment in the summer, waterproofs in the spring, etc. It is possible to use a combined approach, where stock is built up for a stable demand product using the same labour and equipment as the alternative seasonal product to allow more flexibility for the unstable demand.

Table 5.1 Kanban formula (Richards and Grinsted, 2016) and comparison to standardized saw tooth in Figure 2.20

$$\text{Number of Kanbans (N)} = \frac{d \times (t + s)}{c} = \frac{12.5 \times (7 + 2)}{5} = 23$$

Where N = number of Kanbans	Example
d = hourly demand	d = 100/8 hours 12.5 units per hour
c = capacity of container	c = 5 units per box
t = average time to obtain a replacement box (in hours)	t = 7 hours
s = safety stock in hours	s = 2 hours

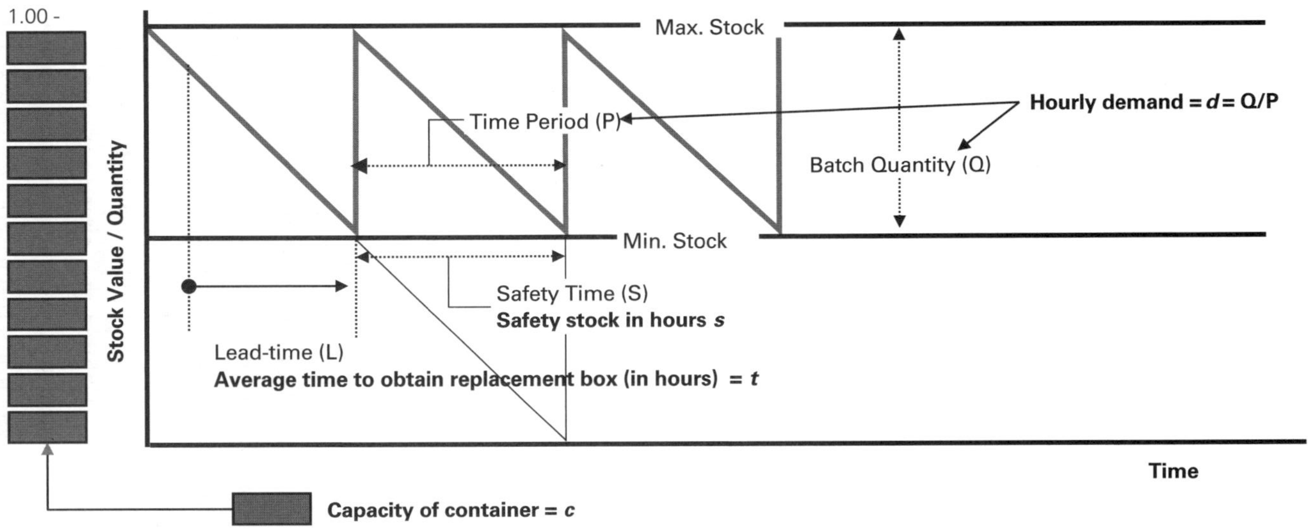

Comparison with standardized saw-tooth showing batch and safety stock linkages

Decoupling inventory

Decoupling inventory allows the production tasks or networks to be disconnected. It is typically used between businesses or major operations. As the amount of decoupling inventory is reduced there is a greater reliance on the 'connectedness' of the processes, that is to say the closeness of the relationship between the businesses or the ability of the operations to remain synchronized. Thus, decoupling inventory is another form of safety stock, but with the specific purpose of allowing processes/business to operate independently and without having an immediate impact on each other. With globalization, decoupling inventory has a significant strategic implication; as discussed by Ray (2011) when examining the effects of the Japanese earthquake, the reduction or elimination of decoupling inventory can expose the supply chain to unplanned events.

DDMRP strategic buffer

Demand-driven materials requirements planning (DDMRP) was mentioned in Chapter 2 and Figure 2.16. It is a methodology used for the positioning and evaluation of the amount of safety stock planned. The exponents of the methodology (Ptak and Smith, 2016) cite three reasons for the DDMRP strategic buffer:

- Shock absorption – this is a form of decoupling inventory.
- Lead-time compression – this is similar in function to finished goods stock, but in the intermediate processes.
- Supply order generation – this is similar to the minimum/maximum parameter definitions in traditional MRP that are used to define the optimum inventory range and trigger when new orders are planned.

Overall, DDMRP is a more sophisticated version of traditional MRP that attempts to answer some of the recognized failings of MRP. DDMRP technique calculates and places within the manufacturing process 'managed' stacks of inventory using a simple traffic light system to indicate if replenishment action is required.

The previous section has shown the wide variety of uses for an inventory stack and has outlined that there are many types of inventory that are held as a stack. In most cases, the tools for optimizing the amount of inventory to be held, which are discussed in the next chapter, focus on the individual part and the quantity. These are important from a business system planning viewpoint, but do not allow the planner to fully appreciate the 'product view' and the value of inventory held in inventory stacks. If we express inventory in monetary terms, we can combine parts based on their value, which is useful when we would like to consider the investment needed to manage an individual product. For example, if we take the parts from the Snow Shovel Final Assembly N123456, shown in Table 5.2, at a part level and in the view of the production and planning staff the N123444 Scoop Assembly is equally important to the assembly as the N123666 Bar Code Sticker: both are essential to the assembly of the finished product irrespective of their individual unit cost. However, as an inventory planner/manager we will need to consider the inventory value. To demonstrate this, when we consider the Scoop Assembly the inventory manager will see a different picture to the planning manager. Looking at Table 5.2, what becomes clear is that the Scoop Assembly N123444 is the most valuable inventory item, whilst the Bar Code Sticker, which is held in greater quantity by planning, is by comparison of little inventory value. Thus, when planning *inventory*, it is crucial that we focus on value. It is obvious that we could easily afford to hold a lot more stock of the Bar Code Sticker than the Scoop Assembly. What would be useful would be to express the product in inventory terms to assist in planning the inventory at a strategic/tactical level.

Table 5.2 Comparison of stock quantity and inventory value

Part	Description	Quantity Each	Unit Cost	Batch Quantity	Inventory Value
N123444	Scoop Assembly	1	£12.72	50	£636.00
N123222	Handle	1	£2.25	50	£112.50
N123555	Shaft Assembly	1	£3.83	25	£95.63
N123111	Screws (x3)	3	£0.02	1,000	£60.00
N123666	Bar Code Sticker	1	£0.01	1,000	£10.00

Weighted average profile – inventory stack

As demonstrated in Table 5.2, the choice of the size of the batch being delivered into the stack is an important part of the materials requirements planning processes. The position or quantity of an inventory stack is used to facilitate the production and materials planning but will not help in optimizing the overall value of product inventory in the business unless unit cost of the components is also considered. In order to focus on the inventory value, we need to simply represent an inventory stack as a value. To do this we can utilize the traditional saw tooth first shown in Figure 2.20 as a way of expressing the stack as value by using the unit cost. If we use the N123444 Scoop Assembly as an example, in Figure 5.2 the saw tooth shows that the batch stock/cycle stock is used up and replenished; here it is appropriate to use the average to indicate the 'steady state' stock level. However, for safety stock, which is a permanent stock holding and therefore is always there, we use the total value. When planning inventory, we are concerned with investment; this has two components – value and time. Let us assume for this example that the N123444 Scoop Assembly has an average demand of 25 per day, the planning batch quantity of 50, safety stock of 25 and a unit cost of £12.72. Expressing the Scoop Assembly as inventory value, the average batch inventory value is £318.00, which is replenished every two days and represents an average of one day's inventory. Similarly, for the safety stock, the inventory value is £318.00, and the amount of safety expressed as time would be one day.

If we use this approach for the Snow Shovel Final Assembly, we have to evaluate five component parts. Each part that is stocked will have different batch quantities and safety stock quantities determined by the materials planning team. We use the unit costs, which are based on the purchased price, or the total assembly/manufactured costs, which will include the labour costs for the assembly or manufactured part. It would be useful to represent the inventory investment for the Snow Shovel Assembly, which is five components stacks similar to Figure 5.2, as a single value and time. The calculations can be seen in Figure 5.3 and show how the weighted average is calculated creating a total inventory value for each item, which when totalled represents the total inventory investment. We can see that our Snow Shovel Final Assembly has an average day of supply of 1.77 days or weighted average days of inventory, which is equivalent to drawing a simple square with the same area as the five components represented by the dotted line (6). The extended value can help allow us to compare the different parts in our product to identify which has the highest inventory value and allow some strategic/tactical planning based on inventory values. We can also look at the values of each part to see which stack has the highest value. For example:

Figure 5.2 Inventory stack as traditional saw tooth

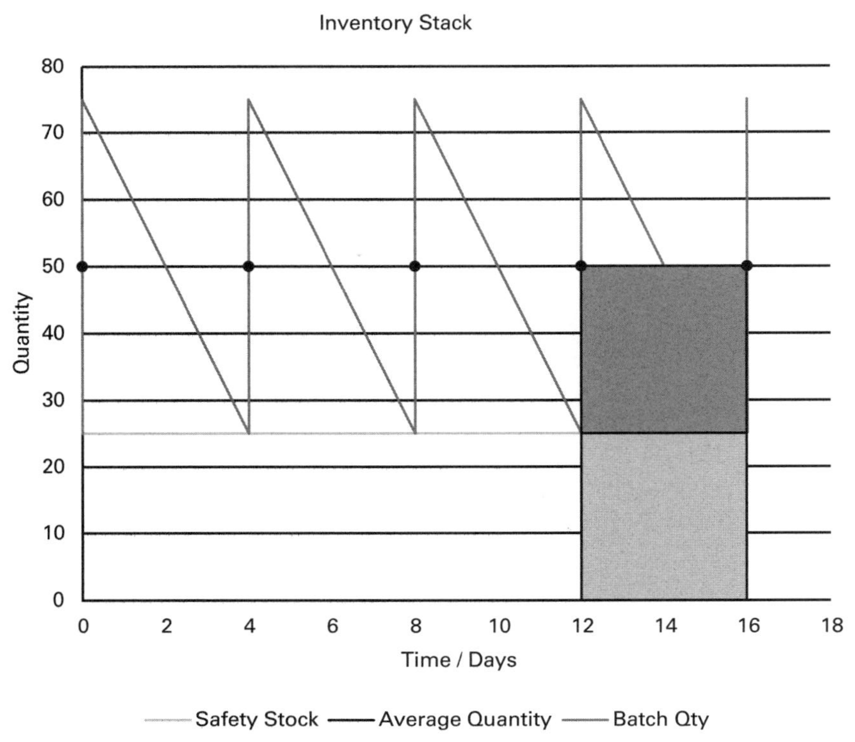

Inventory Investment N123444 Scoop Assembly

Parameters

D	Daily Going Rate	25
Q_b	Batch Quantity	50
Q_s	Safety Quantity	25
p	Unit Price	£12.72

Days of Supply

$$\frac{Q_b}{2D} = B_d \qquad = 1 \text{ Day}$$

Safety Time

$$\frac{Q_s}{D} = S_d \qquad = 1 \text{ Day}$$

Value of Batch Inventory

$$\frac{Q_b p}{2} \text{ or } B_d * p * D = V_b \qquad £318.00$$

Value of Safety Inventory

$$Q_s p \text{ or } S_d * p * D = V_s \qquad £318.00$$

Figure 5.3 Show shovel weighted average profile (WAP)

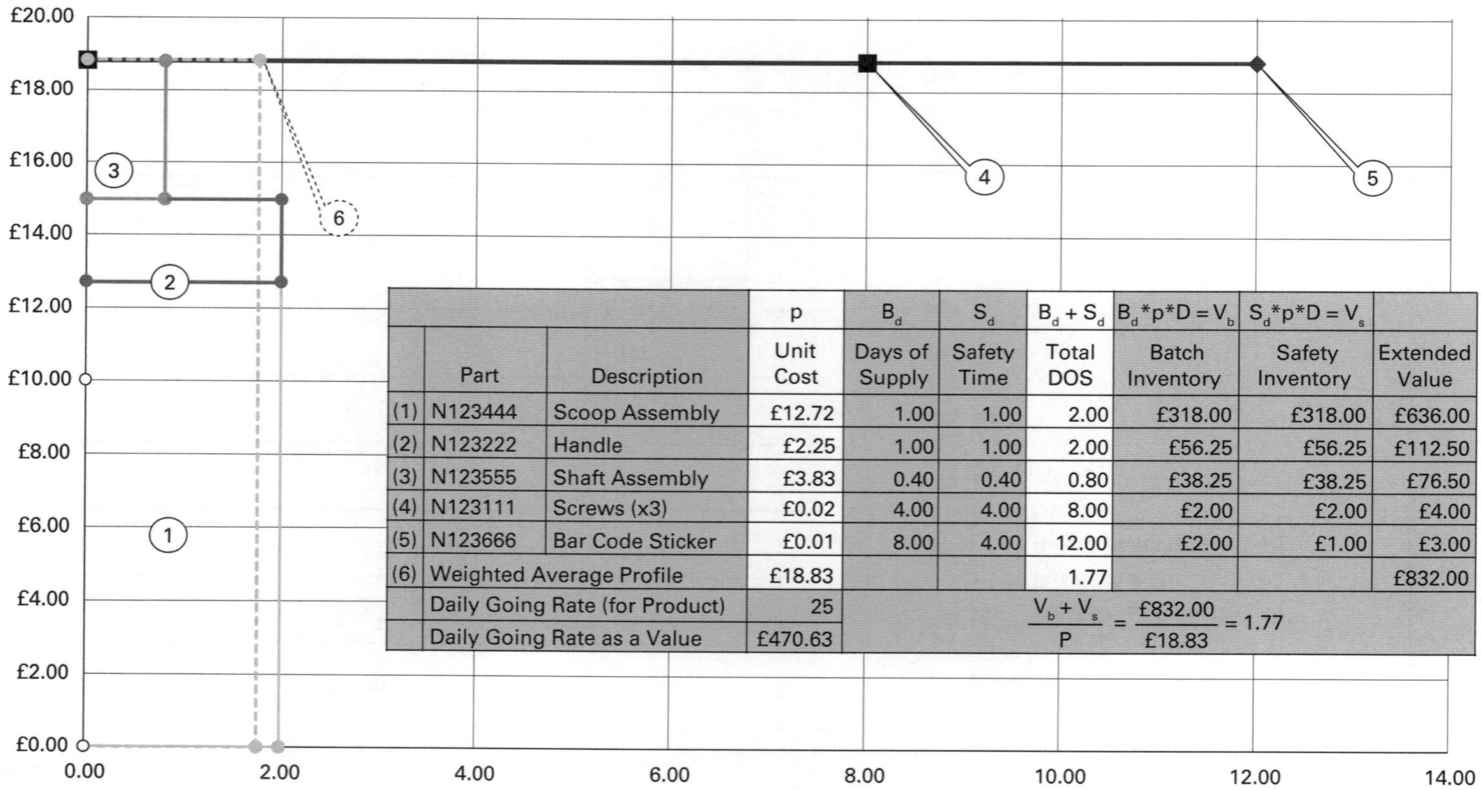

			p	B_d	S_d	$B_d + S_d$	$B_d*p*D = V_b$	$S_d*p*D = V_s$	
	Part	Description	Unit Cost	Days of Supply	Safety Time	Total DOS	Batch Inventory	Safety Inventory	Extended Value
(1)	N123444	Scoop Assembly	£12.72	1.00	1.00	2.00	£318.00	£318.00	£636.00
(2)	N123222	Handle	£2.25	1.00	1.00	2.00	£56.25	£56.25	£112.50
(3)	N123555	Shaft Assembly	£3.83	0.40	0.40	0.80	£38.25	£38.25	£76.50
(4)	N123111	Screws (x3)	£0.02	4.00	4.00	8.00	£2.00	£2.00	£4.00
(5)	N123666	Bar Code Sticker	£0.01	8.00	4.00	12.00	£2.00	£1.00	£3.00
(6)	Weighted Average Profile		£18.83			1.77			£832.00
	Daily Going Rate (for Product)		25			$\frac{V_b + V_s}{P} = \frac{£832.00}{£18.83} = 1.77$			
	Daily Going Rate as a Value		£470.63						

N123222 Handle (2) has a lower unit cost (p), however its Extended Value £112.50 ($V_b + V_s$) is higher than the N123555 Shaft Assembly (3). This is because the Total DOS Days of Supply ($B_d + S_d$) is longer.

By looking at the extended values we are able identify the greatest inventory reduction opportunities by ranking the DOS highest to lowest.

Inventory flow

Having considered the inventory stack, we can now take a close look at the flow inventory. Here we are concerned with material that is being transformed, which occurs in two ways. First, we change a component from one form to another. This can be by machining, moulding, cutting or any other process that changes the component from one state to another. The component part number is usually changed at this point and the cost of the work performed on the component is added to the component value. The second transformation is where we assemble a number of components to form an assembly or sub-assembly. Here we take the components and assemble, by welding, screwing, bonding or any other process that brings the components together. The costs here are the value of the components and the cost of the assembly processes. Also important when the inventory is in a flow state is the need to minimize or optimize the length of the pipeline or time it takes to complete the process of transformation/assembly. Within the transformation process there are two times that are relevant: the 'value-add' time and the 'elapsed' time. The value-add time is the time the process actually takes, whereas the elapsed time is the time from when the components are released (from a stack) to the assembly process to when they are returned (to a stack) completed. The value-add time is more commonly known as the process time and is used in a number of ways to identify the added value through labour, and the equipment and resources required. The elapsed time is more commonly known as the lead time and represents the time used in the BOM to help MRP plan to ensure that materials are available at the correct time. Within planning systems, we use the BOMs and routing to define these values within the transformation process. Table 5.3 shows the BOM and routing for the N123456 Snow Shovel Final Assembly. We can see that the BOM for the Final Assembly defines what is required, the part numbers, quantity required, lead times as well as costs and assembly times. The assembly time represents the elapsed time and the labour hours represents the value-add time.

Table 5.3 BOM and routing for final assembly of Snow Shovel Scoop Assembly N123456

Part Number	Description	Qty	UOM	Lead-time	Labour Cost	Material Cost
N123456	Snow Shovel	1	Each	5	£10.10	£28.97
N123444	Scoop Assembly	1	Each	5		£12.72
N123222	Handle	1	Each	30		£2.25
N123555	Shaft Assembly	1	Each	5		£3.83
N123111	Screws (x3)	3	Each	5		£0.06
N123666	Bar Code Sticker	1	Each	15		£0.01
					Total	£47.84

Operation	Description	Resource	Time in hours	Rate per hour	Cost
Number					
10	Issue components from store				
20	Screw N123222 Handle to N123555 Shaft Assembly with screw N123111	Semi-skilled fitter	0.10	£15.00	£1.50
30	Screw N123444 Scoop Assembly to N123555 Shaft Assembly with 2 x screws N123111	Semi-skilled fitter	0.20	£15.00	£3.00
40	Stick N123666 Bar Code Label to lower shaft	Skilled assembler	0.20	£18.00	£3.60
50	Inspect	Inspector	0.10	£20.00	£2.00
60	Deliver N123456 Snow Shovel final Assembly to store				
		Total	0.60	Total	£10.10

Product planning

The BOM lead times are used by the MRP (planning systems) to determine when the materials need to be available for assembly. In Chapter 4, Table 4.4, we discussed the way MRP offsets the lead times to ensure the materials are ordered in good time. It would be useful to know how long it would take to make the product from scratch, ie that is if we had no stock at all and had to buy all materials and build the total product: this is known as the 'production time' (P). We can then compare this total time with the time we know the customer is prepared to wait, called the 'demand time' (D). This type of comparison is a useful strategic planning tool in that it helps identify where the constraints/bottlenecks are in the product manufacture and assembly processes. This relationship between the customer demand time (D) and the product production time (P) is known as the P:D ratio.

P:D ratio

A detailed explanation, used by Slack, Brandon-Jones and Johnston (2016), is shown summarized in Figure 5.4. The demand time is usually known and to remain competitive would also be constantly compared to the competition. The production time is the cumulative lead time of the product from raw materials and components through sub-assembly to finished product.

A comparison between the two times helps planners decide whether to forecast/hold stock of items, sub-assemblies or assemblies. There are many permutations but only two situations that affect the planning process.

1 Production time = demand time (P:D = 1). Here the product can be built, including the purchase of materials, in the same amount of time the customer is prepared to wait. So, the business can wait until the customer has signed a contract or confirmed the order before committing to purchase the raw materials: this minimizes our risk. This is described as 'resource to order'. If we could include the design/engineering as well we would classify the business as 'design to order' or 'engineer to order': these are typically bespoke products or services. In all cases there is minimal risk for stock holding.
2 Production time > demand time (P:D >1). In this situation we cannot make the product if we wait till the customer has ordered the product. There are different categories, which Slack, Brandon-Jones amd Johnston (2016)

Figure 5.4 P:D ratio

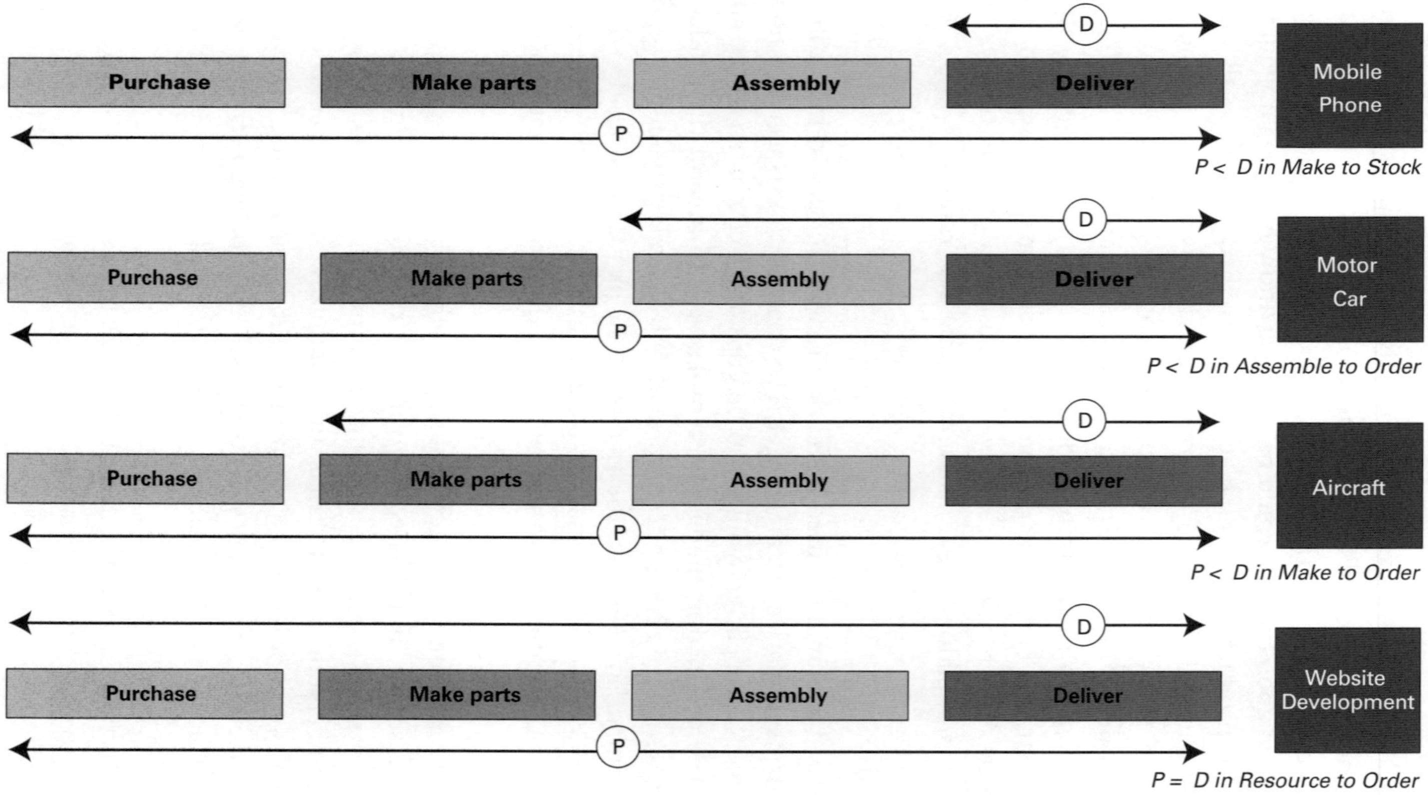

SOURCE Simplified from Slack, Brandon-Jones and Johnston, 2016, p 325

look at in detail. With respect to inventory planning we will concern ourselves with the four simple steps shown in Figure 5.4 – Purchase, Make Parts, Assembly and Deliver – as these have an inventory implication. In this case there are three scenarios where the P:D ratio is > 1:

a Make to Order: In this case the demand time covers making the parts, assembly and delivery, which means that we can wait until we have an order before we use any of our raw materials, so all we need to do is manage/forecast the stock of raw materials which, depending on our products/processes, may be straightforward.

b Assemble to Order: In this case the demand time only covers the last two processes of assemble and deliver, which means that we will need to have made the components from our raw materials. This may mean that we have to make parts specific to a customer before we have the firm order – thus we have to forecast, and as the parts are potentially specific to the customer we have increased the risk of scrap or excess stocks.

c Make to Stock: In this final case the demand time only covers the delivery time, which means that we will have to complete the product and hold it in finished goods stock prior to the customer order. This is the riskiest, as we will be almost entirely dependent on the accuracy of our forecast. In this situation, businesses focus on developing generic products or utilize 'late customization' as a design approach to minimize the risk.

From the above we can see that if the P:D ratio is > 1 we will need to forecast some or all of the raw materials, components or assemblies. In this case we need to take a careful look at the way the production time is built up, from both manufacturing planning and inventory planning aspects. To do this we can use a 'set-back' or stick chart. A set-back chart is the official term used by APICS in their dictionary, but the authors have tended to use the term 'stick chart'. The use of this technique helps us identify where we should begin to look if we want to improve our P:D ratio and thus our delivery capability to our customer. The first step is to determine the total production time or cumulative lead time.

Cumulative lead times

If we look at the snow shovel example in Chapter 2, Table 2.3 and Figure 2.19, we see two different ways of expressing the structure of the snow shovel. If we want to know what lead time to offer a customer, we need to know how long it would take to build the shovel from scratch. To do this we need to know what the lead time is for each of the components, sub-assemblies and assembly. This information is usually determined by the manufacturing and purchasing organizations within the business and used as part of the MRP system. Table 5.4 expands Table 2.3 and adds for each step the lead time for each item based on the low-level code (LLC), which is used by MRP to signify where the part is in the BOM structure.

Looking at Table 5.4 (and relating to Figure 2.19), you can see that there are two assemblies and three components made from raw materials to make the snow shovel. The two assemblies use a combination of manufactured and purchased parts.

- Scoop assembly N123444 is made from:
  - N123445 scoop, a purchased part;
  - N123442 aluminium edge (cut to length), a manufactured part.
- N123555 shaft assembly is made from:
  - N123566 shaft (cut to length) manufactured parts;
  - N123511 grip (cut to length) manufactured parts.

We can see from Table 5.4 that there are three levels below the final assembly. The table shows the lead time for each level and the total in the column on the right. For example, N123445 scoop is purchased on a lead time of 30 days from a supplier. It has N123442 aluminium edge added in sub-assembly N123444 scoop assembly, which has a lead time of five days. The scoop assembly is then assembled into the final product, which takes another five days. This means the total time taken is 40 days from the supplier receiving the order for the scoop to the final assembly being available to the customer. The N123442 aluminium edge is manufactured from extruded aluminium and cut to length, which takes 10 days to manufacture and the supplier of the uncut aluminium edge needs a lead time of 15 days. Adding all this together we get 35 days in total, which although more complex is a shorter cumulative lead time than the scoop. The stick chart (lead time set-back chart) in Figure 5.5 allows us to look at the information in Table 5.4 visually. It is now much easier to see where the longest lead time exists in the process.

Inventory stick chart (lead time set-back chart)

Inventory stick charts are useful for understanding the cumulative lead time and the relationship of the lead time to the bills of material. They also determine the amount of the materials that have to be forecast (ie those

Table 5.4 Cumulative lead time for snow shovel

Item	Description	Quantity	Unit of Measure	Item type	Low level code	Lead-time	LLC 0	LLC 1	LLC 2	LLC 3	Cum Lead-time
N123456	Snow Shovel	1	Each	Assembly	0	5	5	0	0	0	5
N123444	Scoop Assembly	1	Each	Assembly	1	5	0	5	0	0	10
N123445	Scoop	1	Each	Purchased	2	30	0	0	30	0	40
N123442	Aluminium Edge (cut to length)	1	Each	Manufactured	2	10	0	0	10	0	20
N123441	Length of Aluminium Bar	340	Millimetres	Purchased	3	15	0	0	0	15	35
N123222	Handle	1	Each	Purchased	1	30	0	30	0	0	35
N123555	Shaft Assembly	1	Each	Assembly	1	5	0	5	0	0	10
N123566	Shaft (cut to length)	1	Each	Manufactured	2	10	0	0	10	0	20
N123565	Metal Tubing	1.02	Metres	Purchased	3	15	0	0	0	15	35
N123511	Grip (cut to length)	1	Each	Manufactured	2	5	0	0	5	0	15
N123512	Grip Tubing	200	Millimetres	Purchased	3	5	0	0	0	5	20
N123111	Screws (x3)	3	Each	Purchased	1	5	0	5	0	0	10
N123666	Bar Code Sticker	1	Each	Purchased	1	15	0	15	0	0	20

which have a cumulative lead time beyond the customers' acceptable order period). This in effect determines where a part sits on the P:D ratio and if it can be produced or assembled after customer orders are received.

Figure 5.5 Stick chart for snow shovel

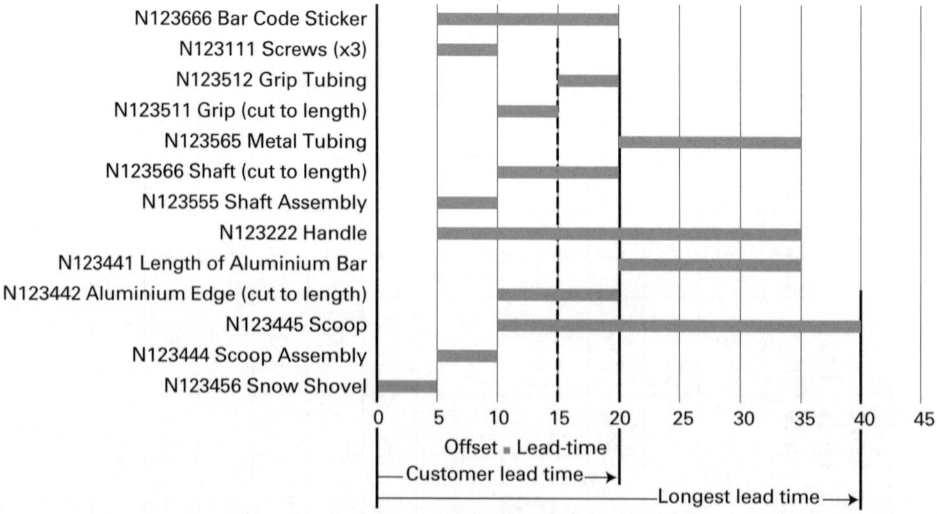

By kind permission of Geoff Relph, Inventory Matters

Examining the stick chart for the snow shovel, we can see that the longest lead time is 40 days. If we are offering a 20-day lead time to our customer, by examining the stick chart we can see that there are four components that need to be on order prior to the customer order being received. These are N123445 scoop, N123441 length of aluminium bar, N123222 handle and N123565 metal tubing. If we are offering the alternate red snow shovel, we need to take account that the black scoop is specific to the product and cannot be used in alternative products; the aluminium bar and metal tubing are common to other products, and we only need to cut to length within the customer lead time.

If the customer requests a lead time of under 15 days, the number of components that need to be on order increases to seven out of a total of 12 parts. However, N123666 Bar Code Sticker would be the only black snow shovel part. The cutting to length would need to be undertaken prior to the customer order and the other general use component would also need to be forecast. This begins to present a significant amount of speculation time and risk for us as the supplier of the snow shovel, which is a highly seasonal product and difficult to predict.

By examining the stick chart we can see where precisely in the process the lead times are causing a major impact on the cumulative lead time. The two purchased components scoop and handle can be clearly seen to have the longest lead times. The opportunity for improvement would be to negotiate a lead time reduction with the supplier. This is unlikely to bring it inside the critical lead time from the customer, but would reduce the risk when forecasting, and a degree of flexibility could be negotiated in the last 10 days before delivery.

Both the manufactured processes have a lead time of five days. If we look at Table 5.3 we can see that the process time is 20 minutes (0.3 hours), and if we made the snow shovel in batches of 10, it would require three hours per batch. This is less than a working day, thus there is opportunity to see if we could reduce the lead time to, say, two days, which would leave one day to process paperwork and move materials to and from the manufacturing area. Whilst this would not bring the purchase of the raw materials inside the customer's requested time of 15 days, it would, however, mean that we would not cut metal until we have a customer order, again reducing the risk. In this analysis we have focused on time only, and as we identified earlier, inventory optimization here is also about value. In Figure 5.5 the stick chart is useful for showing and analysing the effect of the P:D ratio and identifying the focus on the lead time sub-assembly and cumulative effect. However, the stick chart does not identify where within the production sequence of the product the value of the inventory is held; this means we will take a product planner's view, which is an important first stage. To be able to represent the inventory planner's view we need to add the inventory value, for which there is a simple mathematical step. This is done by multiplying the lead time by the inventory unit cost, representing the stick chart as an inventory profile showing each stage of manufacture in inventory value days or IV days.

Product value profiling

Product value profiling (PVP) is a technique learned by the author during his time at IBM. It is similar to the weighted average profile (WAP) discussed earlier in the chapter, as it represents the inventory in time and value, ie IV days. The PVP allows us to determine where the highest values exist in the flow inventory. It can be presented as a table or pictorially and is a mathematical way of showing where the inventory value sits. Looking at the data as a simple stick chart it is difficult to see the inventory investment required. What we know for each component and their assembly is the costs and time.

It would be useful if we could draw a picture of this to represent the inventory investment in the same way as we have for the inventory stack.

The profile in Figure 5.6 shows all the parts related to the N123444 Scoop Assembly in a similar way to the stick chart. In this example we have taken account of the unit cost of each part, which now means the profile represents the value of the parts and the time they are in the flow process, representing the inventory value of each part. However, there is an additional distinction for the purchased parts, which until delivered are not part of the 'on-site' inventory for the company, but as they have been ordered they represent a 'commitment' by the company to purchase, which will depend on the contract terms. In Figure 5.6 some parts are represented as rectangles and others are shown as trapezoidal. The rectangular shape indicates that there is no value added during the lead time, and the trapezoidal shape shows the added value during the manufacturing or assembly processes. Parts are shown in the same position as they appear in the BOM/stick chart.

If we look at the table at the bottom of Figure 5.6 we can see that the total product value profile is £197.28, of which £132.60 (66 per cent) is committed purchases of product and £64.68 (34 per cent) is the manufacturing and assembly processes. We can start to look at the individual elements of the profile. First, if we look at the purchased parts, the scoop represents £127.50 (64 per cent) of the commitment, which reinforces the analysis from the stick chart that we should focus on reducing the lead time for this part. In Figure 5.6 we can see both a visual representation and a table; whilst the visual is often useful for providing a simple representation of the product, which may help quickly identify where and which products need attention, the numbers are much easier to create in a simple excel spreadsheet.

If we assume both come from the same plastic moulding supplier, who also supply the red version of the scoop and handle, we should negotiate a shorter lead time based on better communications and perhaps improved payment terms. If we were able to reduce the lead time from 30 to 20 days, we would reduce the inventory commitment from £127.50 to £85.00, a saving of £42.50 (33.3 per cent) on the whole product value profile. The manufacturing inventory value is very small for the cutting of the aluminium edge and the scoop assembly. The major values are for the scoop itself, but the lead time is already only five days, which we identified as being possible to reduce to two days based on the analysis of the stick chart in Figure 5.5. The opportunity with the aluminium edge would be to combine the cutting operation with the fitting of the edge to the scoop. In BOM terms we would make the part a phantom, which would also avoid stocking the edge (cut to length),

Figure 5.6 Key elements of product value profile

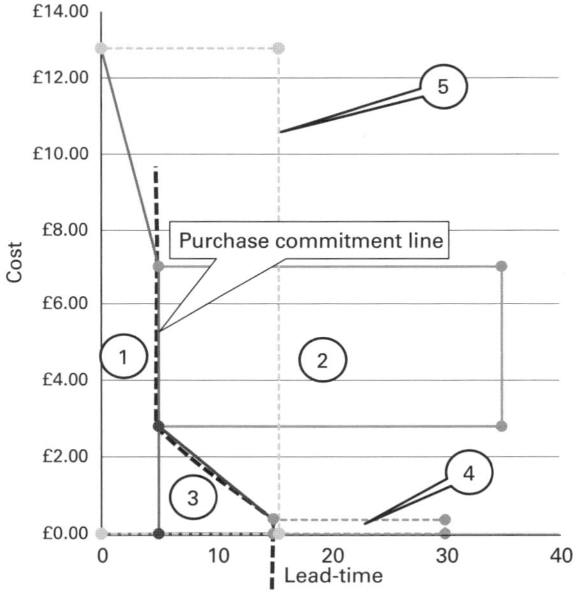

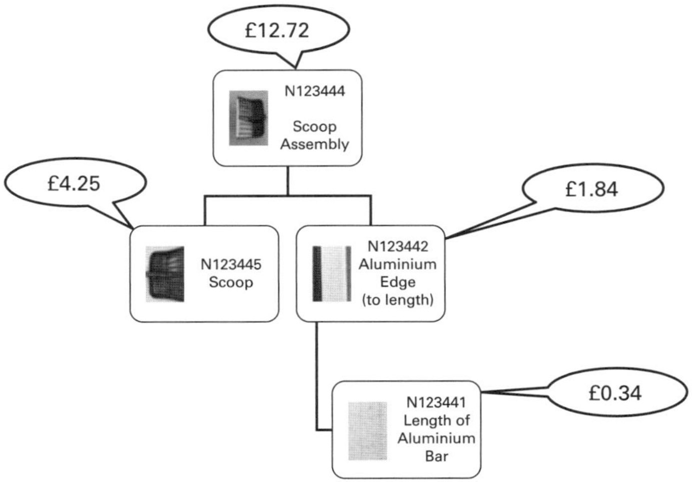

				p		L_c		M_c	$M_c + L_c = C_c$	$Lt \times (M_c + C_c)/2$
	Item	Description	Qty	Unit Cost	Unit Of Measure	Labour Cost	Lead-time	Material Cost	Material & Labour	Inventory Value Days
1	N123444	Scoop Assembly	1	£12.72	Each	£5.73	5	£6.99	£12.72	£49.28
2	N123445	Scoop	1	£4.25	Each		30	£4.25	£4.25	£127.50
3	N123442	Aluminium Edge (cut to length)	1	£2.74	Each	£2.40	10	£0.34	£2.74	£15.40
4	N123441	Length of Aluminium Bar	340	£0.34	mm		15	£0.34	£0.34	£5.10
										£197.28
5	Product Value Profile Days		Total IV days [Lt × (Mc + Lc)/2] = £197.28 Unit cost for Scoop N123444 12.72			=	15.51			

which according to Figure 5.6 is £15.40; the £2.40 labour would still be required. These changes are shown in Figure 5.7; looking at the table at the bottom we can see a total saving of £39.82.

Since both stock WAP and PVP are both expressed in inventory value days it would be easy to combine them. The PVP is expressed as a single unit of product whereas the WAP is based on the daily going rate. To make the data compatible we simply need to express the PVP at the same rate of production as the WAP. In Figure 5.3 for the snow shovel assembly we used a Daily Going Rate for the product of 25 per day.

Table 5.5 shows the equivalent values for the sub-assembly N123444 Scoop Assembly. The batch size and safety stock parameters are converted into days of supply, which are now compatible with the PVP value. If we now combine the values of stacked inventory (1–4) and the flow inventory as shown in Figure 5.8 we get a complete view of the inventory in the process based on time and the unit cost of each part. The table at the bottom of Figure 5.8 shows the calculations and the inventory value days for each element and the product value profile days at 18.74 days (5). By looking at the Inventory Value Days we can prioritize which parts/lead times are driving the inventory value in the product.

Product analysis and planning will also identify opportunities to order later and/or bring in the sub-components finished; for example we could arrange for the red and black scoops to be delivered ready for final assembly both with or without the aluminium edge. This may increase the stock of the components, but it will be offset by the time reduction in the production process. The total product inventory value represents a single product flowing through the process. If our daily going rate for the product was 25 scoop assemblies per day the total inventory in the process would be £12.72 × 18.74 days × 25 units/day = £5,958.31 inventory value days. The WAP/Stack portion is £41.06 × 25 units = £1,026.43 (17 per cent) and the PVP/Flow portion £197.28 × 25 units = £4,931.88 (83 per cent). As we have the average profile it is a very simple exercise to be able to see the effect of increasing production on inventory. Say we wanted to increase production from 25 units to 30, we simply multiply the PVP by the new production rate, thus £12.72 × 18.74 days × 30 units/day = £7,149.97.

In conclusion, the stack and flow tools focus on the product and how, by using both the dimension of the unit cost and the lead time days/days of supply, we can see the inventory value. This helps the production and purchasing planning processes and helps the team focus on where the most business

Figure 5.7 New product value profile after analysis and changes

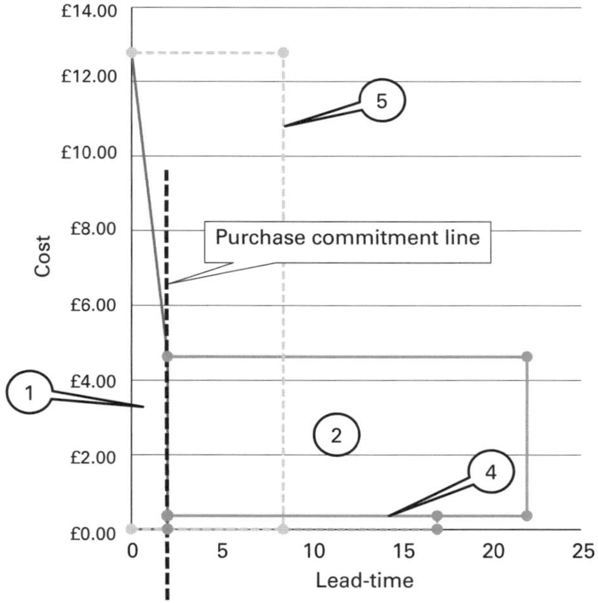

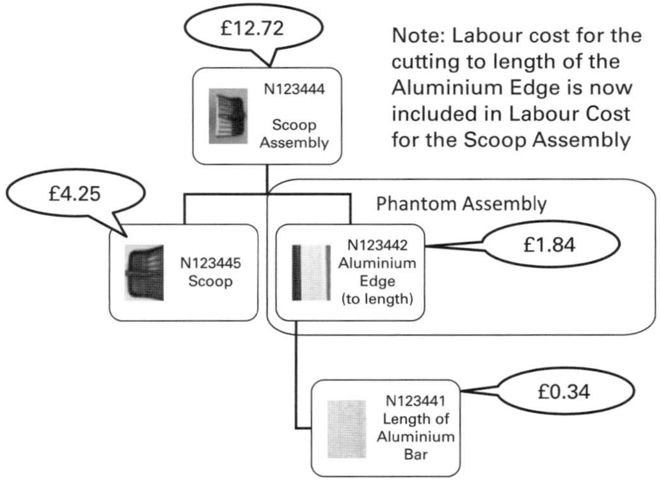

				p		L_c		M_c	$M_c + L_c = C_c$	$Lt \times (M_c + C_c)/2$
	Item	Description	Qty	Unit Cost	Unit Of Measure	Labour Cost	Lead-time	Material Cost	Material & Labour	Inventory Value Days
1	N123444	Scoop Assembly	1	£12.72	Each	£8.13	2	£4.59	£12.72	£17.31
2	N123445	Scoop	1	£4.25	Each		20	£4.25	£4.25	£85.00
	N123442	Aluminium Edge (cut to length)	1							
4	N123441	Length of Aluminium Bar	340	£0.34	mm		15	£0.34	£0.34	£5.10
								£12.72		£107.41
5	Product Value Profile Days		Total IV days [Lt × (Mc + Lc)/2] = £107.41 Unit cost for Scoop N123444 12.72			=	8.44			

Table 5.5 Weighted average profile for scoop assembly showing days of supply

	Part	Description	Quantity Each	Unit Cost	Batch Quantity	Safety Quantity	Days of Supply	Safety Time	Total DOS	Batch Inventory	Safety Inventory	Extended Value
1	N123444	Scoop Assembly	1	£12.72	50	25	1.00	1.00	2.00	318.00	£318.00	£636.00
2	N123445	Scoop	1	£4.25	100	25	2.00	1.00	3.00	212.50	£106.25	£318.75
3	N123442	Aluminium Edge (cut to length)	1	£2.74	25	10	0.50	0.40	0.90	34.25	£27.40	£61.65
4	N123441	Length of Aluminium Bar	340	£0.34	10,000	5,000	0.59	0.59	1.18	5.00	£5.00	£10.00
5	Weighted Average Profile			£20.05				WAP	2.05			£1,026.40
	Daily Going Rate (for Product)			25								
	Daily Going Rate as a Value			£501.25								

Figure 5.8 Weighted average profile and product value profile

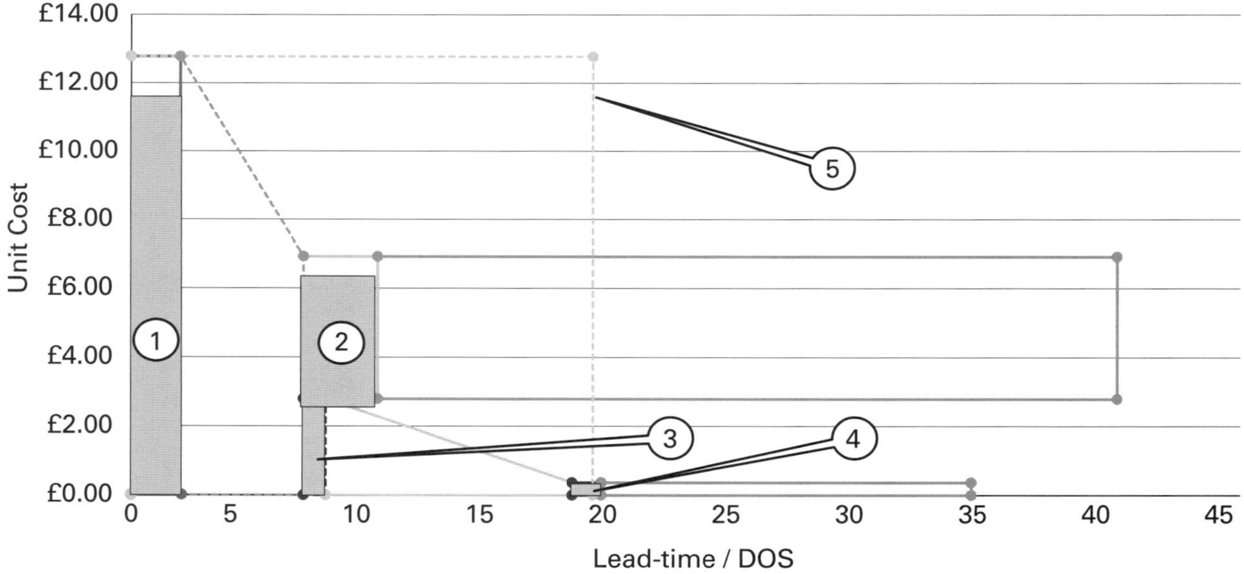

				p		L_c			M_c	$M_c + L_c = C_c$	$Lt \times (M_c + C_c)/2$
	Item	Description	Qty	Unit Cost	Profile	Cost	Lead-time	DOS	Material Cost	Material & Labour	Inventory Value Days
1	N123444	Scoop Assembly	1	£12.72	WAP / Stack			2	£12.72	£12.72	£25.44
	N123444	Scoop Assembly	1	£12.72	PVP / Flow	£5.73	5		6.99	12.72	£49.28
2	N123445	Scoop	1	£4.25	WAP / Stack			3	£4.25	£4.25	£12.75
	N123445	Scoop	1	£4.25	PVP / Flow		30		4.25	4.25	£127.50
3	N123442	Aluminium Edge (cut to length)	1	£2.74	WAP / Stack			0.9	£2.74	£2.74	
	N123442	Aluminium Edge (cut to length)	1	£2.74	PVP / Flow	£2.40	10		0.34	2.74	£15.40
4	N123441	Length of Aluminium Bar	340	£0.34	WAP / Stack			1.18	£0.34	£0.34	£0.40
	N123441	Length of Aluminium Bar	340	£0.34	PVP / Flow		15		0.34	0.34	£5.10
									12.72	Total	£238.33
5	Product Value Profile Days		Total IV days [Lt × (Mc + Lc)/2] = £197.28 Unit cost for Scoop N123444 12.72			=	18.74				

value can be obtained. It makes the WAP and PVP very useful for both analysis of where inventory value is held in the process as well as a strategic planning tool. When looking at inventory planning as part of the strategic planning process we want to deal with high-level numbers rather than part detail.

Financial planning: strategic, tactical and operational

In this last section we will explore inventory planning from a financial planning perspective. The stack and flow approach has shown the importance of understanding the total investment in inventory within the product build and how to analyse and identify where in the process the greatest value of inventory sits. The stick chart, WAP and PVP analysis tools allow us to focus on the product, the inventory value and the purchase commitments. However, it may not be the product or even the parts but the overall business processes that influence the inventory planning processes. To understand this, we need to examine the business operations planning processes.

Business operations planning

The three different levels of business operations planning are:

- Strategic – long-term horizon – three to five years.
- Tactical – medium horizon – one to three years.
- Operational – short horizon – weeks to one year.

It is important to keep all the different plans synchronized. To do this we need to set up a series of planning cycles as shown in Figure 5.9:

- Strategic planning cycle is the beginning of an annual review process, with a review and update at the mid-point of the year. This review will set the targets for sales and inventory, which then gives the purchasing budget.
- Tactical planning cycle will be based on the strategic plan and provide a quarterly update. This will look at the progress towards achieving the plan and through discussion determine what corrective and improvement actions are needed.

- Business operations reviews take place monthly and weekly and provide the current status. These will ensure that early action is taken where necessary to ensure that the annual targets are achieved.

Figure 5.9 Annual planning calendar

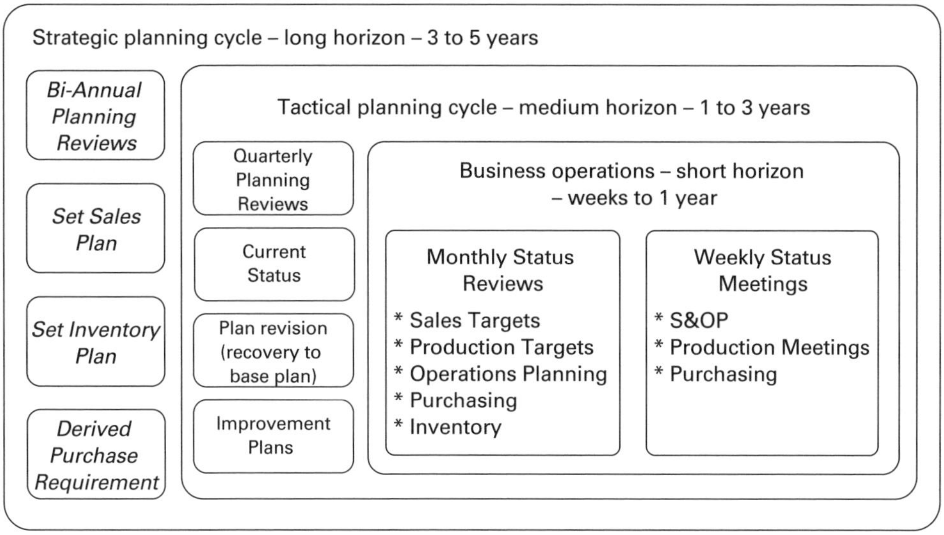

Strategic, tactical and operational inventory planning

The analogy of inventory as a fluid is often used. Slack, Brandon-Jones and Johnston (2016) draw a very simple picture, shown in Figure 5.10, which uses this analogy. We see a supply pipe with a tap, a tank which holds the water and an output pipe with a tap connected to the tank. We can also overlay the stack and flow, which matches this model. First, let's consider the tank at strategic/tactical and operational levels. There are at least three decisions that need to be taken:

- Strategic: the size of tank – how big a tank do I need or what is the size of the stack?
- Tactical: the control of in and out – how do I adjust the flow and manage the level of the stack?
- Operational: the size of pipes in and out – the volume of the flow, fast or slow deliveries?

Figure 5.10 Inventory as a fluid

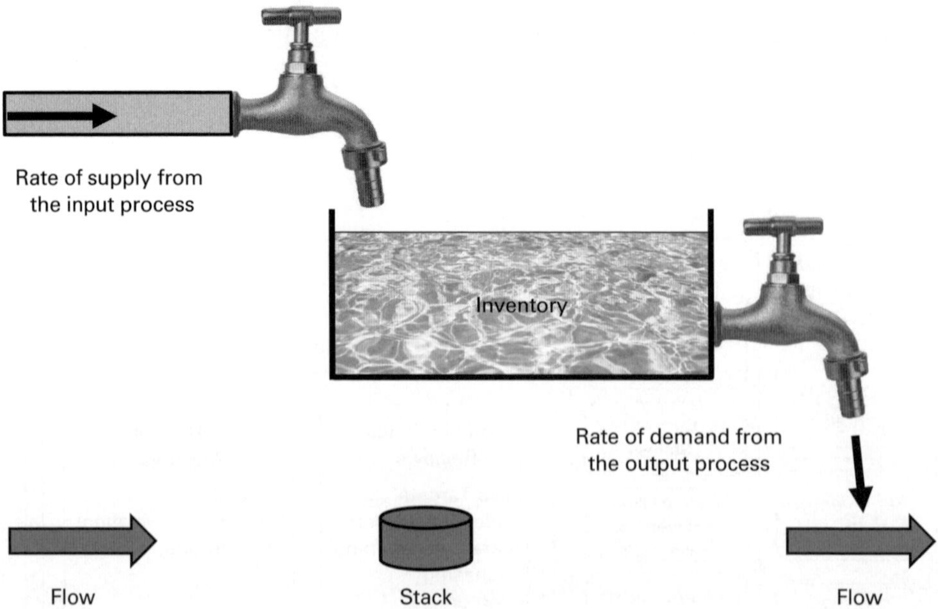

SOURCE Slack, Brandon-Jones and Johnston (2016) p 435 (adapted Figure 13.2)

Strategic: the size of the tank/stack

When we consider the size of the tank/stack at a strategic level we are no longer concerned with the product but now need to consider the business as a whole. If we look again at Figure 5.1 we see there are warehouses for raw materials and finished goods. At a strategic level, we would need to consider:

- space required to store (and manufacture) the product;
- type of space needed.

This first step is an example of the strategic decisions needed, ie the sizing of the stack or the size of the tank to hold the water. The decision of the size of the stack will determine how much and what type of warehouse space is needed. If the product only requires clean and dry storage then a basic warehouse will suffice. If, however, we are dealing with chilled/frozen product then the cost would escalate as we would need a temperature-controlled environment which will drive up the costs both of buying and using the space. Once the decision is made, we then need to consider:

- How much cash do I need to buy the space needed?
- How much do I need to invest in inventory?

- When do get paid for my sales?
- When do I have to pay for my purchases?

This will determine how much money we need to purchase the inventory. The purchased inventory will therefore have a value. There are two ways of valuing inventory – as a liability or as an asset. The accounting view of inventory is an asset, as part of the working capital, but other parts of the organization will view inventory as a liability tying up capital and costing money to store. Viewing inventory as a liability would consider the cost of purchasing and holding. If we only view inventory in this way, we will reinforce the view that it is a liability and will drive the business to minimize. Viewing it as an asset considers the cost of not having inventory, ie the costs associated with not having stock available. This is most recognizable in the term AOG (Aircraft on Ground), ie when an aircraft is grounded because a spare/service part is not available. This can cost the airline many thousands of pounds an hour. If we are in a business where the cost of shortage is significant then we will view inventory as an asset. Thus, at a strategic level we need to understand:

- What value does the inventory holding bring to the business?
- What type of storage is acceptable?
- How much space do I really need?

This not only applies to the 'main' stores but to any location/stocks of inventory used in the business. Which brings us back to the dichotomy of inventory we identified in Chapter 1.

Retail example of cash flow

Joe Devon has contacted the manufacturer of the snow shovel, Eleanor Winter Gear Ltd. He agrees to buy them for £25 and sells them for £35. Joe sells the snow shovels at a local Christmas fair held each week. He decides he can sell about 10 snow shovels and wants to buy 10 as an initial stock; thereafter he will buy enough to replace what he sells. He buys on a Friday for the Christmas fair on Saturday. Joe needs to borrow for the initial purchase, and his mentor Kate suggests that he should see if he can buy on credit. He needs convincing, so Kate shows him alternative payment terms and the effect on the cash balance. The alternatives can be seen in Table 5.6: if both customer and supplier work on a cash basis, then Joe must pay out the £250 before he goes to his first Christmas fair. If in his first week he is only able to sell eight snow shovels, and his plan is to buy what he sells (ie he will buy another eight shovels), he will still be in debt. In week three sales improve and he sells nine and thus buys nine, so his cash position is now positive at the end of the week. If he were to negotiate a delay in payment of one week, he would be cash positive at the end of the second week.

Table 5.6 Cash flow and delayed payment analysis

	Weeks								
	1	2	3	4	5	6	7	8	9
Sales		8	9	10	11	8	10	10	10
Purchases	10	8	9	10	11	8	10	10	10
Inventory	10	10	10	10	10	10	10	10	10
Supplier and Customer cash payment									
Cash in bank start of week	£0	–£250	–£170	–£80	£20	£130	£210	£310	£410
Accounts Receivable	£0	£280	£315	£350	£385	£280	£350	£350	£350
Accounts Payable	£250	£200	£225	£250	£275	£200	£250	£250	£250
Cash in bank end of week	–£250	–£170	–£80	£20	£130	£210	£310	£410	£510
Supplier one week payment terms and Customer cash payment									
Cash in bank start of week	£0	£0	£30	£145	£270	£405	£410	£560	£660
Accounts Receivable	£0	£280	£315	£350	£385	£280	£350	£350	£350
Accounts Payable		£250	£200	£225	£250	£275	£200	£250	£250
Cash in bank end of week	£0	£30	£145	£270	£405	£410	£560	£660	£760
Supplier two week payment terms and Customer cash payment									
Cash in bank start of week	£0	£0	£280	£345	£495	£655	£685	£760	£910
Accounts Receivable	£0	£280	£315	£350	£385	£280	£350	£350	£350
Accounts Payable			£250	£200	£225	£250	£275	£200	£250
Cash in bank end of week	£0	£280	£345	£495	£655	£685	£760	£910	£1,010

What Joe soon realizes is that this has given him more flexibility to invest in inventory. This is of interest as he has identified a second Christmas fair. Table 5.7 shows how the one-week delay facilitates his business expansion plans, since he is able to increase the purchases without having to pay until he has been able to sell the snow shovels. Even if the sales are a little low to start, he still remains cash positive.

Table 5.7 Business expansion based on delayed payment analysis

	Weeks								
	1	2	3	4	5	6	7	8	9
Sales (Christmas Fair 1)		8	9	10	11	8	10	10	10
Sales (Christmas Fair 2)			7	8	11	9	11	9	11
Purchases	10	8	16	18	22	17	21	19	21
Inventory	10	10	10	10	10	10	10	10	10
Supplier one week payment terms and two Christmas Fairs cash payment									
Cash in bank start of week	£0	£0	£280	£590	£1,020	£1,390	£1,535	£1,720	£1,960
Accounts Receivable	£0	£280	£560	£630	£770	£595	£735	£665	£735
Accounts Payable			£250	£200	£400	£450	£550	£425	£525
Cash in bank end of week	£0	£280	£590	£1,020	£1,390	£1,535	£1,720	£1,960	£2,170

The relation between paying for products and receiving payment for the sales becomes a key consideration in the strategic planning of inventory. The longer we can defer payment to the suppliers compared to receiving payment from the customers the less pressure there is on holding inventory. If we return to our tank of water:

- if we had to pay for the water in the tank before we were able to sell it we would try to minimize the amount;
- if, on the other hand, we could get the customer to pay on demand and defer payment to the supplier then we would not worry quite so much about the amount of water in the tank.

> **The inventory dichotomy**
>
> Inventory held ties up working capital (because it costs money and therefore less is better) but it is needed in order to have something to add value to and sell (because we need the inventory to ensure product availability).

Tactical: the control of in and out inventory flow

The next decision is tactical – the medium-term horizon. At this level we need to understand:

- How do I adjust the flow?
- How reactive are my suppliers?
- How do I know how much I have?
- What is the demand from my customer?
- Management of tank.
- Management of level.
- Method of linkage and improvement.

Figure 5.11 Tactical flow as a fluid

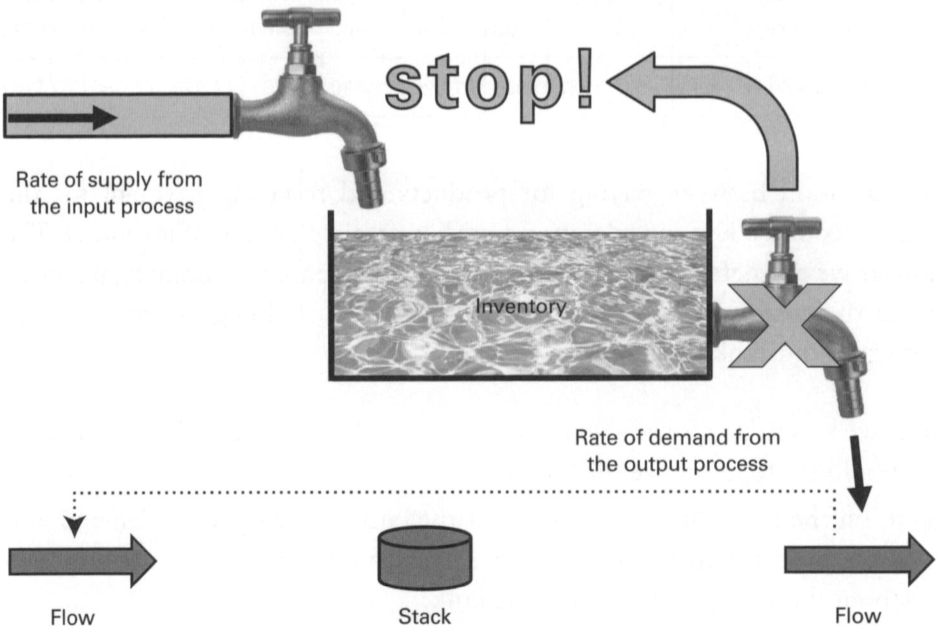

SOURCE Modified from Slack, Chambers and Johnston (2016) p 435 (adapted Figure 13.2)

One of the key considerations is related to its cost and will depend on our relationship with our customer and suppliers. This is expressed in the financial terms as net liabilities, accounts payable (money out) and accounts receivable (money in). To supply a customer, inventory must be bought, made saleable and then sold. If we can sell the product before we pay for the components, we can afford to hold higher stocks. Consider a simple retail example of buying and selling the snow shovels.

Tactical inventory planning: sales/inventory/production and purchase

In Chapter 2 we looked at the simple supply/demand/inventory relationship. In Figures 2.14 and 2.15 we explored the supply demand inventory mechanism. This mechanism works at all levels, not just at the item level. At a tactical level we can use it to build a model which will project the sales, purchases and inventory at a business level. If we want to create a plan for the manufacture of the snow shovel, we can use the planning information from our analysis of the snow shovel, combined with the marketing sales plan and a manufacturing strategy based on an understanding of the forecasted demand:

- Snow shovel product detail.
  - Options:
    black = 75%;
    red = 25%.
  - Weighted average profile (WAP) = 1.5 days.
  - Product value profile (PVP):
    manufactured/assembled = 7.81;
    purchased = 7.19;
    total PVP = 15.00.
  - Cost price = £30.76.
  - Sales price = £45.00.
- Snow shovel sales plan.
  - UK = 40%;
  - Europe = 60%.
- Manufacturing strategy.
  - Level build through year = 25 units/day for 250 days = 6,250 units.
  - Stock build for peak demand in Winter.

We can use the above data to determine other key measures for the business. If Eleanor Winter Gear Ltd was now forecasting sales for the next year based on the last nine weeks sales from Joe Devon, they would conclude that sales would be high in the winter and spring and low in the summer and autumn. The projected sales volume, shown in Tables 5.8 and 5.9, can be used to determine the sales value, profit and cost of good sold. From the WAP and PVP we can set stock turn targets. Finally, based on the manufacturing volume and using the supply demand inventory mechanism, we can derive the expected inventory levels for raw materials, finished goods and the purchases budgets. An example is shown in Table 5.8 and Table 5.9. These targets would then be discussed at the main board level where each function would take away their responsible budget items and create detailed plans for the year.

Table 5.8 Tactical annual planning targets

	Annual Totals
Sales Volume	6,250
Sales Price	£45.00
Sales	£281,250
Margin	£14.24
Total Profit	£89,000
Finished Goods Cost	£30.76
Purchased	£9.81
COGS	£192,250
Average FGS Inventory	£27,437
Year End FGS Inventory	£30,000
FGS Stock Turn	7
Average Inventory	£2,375
Raw Materials Stock Turn	81
Manufacturing Volume	6,250
Throughput Value	£192,250
Purchases	£61,281
Daily Going Rate	25
Working days	250

Table 5.9 Annual sales plan for the snow shovel

	Jan	Feb	Mar	Apr	May	Jun	Jul	Aug	Sep	Oct	Nov	Dec
Working days in month	21	22	21	23	19	20	21	19	22	21	20	21
Sales Volume	1,000	750	750	500	250	100	100	250	250	500	800	1,000
Sales	£45,000	£33,750	£33,750	£22,500	£11,250	£4,500	£4,500	£11,250	£11,250	£22,500	£36,000	£45,000
Profit	£14,240	£10,680	£10,680	£7,120	£3,560	£1,424	£1,424	£3,560	£3,560	£7,120	£11,392	£14,240
COGS	£30,760	£23,070	£23,070	£15,380	£7,690	£3,076	£3,076	£7,690	£7,690	£15,380	£24,608	£30,760
Finished Goods Inventory	£15,389	£9,237	£2,316	£4,623	£11,544	£23,848	£36,921	£43,842	£53,070	£53,839	£44,611	£30,000
Raw Materials Inventory	£2,375	£2,375	£2,375	£2,375	£2,375	£2,375	£2,375	£2,375	£2,375	£2,375	£2,375	£2,375
WIP	£6,361	£6,361	£6,361	£6,361	£6,361	£6,361	£6,361	£6,361	£6,361	£6,361	£6,361	£6,361
Manufacturing Volume	525	550	525	575	475	500	525	475	550	525	500	525
Throughput Value	£16,149	£16,918	£16,149	£17,687	£14,611	£15,380	£16,149	£14,611	£16,918	£16,149	£15,380	£16,149
Purchases	£9,805	£7,354	£7,354	£4,903	£2,451	£981	£981	£2,451	£2,451	£4,903	£7,844	£9,805

Operational: stack and flow planning, balancing and control

- In-flow.
- Out-flow.

Finally, let's consider the operational level, which is the short term. In the short term, it will be about the amount in stock, the use of resources and the cash in the bank. If we consider the example of the tank, we would be concerned with:

- The height of water in the tank.
- Have we enough water being supplied to meet the demand?
- Are there any leaks in the tank?
- Is the water in the tank saleable?

Figure 5.12 Operational interconnected fluid in tank

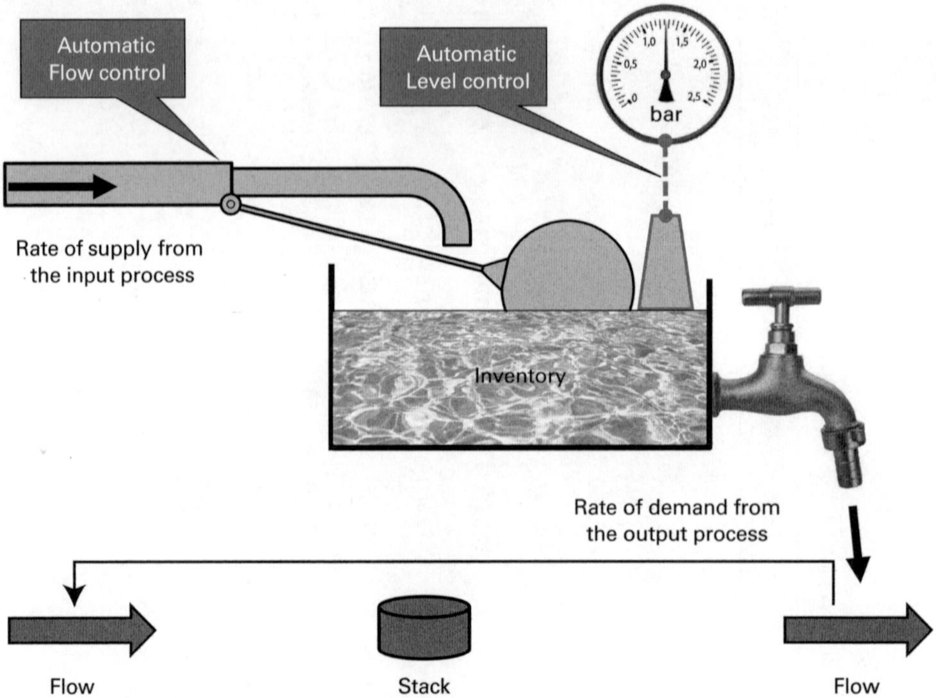

Modified from Slack, Chambers and Johnston (2016) pg 435 (adapted Figure 13.2)

In answering some of these questions we now need to include inventory balancing and control as we are executing the plan at an operational level.

In our water tank example, we could consider the use of automatic control of the flow based on the level of water in the stack as shown in Figure 5.12. The use of 'automatic' level and flow control equates to the use of systems like Kanban and MRP planning. The use of these tools would allow us to operate with less water in the tank, ie working with lower inventory levels. We could then consider a smaller tank, ie reducing the amount of warehousing we invest in. This shows the effect of the inventory exchange curve principle first described in Chapter 3, ie since, as the *capabilities* in managing the in-flow and out-flow of the water (*inventory*) are increased, the amount of water that we need to hold reduces. Inventory control would ensure that any leaks in the tank were identified and managed by comparing the in-flow and out-flow with the automatic level. Finally, the payments would be covered by cash flow management.

Summary

In this chapter we have extended our understanding of materials planning from earlier chapters to show the importance of adding the unit cost and the value of inventory to the planning processes for products and business planning. We have used the principles of 'Stack' and 'Flow' to help logically build the inventory values and look at how this can be analysed to reveal the opportunities. In some cases, it requires us to think differently and lends itself to the Lean and Agile improvement approaches discussed earlier in the book, which ensure that we remain connected to real-world thinking. There is an important distinction between manufacturing and materials planners and inventory planners: to a materials planner the smallest screw is just as capable of stopping production as the scoop moulding. The inventory planner helps focus the production and purchasing activities to ensure that time spent managing stock relates in some way to the inventory value without losing sight that a simple screw is just as capable of stopping the production line.

The second part of the chapter focused on business planning and examined the issues faced by the inventory planner and why it appears that some businesses place emphasis on inventory reduction whilst others are happy to hold significant stock and focus on warehouse space and transport logistics. The chapter concluded with the different approaches to strategic, tactical and operation planning/inventory planning using a water tank analogy to show the different issues raised at each level.

Tools and techniques discussed in this chapter

- Product planning tools:
  - Set-back chart/stick chart.
  - Weighted average profile (WAP).
  - Product value profile (PVP).
- Strategic inventory planning tools:
  - Stock turnover – setting targets in tactical inventory plans
  - Planning calendar – linking vision and operational plan.

References

Ptak, C and Smith, C (2016) *DDMRP Demand Driven Requirements Planning*, Industrial Press Inc, Connecticut

Ray, S A (2011) The Downside of Just-in-Time Inventory. Retrieved April 2019, from https://www.bloomberg.com/news/articles/2011-03-24/the-downside-of-just-in-time-inventory

Richards, G and Grinsted, S (2016) *The Logistics and Supply Chain Toolkit* (2nd ed) Kogan Page, London

Slack, N, Brandon-Jones, A and Johnston, R (2016) *Operations Management*, Pearson

You do the maths

In this chapter we have looked at the importance of the P:D ratio and the need to understand the total lead time not just the part lead time. This exercise will focus on how to generate a cumulative lead time chart and how to identify improvements.

Outline brief for product lead-time exercises

Control Box UK PLC manufacture control boxes, and the sales department has found that the competition is now offering a 45-day lead time on their standard boxes. They would like to reduce the current lead time offer to customers from 65 days to match the competition for CB-87485-1 Control Box 4I-90.

The cumulative lead time has been 95 days up to now. However, by agreement with the casting supplier, the castings IC-25376-1 and IC26345-1 are forecast, with a confirmation/call-off order agreed at 20 days prior to delivery. This means that at 65 days all parts are based on agreed customer orders, and the cumulative lead time has effectively been reduced by 30 days. Nevertheless, this is still 20 days longer than your competitors.

You are the operations planner and have been asked to review the existing BOM and identify which additional parts if any would need to be forecast to be able to offer a 45-day lead time. As the demand is volatile, forecasting should be avoided or kept to a minimum.

Exercise 1: Product lead-time improvement

Using the indented bill of materials for CB-87495-1 in Appendix A, prepare a bill of materials stick chart/set-back chart using Table 5.10.

If you are required to offer a 45-day lead time, which components will you need to forecast?

What are the opportunities for lead-time reduction when considering:

- **a** MRP planning lead-times.
- **b** Purchased components.
- **c** Manufacturing/assembly processes?

In Table 5.10 the first five components have already been shaded in as an example of the required approach.

Answer stick chart

Overall the stick chart shows that there are four components that are outside the 45-day lead time:

- Base Casting BC-24919-6.
- Top Cover TC-57843-4.
- Input Casting panel IC-25376-1.
- Output Panel IC26345-1.

From the briefing notes we can see that the castings IC-25376-1 and IC-26345-1 already have a special arrangement which means that the orders are confirmed 20 days prior to delivery. This still places the order confirmation at 50 days cumulative.

If this arrangement could be improved to 15 days prior to delivery, then it would bring the input and output panel castings call off within the 45 days.

The current lead time for the Base Casting BC-24919-6 and Top Cover TC-57843-4 is 60 days. However, they have the same supplier as the Input Casting panel IC-25376-1 and the Output Panel IC-26345-1. If the agreement can be extended this would mean the call-off order confirmation would happen within the 45-day lead time.

Both Input Casting panel IC-25376-1 and the Output Panel IC-26345-1 are subject to a 15-day machining process. The planner should investigate to see if there is really a

Table 5.10 Exercise 1: Worksheet 1 for CB-87495-1 stick chart for cumulative lead-time build-up

Part Number	Description	Qty	UOM	Type	LLC	Lead-time	WK 0	WK 5	WK 10	WK 15	WK 20	WK 25	WK 30	WK 35	WK 40	WK 45	WK 50	WK 55	WK 60	WK 65	WK 70	WK 75	WK 80	WK 85	WK 90	WK 95	WK 100
CB-87495-1	Control Box 4I-9O	1	ea	F	02	5																					
.BC-24919-6	Base Casting Common	1	ea	P	03	60																					
.TC-57843-4	Top Cover	1	ea	P	03	60																					
.LC-87650-4	Logic Card	1	ea	X	03	5																					
..RC-67896-8	Raw Card	1	ea	P	04	30																					
..LD-25376-2	Logic Device	2	ea	P	04	30																					
..RV-23458-7	Resistor 1Meg	8	ea	P	04	10																					
..WR-14259-2R	Wire – Red	6	mtr	R	07	5																					
.IP-4682-A4I	Input Panel Assy 4I	1	ea	S	03	5																					
..IP-23572-4I	Input Panel 4I	1	ea	C	04	15																					
...IC-25376-1	Input Panel Casting	1	ea	R	05	60																					
..IP-3654-A2R	Input Socket – Red Assy	4	ea	A	04	15																					
...CB-47898-7	Connector – Common	4	ea	P	05	15																					
...IP-35367-2R	Input Socket – Red	4	ea	P	05	15																					
...FS-56124-1	Fixing Screw	8	ea	P	05	10																					
..GT-25833-1	Gasket 4I	1	ea	C	04	5																					
...GP-42317-4	Gasket Paper (2" Strip)	4	in	R	05	15																					

..FS-56124-1	Fixing Screw	4	ea	P	07	10																					
.OP-67236-A9O	Output Panel Assy 9O	1	ea	S	03	15																					
..OP-89712-9O	Output Panel 9O	1	ea	C	04	15																					
...IC-26345-1	Output Panel Casting	1	ea	R	05	60																					
..OL-26877-19O	Output Lead Assy 9O	1	ea	A	04	5																					
...OC-25369-1R	Output Connector – Red	4	ea	P	05	15																					
...OC-25679-1B	Output Connector – Black	4	ea	P	05	15																					
...OC-25754-2G	Output Connector – Green	1	ea	P	05	15																					
...WR-14259-2R	Wire – Red	4	mtr	R	07	5																					
...WB-14625-5B	Wire – Black	4	mtr	R	07	5																					
...WG-14765-5G	Wire – Green	1	mtr	R	07	5																					
...SS-32992-2	Shrink Sleeve	3	mtr	R	07	5																					
...FS-56124-1	Fixing Screw	18	ea	P	07	10																					
..GT-46573-2	Gasket 9O	1	ea	C	04	5																					
...GP-42317-4	Gasket Paper (2" Strip)	4	in	R	05	15																					
..FS-56124-1	Fixing Screw	4	ea	P	07	10																					
.FS-56124-1	Fixing Screw	4	ea	P	07	10																					

Figure 5.13 Stick Chart for CB-87495-1 showing cumulative lead-time build-up

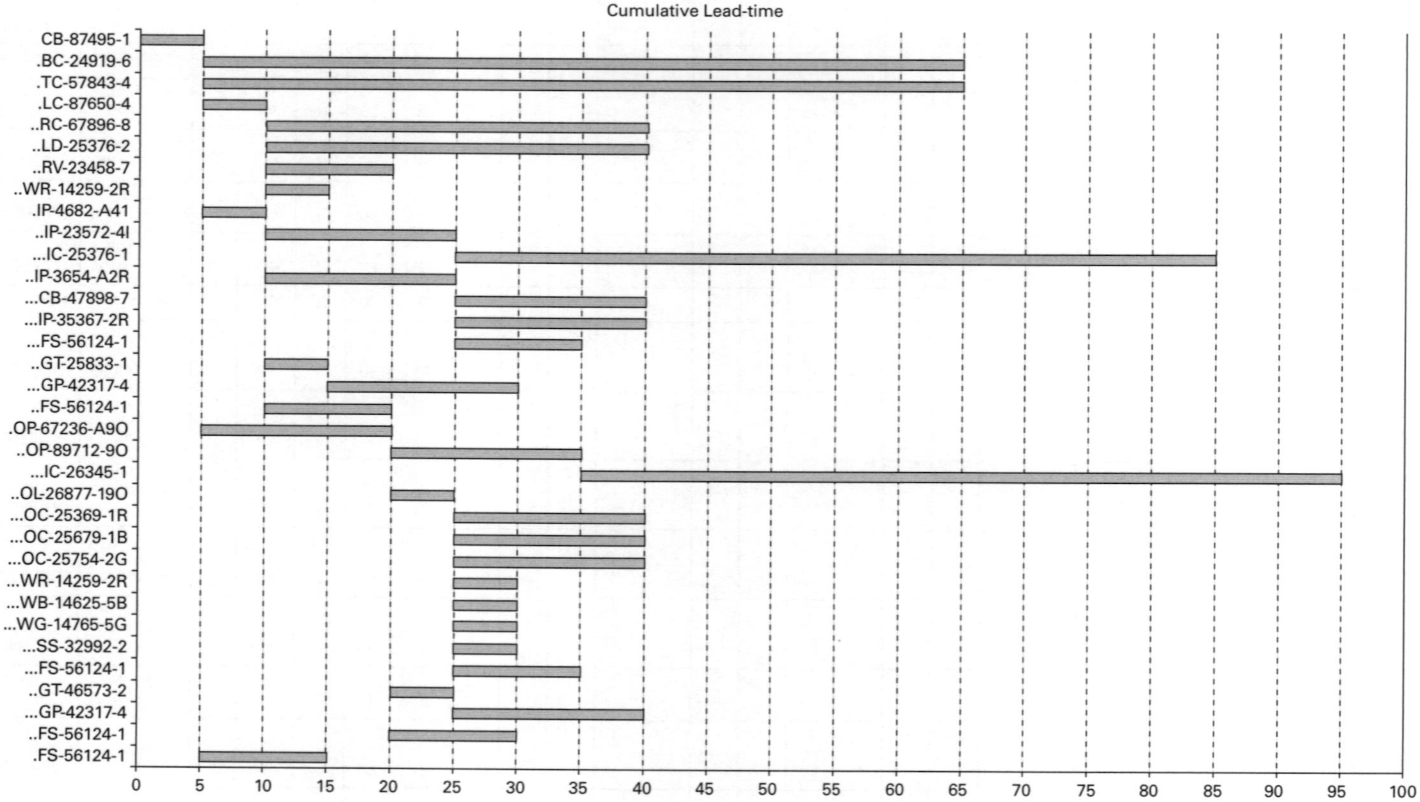

need for a 15-day MRP lead time for a repetitive batch process – could the machining process be completed in a week or 10 days? The 15 days should be challenged. The BOM lead time should be challenged to see if it could be reduced by 5 or 10 days.

However, the Output Panel has a 15-day assembly process. This should be examined to see if it can be reduced to match the Input Panel assembly time of 5 days.

Learning points: stick chart/set-back chart

It is important to understand how useful the stick chart/set-back analysis can be in identifying issues and opportunities related to the P:D ratio.

When working at this level, although there is often no clear answer, the identification of what is driving overall lead time and which items are problematic is enough to direct the next step of the analysis.

The planner will have to develop a list of items to be raised with planning, purchasing or engineering to see if improvements can be made.

Areas to focus on when looking to improve the lead time:

- The purchased products with the longest lead times will need to be forecast.
- Look at BOM structure for manufacturing and assembly to see if they can be shortened or combined.
- Look at the difference between the lead time, the process time and possibly the batch size:
  - It is the lead time which drives the overall cumulative lead time, and may include additional time for administration, inspection and other processes that could be eliminated or shortened.
  - MRPs typically have default lead times which may have been set a long time ago and not reviewed for several years.

Traditional thinking in inventory optimization

06

Introduction

The need to manage inventory is not new. Ever since the Industrial Revolution, when the manufacture of goods moved from cottage industry to mass production through the division of labour, we have been tied to batch manufacture. In order to achieve the 'right product, right place, right amount and right time', researchers have focused on the development of a variety of methods for planning, controlling and balancing inventory. The development of these inventory management techniques is driven by the need to minimize the investment in stock. A vast array of complex techniques have been developed from a relatively small base of principles. In this chapter we will examine the principles which we believe form the basis for most manufacture and retail inventory. This chapter looks at:

- re-order point (ROP) decisions;
- inventory saw tooth;
- economic order quantity (EOQ) and economic order period (EOP);
- statistical safety stock;
- safety time;
- hybrid safety stock;
- Pareto ABC or 80/20 rule;
- Pareto exchange curve;
- runner repeater stranger;
- inventory matrix;

- overage;
- a diagnosis of the five levels which businesses reach as they progress through their inventory management operation.

Inventory saw-tooth

The inventory saw-tooth diagram, which we first discussed in Chapter 2, Figure 2.20, easily defines the essential challenge for inventory management. For any item we use, we have a stock of the item, which we use over time, at some point in the future we will run out of the item. To make sure we are not inconvenienced by running out we attempt to predict when we will run out, then order new supplies to arrive at about the time we will run out. We need to decide how much to order, and how confident we are about our prediction of how many we use, and how reliable our supplier is at delivering on time. We may hold some stock in contingency in case we experience more demand or our supplier is late.

If we examine Figure 6.1 we can see each element of the above statement. The prediction of demand is the usage rate or DGR (daily going rate); to ensure the order arrives on time we calculate the ROL (re-order level) based on the predicted usage (DGR) and the time to get more stock, the lead time (L). To determine the amount we buy, we specify a re-order quantity (ROQ) or make an estimate of quantity needed to last a known period (P), ie a week

Figure 6.1 Standard inventory saw-tooth model for ROP logic, based on Figure 2.20, with re-order point (ROP) logic added

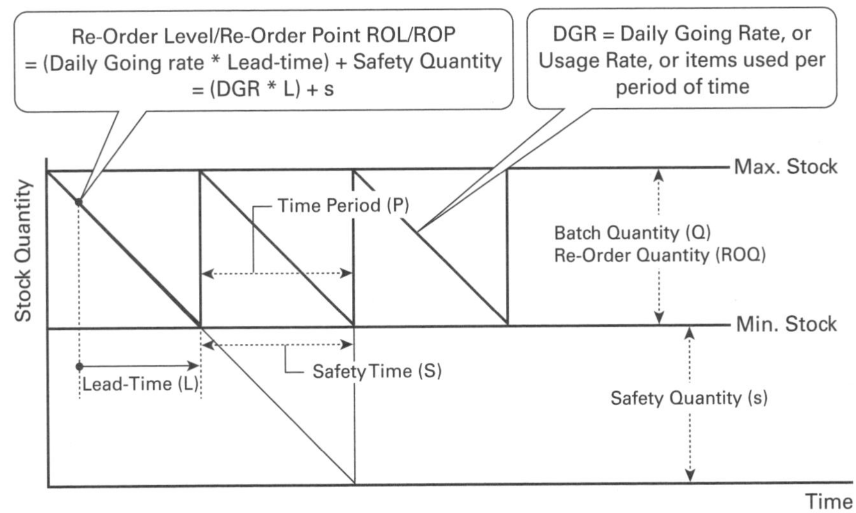

of usage. To protect against high demand and late deliveries we add safety quantity (s) or safety time (S). The figure is stylized as it shows the usage as a straight line; although we know that parts are not usually used in a uniform manner, for simplicity it is usually shown as a straight line. In summary, to define the inventory plan we need to make three decisions:

- How much do we order or how often do we order?
- How much do we protect against supply and demand uncertainties?
- How long will it take to make/supply them?

As mentioned in Chapters 2 and 4 there are principally two approaches to answering the above questions. The first approach is to use ROP logic, which is a combination of the ROP which includes safety and ROQ for ordering; this approach works when the future demand is not known and the DGR is calculated based on usage history. The second approach is to use MRP logic which, as discussed in detail in Chapter 4, uses the future demand (independent or dependent) and order and safety parameters to project future stock and thus place orders to maintain stock levels. However, both approaches rely on the planner specifying the order quantity/time and the safety quantity/time. The following sections covers the possible approaches available to the planner if they wish to apply science to the problem.

Determining the order size

Once we have understood that we need to determine how much we need to order and how much we might provision for higher than expected demand and late deliveries from our suppliers, we can divide the problem into two halves. What is important to note is that MRP systems, as discussed in Chapter 2, require these same decisions to be made and input into their item master data for the MRP system to manage the materials supply. Thus paying attention to determining the optimum value for the orders and safety will pay significant dividend in helping MRP to run efficiently. The first challenge is how much to order.

How much do I order?

In the absence of any guidance most planners/buyers will usually rely on the quantity specified by the supplier. In most cases the supplier has a preferred minimum order quantity, which can be based on their manufacturing process, packaging or transport considerations. For example, we may decide that as the supplier delivers once a week that we should buy a week's worth at a time; if we use 10 a day then we will order 50 at a time. If, however, when we talk to the supplier he advises that he will only supply in 100's then we will more usually accept his conditions and buy 100 at a time, every two weeks. Now this 'instinctive' approach takes no account of the consequences of the decision. It is worth considering the example of the two for one deal often used by retailers to encourage shoppers to buy larger quantities (batches). If the goods purchased are, say, dishwasher tablets, then all this will do is delay the time of the next purchase. However, if it is Seville oranges, then there is a risk that they will deteriorate before they have all been consumed, leading to waste. The planner must therefore know that if larger quantities are purchased they will not deteriorate before they are required to be used. This is discussed again in the 'inventory matrix' section later in this chapter. The best-known method for determining the most economic order quantity using the product's value was determined by Harris (1913) and popularized by Wilson in the early part of the 1920s.

EOQ (Economic Order Quantity)

To understand the principles of economic ordering first proposed by Harris (1913) let us consider the young entrepreneur Sam Cornish. Sam has spotted an opportunity to buy and sell footballs; he has found a supplier who will sell him footballs for £1 each; and he can sell for £2 after applying the club badge. His supplier Clare's Sports Plc charges him £10 per order and £20 to deliver, irrespective of the quantity ordered. Sam estimates that he can sell 100 footballs each week. Sam needs to decide how many footballs to buy. If he buys 100 footballs they will last him a week, and it will cost him £30 for ordering and delivery; this is known as the order cost. If he does this each week it will cost him £30 × 52 weeks or £1,560. If, however, he buys enough for two weeks – 200 – he will need to order 26 times in a year which will cost him 26 × £30 or £780. Thus it appears to be cheaper to order more. To find the best order size Sam evaluates a number of options. The results are shown in Table 6.1. What is clear from the table is that the lowest cost would be to order the entire year's worth in one go.

If Sam went ahead he would now have a storage problem. So Sam goes and talks to his brother Ollie who works for Warehouses Unlimited Ltd to arrange for some storage space. Ollie can provide space but will charge based on the average number of footballs in stock each day. The charge is £1 per 100 footballs per week. The cost of storing the footballs can be calculated as

Table 6.1 Evaluation of ordering costs from suppliers

- We have set up a small business selling Footballs
- I can buy for £1 and sell for £2
- The supplier will charge £10 per order and £20 to deliver
- Our expected demand is 100 units per week
- How many should I order?
- I need to consider the cost of ordering
- Evaluate the cost over a year
- Which is the best order quantity?

Order period	1 week	2 weeks	4 weeks	8 weeks	13 weeks	26 weeks	52 weeks
Quantity	100	200	400	800	1300	2600	5200
Cost	£100	£200	£400	£800	£1,300	£2,600	£5,200
Orders in a year	52	26	13	6.5	4	2	1
Order/Delivery Cost in year	£1,560	£780	£390	£195	£120	£60	£30

Table 6.2 However we need to consider the cost of storing goods

- If I buy a week's stock I need space to store
- I can rent space from a warehouse, at a cost of £1 per 100 footballs per week
- I only pay for space I use
- How many should I store?
- I need to consider the cost of buying the storage
- Evaluate the cost of holding over a year
- What is the best quantity to store?

Order period	1 week	2 weeks	4 weeks	8 weeks	13 weeks	26 weeks	52 weeks
Quantity to be stored	100	200	400	800	1,300	2,600	5,200
Average quantity in stock	50	100	200	400	650	1,300	2,600
Cost/football/year	£0.52						
Holding Cost per year	£26	£52	£104	£208	£338	£676	£1,352

follows. If one week's worth of footballs were purchased at the beginning of the week there would be 100 footballs in stock and all being well by the end of the week there would be none left. Thus if we wanted to know the average number we could take the stock at the beginning and the stock at the end and divide by two. So the average stock is 50. If the charge is £1 per 100 footballs per week or 1p per football per week, to store one football for a year or 52 weeks is £0.52p. This cost is known as the inventory holding cost, and if we divide this cost of the unit cost (P) £1.00 we get 52 per cent pa. This is known as the inventory holding cost (i) as a percentage. We now consider the various options and construct a table showing the cost of holding stock, as shown in Table 6.2.

Now this presents an entirely different picture. The highest cost is when the entire year's stock is purchased. Sam goes to his Finance Director Emily for advice. She suggests that adding the two costs would be a simple way to see what the total costs are. This evaluation is shown in Table 6.3.

What is clear to Sam is that as one cost increases the other decreases. By adding up we can see that at some point there is a balance between increasing and decreasing costs. In this case it is around eight weeks, thus the best option would be to order from Clare's Sports every eight weeks and store an eight-week order, an average stock of 400, at Ollie's Warehouse. To get a better view of this we can view it as a graph, shown in Figure 6.2.

Figure 6.2 Graph of inventory costs (ordering and holding)

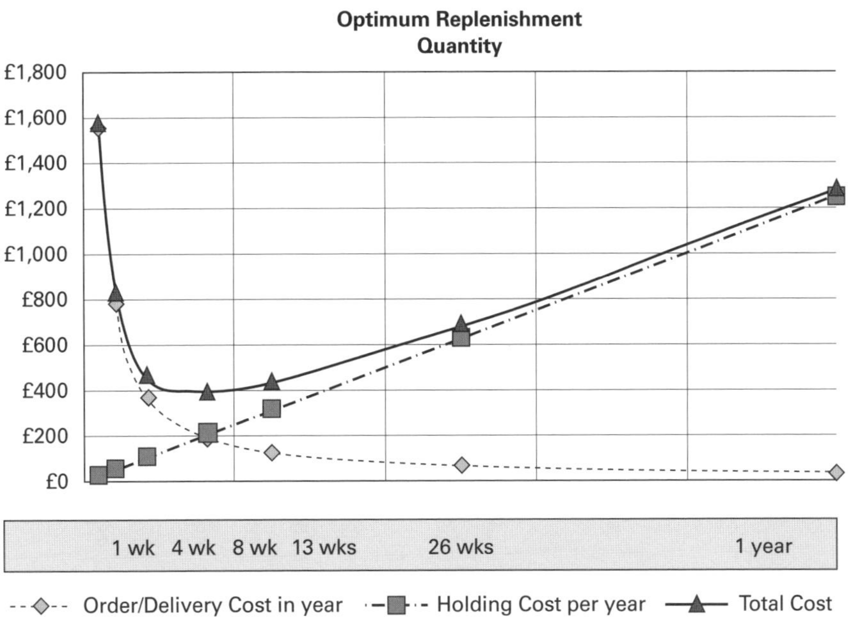

Table 6.3 Total inventory costs over the year

- Increasing the order size reduces the Order cost, but
  - Reducing the order quantity reduces the storage cost so is there a solution?
- Consider both, thus the total cost of storing and holding...

	1 week	2 weeks	4 weeks	8 weeks	13 weeks	26 weeks	52 weeks
Order Quantity	100	200	400	800	1300	2600	5200
Order/Delivery Cost in year	£1,560	£780	£390	£195	£120	£60	£30
Holding Cost per year	£26	£52	£104	£208	£338	£676	£1,352
Total Cost	£1,586	£832	£494	£403	£458	£736	£1,382

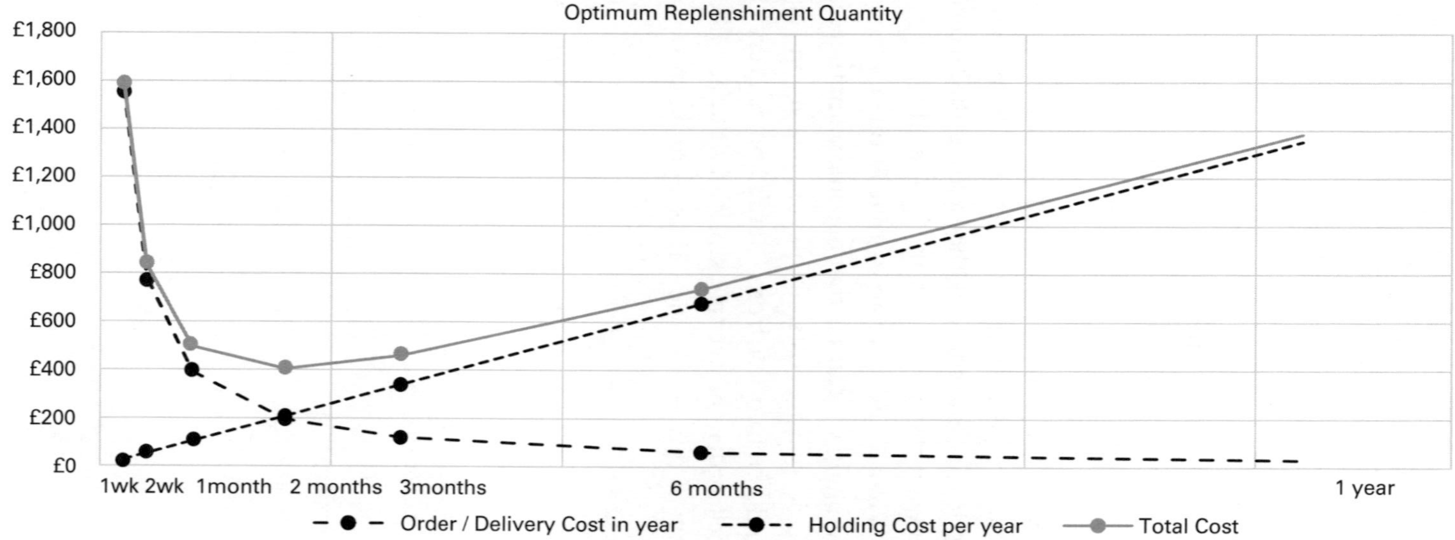

If we look at this graph it is clear that there is a balance between the cost of ordering and the cost of holding stock. What Harris noted, all those years ago, was that this balance point was when the order cost = the holding cost. What Harris did was to express the evaluation as an equation. Figure 6.3 shows the development of the economic formula used by Harris.

Figure 6.3 The classic economic order quantity formula (Harris, 1913)

Based on Sam's footballs

D = Annual Demand Quantity C = Cost of Ordering/Set-up P = Unit Cost i = inventory holding rate as %		5,200 £30.00 £1.00 52%	
Annual Ordering Costs = $\frac{\text{Annual Demand * Ordering Cost}}{\text{Quantity}}$		$OC = \frac{D * C}{Q}$	$\frac{5{,}200 * £30.00}{Q}$
Annual Holding Costs = $\frac{\text{Quantity Ordered * Inventory Holding Cost}}{2}$ Inventory Holding Costs = holding cost % * the cost per item		$HC = \frac{Q * i * P}{2}$	$\frac{Q * 52\% * £1.00}{2}$
Balance is achieved when OC = HC	$\frac{D * C}{Q} = Q * i * P$	$\frac{£156{,}000}{Q} = £52.00 * Q$	
Economic Order Quantity	$\sqrt{Q^2} = \frac{2 * D * C}{P * i}$	$Q = \sqrt{\frac{2 * 5{,}200 * £30.00}{£1.00 * 52\%}}$	774.60

The result shows the calculated EOQ is in reality 774.59, which is usefully precise, but practically we would round up to 800 or eight weeks' supply. In our example we took a very simplistic view of the order and holding costs. If we consider these more carefully we would come up with the following:

- Ordering cost:
  - cost of placing an order, eg administration costs – staff, paperwork;
  - cost of transporting goods;
  - costs for receiving/issuing materials for manufacturing; and
  - cost of transit packaging/pallets.

- Holding cost
  - storage costs, eg renting, heating, lighting, insurance, personnel, containers;
  - capital costs, eg interest on loans (working capital costs), land, building, equipment;
  - risk costs, eg obsolescence, deterioration, shrinkage or evaporation; and
  - opportunity costs, eg lost opportunity to invest elsewhere, opportunity to reduce purchase price.

The costs indicated above are the more obvious; later academics expanded this to include the cost of shortage. There are issues with this formula in that while it is logical and important to find the balance between conflicting costs of inventory, the key elements of the EOQ formula are difficult to calculate accurately, ie the cost of holding inventory and the cost of placing an order. If we are able to get an estimate of the costs the approach is beneficial because it is common to all parts being managed and is equally applicable to all. It also assumes that the demand is constant, which is not always true. This is easily overcome by frequent re-validation. The formula can easily be expressed as a handy calculator in Excel, as seen in Excel 6.1.

Excel 6.1 Simple EOQ calculator

	A	B	C	D
1	Annual Demand Quantity	D	£5,200	
2	Order Cost	C	£30.00	
3	Cost per Part	P	£1.00	
4	Inventory Holding Cost as a percentage	i	52%	
5				
6				
7	Economic Order Quantity		£774.60	
8				
9				
10				

Enter this formula

Cell C7	= SQRT((2*C*D)/(P*i))	= SQRT((2*C2*C1)/(C3*C4))

EOP: extending EOQ to represent days of supply

In our example, once we had calculated the EOQ we mentally converted to a time period. If we think how we normally relate to our suppliers we tend to use regular deliveries, daily, weekly, usually a specific day in the week, monthly etc. Thus it would be useful to express the EOQ as a time period. Figure 6.4 shows the extension of the formula which, when calculated, gives 37.24 days or approximately two months based on four weeks a month.

Figure 6.4 EOQ extended to calculate the economic order period

Based on Sam's footballs

D = Annual demand quantity C = Cost of Ordering / Set-up P = Unit Cost i = inventory holding rate as % £0.52 per year or 52% of the unit cost W = working days in a year		5,200 £30.00 £1.0 52% 250	
Economic Order Quantity	$Q = \sqrt{\frac{2*D*C}{P*i}}$	$Q = \sqrt{\frac{2*5{,}200*30.0}{£1.0*52\%}}$	774.60
Economic Order Period (EOP)	EOQ / D		774.60 / 5,200 0.148 years
	(EOQ / D) * W	0.148 * 250	37.24 days
Economic Order Period (EOP)	$\left\{\frac{\sqrt{\frac{2*D*C}{P*i}}}{D}\right\} *W$	$EOP = \left\{\frac{\sqrt{\frac{2*5{,}200*30.0}{£1.0*52\%}}}{5{,}200}\right\} * 250$	774.60 / 5,200 * 250 0.148 years * 250 37.24 days

This is easily converted to a simple Excel sheet to provide a handy calculator shown in Excel 6.2.

Excel 6.2 EOQ calculation extended to show economic order period (EOP)

	A	B	C	D
1	Annual Demand Quantity	D	5,200	
2	Order Cost	C	£30.00	
3	Cost per Part	p	£1.00	
4	Inventory Holding Cost	i	52%	
5	Working Days a year	W	250	
6				
7	Economic Order Quantity		774.597	Units
8	Economic Order Period in Days		37.240	Days
9	Economic Order Period in Days		37.240	Days
10				

Enter these formulae

Cell C7 = SQRT((2*C*D)/(p*i)) = SQRT((2*C2*C1)/(C3*C4))
Cell C8 = (EOQ / D) * W = (C7/C1)*C5
Cell C9 = (SQRT((2*C*D)/(p*i))/D)*W = (SQRT((2*C2*C1)/(C3*C4))/C1)*C5

EOQ and price breaks

The last twist in the tale is the possibility that the supplier, in an effort to induce you to buy larger quantities, will offer a price reduction, say if you buy 1,000 footballs I will let you have them for £0.95p and if you buy 2,000 then you can have them for £0.90p. In simple terms we would calculate the EOQ and EOP for the two price breaks; a simple modification to the Excel 6.2 would create an easily used ready reckoner, as shown in Excel 6.3.

Excel 6.3 EOQ calculation extended to show effect of unit cost variation

	A	B	C	D
1	Annual Demand Quantity	D	5,200	
2	Order Cost	C	£30.00	
3	Cost per Part	P	£75.00	
4	Inventory Holding Cost	i	52%	
5	Working days	W	250	
6	Economic Order Quantity	= SQRT((2*C*D)/(P*i))		
7				
8	Supplier Order Quantity	Cost per Part	EOQ	EOP Days
9	up to 1000	£1.00	774.597	37.240
10	> 1000	£0.95	794.719	38.208
11	> 2000	£0.90	816.497	39.255

Enter these formulae

Cell C9, *then copy down* = SQRT((2*$C$2*$C$1)/(B9*$C$4))
Cell D9, *then copy down* = (C9/$C$1)*$C$5

By looking at the result we can easily see that on this occasion we should resist the temptations of our supplier to buy more. The initial rounding to 40 days is not exceeded by even the most generous discount.

Economic ordering summary

We have looked at a number of ways we can use the principles of economic ordering and a couple of formulas. The debate still continues nearly 100 years after Wilson and Harris first proposed the EOQ formula. Many other academics have extended and modified the formula, but at its heart it is seeking to balance the between the cost of ordering and the cost of holding stock. The issues of how to determine the costs will be addressed in Chapter 7, but the simple truth is that there is 'a balance point between a small number of big orders and a large number of small orders'.

Protecting against supply and demand issues

We know that all the best laid plans can go awry – in the case of operations planning and MRP systems we make a forecast of what we think our customers want and we plan deliveries, based on a given lead time with deliveries to arrive 'just' before the stock we have runs out. There are four possible outcomes:

- Supplier delivers late.
- Supplier delivers early.
- Demand is higher than expected.
- Demand is lower than expected.

These four possibilities are shown in Figure 6.5: if the supplier delivers late then we will likely run out of stock; conversely, if the supplier is early then we will have still have some left. If the demand is higher than expected then again we will run out before the next delivery from the supplier, and if the demand is lower we will have some in hand when the next delivery arrives. Thus we only need to focus on two scenarios: late deliveries and higher than expected demand.

Figure 6.5 Supply demand variations effect on the inventory saw-tooth

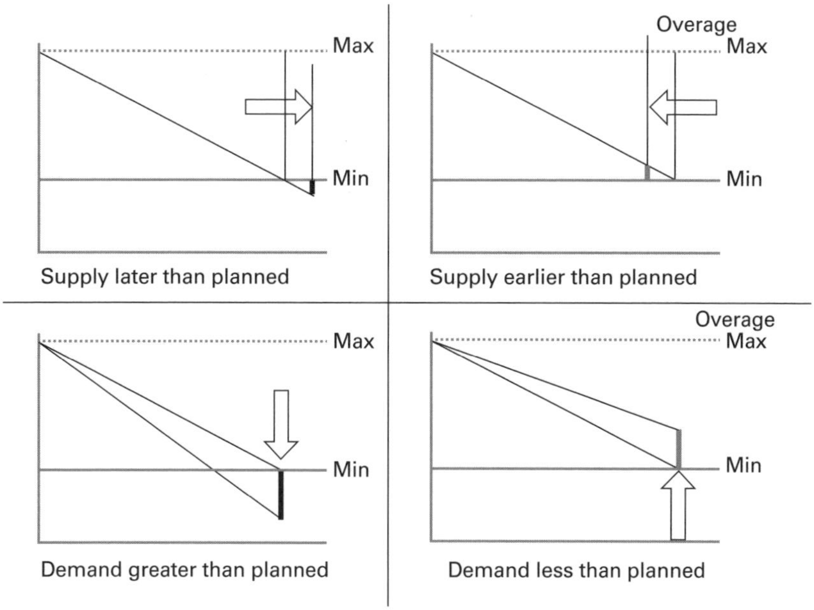

Forecast error

In Chapter 2 we mentioned the importance of forecasting in the management of demand; it was also made clear that the forecast would likely be wrong. This not a failure of an individual, weak business processes or poor quality software, it is merely a fact of life. Predicting the future is impossible; we can often get close but there will always be an event on the horizon which will not be expected. Forecast and inventory planning systems have come a long way and utilize statistics to help protect against a predictable amount for forecast error. Most forecast error and statistical safety stock systems utilize the Normal and Poisson distributions.

Normal distribution and Poisson distribution

If we measure the accuracy of a forecast, we will find that in most cases it behaves like a 'normal' distribution. If a forecast is behaving with a normal distribution, then:

- on most occasions, the forecast will be only slightly above or below the prediction;
- on far fewer occasions the demand is *significantly* higher or lower than the forecast;
- on rare occasions the demand is *very significantly* higher or lower.

A typical normal distribution curve is shown on the left in Figure 6.6. The normal distribution holds true for all but the very low levels of demand when the distribution is said to be a Poisson distribution, also shown in Figure 6.6. Looking at Figure 6.6 it can be seen that as the average demand increases the Poisson distribution begins to look similar to the normal. The key is that both are used to provide a link between customer service level and the determination of safety stock. The similarity between the two types of distribution is not really a surprise as we are looking to determine the probability of an event happening. These distributions are used by all disciplines when estimating the probability of an occurrence.

Figure 6.6 Comparisons of Poisson and normal distributions

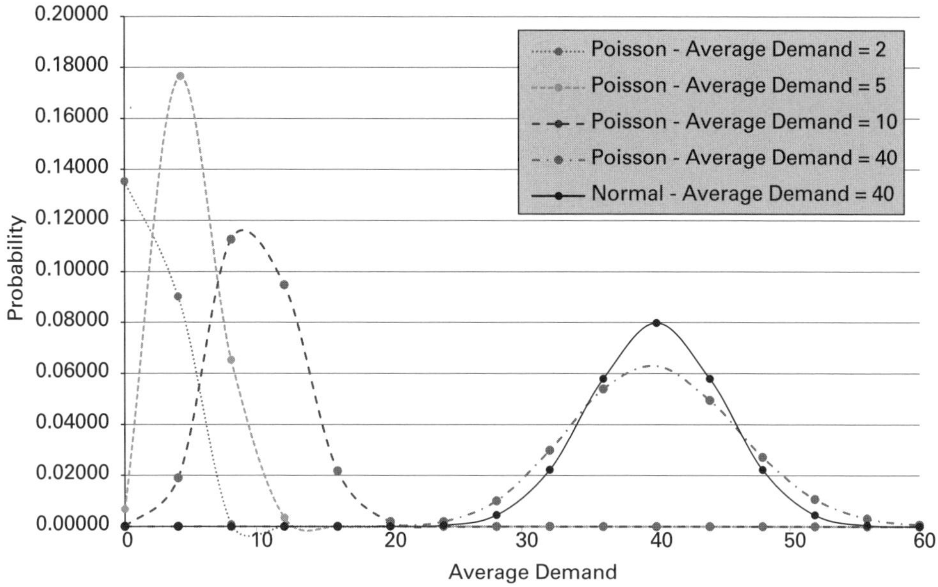

Normal distribution roles in safety stock

To understand how we can use normal distribution let us consider some more young entrepreneurs, Harry and Jack, who run Set and Smash Ltd. Harry Oxbridge, Sales Director, knows he can sell volleyballs to the Varsity Volley Ball Clubs in the UK (product VB001 code), and over the last year they have sold an average of 40 per day. Harry has analysed the demand and found it behaves with a normal distribution, with a total annual demand of 14,600 balls or an average of 40 per day, based on 365 days of internet sales, and a standard deviation of 25 balls per day. Harry has developed a chart and table to represent the normal distribution for his demand in Figure 6.7. Harry can see that 50 per cent of the time demand will be met if the average demand of 40 volley balls a day is achieved.

In the case of safety stock, Harry can use these distributions to help deliver a given customer service level. Thus, looking at the shaded area in Figure 6.7, we can see that in the normal distribution, the annual demand of 14,600, shown as an average demand of 40 per day, represents half of the area of the curve; the average demand or a probability of 50 per cent. If Set and Smash Ltd only held enough stock for a forecasted demand of 40 per day, they would only meet the demand 50 per cent of the time and their service level would be said to be 50 per cent. If, however, they wanted to ensure that they

Figure 6.7 Normal distribution and demand probability for Set and Smash Ltd

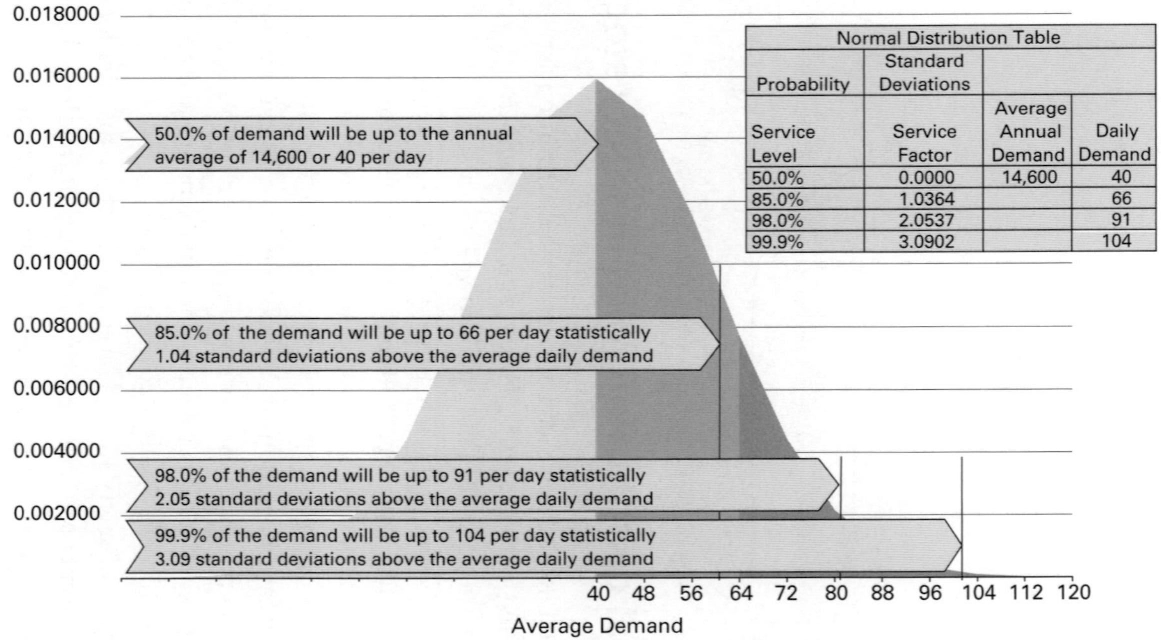

Normal Distribution Table			
Probability	Standard Deviations		
Service Level	Service Factor	Average Annual Demand	Daily Demand
50.0%	0.0000	14,600	40
85.0%	1.0364		66
98.0%	2.0537		91
99.9%	3.0902		104

satisfied their customers 98 per cent of the time they would need to hold enough in stock for a forecasted demand of 91, which is statistically represented as 2.0537 standard deviations of the average demand. Harry is pragmatic enough to know that Set and Smash Ltd could never achieve 100 per cent customer satisfaction, but if he wanted to ensure that he satisfied his customers 99.9 per cent of the time he would need to hold enough in stock for a forecasted demand of 104, which is statistically represented as 3.0902 standard deviations of the average demand.

Discussing this, his business partner Jack Lancaster, the Procurement Director of Set and Smash Ltd, knows that their supplier Clare's Sports can resupply orders on a 15-day lead time. Jack thinks Harry ought to take into account the time to re-supply and the reliability of Clare's Sports when considering what to hold in stock. His friend Sam Cornish, an expert on economic batch quantity, suggests that batch size may also be an important factor.

The next section will look at the various formulae that Jack and Harry can use to take into account all the information they have gathered about their customers and supplier to determine safety stock.

Statistical safety stock

The simplest way to protect against higher than expected demand is to keep an additional quantity in stock as a reserve against unexpected demand. However, academics have utilized this 'normal' relationship that naturally results from forecasting/demand to develop formula that help us to calculate safety stock. There is a wide range of formulas which will attempt to cover all types of eventualities. We have focused on the three most commonly used safety stock formulas when applying statistics to calculate safety stock:

- Demand safety considers demand variation and lead time.
- Demand and supply safety considers demand variation, lead time and supply variation expressed as variation in the given lead time.
- Safety stock, including effect of batch size, considers demand variation, lead time, supply variation expressed as variation in the given lead time, and the agreed batch size.

Demand safety

If we are only concerned with demand variability and assume that it behaves 'normally' then we can use the simple formula shown in Figure 6.8.

Figure 6.8 Safety stock to protect against demand variation (Waters, 2003: 174)

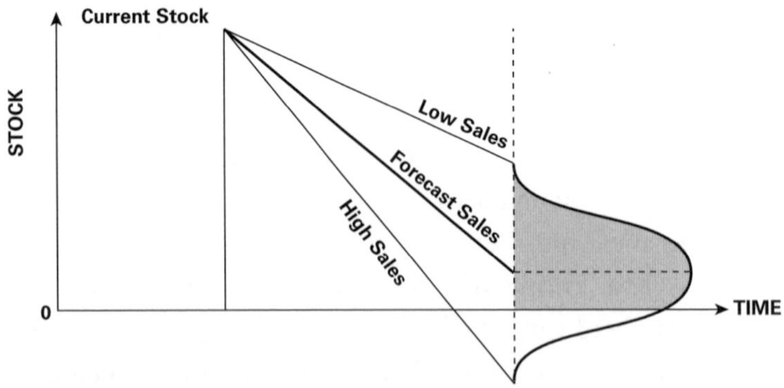

Normal Distribution Table	
Service Level	Standard Deviations
50.000%	0.0000
60.000%	0.2533
70.000%	0.5244
80.000%	0.8416
85.000%	1.0364
90.000%	1.2816
95.000%	1.6449
96.000%	1.7507
97.000%	1.8808
98.000%	2.0537
99.000%	2.3263
99.500%	2.5758
99.900%	3.0902
99.950%	3.2905
99.990%	3.7190
99.997%	4.0128

Annual demand	14,600
Daily demand (based on 365 days a year)	40
Lead time to re-supply	15 days
Standard Deviation (Forecast Error as a quantity)	25 Units / Day

Service factor is the number of standard deviations to achieve the desired service level

Thus to deliver a Service Level (to the customer) of 98% the Service Factor from the Table is 2.054

Safety stock = Service Factor x Standard Deviation x SqRt of Lead-time $= 2.054 * 25 * \sqrt{15}$
$= 199$

Safety stock to protect against demand variation has three elements:

1 Desired service level.

2 Demand variation per day.

3 Square root of time to re-supply in days.

The three elements are explained in detail below.

- Service factor – this is the conversion of the desired service level into a 'factor' that represents the number of standard deviations from the average demand. If you look at the normal distribution table in Figure 6.8 you will see that to achieve a service level of 85 per cent you will need a service factor of 1.0364; this would result in disappointing 15 per cent of your customers. To achieve 98 per cent will require a service factor of 2.0537; here only 2 per cent of your customers will be disappointed. High-volume business would need to aim for a much higher level, say 99.9 per cent service or 0.1 per cent or 1 in a 1,000 customers. To achieve this a service factor of 3.0902 would be needed.
- Demand variation – this is the variability of the demand, either by looking at the demand history over time or by comparing the forecast with the actual demand and calculating the error. Either way it is expressed as a

variation per (day) unit time. For example, we have an average sales of 40 units per day ± 25 units, that is the demand could be as low as 15 or as high as 65.

- Lead-time (of the replenishment order) – this is needed as we state the demand variation per unit time, so if we have to wait a long time for the next order the risks are much higher. The lead time sits on the base of the saw-tooth triangle and the variation occurs on the hypotenuse, thus the increase is based on the square root of the lead-time and not a direct relationship.

Looking at the results we can see that for a planned service level of 98 per cent we need to have 199 units of safety stock; to understand this we can convert to time based on the daily demand, thus the safety stock represents 199/40 = 4.75 days or approximately five days. If you also express the demand variation as days 0.625, just over half a day. From this we can see that our demand is very variable; when we place an order for a product it will be 15 days before it will arrive. On this basis this amount of safety stock begins to seem reasonable. This can be easily expressed as an Excel formula as shown in Excel 6.4.

The Excel model makes it very easy to see the effect of varying the service level. For example, the model shows that to move to a planned service level of 98 per cent requires a safety stock of 198.5 units, and to go up to a service level of 99 per cent the safety stock needs to increase to 225.25 units. The next problem is to consider the value for money against the protection provided. Let us say that we can buy this product for £10 and sell it for £15. As we said earlier, if we achieve a 98 per cent service level we will disappoint 2 per cent of our customers. This would potentially result in lost sales. If we are selling 14,600 units a year and we lose 2 per cent of sales we will miss the opportunity to sell:

14,600 × 2% = 292 @ £15 each = £4,380 of lost sales

If we compare this to our investment of 199 units of safety stock @ £10 = £1,990 it begins to look like a good deal. We need to be careful to make sure we do not get carried away and evaluate the lost sales with the investment in safety stock. By comparing the investment with the service level we can quickly come to a decision on the most appropriate safety stock level. An evaluation table can easily be built in Excel as shown in Excel 6.5.

A quick examination of the table will show that a service level of 95 per cent and the investment in safety is too low when compared to the lost sales;

Excel 6.4 Simple safety stock based on demand variation

	A	B	C	D	E	F	G
1	Annual Demand	14,600	Units			Service Level	Standard Deviations
2	Daily Demand	40	Units			50.000%	0.0000
3	Leadtime to re-supply	15	Days			60.000%	0.2533
4	Standard Deviation	25	Units			70.000%	0.5244
5						80.000%	0.8416
6						85.000%	1.0364
7						90.000%	1.2816
8						95.000%	1.6449
9						96.000%	1.7507
10	Safety Stock for	98%	=	198.853		97.000%	1.8808
11						98.000%	2.0537
12	Safety stock as days of demand			4.971		99.000%	2.3263
13						99.500%	2.5758
14						99.900%	3.0902
15						99.950%	3.2905
16						99.990%	3.7190
17						99.997%	4.0128

Enter these formulae

Cell D10	= NORMSINV(B10)*B4*SQRT(B3)
Cell D12	= +D10/B2
Cell G2 *then copy down to* G17	= NORMSINV(F2)

by increasing the service level to 98 per cent a small increase in investment of £395.91 potentially prevents £6,570 in lost sales. However, investing the next £263.95 would reduce the lost sales by £2,190, a much lower figure, a total investment of £2,252.48, a little more than the lost sales prevented. The argument is not quite so straightforward as the safety inventory investment is still available the following year and for no additional investment, however it does cost to hold the safety stock year on year. What is clear is that (in this example) less than 98 per cent of the losses are too high and much above 98 per cent the additional cost makes the ROI questionable.

Demand/supply safety

If we want to extend the safety to cover the performance of our supplier it would make sense to use a formula that covers both. Waters (2003) extends his demand safety formula as shown in Figure 6.8. The additional variation

Excel 6.5 Safety stock based on demand variation showing lost sales

	A	B	C	D
1	Annual Demand	14600	Units	
2	Daily Demand	40	Units	
3	Leadtime to re-supply	15	Days	
4	Standard Deviation	25	Units	
5	Unit Cost	£10.00	Each	
6	Selling Price	£15.00	Each	
7				
8	Service Level	Safety Quantity	Safety Value	Lost Sales
9	95.000%	159.26	£1,592.62	£10,950.00
10	98.000%	198.85	£1,988.53	£4,380.00
11	99.000%	225.25	£2,252.48	£2,190.00
12	99.900%	299.21	£2,992.10	£219.00
13	99.997%	388.54	£3,885.39	£6.57

Enter these formulae

Cell B9 *then copy down to* B13	= NORMSINV(A9)*$B$4*SQRT($B$3)
Cell C9 *then copy down to* C13	= B9*$B$5
Cell D9 *then copy down to* D13	= (1-A9)*$B$1*$B$6

used is the supplier lead-time variation, for example if we were to monitor our supplier we may find that on average his lead-time is 15 days, but that he could be five days early or five days late (when measuring one standard deviation).

There is quite a significant effect by adding supply variation, which will possibly affect what would be a cost-effective service level. This formula is simple enough to convert into an Excel as shown in Excel 6.6.

By adding the supply safety the cost-effective service level has been lowered. It is now somewhere between 97 per cent and 98 per cent, rather than 98 per cent and 99 per cent.

Safety stock including the effect of batch size

Having protected against supply and demand, we have focused on the point of time when the supply is just due to arrive. In reality, for most of the time there is a considerable amount of stock, which gives a natural protection. It is therefore no surprise to find that academics have considered the size of the incoming order as well as supply/demand. Figure 6.10 shows this graphically.

Excel 6.6 Safety stock based on demand/supply variation with lost sales

	A	B	C	D
1	Annual Demand	14600	Units	
2	Daily Demand	40	Units	
3	Leadtime to re-supply	15	Days	
4	Standard Deviation Demand	25	Units	
5	Standard Deviation Supply	5	Days	
6	Unit Cost	£10.00	Each	
7	Selling Price	£15.00	Each	
8				
9	Demand Safety			96.825
10	Supply Safety			200.000
11	Total Safety for	98%	=	456.353
12				
13	Service Level	Safety Quantity	Safety Value	Lost Sales
14	95.000%	365.49	£3,654.94	£10,950.00
15	97.000%	417.92	£4,179.21	£6,570.00
16	98.000%	456.35	£4,563.53	£4,380.00
17	99.000%	516.93	£5,169.26	£2,190.00
18	99.500%	572.36	£5,723.62	£1,095.00

Enter these formulae

Cell D9	= B4*SQRT(B3)
Cell D10	= B2*B5
Cell D11	= NORMSINV(B11)*SQRT((D9*D9)+(D10*D10))
Cell B14 *then copy down to* B18	= NORMSINV(A14)*SQRT(($D$9*$D$9)+($D$10*$D$10))
Cell C14 *then copy down to* C18	= B14*$B$6
Cell D14 *then copy down to* D18	= (1–A14)*$B$1*$B$7

Looking at the left of Figure 6.10 we can see that the larger order size would only reach a level where safety may be needed three times in a given period, whereas as can be seen on the right the smaller order size will be in the 'zone' five times. Conversely, since we know that the demand safety is based on the time between orders, that small orders may require less safety, which is a bit of a contradiction. Schmidt, Hartmann and Nyhuis (2007) investigated this anomaly and derived a formula which attempts to take this into account. The formula is shown in Figure 6.11.

A closer look at the formula shows that it is essentially the same as the Supply Demand Safety formula with an additional factor to account for the effect of the batch size. The effect of this factor here is to reduce the safety

Figure 6.9 Safety stock to protect against demand and supply variation

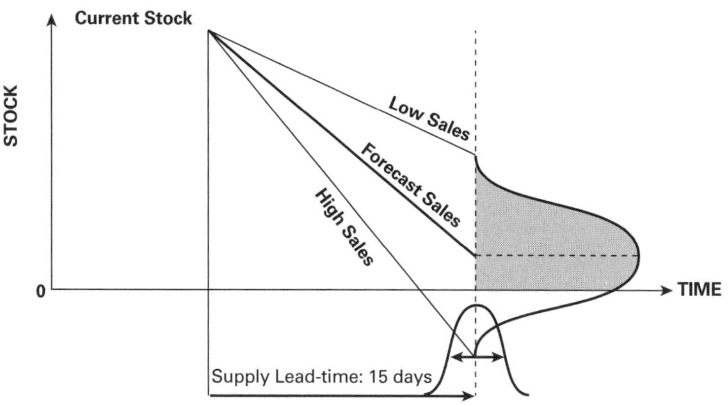

Normal Distribution Table	
Service Level	Standard Deviations
50.000%	0.0000
60.000%	0.2533
70.000%	0.5244
80.000%	0.8416
85.000%	1.0364
90.000%	1.2816
95.000%	1.6449
96.000%	1.7507
97.000%	1.8808
98.000%	2.0537
99.000%	2.3263
99.500%	2.5758
99.900%	3.0902
99.950%	3.2905
99.990%	3.7190
99.997%	4.0128

Annual demand	14,600
Daily demand (based on 365 days a year)	40
Lead time to re-supply	15 days
Standard Deviation (Forecast Error as a quantity)	25 Units / Day
Standard Deviation of lead-time (delivery performance)	±5 days

Service factor is the number of standard deviations to achieve the desired service level
Thus to deliver a Service Level (to the customer) of 98% the Service Factor from the Table is 2.054

Safety Stock $= \text{Service Factor} \times \sqrt{(\text{Demand Safety})^2 + (\text{Supply Safety})^2}$

Demand Safety $= \text{Standard Deviation of Demand} \times \sqrt{\text{lead-time}}$ $= 25 * \sqrt{15}$

Supply Safety $= \text{Standard Deviation of Supply} \times \text{Demand}$ $= 5 * 40$

Safety Stock $= 2.054 * \sqrt{(25 * \sqrt{15})^2 + (5 * 40)^2}$ $= 456$

Figure 6.10 Effect of order quantity on the need for safety stock

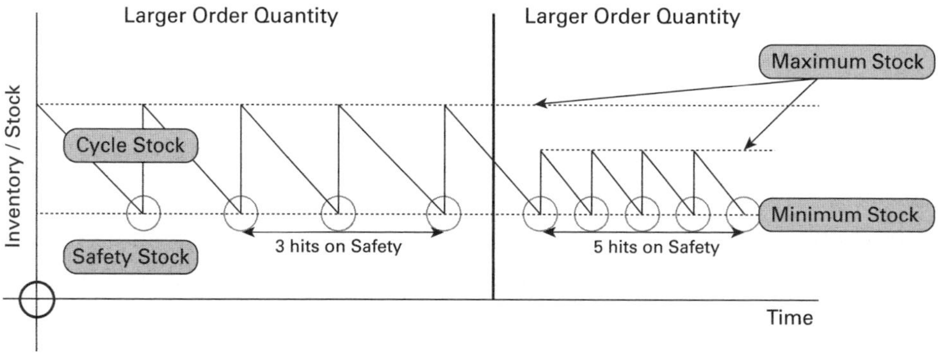

stock by a small amount which recognizes that the size of the batch naturally protects for a period of time. Overall, the effect in simple terms is that the higher the order size the lower the safety stock, when compared with the supply demand safety. The caveat that Schmidt, Hartmann and Nyhuis (2007) apply to the formula is that it is only valid when the order size is greater than

Figure 6.11 Supply demand safety considering order size and replenishment time

SL = Service Level SF = Service factor QRP = replenishment quantity TRP = replenishment time (lead-time) D = Demand σ_n = standard deviation of demand σ_{trp} = standard deviation of replenishment time		98% 2.0542 900 units 15 days 14,600 / 40/day ±25 units ±5 units
Safety Stock =	$SF(1-\frac{(1-SL)(QRP)}{(TRP)(D)})\left(\sqrt{(TRP)(\sigma_N^2)+(D^2)\ (\sigma_{TRP}^2)}\right)$	
	$(1-\frac{(1-SL)(QRP)}{(TRP)(D)})$ * Safety Stock Supply & Demand	
	$(1-\frac{(1-98\%)(900)}{(15)(40)}) \times 2.054 * (25 * 15)^2 + (5 * 40)^2$	= 0.9700 * 456 = 442.32

the quantity used during the lead time, that is to say where there is only one order being processed at any time. Where the quantity used during the lead time is greater than the order size, ie there would more than one order being processed at any time, this is typically what happens in MRP systems. The time to replenishment (lead time) is, in reality, the time between batches which is in effect the order size, in which case the formula simplifies to: Safety Stock = Service Level Percentage × Supply Demand Safety Stock.

This formula is a little more complex to convert into an Excel and is shown in Excel 6.7.

Safety time

There is a simple alternative to the complex statistical-based safety stock which simply adds time, to protect against the supply and demand variations. As discussed in earlier chapters, the advantage of using a time-based parameter is that it will require less maintenance. It would be possible to convert any safety stock determined as a quantity to time by dividing by the demand. It is common to use in combination with Pareto, which is discussed in the next section, and specify a number of days per value class.

Hybrid safety stock

It is possible to combine safety quantity and time to create hybrid approaches which can resolve some of the issues. There are three options when using this approach:

Excel 6.7 Safety stock based on demand, supply and order size variation

	A	B	C	D
1	Annual Demand	14600	Units	D
2	Daily Demand	40	Units	d
3	Leadtime to re-supply	15	Days	TRP
4	Standard Deviation Demand	25	Units	σ_D
5	Standard Deviation Supply	5	Days	σ_{TRP}
6	Order Size	900	Units	QRP
7	Unit Cost	£10.00	Each	
8	Selling Price	£15.00	Each	
9				
10	Demand Safety			96.82
11	Supply Safety			200.00
12	SD Safety			222.20
13	QRP Function			0.9700
14	Total Safety for	98%	=	442.66

Enter these formulae

Cell D10	= B4*SQRT(B3)
Cell D11	= B2*B5
Cell D12	= SQRT((D10*D10)+(D11*D11))
Cell D13	= (1-((1-B14)*B6)/(B3*B2))
Cell D14	= NORMSINV(B14)*D13*SQRT((D10*D10)+(D11*D11))

- Calculate both, then take the least of the two values – this is useful if you are looking to minimize the safety stock holdings, and service level is not a significant issue. It will tend to under-protect the very high-value items, which should already be focus items.
- Calculate both, then take the higher of the two values – this is useful if you want to focus on customer service level and inventory holding is not a specific issue. It will tend to over-protect the low-value items.
- Use a combination of both, ie safety time of five days plus safety quantity of 100. This approach will give the advantages of adjusting as the demand varies up and down, but retain a minimum if the demand falls below a certain level. A common method of determining the values is to calculate a statistical safety stock and then allocate part of the safety quantity as safety time based on the daily going rate of the product.

Safety stock summary

Before we leave the topic of safety stock tools it is worth just summarizing the advantages and disadvantages of the various approaches.

Advantages of statistical-based safety stock

Statistical-based safety stock protects against the real world of variations of supply, demand and order size. There is significant research that continues to refine these formulas as well as compare and contrast their performance. The real challenge with any formula is the collection of the data required, as well as interpreting the results.

Disadvantages of statistical-based safety stock

The disadvantages of statistical-based safety stock are that it protects at any cost, with no checks and balances against the unit cost. It is a formula requiring increasing amounts of data which may not be readily available.

Advantages of safety time

Safety time will require less maintenance as it will rise and fall as the demand increases and decreases.

Disadvantages of safety time

In its simplest form it has no recognition of the variations of supply, demand and order size; however, safety quantity can simply be converted to time, overcoming this weakness.

A hybrid safety approach offers a way of mitigating the disadvantages and capitalizing on the advantages of each of the different solutions.

In the second half of the chapter the focus has been on understanding the importance of identifying the correct attributes of the parts being managed. These attributes should then be used as the determining factor for categorizing the parts into groups; each group can then be managed based on its importance to the business. This led naturally on to the development of a plan utilizing techniques like Pareto which can be manipulated to both determine an initial plan as well as to evaluate options for improving the plan year on year. Finally, we looked at the importance of looking into overage to ensure that we cover all four possibilities for supply and demand variation. Thus, we can be confident that an inventory plan has considered all the components needed to ensure that it is realistic and achievable. The next chapter will look at some of the weaknesses identified in these traditional inventory management methods, and the techniques that have been developed to overcome them.

Parts classification

When managing large numbers of items it is often useful to segregate into groups by:

- commodity;
- supplier;
- depot;
- buyer; and
- planner.

All these groupings do not consider the attributes of the item itself, they are focused on the management grouping and thus may not be the most effective way to allow for inventory analysis and/or optimization. Parts/products have different attributes:

- value;
- volumes;
- volatility – variation of the demand of the product;
- physical size;
- shelf-life; and
- product lifecycle.

It is these attributes that will affect the way you want to manage each part, and thus if we can classify the product using these attributes we can divide our parts into useful sub-groups for inventory management. In this section we will look at a number of the most popular techniques and how they can be combined to define inventory policy to produce inventory plans.

ABC/Pareto classification

ABC or Pareto planning is a very common classification technique. It is based on the observation of the economist Vilfredo Pareto in 1906. Pareto identified that 80 per cent of the wealth was held by 20 per cent of the population. This observation was developed by Juran and others in the period after

World War II as part of the drive to improve production efficiency. This work gave rise to the use of the Pareto Curve in operations management, in inventory planning, inventory control and quality and problem solving. The ABC classification for inventory planning will take a group of parts and divide into three groups, based on their annual usage value. That is to say the number of pieces used in 12 months times the unit cost. This group of parts is then ranked highest spend parts at the top and lowest at the bottom. They are then divided into three groups based on the following rule:

- A Class – the top 80 per cent of parts by value, normally about 20 per cent of the parts.
- B Class – the next 15 per cent (95 per cent of the total value), normally the next 30 per cent of parts.
- C Class – the last 5 per cent of parts by value, which is the remaining 50 per cent of parts.

The benefit of this approach is that you can take a large number of parts that you are trying to manage and identify the parts that are the most financially important. To understand this a little better we can look at a sample group of parts. If we take a sample group of 27 parts as shown in Appendix B we can create a Pareto curve and divide the parts into the three categories, by following the following steps:

- Calculate the annual usage spend (use Table B1 from Appendix B).
- Sort annual spend highest at top.
- Cumulate the annual spend.
- Calculate the percentage of cumulative annual spend.
- Calculate percentage of items.

Once you have calculated the cumulative spends you will be able to divide the list into three parts by applying the Pareto rules above. An example of this process is shown in Excel 6.8.

If we look at the list we can see that if we were to simply look at the list in part number order the first part would have been A0889030013. However, this is the 25th in importance rank in our Pareto list, and the most important part B78811ZD is eighth in the alphabetical list, in Appendix B1, effectively buried somewhere in the middle of the list. In this example we have one part that accounts for about one quarter of our annual spend. The likelihood is that this part already receives a lot of attention as it is probably a very important

Excel 6.8 Pareto classification

	A	B	C	D	E	F	G	H	I
1	Count	Part Number	Annual Usage or Demand	Cost Per Part	Annual Spend Value £	Cumulative Annual Spend £	Cumulative percentage of Annual Spend	Cumulative percentage of Parts	ABC
2	1	B78811ZD	1324	£42.84	£56,720.16	£56,720.16	26.6%	3.7%	A
3	2	B78812ZF	987	£41.87	£41,325.69	£98,045.85	45.9%	7.4%	A
4	3	B78810741A	1012	£18.50	£18,722.00	£116,767.85	54.7%	11.1%	A
5	4	N6554004M0256	523	£35.08	£18,346.84	£135,114.69	63.3%	14.8%	A
6	5	SK98751	46	£316.19	£14,544.74	£149,659.43	70.1%	18.5%	A
7	6	LE763	781	£11.11	£8,676.91	£158,336.34	74.2%	22.2%	A
8	7	D0883030014C	267	£27.54	£7,353.18	£165,689.52	77.6%	25.9%	A
9	8	C78810742A	360	£16.87	£6,073.20	£171,762.72	80.4%	29.6%	B
10	9	D0862060018Y	163	£33.26	£5,421.38	£177,184.10	83.0%	33.3%	B
11	10	C78810761A	567	£8.43	£4,779.81	£181,963.91	85.2%	37.0%	B
12	11	LE02	396	£11.09	£4,391.64	£186,355.55	87.3%	40.7%	B
13	12	B78812001B	458	£7.10	£3,251.80	£189,607.35	88.8%	44.4%	B
14	13	KN552130	10	£319.98	£3,199.80	£192,807.15	90.3%	48.1%	B
15	14	A0906030015	18	£150.22	£2,703.96	£195,511.11	91.6%	51.9%	B
16	15	B78810721A	749	£3.44	£2,576.56	£198,087.67	92.8%	55.6%	B
17	16	D0991020012	164	£14.60	£2,394.40	£200,482.07	93.9%	59.3%	B
18	17	D0862070019Y	60	£35.25	£2,115.00	£202,597.07	94.9%	63.0%	B
19	18	D0978040014	35	£57.63	£2,017.05	£204,614.12	95.8%	66.7%	C
20	19	A78810601E	450	£4.20	£1,890.00	£206,504.12	96.7%	70.4%	C
21	20	B78818AE	35	£49.57	£1,734.95	£208,239.07	97.5%	74.1%	C
22	21	C78810762A	199	£7.44	£1,480.56	£209,719.63	98.2%	77.8%	C
23	22	D0753100033	75	£15.36	£1,152.00	£210,871.63	98.8%	81.5%	C
24	23	D1017040014	10	£95.36	£953.60	£211,825.23	99.2%	85.2%	C
25	24	KDB300600	8	£93.75	£750.00	£212,575.23	99.6%	88.9%	C
26	25	A0889030013	52	£9.59	£498.68	£213,073.91	99.8%	92.6%	C
27	26	B30880112C	700	£0.45	£315.00	£213,388.91	99.9%	96.3%	C
28	27	B30880113C	105	£1.18	£123.90	£213,512.81	100.0%	100.0%	C
29		**Totals**			**£213,512.81**				

Enter these formulae

Cell E2 *then copy down to* E28 = C2*D2
Sort Range A1:E27, using Column E (Annual Spend Value £) Order [largest to smallest]
Cell F2 *then copy down to* F28 = SUM(E$2:E2)
Cell G2 *then copy down to* G28 = F2/MAX($F$2:$F$28)
Cell H2 *then copy down to* H28 = A2/MAX($A$2:$A$28)

part of the range of products or a key part of the product we are making. We would tend to manage this part very closely and only bring into stock at the last minute. We would use JIT to manage the flow for either purchasing or manufacture. Once we have divided the parts into groups we would define a policy approach to the management of the parts in the group based on the class the part falls into. Table 6.4 summarizes the key policy considerations.

Table 6.4 Action/focus for the three Pareto inventory classes

Class	Percentage of Spend	Cumulative Percentage of Spend	Percentage of Parts	Cumulative Percentage of Parts
A	80%	80%	20%	20%
B	15%	95%	30%	50%
C	5%	100%	50%	100%

Class	Percentage of Spend	Percentage of Parts	Action/Focus
A	80%	20%	A small number of very important and valuable items needing close management
B	15%	30%	A larger number of parts which are considerably less valuable but need to be managed efficiently
C	5%	50%	A large number of parts of little monetary value that need to be managed in a way that they minimize the time to manage

For the A Class we are dealing with high-value key components/products. We want to ensure that they arrive 'at the last possible moment' or JIT and in small quantities, which means very frequent deliveries often daily. For our C Class parts we have to manage a large range of products but they are in inventory value terms of little consequence, but do not forget that they are still capable of stopping production. To paraphrase the proverb:

> For the want of a nail, the horse was lost, for want of the horse the army was lost.

So although these are of no financial value they still have the potential to disrupt the business, thus we must ensure we have sufficient without spending time managing.

We can summarize into a simple inventory law:

If I am going to manage inventory I want small amounts of high-value inventory received frequently, and large amounts in low-value inventory received infrequently.

Pareto is always represented as a Pareto Curve which is shown in Figure 6.12. This curve is achieved by plotting Columns H and G using the Excel XY chart type. In this case the curve of our 27 parts does not strictly confirm the 80/20 rule, although it clearly shows the important few and the trivial many.

Figure 6.12 Pareto Curve of parts list in Excel 6.8

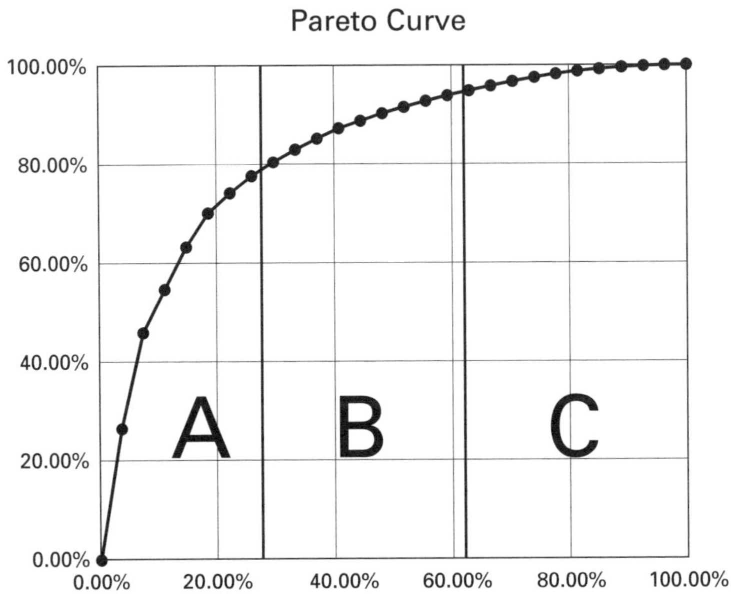

Using Pareto to plan inventory using cycle and safety stock

Pareto inventory policy and estimate

Once the principle is understood, the next important step is to look at how we can utilize this in the process of inventory planning, how to develop an inventory policy and use it to calculate inventory based on Pareto. As we are dealing with a group of parts we do not want to make individual decisions about how many to hold for each part, so we can use the order period as a representation of the order size. We could consider holding a week of stock, two weeks, one month etc.

It would be easy to guess at the appropriate days of supply, but by using a simple table, as shown in Table 6.5, we can put some logic behind the decision. First, we summarize the list of parts into the three Pareto classes ABC, next we take the cumulative value for each group, and the number of parts. If we assume that the working year is 250 days then we can calculate the daily going rate, the amount of value used in a working day. We can also list, for reference, the number of parts in each group. If we now create a table with an evaluation of 5, 10, 20 etc days of supply we can see how much inventory we would need to invest if we were to adopt a particular days of supply policy. Looking at Table 6.5, it now becomes clear that even at five days for Class A the investment is significant when compared to the other groups. However, for Class C we can easily afford to buy much larger quantities – the benefit of this is less frequent orders, for example if we bought weekly we would have to process 10 orders a week for 52 weeks in the year (a total of 520); if we bought 80 days supply we would only need to process 3–4 orders a year for the 10 parts (a total of 30–40), which is a considerable saving in time, which can then be spent focusing on the A class parts. Thus we are, in effect, exchanging a higher inventory level for less time and effort. Using this analysis we can see the logic behind the typical ABC policy shown below in Table 6.6.

Table 6.6 shows all the summarized information, along with the policy decisions, which will clearly define what needs to be done to implement the policy. Note the average inventory is half the days of supply, as for planning we assume the average inventory is half the order size. Having defined the plan we can communicate our decision to the planner. All the planner needs to do to implement it would be to look up their part in the Pareto list in Excel 6.8 and he would be able to determine what order policy he should apply. For example, Part C78810742A is a B Class product and should as a result be ordered every 20 days. The planner knows that 360 are used a year, so an order of 360 divided by 250 (working days in a year) multiplied by a 20 days order cycle will give 28.8 as a recommended order size, which would be rounded to 30 (a month's supply). In addition to making the decision about the order size we must also consider the safety stock. We can apply the same approach by looking at the value of safety based on time (Table 6.7).

The table is essentially the same as the days of supply, however the decision here is not the amount to be ordered but the amount of demand/supply

Table 6.5 Determining inventory policy based on Pareto analysis

Class	Total Annual Spend	Daily Going Rate	No of parts	Days of Supply					
				5	10	20	40	80	160
A	£165,689.52	£662.76	7	£3,313.79	£6,627.58	£13,255.16	£26,50.32	£53,020.65	£106,041.29
B	£36,907.55	£147.63	10	£738.15	£1,476.30	£2,952.60	£5,905.21	£11,810.42	£23,620.83
C	£10,915.74	£43.66	10	£218.31	£436.63	£873.26	£1,746.53	£3,493.04	£6,986.07
	£213,512.81	£854.05	27						

Table 6.6 Inventory policy statement

Class	Annual Spend Value £	Daily Going Rate	Class Limits	No of Parts	Days of Supply	No of Orders	Average Inventory
A	£165,689.52	£662.76	80.0%	7	5	350	£1,656.90
B	£36,907.55	£147.63	95.0%	10	20	125	£1,476.30
C	£10,915.74	£43.66		10	80	31.25	£1,746.52
Totals	£ 213,512.81	£854.05		27		506.25	£4,879.72

protection, thus we would be saying that for Class A we can only afford five days, whereas for C Class having 20 days' extra stock to protect against late deliveries or higher than expected demand is more than sufficient. We can now add these decisions to our inventory plan/policy. The final results can be seen in Table 6.8.

The table now shows the days of supply and safety stock decisions we have made, so we now have a clearly defined policy for each Pareto inventory class which can be implemented by the planner. Thus for our example, part C78810742A, we have also indicated the amount of safety; either it can be set to 10 days safety time or a quantity of 14.4, rounded to 15.

Pareto exchange curve

It goes without saying that any business will focus on year on year improvements on all aspects of the business. As a result we can expect a request to reduce inventory each year. To achieve a reduction we will have to change one or more elements of the policy. The two options we have are:

1. Change the days of supply/safety stock for each Pareto Class.
2. Change the number of parts in each Pareto Class.

To understand which of these is better we can look at the effect on each policy to see which option is the most effective way to reduce inventory.

Change the days of supply/safety stock for each Pareto Class

For this we could consider first reducing the safety stock on the A class parts by one day – these are the most closely managed parts and we should be able to manage. The days of supply for C Class parts could be reduced from 80 days to, for example, 60 days. If we evaluate these changes the results would be as shown in Table 6.9.

By applying these changes we have reduced the inventory from £10,543.49 to £9,444.07, some £1,098.81 or about 10 per cent.

Change the number of parts in each Pareto Class

If we decide to alter the class limit in order to reduce the inventory we will need to increase the number of parts in A Class and reduce the number in C Class, thus changing the limit from 80 per cent to 82 per cent and similarly shifting 95 to 97 per cent. We will move parts from B to A and from C to B. The results can be seen in Table 6.10.

Table 6.7 Determining inventory policy based on Pareto analysis

Class	Total Annual Spend	Daily Going Rate	No of parts	Days of Safety					
				5	10	20	40	80	160
A	£165,698.95	£662.80	7	£3,313.98	£6,627.96	£13,255.92	£26,511.83	£53,023.66	£106,047.33
B	£36,909.20	£147.64	10	£738.18	£1,476.37	£2,952.74	£5,905.47	£11,810.94	£23,621.89
C	£10,915.79	£43.66	10	£218.32	£436.63	£873.26	£1,746.53	£3,493.05	£6,986.10
	£213,523.93	£854.10	27						

Table 6.8 Inventory policy statement including safety stock

Class	Annual Spend Value £	Daily Going Rate	Class Limits	No of Parts	Days of Supply	Safety Stock Days	No of Orders	Average Cycle Inventory	Safety Stock Value	Total Planned Inventory
A	£165,698.95	£662.80	80.00%	7	5	5	350	£1,656.99	£3,313.98	£4,970.97
B	£36,909.20	£147.64	95.00%	10	20	10	125	£1,476.37	£1,476.37	£2,952.74
C	£10,915.79	£43.66		10	80	20	31	£1,746.53	£873.26	£2,619.79
Totals	£213,523.93	£854.10		27			506	£4,879.88	£5,663.61	£10,543.49

Table 6.9 The effect of changing days of supply and safety stock

Class	Annual Spend Value £	Daily Going Rate	Class Limits	No of Parts	Days of Supply	Safety Stock Days	No of Orders	Average Cycle Inventory	Safety Stock Value	Total Planned Inventory
A	£165,698.95	£662.80	80.00%	7	5	4	350	£1,656.99	£2,651.18	£4,308.17
B	£36,909.20	£147.64	95.00%	10	20	10	125	£1,476.37	£1,476.37	£2,952.74
C	£10,915.79	£43.66		10	60	20	42	£1,309.89	£873.26	£2,183.16
Totals	£213,523.93	£854.10		27			517	£4,443.25	£5,000.81	£9,444.07

Table 6.10 The effect of changing class limits in inventory plan

Class	Annual Spend Value £	Daily Going Rate	Class Limits	No of Parts	Days of Supply	Safety Stock Days	No of Orders	Average Cycle Inventory	Safety Stock Value	Total Planned Inventory
A	£171,770.91	£687.08	82.00%	8	5	5	400	£1,717.71	£3,435.42	£5,153.13
B	£34,744.33	£138.98	97.00%	11	20	10	137.5	£1,389.77	£1,389.77	£2,779.55
C	£7,008.69	£28.03		8	80	20	25	£1,121.39	£560.70	£1,682.09
Totals	£213,523.93	£854.10		27			562.5	£4,228.87	£5,385.89	£9,614.76

We can see from the table that we have achieved a reduction from £10,543.49 to £9,614.76, or £928.73 or about 9 per cent. This is slightly less than the option of changing the parameters. If we take a close look at this approach we can see a distinct advantage. If we change the parameters we affect every part in the classes affected, thus to execute the first option we have to take more risk on our seven A class parts by reducing safety and need to discuss with all the suppliers/manufacturing affected by the changes to the days of supply for the 10 Class C parts. However, to execute the second option we only have to change one part from B Class to A Class and two parts from C Class to B Class. The parts can easily be identified by looking at the Pareto listing and marking off the new limits. In the example parts in Excel 6.8, we can see they are C78810742A, D0978040014 and A78810601E. It is a much easier task to look at three parts than 17. Thus we can see that the manipulation of the Class limits is the most effective method of reducing inventory within a Pareto model.

Runner repeater stranger

Dividing parts by their usage value is not the only way of splitting products; as we mentioned earlier in the chapter there are other attributes we can consider to split the parts into groups. Dividing into groups by volume of demand is another popular approach. By dividing products into their volume, the logic is that high-volume parts will, assuming the demand is regular, need to be made often and low-volume parts we may choose to make less often but in larger quantities. The most often cited example is Runner, Repeater and Stranger:

- *Runner*. A runner is typically defined as high-volume products which are typically produced each day or week.
- *Repeater*. A repeater is typically defined as medium-volume products, which are made on a regular basis, possibly fortnightly or monthly.
- *Stranger*. A stranger is the low-volume residue, which are usually only made when sufficient demand is identified; the demand may also be regular. Some people will add an additional category of Aliens, which, as the name implies, are even rarer than the strangers.

Dividing the products into the groups, there is little advice on how to determine these groups. The decision is largely driven by the range of volume in the parts being managed. For example, if we consider automotive manufacturing, Ford GB's output is 75,000 compared with Morgan's output of 1,000 per year. The number of parts to be managed may be similar, but magnitude of the volumes will be entirely different. Table 6.11 below shows possible split approaches using a boundary based on dividing the maximum by 10.

Table 6.11 Runner, repeater, stranger volume comparison

	Total Volume	75,000	1,000
Category	**Usage per vehicle**	**Ford**	**Morgan**
Runner	1,000 to 100	75,000,000 to 7,500,000	1,000,000 to 100,000
Repeater	100 to 10	7,500,000 to 750,000	100,000 to 10,000
Stranger	10 to 0	750,000 to 0	10,000 to 0

A second alternative would be to divide the group of parts into three groups such that the middle group is 50 per cent of the total volume, in the middle of the distribution. The results for our sample groups of parts is shown in Table 6.12.

The first approach divides into >1,000, <1,000 but >100, whereas the second approach takes the total volume of 9, 554 divided by 2, giving 4,777 and then starting from the middle spread up and down till half the volume is covered. The thresholds in the second case are >700, <700 but >35. The second approach produces a more balanced list, although is more complex to implement.

It is also possible to use the Pareto boundary rules of 80 per cent and 95 per cent of cumulative volume as the boundary rules which, when you look at Table 6.12, looks visually wrong, with quite an unbalanced grouping of 10 runners, 6 repeaters and 11 strangers. Finally, we could simply try dividing the list into three even groups; in this case the thresholds are > 450 for runners, <450 but >75 for repeaters and <75 for strangers with nine parts in each group. The choice of which approach to use is very much down to the individual circumstance of the business, the range of volume which, in the example is from 1,324 to 8 per year, and to an extent what policy is applied for each grouping.

Table 6.12 Alternate approaches to the division of sample group into runner, repeater and stranger

	RRS x 10	RRS @ 50%	RRS 80%/95% as pareto	even from centre-point
Runner	2	5	10	9
Repeater	15	17	6	9
Stranger	10	5	11	9
Total	27	27	27	27

Part Number	Annual Usage or Demand	Cumulative Volume	Cumulative Percentage	Count	RRS x 10	RRS @ 50%		
B78811ZD	1,324	1,324	13.9%	1	Runner	Runner	Runner	Runner
B78810741A	1,012	2,336	24.5%	2	Runner	Runner	Runner	Runner
B78812ZF	987	3,323	34.8%	3	Repeater	Runner	Runner	Runner
LE763	781	4,104	43.0%	4	Repeater	Runner	Runner	Runner
B78810721A	749	4,853	50.8%	5	Repeater	Runner	Runner	Runner
B30880112C	700	5,553	58.1%	6	Repeater	Repeater	Runner	Runner
C78810761A	567	6,120	64.1%	7	Repeater	Repeater	Runner	Runner
N6554004M0256	523	6,643	69.5%	8	Repeater	Repeater	Runner	Runner
B78812001B	458	7,101	74.3%	9	Repeater	Repeater	Runner	Runner
A78810601E	450	7,551	79.0%	10	Repeater	Repeater	Runner	Repeater
LE02	396	7,947	83.2%	11	Repeater	Repeater	Repeater	Repeater
C78810742A	360	8,307	86.9%	12	Repeater	Repeater	Repeater	Repeater
D0883030014C	267	8,574	89.7%	13	Repeater	Repeater	Repeater	Repeater
C78810762A	199	8,773	91.8%	14	Repeater	Repeater	Repeater	Repeater
D0991020012	164	8,937	93.5%	15	Repeater	Repeater	Repeater	Repeater
D0862060018Y	163	9,100	95.2%	16	Repeater	Repeater	Repeater	Repeater
B30880113C	105	9,205	96.3%	17	Repeater	Repeater	Stranger	Repeater
D0753100033	75	9,280	97.1%	18	Stranger	Repeater	Stranger	Repeater
D0862070019Y	60	9,340	97.8%	19	Stranger	Repeater	Stranger	Stranger
A0889030013	52	9,392	98.3%	20	Stranger	Repeater	Stranger	Stranger
SK98751	46	9,438	98.8%	21	Stranger	Repeater	Stranger	Stranger
B78818AE	35	9,473	99.2%	22	Stranger	Repeater	Stranger	Stranger
D0978040014	35	9,508	99.5%	23	Stranger	Stranger	Stranger	Stranger
A0906030015	18	9,526	99.7%	24	Stranger	Stranger	Stranger	Stranger
D1017040014	10	9,536	99.8%	25	Stranger	Stranger	Stranger	Stranger
KN552130	10	9,546	99.9%	26	Stranger	Stranger	Stranger	Stranger
KDB300600	8	9,554	100.0%	27	Stranger	Stranger	Stranger	Stranger
	9,554							

Where RRS is appropriate

The RRS approach may be more appropriate than Pareto where the parts values are similar, manufacture process have high set-up time, or the key attribute in the supply chain is the volume throughput not the inventory value. It becomes very much a business judgement as to whether RRS or Pareto is favoured.

Inventory matrix

To overcome this an inventory matrix can be used, which combines these two approaches, thus dividing the parts into two simple three-way splits to create a nine-box matrix. This has the advantage of being able to differentiate between high-value/high-volume products and high-value/low-volume products which may benefit from different planning rules.

Table 6.13 shows how we can use different techniques to provide a more sophisticated approach than the simple division into three groups.

Table 6.13 Inventory matrix of ABC Pareto and runner, repeater and stranger

	Runner	Repeater	Stranger
A	High Volume/High Value JIT style production	Medium Volume/High Value MRP Consider EOQ Ordering	Low Volume/High Value MRP Lot-for-Lot
B	High Volume/Medium Value MRP Consider EOQ Ordering	Medium Volume/Medium Value MRP Consider EOQ Ordering	Low Volume/High Value
C	High Volume/Low Value Vendor Managed Inventory	Medium Volume/Low Value Re-order point Bulk Purchase	Low Volume/Low Value Make to Order

Alternatives matrices

We began this section by talking about the different attributes of the parts and so far we have only focused on value and volume. The inventory matrix approach allows us to possibly consider, within our business operation, the most important attributes for the product. It may be that we are in the business of making products that have a variable shelf-life. Thus we can replace the runner, repeater and stranger with long, medium and short shelf life, which would allow us to alter our policies in line with the difficulty of managing shelf life.

Developing a plan that will succeed

So far we have built an inventory plan/policy based on the sum of the average cycle stock and safety stock; this is also known as the average inventory.

Average inventory is the level of inventory that our MRP system would attempt to achieve based on the specified parameters that define cycle stock (order quantity or order period) and safety stock (quantity or time). As we know, one of MRP's key assumptions is that what is planned to happen actually occurs, which we know is rarely true, more importantly, as we discussed in the earlier chapter, the very purpose of safety stock is to protect against the unplanned increase in demand and/or the late arrival from our supplier.

What is underage and overage?

Thus our plans are built to protect against late orders and higher than expected demand. As we can see in Figure 6.13, there is almost as much chance that the order will be early or the demand lower than planned. If the demand is *less* than predicted or the supplier does deliver *early* then the stock level would be higher than we would have planned. The overstock we shall call overage – which is defined as when the stock level is above the maximum stock. Conversely, if we have made use of the safety stock we are below the minimum and we will define this as underage. If we are between the minimum and maximum stock we can define this as optimum. These definitions are shown pictorially in Figure 6.14. If parts are in overage MRP's logic will attempt to resolve the situation at the earliest opportunity, by recommending that orders are scheduled-out.

Figure 6.13 Supply and demand variations (Relph and Barrar, 2001)

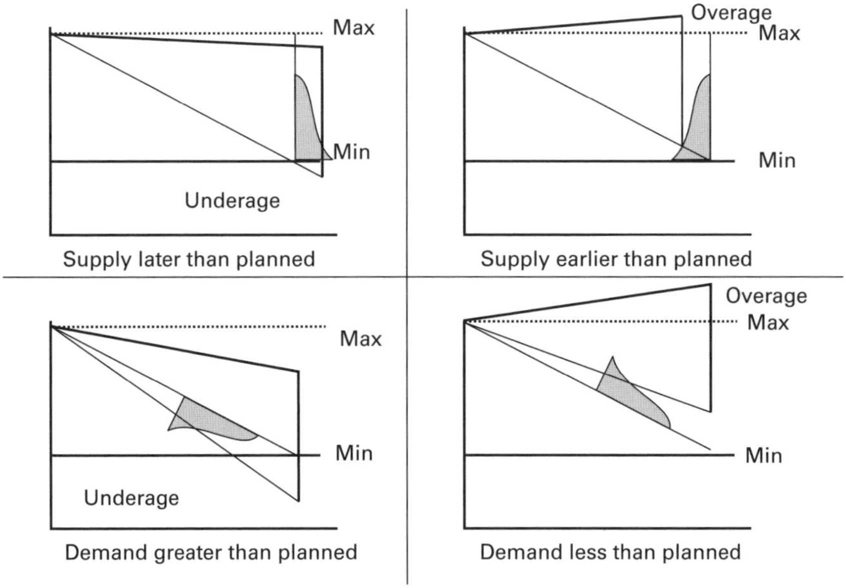

Figure 6.14 Definitions of overage, underage and optimum stock

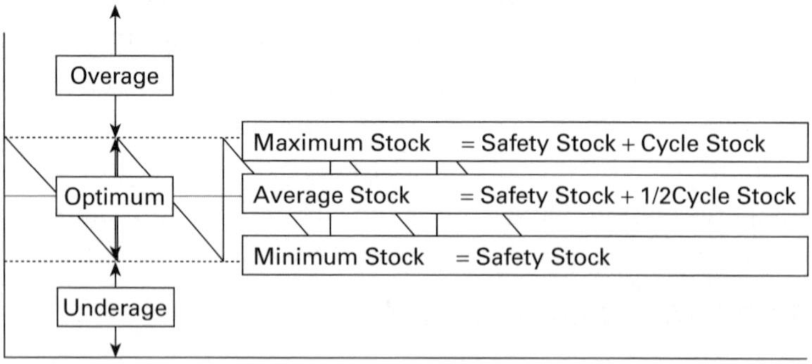

Why is overage important?

In the research conducted by Relph and Barrar (2001) to evaluate the amount of overage in companies, the report abstract summarizes the findings:

> The paper argues that overage is important because there is evidence that, even in well managed businesses a significant proportion of the inventory is in overage at any given time. Evaluations of twenty-inventory profiles from companies in different business sectors show between 10% and 98% of the inventory values were 'in overage'. For most businesses this will not be a trivial amount and any actions that can reduce it will bring significant benefit. The paper concludes that overage should be recognised in the same way as safety stock and thus, formally planned. Hence the effective control of overage will enhance the business's profitability by minimising the inventory investment.

The overage occurs for the same reason that shortage/underage occurs, in that people and systems are not perfect. As a result we get parts moving between shortage, underage, optimum and overage. In the main the MRP system will manage this movement by issuing re-scheduling actions, re-schedule-in for Underage which if ignored will lead to Shortage, at which point the item is the focus of considerable attention. With overage MRP will recommend schedule out or cancel actions; the consequences of ignoring these are less dramatic, in that unlike shortages the immediate effect is not apparent. Assuming the part is current the Overage will eventually be used; the costs of Overage are associated with extra storage, cost of holding and risk of obsolescence. While it can be argued that some overage is inevitable and should be tolerated it is important to ensure that it remains a small amount. As the research showed, companies can operate with up to 98 per cent overage. The important step is to recognize the existence of the overage conditions and then agree upon the appropriate action. This is self-evident as, according to the renowned Management Consultant Peter Drucker, 'What gets measured gets managed'. It is worthwhile being a little more specific about overage to ensure that we do not focus on parts unnecessarily. The two questions related to overage are first how much, and second how long will it last. If we were to focus only on the highest value overages using a simple list in descending overage value order we would identify high-value items but they will be consumed in a short period of time. This is what we call overage dissipation.

What is overage dissipation?

Dissipation is defined as 'how long before the item returns to within the optimum range'.

Figure 6.15 shows a typical stock level above maximum, ie 'in overage' as the part is consumed it falls below the maximum; when this happens the item is no longer in overage. However, the overage dissipation is only complete when the stock reaches the minimum. This is because the next order due will take the item back up to maximum. We can express the overage dissipation as a length of time, ie overage days. The overage days are a simple expression of how long before the item returns to normal. This can provide a useful additional filter to the value, as a high-value overage item whose dissipation is only five overage days is less of a worry than an item that has a dissipation of 50 days.

Figure 6.15 Overage dissipation

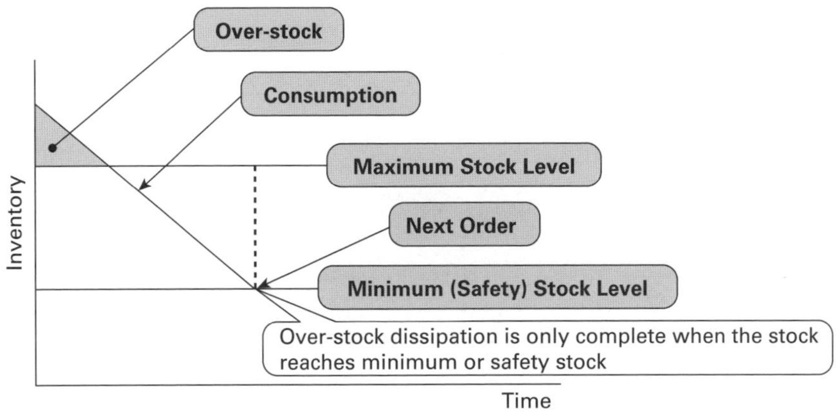

It is useful to provide generalized categories of overage. Table 6.14 shows a typical set of inventory conditions that are often used with inventory reporting.

Table 6.14 Inventory conditions and definitions

Inventory Condition	Definition
Shortage	Stock is 0
Underage	Stock is below the minimum
Optimum	Stock is between the minimum and maximum
Overage	Stock is above the maximum
Severe Overage	Stock is twice the maximum
Excess	Stock is > 12 months demand
Surplus	Stock is > 24 months demand

The benefit of categorization is to be able to simply express the inventory performance and identify appropriate actions/level of management review against each inventory condition. For example, all surplus items should be reviewed by a senior manager, confirmation that all orders have been cancelled etc.

Importance of the next order

When defining overage we specified that it was not truly recovered until the stock level reaches the minimum stock. Figure 6.16 shows that if the order arrives before the stock reaches minimum the item is returned to overage, albeit for a small period of time.

Figure 6.16 Incomplete overage dissipation

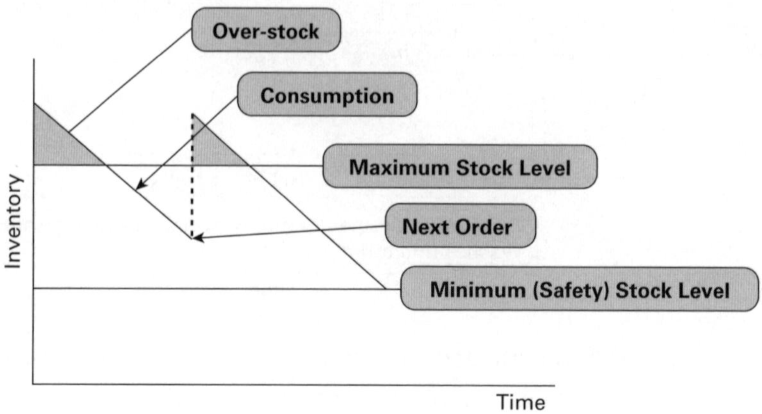

This serves to emphasize the importance of the next order in the management of overage.

It is possible to create a report which identifies items where the next order is due to be received before the overage has dissipated to the minimum stock level. In theory this will mirror the re-schedule out action report, however this list is usually presented in part number order so the 'needle is well hidden in the haystack'. Presenting an action report in inventory value order will ensure that if time is short the highest value items are actioned first.

Summary

In this chapter we have looked at the tools and techniques available for determining the optimum order size and safety stock. They are by their nature complex and need to be carefully considered before use and setting the key parameters of order size and safety stock in MRP. However, just using judgement or blindly accepting the recommendations from suppliers will lead the planners to an inevitable cycle of increasing batch sizes and safety stock, driving up inventory followed by a purge when they are reduced by commands from senior management, only to creep back up as suppliers press for increased order sizes and delivery failure permits the adding of safety stock.

The supplier and the manufacturing departments both have a significant influence over the determination of the order size. In this chapter we looked at tools that the planner can use to ensure the influence of the supplier or manufacturer does not have a detrimental effect on the inventory. The tools help inventory planners to determine if the discount offered by a supplier, for a larger order size, is truly in the company's best interest.

It is worth quickly summarizing the key difference between the use of statistical safety stock and safety time. While statistical safety stock techniques take account of the demand, supply variations and the order size, the formulas do not include the unit cost of the part. Thus, when a safety stock calculation makes a recommendation of 442 units it is irrespective of the unit cost of the part. So if the product was £10 it would only require £4,420 of inventory; if, however, the part was £1,000 the safety stock inventory value would be £442,000. The decision to accept these different levels of investment would be very different. It is therefore important when planning safety inventory always to extend the calculations to include the unit cost and keep an eye on the return on investment, and balance the reduced 'lost sales' with the additional inventory value.

In most businesses the number of parts to be managed is measured in many thousands, thus it quickly becomes impractical to manage them as individual parts and grouping them using predefined rules becomes a useful tool in managing these large numbers. In this chapter we looked at a range of tools that help the parts classification process focus the decision on managing and optimizing the inventory level. We showed that moving the Pareto boundaries was a more effective way to alter the inventory level than changing the order size or safety stocks in any specific group.

Finally, having set the order size and safety stock we saw the importance of focusing on overage and its dissipation as a way of ensuring the right focus. There are always a lot of MRP actions that need to be actioned, and overage analysis helps identify which will have the greatest influence on the inventory level. Utilizing the inventory condition (ie underage as a pre-warning of imminent stock out or late delivery) is an additional way of providing a dynamic parts classification that helps the business focus on inventory planning and balancing.

Tools and techniques discussed in this chapter

- Inventory saw tooth
- Order/batch size
  - Economic order quantity
  - Economic order period
  - Order period
- Safety stock
  - Statistical safety stock
  - Safety time
  - Hybrid safety
- Parts classification
  - Pareto ABC
  - Runner repeater and stranger
  - Classification matrix
- Overage
- Inventory condition

References

Harris, F W (1913) How many parts to make at once, *Factory, The Magazine of Management*, **10**(2), pp 135–36, 152

Relph, G and Barrar, P (2001) Overage inventory – How does it occur and why it is important? *International Journal of Production Economics*, ISIR Proceedings (81–82), pp 163–71

Schmidt, M, Hartmann, W and Nyhuis, P (2007) Simulation based comparison of safety stock calculation methods, *CIRP Annals – Manufacturing Technology*, **61**(1), pp 403–06

Waters, C (2003) *Inventory Control and Management* (2nd edn), John Wiley & Sons, Chichester

You do the maths

Using the formulae for EOQ and EOP from Excel 6.2 extend the Pareto Table in Excel 6.8 and calculate for each part the EOQ and EOP, assuming the cost of ordering is £5.00 and cost of holding is 30 per cent.

1. Now look at the EOP values and compare their values as they change down the Pareto list.
2. In Table 6.8 we divided the list in three, and allocated the days of supply based on Class. How good is that decision compared with EOQ?
3. Now divide the list into six groups. Try:
   - **a** using percent limits,
   - **b** using the EOP as a guide and rounding to the nearest number of days or weeks.
4. Which do you think is the best approach?
5. What happens if you alter the cost of ordering or cost of holding inventory?
6. For example:
   - **a** Only Reduce the Cost of Ordering to £4.50
   - **b** Only Increase the Inventory Holding percentage 34%
   - **c** Change Both

Table 6.15 (Copy of Table 6.8) Inventory policy statement including safety stock

Class	Annual Spend Value £	Daily Going Rate	Class Limits	No of Parts	Days of Supply	Safety Stock Days	No of Orders	Average Cycle Inventory	Safety Stock Value	Total Planned Inventory
A	£165,689.52	£662.76	80.0%	7	5	5	350	£1,656.99	£3,313.98	£4,970.97
B	£36,907.55	£147.63	95.0%	10	20	10	125	£1,476.37	£1,476.37	£2,952.74
C	£10,915.74	£43.66		10	80	20	31	£1,746.53	£873.26	£2,619.79
Totals	£ 213,512.81	£854.05		27			506	£4,879.88	£5,663.61	£10,543.49

NOTE Average Inventory is half Days of Supply

Excel 6.9 You do the maths exercise

	A	B	C	D	E	F	G	H	I	J	K
1	Purchase Order Cost	£5.00									
2	Carrying Rate	30%									
3	Working Days	250									
4											
5											
6	Count	Part Number	Annual Usage or Demand	Cost Per Part	Annual Spend Value	ABC	EOQ	EOP	Rounded EOP	No of Orders	Average Inventory
7	1	B78811ZD	1,324	£42.84	£56,720.16	A	32.10	6.06	5	50	£567.20
8	2	B78812ZF	987	£41.87	£41,325.69	A	28.03	7.10	5	50	£413.26
9	3	B78810741A	1,012	£18.50	£18,722.00	A	42.70	10.55	10	25	£374.44
10	4	N6554004M0256	523	£35.08	£18,346.84	A	22.29	10.66	10	25	£366.94
11	5	SK98751	46	£316.19	£14,544.74	A	2.20	11.97	10	25	£290.89
12	6	LE763	781	£11.11	£8,676.91	A	48.41	15.50	15	17	£260.31
13	7	D0883030014C	267	£27.54	£7,353.18	A	17.98	16.83	15	17	£220.60
14	8	C78810742A	360	£16.87	£6,073.20	B	26.67	18.52	20	13	£242.93
15	9	D0862060018Y	163	£33.26	£5,421.38	B	12.78	19.60	20	13	£216.86
16	10	C78810761A	567	£8.43	£4,779.81	B	47.35	20.88	20	13	£191.19
17	11	LE02	396	£11.09	£4,391.64	B	34.50	21.78	20	13	£175.67
18	12	B78812001B	458	£7.10	£3,251.80	B	46.37	25.31	25	10	£162.59
19	13	KN552130	10	£319.98	£3,199.80	B	1.02	25.52	25	10	£159.99
20	14	A0906030015	18	£150.22	£2,703.96	B	2.00	27.76	30	9	£162.24
21	15	B78810721A	749	£3.44	£2,576.56	B	85.19	28.44	30	9	£154.59
22	16	D0991020012	164	£14.60	£2,394.40	B	19.35	29.50	30	9	£143.66
23	17	D0862070019Y	60	£35.25	£2,115.00	B	7.53	31.39	30	9	£126.90
24	18	D0978040014	35	£57.63	£2,017.05	C	4.50	32.14	30	9	£121.02
25	19	A78810601E	450	£4.20	£1,890.00	C	59.76	33.20	35	8	£132.30
26	20	B78818AE	35	£49.57	£1,734.95	C	4.85	34.65	35	8	£121.45
27	21	C78810762A	199	£7.44	£1,480.56	C	29.86	37.51	40	7	£118.44
28	22	D0753100033	75	£15.36	£1,152.00	C	12.76	42.53	45	6	£103.68
29	23	D1017040014	10	£95.36	£953.60	C	1.87	46.74	45	6	£85.82
30	24	KDB300600	8	£93.75	£750.00	C	1.69	52.70	55	5	£82.50
31	25	A0889030013	52	£9.59	£498.68	C	13.44	64.64	65	4	£64.83
32	26	B30880112C	700	£0.45	£315.00	C	227.71	81.33	80	4	£50.40
33	27	B30880113C	105	£1.18	£123.90	C	54.46	129.67	130	2	£32.21
34			9,554		£213,512.81					376	£5,142.91
35											

EOQ	Cell G6 then copy down to G32	=SQRT((2*C6*$B$1)/(D6*$B$2))
EOP	Cell H6 then copy down to H32	=(G6/C6)*$B$3
Rounded EOP	Cell I6 then copy down to I32	=ROUND(H6/5,0)*5
No of Orders	Cell J6 then copy down to J32	=ROUNDUP($B$3/I6,0)
Average Inventory	Cell K6 then copy down to K32	=(E6/$B$3)*(I6/2)

Notes for Excel 6.9 You do the maths exercise

1 The EOQs do not have any direct relation to their position in the Pareto list, but the EOPs increase as they move further down the list.

This is similar to the approach taken in Tables 6.5 and 6.6.

2 The rounded EOPs for Class A range from 5 to 15 days, compared with the chosen value of 5 days. Similarly, for Class B the EOPs range from 20 to 30 days, compared with 20 days. And finally, for Class C the EOP range is 30 to 130 days, compared with 80 days.

3 If we were to try to divide into the Pareto, based on Annual Spend, in to 6 groups rather than the traditional 3 (ABC) using percentage limits is pure guesswork.

Using rounded EOP as a guide is significantly easier. This is particularly true if you start to alter the order cost and holding cost percentage, as in this exercise. Alter the Order cost value and Holding cost values and look at which parts have a rounded EOP of 15.

4 By changing the holding cost and ordering cost the EOQ and EOP value change which affects the number of orders and the average inventory.

   a Decreasing the cost of ordering from £5.00 to £4.50 will allow more orders to be placed for the same overall cost. This will lead to a reduction in inventory from £5,142.91 to £5,028.00 i.e. £114.91 despite an increase in the numbers of orders from 376 to 382 i.e. 6 more orders.

   b If you increase the inventory holding cost percentage from 30% to 34%, the inventory reduced from £5,142.91 to £4,966.03 i.e. £176.88 but the number of orders increases by 11.

If you change both the inventory reduces to £4,849.10 and the number of orders increases to 395.

k-curve methodology 07

Introduction

This chapter will describe the *k*-curve methodology (KCM) developed in the late 1980s/early 1990s, which built on Murdoch and Brown's work on exchange curves in the 1960s and 1970s. The use of exchange curves in the analysis and evaluation of order size improves upon the strengths of Pareto and EOQ and addresses the weaknesses. First, we will look at the strengths and weaknesses of EOQ, Pareto and exchange curve. Second, a brief history of the development of *k*-curve. Third, how the '*k*-curve' is created and how it resolves the weaknesses of EOQ and Pareto. The chapter concludes with the creation of a composite curve that becomes the basis for planning inventory in MRP systems.

In the previous chapter we looked at the ways in which we can determine the cycle stock and safety stocks for individual items and how using Pareto or the Inventory Matrix we can begin to consider all the parts that we are trying to manage. The key problem facing any operations manager is how to determine the optimum inventory level. The tools described in the previous chapter all, in their own way, help determine the optimum. However, they all have their strengths and weaknesses. It is the weaknesses that remain the key barrier to their effective application in an operations management. So what are these weaknesses?

- EOQ – it needs to know the cost of ordering and the cost of holding inventory; both these values are difficult to determine. I once asked a finance manager for the cost of ordering and after 12 months his considered reply was 'you can have any value from £1 to £100 depending on what resources you wish to consider are part of the cost of ordering'.
- EOQ – it also relies on the assumption that the demand (which is usually based on 12 months) is constant. This is rarely the case, although can largely be overcome by more frequent calculations.

- Safety stock – the main statistical formulae typically do not use the unit cost of the item, so they in effect will 'protect the parts at any cost', which is OK if you have an unlimited budget, but for most organizations this is rarely the case.
- Pareto – this ascribes a rank/importance of the part based on their annual spends, and divides the whole population of parts into three groups. In many businesses simply dividing into three groups is not sufficiently detailed. Dividing into three groups by percentage only requires two decisions: 80/20 and 95/50. Now consider how you might divide into six groups. It is clear very quickly that this is not really practical.
- Pareto – the fundamental principle is correct: the important *few* have to be closely managed, and the low-value *many* are infrequently replenished with large batch sizes, *but* this leads to too many unconnected decisions, *and* it's too simple for anything other than a simple business.
- Pareto forces a predetermined per cent into each class regardless of what's appropriate for each item.
- Pareto – like the EOQ – makes the assumption that demand is constant over 12 months. The effect of this is more serious than its effect on EOQ, and can be seen in Table 7.1. As the demand changes by quarter the classification based on the quarter and the Pareto classification based on the annual average is different.

Table 7.1 Comparison of Pareto classification for different demand patterns during the annual period

Groups	Q1	Q2	Q3	Q4	Annual Demand
Flat	100	100	100	100	400
Seasonal	50	125	150	75	400
End of Life	175	100	75	50	400
New Product	25	75	100	200	400
Pareto rank Demand	**Q1**	**Q2**	**Q3**	**Q4**	**Annual Demand**
Flat	B	B	B	B	B
Seasonal	B/C	A	A	B/C	B
End of Life	A	B	C	C	B
New Product	C	C	B	A	B

It is always easy to criticize, but what is needed is a solution to the problem.

History of *k*-curve

History of the exchange curve

Since the early 1960s the development of scientific inventory control theories by academics such as J Murdoch (1965), C D Lewis (1970), R G Brown (1982) and S Shah (1992), have all built on the principle of the *exchange curve*. The exchange curve principle is shown diagrammatically in Figure 7.1. The development of the principle over the last 50 years has meant that there is a strong academic and operational pedigree and there are a range of software products available based on the principle. In summary the principle states:

The exchange curve principle

> Inventory value can only be reduced in exchange for increased number of transactions.

That is to say, to reduce inventory investment smaller quantities *must* be purchased. This will result in *more* transactions needing to be processed, requiring *better*, more capable processes to achieve this without increasing the risk of failure.

In this chapter we will focus on the *k*-curve methodology (KCM) which was initially developed as part of a PhD by Shah (1992) in collaboration with the inventory planning team at IBM's award-winning manufacturing plant in Havant, Hampshire in the UK.

It was this project which set out to resolve the question 'What does it cost to place an order? The finance manager's response to this question was, after some considerable thought, 'You can have any value from £1 to £100 depending on what resources you wish to consider are part of the cost of ordering.' This response set off a train of thought that concluded that we were trying to solve the wrong problem. It was already stated by both (Lewis, 1970) and (Brown 1982) that you could treat the 2C/i in the EOQ equation as a constant. The extension researched by (Shah 1992) was to ask why not simply vary the constant *k* between a range of values, say, 1 and 100, and look at the result. Thus the *k*-curve was created and the methodology was born. The methodology was used to set the MRP parameters for IBM's Havant Plant in the 1990s and won awards within IBM for its innovation. IBM sponsored

Figure 7.1 Exchange curve principle

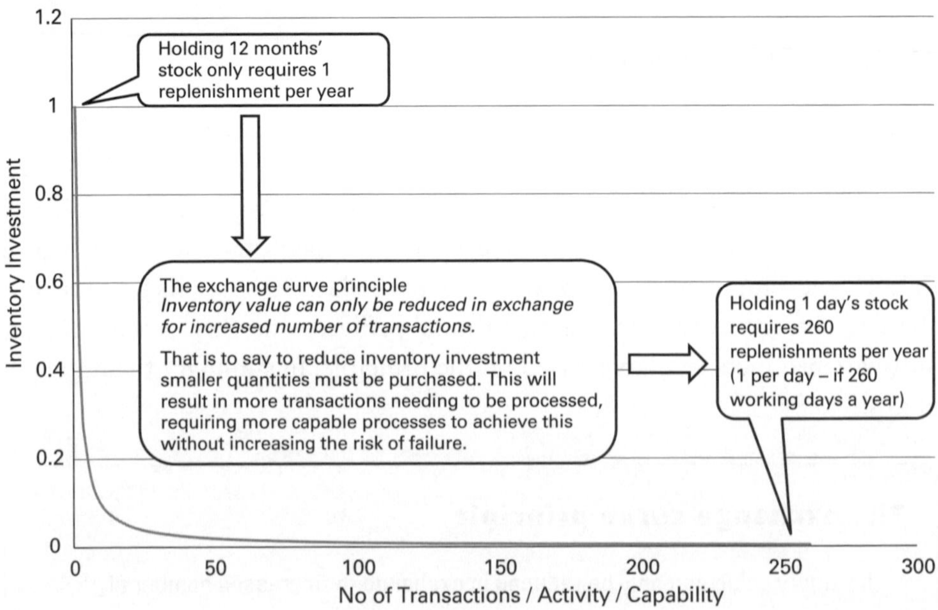

further research (Dupernex, 1993) to examine the optimum number of classes and the effect of different datasets. Following on, Dupernex (1997) went on to extend the optimization to cover batch manufacturing environments where capacity was constrained. In the late 1990s IBM extended the use of the methodology into their consultancy work; it was used during projects with large multinationals like Heidelberg Druken Machin, Wartsila and Mann+Hummell. It was published in academic journals by Burcher, Dupernex and Relph (1996) focusing on theory and Handley (1999) who reviewed the benefits of implementation. IBM developed software AIM (Advanced Inventory Manager) which finally became DIOS (Dynamic Inventory Optimization Solution). Schwarz (2000) extended the methodology, looking at more sophisticated approaches to determining the cycle stock using heuristic optimization. Relph (2006) researched the use of optimization tools that were already built into MRP systems and the potential for implementation of *k*-curve. The research conducted four six-month case studies looking at the current practice and then the effect of using *k*-curve on the planning process. The methodology is still used by IBM consultants for their clients. We continue to champion the methodology when working with our own clients to help them optimize their MRP systems and business operations.

Pareto exchange curve

In Chapter 6 we saw how, in Table 6.10, by changing the Class A/B Pareto percentage limit from 80 per cent to 82 per cent we reduced inventory. We also observed when comparing Table 6.8 and Table 6.10 that this reduction caused an increase in number of orders from 506 to 562.5. We can extend this example by varying the A/B class limit from 75 to 85 per cent in equal steps around 80 per cent and varying the B/C limit from 93 to 97 per cent. The results of this can be seen in Table 7.2; when the numbers are plotted, as shown in Figure 7.2, we can see from the operation of the exchange curve principle for Pareto *that inventory reduction can only be achieved through an increase in orders.*

Table 7.2 Varying values of A/B and B/C Pareto limits to create an exchange curve

	A/B Percentage	B/C Percentage	No of Orders	Average Inventory
1	75.0%	93.0%	436.50	£7,029.74
2	77.5%	94.0%	447.00	£6,527.08
3	80.0%	95.0%	495.00	£5,862.30
4	82.5%	96.0%	543.00	£5,256.55
5	85.0%	97.0%	591.00	£4,697.03

Figure 7.2 Pareto (ABC) exchange curve based on Table 7.2

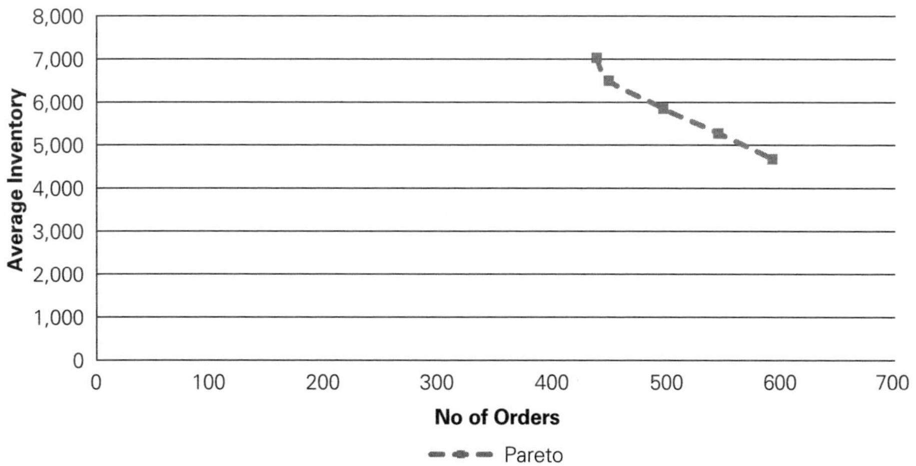

In summary the weaknesses of using Pareto to determine this exchange are:

- With only three groups the granularity is quite coarse.
- The decisions between the Class A/B boundary and the Class B/C boundary are arbitrary and assume a level demand.
- The days of supply for all the classes is arbitrary, with the first 20 per cent, irrespective of what they are, getting the lowest days of cover.

The next sections will cover the development and generation of an alternative approach, the *k*-curve, and show how the *k*-curve brings together the strengths of both Pareto and EOQ, and eliminates their weaknesses.

Generating a *k*-curve

There are three key stages to the creation of the k-curve:

- Stage 1: Expressing the EOQ as an economic period.
- Stage 2: Building a bridge between Pareto and Economic Order Period (EOP).
- Stage 3: The variation of *k* to create an exchange curve.

As we saw in the creation of the Pareto exchange curve in Table 7.2, if we express the order policy in terms of days of supply (DOS) for each value class we can calculate the total average inventory and the total number of deliveries per year. Using these two values we can plot the exchange curve as shown in Figure 7.2.

Stage 1: Expressing the EOQ as the economic order period (EOP)

Figure 7.3 shows the steps for expressing the EOQ as EOP: the first step is to substitute *k* for 2C/i in the EOQ formula (1), which gives us the simplified EOQ (2). You can create it using Excel 7.1 and try out different parts from the '27 parts' list in Appendix B to see the variations for different part numbers.

The next step is to convert the EOQ to an order period by dividing by the annual demand quantity (D) which gives the EOP in years (3). Expressing this using the EOQ formula (4) gives a long-winded formula, but with a little

Figure 7.3 Classical EOQ and simplification (Brown, 1980: 131 with examples)

	D = Annual Demand Quantity C = Cost of Ordering / Set-up P = Unit Cost I = inventory holding rate as %		1,000 £4.50 £75.00 30%	
1	Economic Order Quantity	$Q = \sqrt{\frac{2*D*C}{P*i}}$	$Q = \sqrt{\frac{2*1{,}000*4.50}{£75.00*30\%}}$	20
	Common Factor (k)	2C/i = k	2 * £4.50 / 30%	30
2	Simplified EOQ	$\sqrt{kD/P}$	$\sqrt{30 * 1{,}000 / £75.00}$	20
3	Economic Order Period (EOP)	EOQ / D	20 / 1,000	0.02 years
4	Economic Order Period (EOP)	$\left(\sqrt{\frac{2*D*C}{P*i}}\right) / D$		
5		$\sqrt{k/D*P}$	$\sqrt{30 / 1{,}000 * £75.00}$	0.02 years
	Annual Demand Value = A = D*P Demand Quantity * Unit Cost. It is easier to express the EOP in days, using W (working days) = 250			
6	Economic Order Period (EOP)	$W * \sqrt{k/A}$	$250 * \sqrt{30 / £75{,}000}$	5 days
7	Average Inventory	0.5 * EOP * A/W	$\frac{0.5 * 5 * £75{,}000}{250}$	£750.00
8	No of deliveries	Working days / EOP	250 / 5	50

Excel 7.1 Simplified economic order quantity (EOQ) using *k*

	A	B	C	D	E
1	Annual Demand Quantity	D	1000		
2	Constant 2C/i	k	£30.00		
3	Cost per Part	P	£75.00		
4					
5					
6	Economic Order Quantity		20.00		

Enter this formula

Cell C6 = SQRT((K*D)/P) = SQRT((C2*C1)/C3)

algebra the formula can be simplified to (5). This can be further simplified if we substitute Annual Spend for Demand × Unit Cost; remember that a Pareto curve is created using Annual Spend. Also expressing the EOP in years is cumbersome; it would be better to work in days. Typically we use 250 working days (W) in a year, based on five days in a week. This final substitution leaves us with a very simple formula for the EOP in days (6). From this simple formula we can determine the average inventory (7) held. If we know the order period we also know how may deliveries we will get a year (8); you can create an Excel model using the formulae shown in Excel 7.2.

Excel 7.2 EOP in days based on Excel 7.1 EOQ

	A	B	C	D
1	Annual Demand Quantity	D	1,000	
2	Constant 2C/i	k	30	
3	Cost per Part	p	£75.00	
4	Annual Demand Value	A	£75,000.00	
5	Working Days a year	W	250	
6				
7	Economic Order Period	EOP in Years	0.02	
8		EOP Simplified	0.02	
9	Economic Order Period in Days	EOP in Days = E	5.00	
10				
11		Average Inventory	£187.50	
12		No of deliveries	50	

Enter these formulae

EOP in Years	Cell C7	=SQRT((K*d)/p))/D	=SQRT((C2*C1)/C3))/C1
EOP simplified	Cell C8	=SQRT(k/A)	=SQRT(C2/C4)
EOP in Days = E	Cell C9	=W(SQRT(k/A))	=C5*(SQRT(C2/C4))
Average Inventory	Cell C11	=0.5*EOP * p	=0.5*C9*C3
No of deliveries	Cell C12	=W / EOP	=C5/C9

You can experiment using the parts detailed from Appendix B.

Stage 2: Building a bridge between Pareto and EOP

This next step now applies the EOP calculation to all the parts in the group being managed; in our case with the 27 parts from Appendix B, we can calculate the EOP for each of items. Using the formula derived in Excel 7.2, the results can be seen in Excel 7.3 opposite.

Excel 7.3 Calculation of EOQ and EOP values on 27 sample parts

	A	B	C	D	E	F	G
1	Constant *k*	30					
2	Working Days	250					
3							
4							
5	Count	Part Number	Annual Usage or Demand	Cost Per Part	Annual Spend Value	EOQ	EOP Days
6	1	B78811ZD	1324	£42.84	£56,720.16	30	5.75
7	2	B78812ZF	987	£41.87	£41,325.69	27	6.74
8	3	B78810741A	1012	£18.50	£18,722.00	41	10.01
9	4	N6554004M0256	523	£35.08	£18,346.84	21	10.11
10	5	SK98751	46	£316.19	£14,544.74	2	11.35
11	6	LE763	781	£11.11	£8,676.91	46	14.70
12	7	D0883030014C	267	£27.54	£7,353.18	17	15.97
13	8	C78810742A	360	£16.87	£6,073.20	25	17.57
14	9	D0862060018Y	163	£33.26	£5,421.38	12	18.60
15	10	C78810761A	567	£8.43	£4,779.81	45	19.81
16	11	LE02	396	£11.09	£4,391.64	33	20.66
17	12	B78812001B	458	£7.10	£3,251.80	44	24.01
18	13	KN552130	10	£319.98	£3,199.80	1	24.21
19	14	A0906030015	18	£150.22	£2,703.96	2	26.33
20	15	B78810721A	749	£3.44	£2,576.56	81	26.98
21	16	D0991020012	164	£14.60	£2,394.40	18	27.98
22	17	D0862070019Y	60	£35.25	£2,115.00	7	29.77
23	18	D0978040014	35	£57.63	£2,017.05	4	30.49
24	19	A78810601E	450	£4.20	£1,890.00	57	31.50
25	20	B78818AE	35	£49.57	£1,734.95	5	32.87
26	21	C78810762A	199	£7.44	£1,480.56	28	35.59
27	22	D0753100033	75	£15.36	£1,152.00	12	40.34
28	23	D1017040014	10	£95.36	£953.60	2	44.34
29	24	KDB300600	8	£93.75	£750.00	2	50.00
30	25	A0889030013	52	£9.59	£498.68	13	61.32
31	26	B30880112C	700	£0.45	£315.00	216	77.15
32	27	B30880113C	105	£1.18	£123.90	52	123.02
33		Totals			£213,512.81		

Enter these formulae

EOQ	Cell F6 *then copy down to* F32	=SQRT($B$2*C6/D6)
EOP Days	Cell G6 *then copy down to* G32	=$B$2*SQRT($B$1/E6)

If you examine the calculated values of EOQ and EOP you will see that while the EOQ appear somewhat random the EOP's relationship with the Annual Spend for the items is such that as the Annual Spend Value decreases the EOP increases. This conforms to the logic used when applying the 'estimated' cycle stock for traditional Pareto Planning. Thus we now have a mechanism that will vary the size of the order (in days) in direct relation with the annual spend of the part. As with the original Pareto approach of using five days for Class A, 20 days for Class B and 125 days for Class C, we are keeping the order size small for the high-value parts. However, it is obvious that setting an order size to 5.75 days or 27.99 days makes little sense as no system or supplier will deliver to that level of accuracy. It would be far more logical to use order sizes that reflected what would happen in practice, so order sizes of 5, 10, 20, 40, 80, 160 and so on would be a good place to start. If we plot the Annual Demand Value vs Economic Order Period on a Log/Log scale and draw gridlines at 5, 10, 20 etc we get an interesting result, as seen in Figure 7.4 below.

Figure 7.4 Effect of changing *k* on value class population

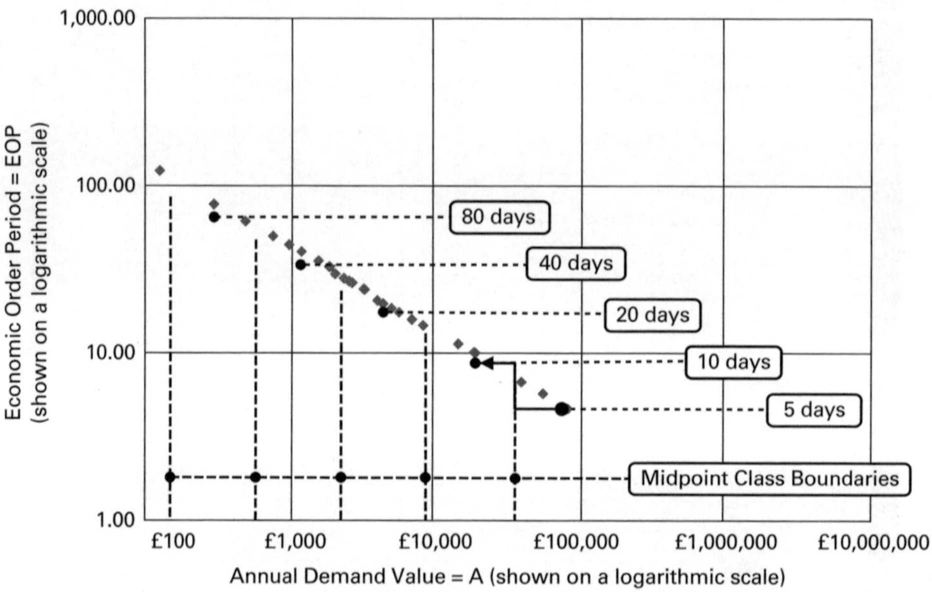

The points represent each of the individual parts from our list of 27 parts; the horizontal lines represent the order sizes of 5, 10, 20 days etc. It would be logical to round our exact EOP calculations to the nearest practical value, as with rounding the most logical place is halfway between each of these values, these points are shown as the vertical dash lines, we can see that the first two parts would be in the five days group, the next few would be in the 10 day grouping. The halfway point between the EOP values of 5 days and 10 days on the log scale can be used to identify the Annual Demand Value that is the switching point for changing from one EOP value to the next. The derivation of the calculations are shown in Figure 7.5, Excel 7.4 and Excel 7.5.

Excel 7.4 Value class tables for EOP

	A	B	C	D	E	F
1	Constant *k*	30				
2	Working Days	250				
3						
4						
5	Value Class	Cycle Days	Class Limit			
6	1	5	£37,500			
7	2	10	£9,375			
8	3	20	£2,344			
9	4	40	£586			
10	5	80	£146			
11	6	160	£0			
12	7		£0			
13	8		£0			
14	9		£0			

Enter this formula

Class Limit Cell C6 *then copy down to* C14 =IF($B7=0,0,+$B$2*$B$2*$B$1/($B6*$B7))
If there are no values in C12 to C14 formula returns a 0

Thus we have now divided the list of parts into classes, similar to the Pareto exercise in Chapter 6. However, this approach has two distinct advantages: first, there are more boundaries, which provides better granularity when dealing with large populations of parts. Second, the order sizes chosen in each group are logical and the parts are selected based on an economic principle, unlike the Pareto approach where the order size is a matter of judgement, with the lowest order size being applied to the first 20 per cent irrespective of their annual spend.

For this to be practical we need to be able to express the information in the Figure 7.5 in a simple tabular form. This will enable the division of the group of parts into 'value classes' as opposed to ABC Class or Pareto Class. This can be done as seen in Excel 7.5; the Class Limit represents the point at which it would be most economical to switch from Class 1 and an order cycle of five days to Class 2 and an order cycle of 10 days.

Figure 7.5 Calculation of the midpoint class boundary

A = Annual Demand Value	£75,000.00		
k= constant	30		
W = working days	250		
EOP = Economic Order Period	$W * \sqrt{k/A}$	$250 * \sqrt{30 / £75,000}$	5 days
First we need to change the formula to give the Annual Spend for a given value of EOP -> E			
Annual Demand = A_1, where EOP = 5	$W^2 * k / E_1^2$	250 * 250 * 30 / 5* 5	£75,000
Annual Demand = A_2, where EOP = 10	$W^2 * k / E_2^2$	250 * 250 * 30 / 10 * 10	£18,750
Next we want to find the Class Limit at the midpoint between A1 and A2 in Figure 7.4, but because it is on the log scale we need to use the Log of A			
Midpoint Demand $Log(A_m)$	$[Log(A_1) + Log(A_2)]/2$	This needs simplifying using Algebra	
	$[Log(W^2 * k / E_1^2) + Log(W^2 * k / E_2^2)]/2 => [Log(W^2 * k / E_1^2 * E_2^2)]/2 => [Log(W^2 * k / E_1 * E_2)]$		
Midpoint Demand A_m	$W^2 * k / E_1 * E_2$	250 * 250 * 30/5 * 10	£37,500

Excel 7.5 Value class and limits applied to list of parts

	A	B	C	D	E	F	G	H
1	Constant *k*	30						
2	Working Days	250						
3								
4								
5	Value Class	Cycle Days	Class Limit					
6	1	5	£37,500					
7	2	10	£ 9,375					
8	3	20	£ 2,344					
9	4	40	£ 586					
10	5	80	£ 146					
11	6	160	£0					
12	7		£0					
13	8		£0					
14	9		£0					
15								
16								
17	Count	Part Number	Annual Usage or Demand	Cost Per Part	Annual Spend Value £	EOP Days	Value Class	Cycle Days
18	1	B78811ZD	1,324	£42.84	£56,720.16	5.75	1	5
19	2	B78812ZF	987	£41.87	£41,325.69	6.74	1	5
20	3	B78810741A	1,012	£18.50	£18,722.00	10.01	2	10
21	4	N6554004M0256	523	£35.08	£18,346.84	10.11	2	10
22	5	SK98751	46	£316.19	£14,544.74	11.35	2	10
23	6	LE763	781	£11.11	£8,676.91	14.70	3	20
24	7	D0883030014C	267	£27.54	£7,353.18	15.97	3	20
25	8	C78810742A	360	£16.87	£6,073.20	17.57	3	20
26	9	D0862060018Y	163	£33.26	£5,421.38	18.60	3	20
27	10	C78810761A	567	£8.43	£4,779.81	19.81	3	20
28	11	LE02	396	£11.09	£4,391.64	20.66	3	20
29	12	B78812001B	458	£7.10	£3,251.80	24.01	3	20
30	13	KN552130	10	£319.98	£3,199.80	24.21	3	20
31	14	A0906030015	18	£150.22	£2,703.96	26.33	3	20
32	15	B78810721A	749	£3.44	£2,576.56	26.98	3	20
33	16	D0991020012	164	£14.60	£2,394.40	27.98	3	20
34	17	D0862070019Y	60	£35.25	£2,115.00	29.77	4	40
35	18	D0978040014	35	£57.63	£2,017.05	30.49	4	40
36	19	A78810601E	450	£4.20	£1,890.00	31.50	4	40
37	20	B78818AE	35	£49.57	£1,734.95	32.87	4	40
38	21	C78810762A	199	£7.44	£1,480.56	35.59	4	40
39	22	D0753100033	75	£15.36	£1,152.00	40.34	4	40
40	23	D1017040014	10	£95.36	£953.60	44.34	4	40
41	24	KDB300600	8	£93.75	£750.00	50.00	4	40
42	25	A0889030013	52	£9.59	£498.68	61.32	5	80
43	26	B30880112C	700	£0.45	£315.00	77.15	5	80
44	27	B30880113C	105	£1.18	£123.90	123.02	6	160
45		Totals			£213,512.81			

Enter these formulae

Combine Excel 7.3 and 7.4 by adding 12 rows after row 4

EOP Days Cell E18 then copy down to E44 =$B$2*SQRT($B$1/E18)

Value Class Cell F18 then copy down to F44=IF(E18>$C$6,1,IF(E18>C$7,2,IF(E18>$C$8,3, IF(E18>$C$9,4,IF(E18>$C$10,5,IF(E18>$C$11,6,IF(E18>$C$12,7, IF(E18>$C$13,8,9))))))))

Cycle Days Cell H18 then copy down to H44 =CHOOSE(G18,$B$6,$B$7,$B$8,$B$9,$B$10,$B$11,$B$12,$B$13,$B$14,)

If we applied these Class Limits to the parts in Excel 7.3, we can see how it compares with the original EOP values. This can be seen in Excel 7.5 below. What you will observe is that some items' actual EOP values are less than the selected Cycle days and some are greater, which is as you would expect when using the midpoint to determine the switching point.

So far so good, but as with the original EOQ we have known what the value of *k* is. If we cannot determine *k* we are no further on.

Stage 3: The creation of the k curve

The next step came from the comment from the finance director: 'You can have any value from £1 to £100.' So what if we were to vary the values of *k* from 1 to 100?

To evaluate this we can use the same technique that was used to create Pareto exchange curve, shown in Figure 7.2, by calculating the total cycle stock and the number of orders, using the formulae described in Figure 7.6, (2) Average Inventory and (3) No of deliveries, we can then sum the average inventory and total the number of expected deliveries as shown in Excel 7.6.

Figure 7.6 Calculation of average inventory and number of deliveries

	D = Demand Quality *k* = Common Factor P = Unit Cost A = Annual Demand Value W = Working Days		1,000 30 £75.00 £75,000.00 250	
1	Economic Order Period (EOP) = E	W * $\sqrt{k/A}$	250 * $\sqrt{30 / £7,500}$	5 days
2	Average Inventory	0.5 * E * A/W	0.5 * 5 * 75,000/250	£750.00
3	No of deliveries	Working days / EOP	250 / 5	50

Using Excel 7.6 we can calculate the totals for the number of orders and the average inventory for the different values of *k* from 1–100; these can then be plotted on a scatter chart as seen in Figure 7.7 and Table 7.3. The results in Figure 7.7 show, as with the Pareto exchange curve which is also shown for reference, how the number of deliveries increases as the inventory decreases, thereby exchanging increased deliveries for a lower level of inventory.

Excel 7.6 Number of orders and average inventory calculations

	A	B	C	D	E	F	G	H	I
1	Constant *k*	30							
2	Working Days	250							
3									
4									
5	Value Class	Cycle Days	Class Limit						
6	1	5	£37,500						
7	2	10	£ 9,375						
8	3	20	£ 2,344						
9	4	40	£586						
10	5	80	£146						
11	6	160	£0						
12	7		£0						
13	8		£0						
14	9		£0						
15									
16									
17	Count	Part Number	Annual Usage or Demand	Cost Per Part	Annual Spend Value £	Value Class	Cycle Days	No of Orders	Average Inventory
18	1	B78811ZD	1,324	£42.84	£56,720.16	1	5	50.00	£567.27
19	2	B78812ZF	987	£41.87	£41,325.69	1	5	50.00	£413.26
20	3	B78810741A	1,012	£18.50	£18,722.00	2	10	25.00	£374.44
21	4	N6554004M0256	523	£35.08	£18,346.84	2	10	25.00	£366.93
22	5	SK98751	46	£316.19	£14,544.74	2	10	25.00	£290.89
23	6	LE763	781	£11.11	£8,676.91	3	20	12.50	£347.17
24	7	D0883030014C	267	£27.54	£7,353.18	3	20	12.50	£294.17
25	8	C78810742A	360	£16.87	£6,073.20	3	20	12.50	£242.88
26	9	D0862060018Y	163	£33.26	£5,421.38	3	20	12.50	£216.84
27	10	C78810761A	567	£8.43	£4,779.81	3	20	12.50	£191.22
28	11	LE02	396	£11.09	£4,391.64	3	20	12.50	£175.73
29	12	B78812001B	458	£7.10	£3,251.80	3	20	12.50	£130.01
30	13	KN552130	10	£319.98	£3,199.80	3	20	12.50	£127.99
31	14	A0906030015	18	£150.22	£2,703.96	3	20	12.50	£108.16
32	15	B78810721A	749	£3.44	£2,576.56	3	20	12.50	£103.19
33	16	D0991020012	164	£14.60	£2,394.40	3	20	12.50	£95.74
34	17	D0862070019Y	60	£35.25	£2,115.00	4	40	6.25	£169.20
35	18	D0978040014	35	£57.63	£2,017.05	4	40	6.25	£161.37
36	19	A78810601E	450	£4.20	£1,890.00	4	40	6.25	£151.20
37	20	B78818AE	35	£49.57	£1,734.95	4	40	6.25	£138.80
38	21	C78810762A	199	£7.44	£1,480.56	4	40	6.25	£118.44
39	22	D0753100033	75	£15.36	£1,152.00	4	40	6.25	£92.16
40	23	D1017040014	10	£95.36	£953.60	4	40	6.25	£76.29
41	24	KDB300600	8	£93.75	£750.00	4	40	6.25	£60.00
42	25	A0889030013	52	£9.59	£498.68	5	80	3.13	£79.79
43	26	B30880112C	700	£0.45	£315.00	5	80	3.13	£50.40
44	27	B30880113C	105	£1.18	£123.90	6	160	1.56	£39.65
45		Totals			£213,512.81			370.31	£5,183.19

Enter these formulae

Using Excel 7.5 delete Column F add Column H & I

No of Orders	Cell H18 then copy down to H44	=$B$2/G18
Average Inventory	Cell I18 then copy down to I44	=0.5*(G18*(C18/$B$2)*D18)

Figure 7.7 *k*-curve curve plot of Table 7.3

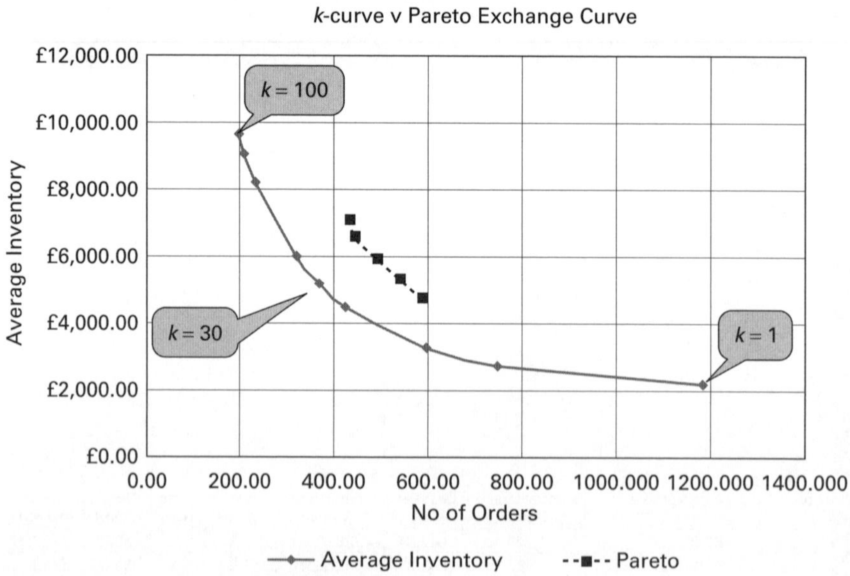

It would be much easier to visualize the data in Table 7.3 if it was presented as a chart. This can be easily done in Excel by using the chart option XY and plotting the data in the columns; number of orders and average inventory, the chart produced is shown in Figure 7.7.

Table 7.3 Comparison of inventory and orders for different values of *k*

k	No of Orders	Average Inventory
1	1187.50	£2,175.54
5	750.00	£2,736.39
10	596.88	£3,265.19
20	425.00	£4,492.33
30	370.31	£5,182.93
40	323.44	£5,963.18
60	235.94	£8,164.83
80	212.50	£8,984.65
100	200.00	£9,568.77

Interpretation of the curve

This is where we finally break the deadlock on our inventory management problem. If we look at this curve in Figure 7.7 and consider the question of which value of *k* do we use, we are now presented with a question statement, which can be expressed as 'How many deliveries can I cope with?' This is in reality a far easier question to answer than 'What does it cost to place an order?' If the parts we are concerned with are purchased, the number of orders generated directly equate to the number of deliveries received by the goods-in department. If they are manufactured they will directly relate to the number of changeovers we can perform in the work area. For a machine shop this will be the number of tool changes, for a moulding shop it will be the number of mould changes, etc. In summary, the number of orders can be said to be the 'capability' of the business to process orders in the work area in question. Thus we can look at this as an inventory capability exchange curve. If we are able to confirm a decision with respect to the number of deliveries that we can cope with we can then simply draw a vertical line and intersect the curve; this will give us the 'optimum' inventory for our capability (to process orders).

So let us imagine that we have spoken to our goods inward supervisor and that he has confirmed that at present they are receiving 400 receipts a year. It is now possible to find the point on the curve where the number of deliveries per year is 400. We can see that at this point on the curve the average inventory is £4,784.60, and by varying *k* in Excel 7.6, determine that 400 deliveries is when *k* = 25.

Once this decision is taken then we can use the list to identify the appropriate batch size for each part. The reverse process is also true, as if the management wanted to achieve an inventory target of say £4,000.00 then again reading of the *k*-curve we can see that we will need to be able to process 471 receipts to achieve an inventory of £4,082, with *k* set to 15. It should be an easy question to ask the goods inwards supervisor if he can increase his department's receipt rate from 400 to 471 per year. If this is possible then it is simply a matter of adjusting the *k* value in Excel 7.6 and the setting for all the parts will be given.

Why is it so useful?

The nirvana for all advocates of the EOQ is to solve the 2C/i question. By using this approach we have turned the question on its head and created a mechanism that allows us to make a rational decision that will 'fix' the EOQ at an 'optimum' value for the business. *k*-curve solves the EOQ weaknesses; instead of needing to find the cost of ordering and cost of holding, we now need to determine the number of batches and/or a target inventory level. It also solves the Pareto weaknesses as the Value Class Table created in Excel 7.4 allows more subdivisions and allocates the order size on an 'economic' order principle, rather than just setting an arbitrary order size to the first 20 per cent. The proof that the *k*-curve is more effective is seen if we compare the results of the *k*-curve with the results of the Pareto exchange curve shown in Table 7.2 and Figure 7.2 and now shown as a dotted line in Figure 7.7. For the same number of orders a much lower level of inventory can be achieved using the *k*-curve. If we examine the two scenarios it is obvious as Pareto goes from five-day ordering to 20-day ordering, whereas *k*-curve goes from 5 days to 10 days to 20 days – a much more granular approach.

What is also of significance is that, as seen in Excel 7.7, if the value of *k* is varied the population in each group will alter. For example, with *k* set to 50 there are no Class 1 parts, which says that when *k* = 50 it is appropriate for your business not to order any parts on a weekly basis. This differs from Pareto approach which advises that the first 20 per cent will always be on the lowest order cycle, typically five days ordering, or whatever policy is chosen for the Class A parts.

k-curve for business case analysis

Usually, when asking to spend money, a business case has to be prepared to answer the question 'If I spend X how much benefit will I get?' It is not often that the reverse is tested. Inventory reduction is assumed to cost nothing to achieve, just hard work. We can now see that the capability to process receipts or that the capability to increase the number of tool changes is directly related to the inventory reduction, as we have demonstrated with the *k*-curve. Thus we can now compare the cost of increasing the business's capability to meet the proposed inventory benefit. We can use the model created in Excel 7.6 and can vary *k* until we get the required inventory levels. Say we wish to reduce the inventory level from £5,000 to £4,000 then £3,000, the results are shown in Figure 7.8, and we see the need to increase the number of orders from 383 to 472 for the first £1,000 and from 472 to 641 for the second £1,000. Let us consider how to use this tool. It is useful when examining how two possible different scenarios, based on the same data in Figure 7.7, could be resolved first in a goods-inwards department and then in the more complex example of a machine shop.

Excel 7.7 Shown with *k* set to 50

	A	B	C	D	E	F	G	H	I
1	Constant *k*	50							
2	Work Days	250							
3									
4									
5	Value Class	Cycle Days	Class Limit						
6	1	5	£62,500						
7	2	10	£15,625						
8	3	20	£3,906						
9	4	40	£977						
10	5	80	£244						
11	6	160	£0						
12	7		£0						
13	8		£0						
14	9		£0						
15									
16									
17	Count	Part Number	Annual Usage or Demand	Cost Per Part	Annual Spend Value £	Value Class	Cycle Days	No of Orders	Average Inventory
18	1	B78811ZD	1,324	£42.84	£56,720.16	2	10	25.00	£1,134.40
19	2	B78812ZF	987	£41.87	£41,325.69	2	10	25.00	£826.51
20	3	B78810741A	1,012	£18.50	£18,722.00	2	10	25.00	£374.44
21	4	N6554004M0256	523	£35.08	£18,346.84	2	10	25.00	£366.94
22	5	SK98751	46	£316.19	£14,544.74	3	20	12.50	£581.79
23	6	LE763	781	£11.11	£8,676.91	3	20	12.50	£347.08
24	7	D0883030014C	267	£27.54	£7,353.18	3	20	12.50	£294.13
25	8	C78810742A	360	£16.87	£6,073.20	3	20	12.50	£242.93
26	9	D0862060018Y	163	£33.26	£5,421.38	3	20	12.50	£216.86
27	10	C78810761A	567	£8.43	£4,779.81	3	20	12.50	£191.19
28	11	LE02	396	£11.09	£4,391.64	3	20	12.50	£175.67
29	12	B78812001B	458	£7.10	£3,251.80	4	40	6.25	£260.14
30	13	KN552130	10	£319.98	£3,199.80	4	40	6.25	£255.98
31	14	A0906030015	18	£150.22	£2,703.96	4	40	6.25	£216.32
32	15	B78810721A	749	£3.44	£2,576.56	4	40	6.25	£206.12
33	16	D0991020012	164	£14.60	£2,394.40	4	40	6.25	£191.55
34	17	D0862070019Y	60	£35.25	£2,115.00	4	40	6.25	£169.20
35	18	D0978040014	35	£57.63	£2,017.05	4	40	6.25	£161.36
36	19	A78810601E	450	£4.20	£1,890.00	4	40	6.25	£151.20
37	20	B78818AE	35	£49.57	£1,734.95	4	40	6.25	£138.80
38	21	C78810762A	199	£7.44	£1,480.56	4	40	6.25	£118.44
39	22	D0753100033	75	£15.36	£1,152.00	4	40	6.25	£92.16
40	23	D1017040014	10	£95.36	£953.60	5	80	3.13	£152.58
41	24	KDB300600	8	£93.75	£750.00	5	80	3.13	£120.00
42	25	A0889030013	52	£9.59	£498.68	5	80	3.13	£79.79
43	26	B30880112C	700	£0.45	£315.00	5	80	3.13	£50.40
44	27	B30880113C	105	£1.18	£123.90	6	160	1.56	£39.65
45		Totals			£213,512.81			270.31	£7,155.63

Goods *inwards*

In this case we can ask the goods inwards supervisor to increase the number of receipts by 22 per cent in the first case; his response may be 'more overtime' – this can then be costed, let's say £500, the business case is then passed easily. The second tranche is a 35 per cent increase in receipts but overall nearly 67 per cent, at which point there may be a request for additional labour or new equipment. Again this can be costed, so the options are say £13,000 for labour or £6,000 for new equipment; in this case it is clear that there is no longer a basic case as the costs of improving the capability of the goods inwards department outweigh the inventory benefits.

Machine shop

The machine shop scenario is interesting as the likely response is that in order to achieve more changeovers it would be perceived that all the tooling would need to be improved. The *k*-curve analysis would show which parts are to change from fortnightly processing to weekly processing. In Table 7.4 we can see the lists of parts, their classes for each of the *k* values and the recommended cycle days.

What can be seen is that to get the first £1,000 savings, moving from *k* = 27.5 to *k* = 15 as shown in Figure 7.8, only four parts need to move from monthly to fortnightly tool-changeover, and one from bi-monthly to monthly.

Figure 7.8 Using *k*-curve for business case analysis

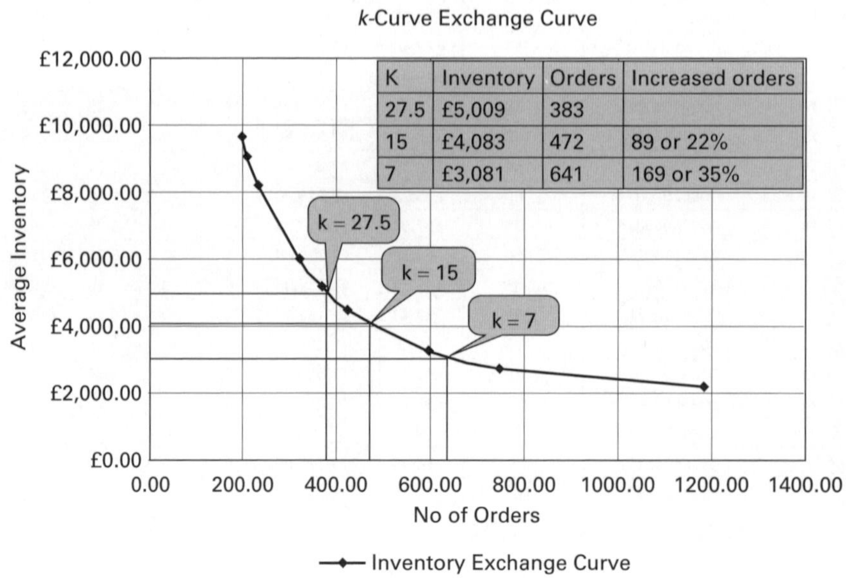

Table 7.4 Effect of changing *k* on value class population

Count	Part Number	Annual Usage or Demand	Cost Per Part	Annual Spend Value £	*k* = 27.5		*k* = 15		*k* = 7	
					Value Class	Cycle Days	Value Class	Cycle Days	Value Class	Cycle Days
1	B78811ZD	1,324	£42.84	£56,726.63	1	5	1	5	1	5
2	B78812ZF	987	£41.87	£41,325.69	1	5	1	5	1	5
3	B78810741A	1,012	£18.50	£18,722.00	2	10	2	10	1	5
4	N6554004M0256	523	£35.08	£18,346.42	2	10	2	10	1	5
5	SK98751	46	£316.19	£14,544.64	2	10	2	10	1	5
6	LE763	781	£11.11	£8,679.28	2	10	2	10	2	10
7	D0883030014C	267	£27.54	£7,354.28	3	20	2	10	2	10
8	C78810742A	360	£16.87	£6,071.97	3	20	2	10	2	10
9	D0862060018Y	163	£33.26	£5,420.88	3	20	2	10	2	10
10	C78810761A	567	£8.43	£4,780.58	3	20	2	10	2	10
11	LE02	396	£11.09	£4,393.19	3	20	3	20	2	10
12	B78812001B	458	£7.10	£3,250.36	3	20	3	20	2	10
13	KN552130	10	£319.98	£3,199.83	3	20	3	20	2	10
14	A0906030015	18	£150.22	£2,703.97	3	20	3	20	2	10
15	B78810721A	749	£3.44	£2,579.83	3	20	3	20	2	10
16	D0991020012	164	£14.60	£2,393.59	3	20	3	20	2	10
17	D0862070019Y	60	£35.25	£2,115.00	4	40	3	20	3	20

Whereas to get the next £1,000, three parts need to move to weekly, six need to change to fortnightly, leaving only one at monthly. The business case for the inventory reduction can be built on some very specific costs for the improvement to tooling, which can be identified at an item level.

In summary, the use of the *k*-curve analysis tool use extends well beyond a simple inventory ready reckoner as it can deliver detailed information at part level.

In simple terms, by using a *k*-curve you can establish the true cost/benefit of the inventory reduction, by understanding the costs of increasing the 'capability' prior to going ahead with an inventory reduction. This is likely to be better than having an irate goods inwards supervisor complaining bitterly that his people are overworked and the processing of goods is delayed causing problems on the shop floor. Similarly, discussing which tools need to be upgraded is better than being berated by a machine shop foreman complaining that the increase in tool changeovers has consumed valuable machine shop capacity.

Creating a composite curve

Adding safety stock

The use of basic formulae and the concept of using variable service level rates for each class

Having established the basic inventory capability exchange curve, the next logical step is to consider the addition of safety stock. We saw in Chapter 6 a wide range of safety stock options, from simple to complex statistical formula which are essentially based on the customer service levels desired, second the more straightforward safety time and finally the more sophisticated hybrid safety stock which combine both time and quantity. All require a 'parameter' to be decided which will affect the amount of safety stock held. These decision points are shown in Table 7.5.

Typically, there is one parameter that drives each of the safety calculations. The result of the decision, as seen in Chapter 6, will increase or decrease the amount of safety. When used in the Pareto calculation the key decision was for the top value class to have the least value of safety stock, either by keeping the number of days to a minimum or lowering the expected service level. We can apply the same logic to the *k*-curve and assign different levels of

Table 7.5 Safety stock parameter decision focus

Safety Stock Formula	Decision parameter	Focus	Ignores
Demand Variation	Service Level %	Service level to customer	Costs
Supply & Demand Variation	Service Level %	Service level to customer and from supplier	Costs
Batch, Supply & Demand Variation	Service Level% and Batch Size	Relationship between batch size and service levels	Costs
Time	No of Days	Inventory cost	Customer service
Hybrid	Greater or lesser of the Time / Quantity	Forces decision between cost or customer service	
Combination	Service Level % and No of Days	Elements of cost and customer service	

safety for different classes. Once this decision is made it is relatively simple to add this to the inventory calculation. The results in our excel example can be seen in Excel 7.8. For simplicity we have chosen to use safety days. If we had demand variation data we could easily use statistical safety stock calculations in the same column, with the variation being the service level.

The choice of the number of days of safety is essentially judgement, starting from the lower values for the higher spend items, of which there are fewer. Now that we are making more detailed decisions what is becoming apparent is that it would be useful to display the subtotals for each column. This will mean that we can see both the 'detail' and inventory sub-totals by each value class. Excel 7.9 shows a class-level inventory model; the columns have been rearranged into a logical flow that enables the use of DSUM and DCOUNT functions of Excel to work effectively. The formula have been designed to be copied easily.

This model now provides a clear summary picture of where the inventory is invested, and will enable easy examination of various scenarios, with

Excel 7.8 Safety stock (in days) added to the inventory model in Excel 7.7

	A	B	C	D	E	F	G	H	I	J	K
1	Constant *k*	30									
2	Working Days	250									
3											
4											
5	Value Class	Cycle Days	Class Limit	Safety Days							
6	1	5	£37,500	5							
7	2	10	£9,375	5							
8	3	20	£2,344	10							
9	4	40	£586	15							
10	5	80	£146	20							
11	6	160	£0	25							
12	7		£0								
13	8		£0								
14	9		£0								
15											
16											
17	Count	Part Number	Annual Usage or Demand	Cost Per Part	Annual Spend Value £	Value Class	Cycle Days	Safety Days	No of Orders	Average Cycle Inventory	Safety Inventory
18	1	B78811ZD	1324	£42.84	£56,720.16	1	5	5	50	£567.20	£1,134.40
19	2	B78812ZF	987	£41.87	£41,325.69	1	5	5	50	£413.26	£826.51
20	3	B78810741A	1012	£18.50	£18,722.00	2	10	5	25	£374.44	£374.44
21	4	N6554004M0256	523	£35.08	£18,346.84	2	10	5	25	£366.94	£366.94
22	5	SK98751	46	£316.19	£14,544.74	2	10	5	25	£290.89	£290.89
23	6	LE763	781	£11.11	£8,676.91	3	20	10	12.5	£347.08	£347.08
24	7	D0883030014C	267	£27.54	£7,353.18	3	20	10	12.5	£294.13	£294.13
25	8	C78810742A	360	£16.87	£6,073.20	3	20	10	12.5	£242.93	£242.93
26	9	D0862060018Y	163	£33.26	£5,421.38	3	20	10	12.5	£216.86	£216.86
27	10	C78810761A	567	£8.43	£4,779.81	3	20	10	12.5	£191.19	£191.19
28	11	LE02	396	£11.09	£4,391.64	3	20	10	12.5	£175.67	£175.67
29	12	B78812001B	458	£7.10	£3,251.80	3	20	10	12.5	£130.07	£130.07
30	13	KN552130	10	£319.98	£3,199.80	3	20	10	12.5	£127.99	£127.99
31	14	A0906030015	18	£150.22	£2,703.96	3	20	10	12.5	£108.16	£108.16
32	15	B78810721A	749	£3.44	£2,576.56	3	20	10	12.5	£103.06	£103.06
33	16	D0991020012	164	£14.60	£2,394.40	3	20	10	12.5	£95.78	£95.78
34	17	D0862070019Y	60	£35.25	£2,115.00	4	40	15	6.25	£169.20	£126.90
35	18	D0978040014	35	£57.63	£2,017.05	4	40	15	6.25	£161.36	£121.02
36	19	A78810601E	450	£4.20	£1,890.00	4	40	15	6.25	£151.20	£113.40
37	20	B78818AE	35	£49.57	£1,734.95	4	40	15	6.25	£138.80	£104.10
38	21	C78810762A	199	£7.44	£1,480.56	4	40	15	6.25	£118.44	£88.83
39	22	D0753100033	75	£15.36	£1,152.00	4	40	15	6.25	£92.16	£69.12
40	23	D1017040014	10	£95.36	£953.60	4	40	15	6.25	£76.29	£57.22
41	24	KDB300600	8	£93.75	£750.00	4	40	15	6.25	£60.00	£45.00
42	25	A0889030013	52	£9.59	£498.68	5	80	20	3.12	£79.79	£39.89
43	26	B30880112C	700	£0.45	£315.00	5	80	20	3.12	£50.40	£25.20
44	27	B30880113C	105	£1.18	£123.90	6	160	25	1.56	£39.65	£12.39
45		Totals			£213,512.81				370.31	£5,182.93	£5,829.17

Enter these formulae

Using Excel 7.6 add Column between G and H and add Column K

Safety days G18 *then copy down to* G44 =+CHOOSE(F18,$D$6,$D$7,$D$8,$D$9,$D$10,$D$11,$D$12,$D$13,$D$14)

Safety Inventory K18 *then copy down to* K44 =(H18*(C18/$B$2)*D18)

Excel 7.9 Inventory model summary table added to Excel 7.8

	A	B	C	D	E	F	G	H	I	J	K
1	Constant *k*	30									
2	Working Days	250									
3											
4											
5	Value Class		Class Limit		No of Parts in Class	Annual Spend Value £	Cycle Days	Safety Days	No of Orders	Average Cycle Inventory	Safety Inventory
6	1		£37,500		2	£98,045.85	5	5	100	£980.46	£1,960.92
7	2		£9,375		3	£51,613.58	10	5	75	£1,032.27	£1,032.27
8	3		£2,344		2	£16,030.09	20	10	25	£641.20	£641.20
9	4		£586		0	£0.00	40	15	0	£0.00	£0.00
10	5		£146		0	£0.00	80	20	0	£0.00	£0.00
11	6		£0		0	£0.00	160	25	0	£0.00	£0.00
12	7		£0		0	£0.00			0	£0.00	£0.00
13	8		£0		0	£0.00			0	£0.00	£0.00
14	9		£0		0	£0.00			0	£0.00	£0.00
15				Total	7	£165,689.52			200	£2,653.93	£3,634.39
16											
17	Count	Part Number	Annual Usage or Demand	Cost Per Part	Value Class	Annual Spend Value £	Cycle Days	Safety Days	No of Orders	Average Cycle Inventory	Safety Inventory
18	1	B78811ZD	1324	£42.84	1	£56,720.16	5	5	50.0	£567.20	£1,134.40
19	2	B78812ZF	987	£41.87	1	£41,325.69	5	5	50.0	£413.26	£826.51
20	3	B78810741A	1012	£18.50	2	£18,722.00	10	5	25.0	£374.44	£374.44
21	4	N6554004M0256	523	£35.08	2	£18,346.84	10	5	25.0	£366.94	£366.94
22	5	SK98751	46	£316.19	2	£14,544.74	10	5	25.0	£290.89	£290.89
23	6	LE763	781	£11.11	3	£8,676.91	20	10	12.5	£347.08	£347.08
24	7	D0883030014C	267	£27.54	3	£7,353.18	20	10	12.5	£294.13	£294.13

Enter these formulae

NOTE: Only Rows 1–24 are shown in this extract. All 27 parts are still used in Excel 7.9. Using Excel 7.8, first move Column E to F, and F to E. Next move B5–B14 to G5–G14, and D5–D14 to H5–H14.

Cell E6 *and copy down to* E14 = DCOUNT($E$17:$K$44,$E$17,$A$5:A6)-SUM(E$5:E5)

Cell F6 *and copy down to* F14 = DSUM($E$17:$K$44,F$17,$A$5:$A6)-SUM(F$5:F5)

Cell I6 *and copy down and across to* K14 = DSUM($E$17:$K$44,I$17,$A$5:$A6)-SUM(I$5:I5)

differing cycle days and safety days, as well as easily allowing you to vary *k* to produce a curve which represents the sum of average inventory and safety. Figure 7.9 shows the *k*-curve generated showing the Average Cycle Inventory and Average Cycle Inventory + Safety Inventory.

We are now beginning to develop a clearer picture of the inventory and the key decisions that will enable us to manage the inventory at an aggregated level. The top line represents the optimum curve for a given set of parts. This can then be tested against the budget and capabilities of the department managing these parts.

Figure 7.9 *k*-curve of cycle and safety stock

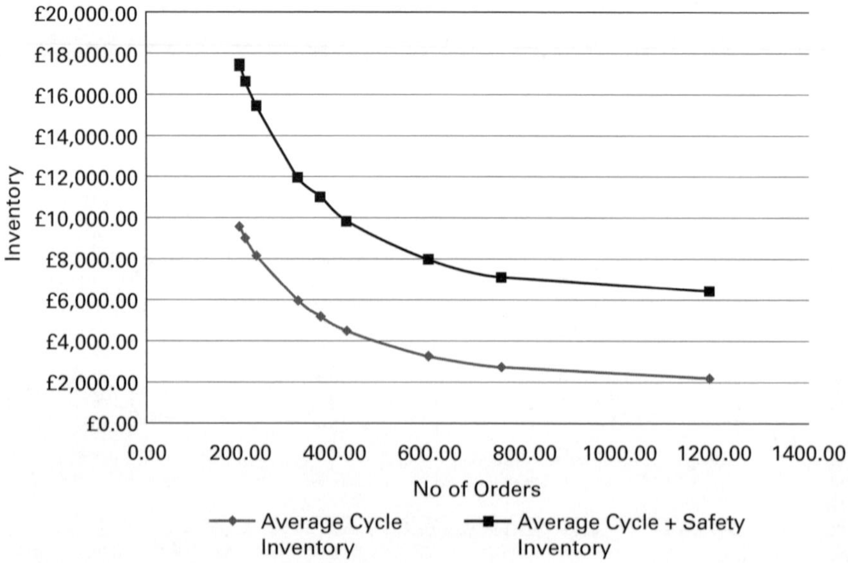

Adding overage to the k-curve

Why include overage in the composite curve?

In Chapter 6 we discussed the existence of overage and how it can be managed; we saw the importance of overage as part of overall inventory evaluation. Therefore it is worthy of consideration when developing a realistic inventory plan. Including overage takes account of the 'real world environment' in order to make a realistic commitment.

Therefore the addition of overage into the inventory plan is important as what we are trying to do is prepare a plan that we intend to achieve. In the words of Benjamin Franklin: 'By failing to prepare, you are preparing to fail.'

If we do not include overage in the plan calculations then, as we have shown in Chapter 6, we are guaranteeing that we will exceed the plan. We know overage will occur, and ignoring it will not make it go away. As any experienced manager knows, the result of missing a plan is a lot of management attention in explaining why we are over plan.

Overage logic

It would be easy to create a clever and complicated algorithm for adding overage to the plan, but the research by Relph (2006) showed that adding a percentage to the maximum stock is as accurate as any more complex method. The formula is shown on the left-hand side of Figure 7.10; this may look counterintuitive as it would be more straightforward to simply add a percentage to the maximum stock. However, when you consider measuring the actual overage, the known values are the actual inventory and the maximum stock, thus the overage would be Actual – Maximum, shown on the right-hand side of Figure 7.10, which is more straightforward and can be used when analysing the actual inventory performance, which is covered in the next chapter.

Figure 7.10 Overage formula to determine the planned level of overage

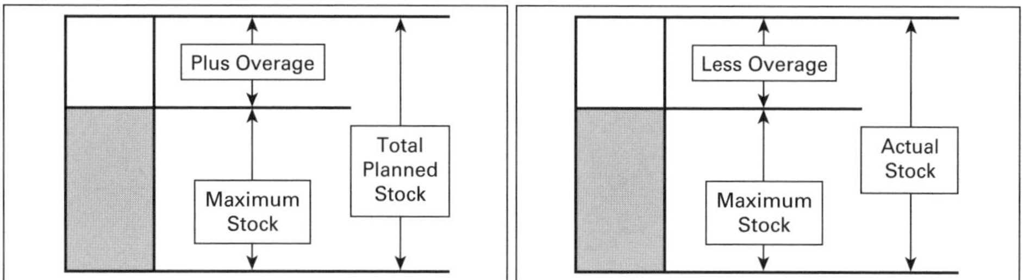

Formula to determine the Planned level of inventory	Formula to determine the Overage Performance
Maximum Stock = Safety + Cycle Stock = M Overage Estimate percentage = O_p Planned Stock = P Overage = O Planned Stock = $\frac{M}{(1 - O_p)}$ Overage = P – M	Maximum Stock = Safety + Cycle Stock = M Actual Stock = A Overage = O Overage percentage = O_p Overage = A – M Overage Percentage = $O_p = \frac{O}{A}$
Maximum Stock = Safety + Cycle Stock = M = 150 Overage Estimate percentage = O_p = 25% Planned Stock = P = 150 / (1-).25) = 150 / 0.75 – 200 Overage = O = 200 –150 = 50	Maximum Stock = Safety + Cycle Stock = M = 150 Actual Stock = A = 200 Overage = O = A – M = 200 –150 = 50 Overage percentage = O_p = O / A = 50 / 200 = .25 = 25%

This can be applied to the summary data; there is no real benefit in applying this to the part number level of the data.

Overage can be refined by adding a different percentage for each value class as you would expect to manage the parts in the higher value classes more closely. Excel 7.10 shows our sample parts with overage built into the plan; you can see the two parts in Value Class 1 have significantly more overage than the two parts in Value Class 5. We can now create a *k*-curve to include safety and overage; as a result we can be confident that it is a good representation of the optimum inventory envelope that could be achieved. Since the *k*-curve is based on a set of cycle days, a safety policy (in this case safety days) and an estimation of the expected overage, it completely defines for the group of parts being managed the range of possible inventory levels. These rules are, in effect, a statement of the inventory plan in a set of policy rules, which can be documented as an inventory plan. Figure 7.11 shows the complete composite curve for the sample 27 parts. The only remaining decision is to identify the target inventory level, which is usually a given based on the business needs.

To be able to create Figure 7.11, using the Excel XY Chart function we need to create a table, shown in Table 7.6, where the three columns are cumulative rather than the specific values. Thus the three lines to be plotted are based on the values in Excel 7.10.

Figure 7.11 Complete inventory *k*-curve

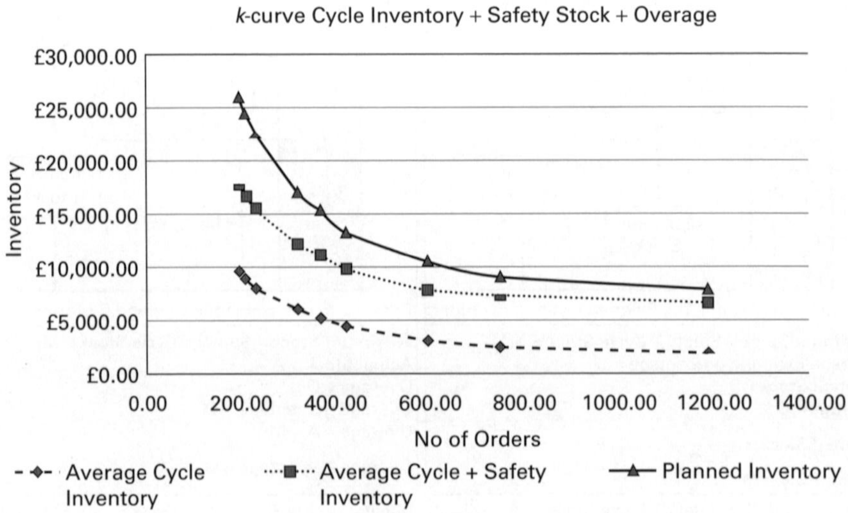

Table 7.6 Table of *k* values and the resultant inventory

k	No of Orders	Average Cycle Inventory	Average Cycle + Safety Inventory	Planned Inventory
1	1187.50	£2,175	£6,449	£8,075
5	750.00	£2,736	£7,121	£9,130
10	596.88	£3,265	£7,986	£10,474
20	425.00	£4,492	£9,834	£13,365
30	370.31	£5,183	£11,013	£15,273
40	323.44	£5,963	£11,962	£16,842
60	235.94	£8,165	£15,455	£22,371
80	212.50	£8,985	£16,636	£24,428
100	200.00	£9,569	£17,439	£25,841

Excel 7.10 Inventory model including overage

	A	B	C	D	E	F	G	H	I	J	K	L	M
1	Constant *k*	30											
2	Working Days	250											
3													
4													
5	Value Class		Class Limit	Overge Percentage	No of Parts in Class	Annual Spend Value £	Cycle Days	Safety Days	No of Orders	Average Cycle Inventory	Safety Inventory	Planned Overage	Total Inventory
6	1		£37,500	20%	2	£98,046	5	5	100	£980	£1,961	£735	£3,677
7	2		£9,375	25%	3	£51,614	10	5	75	£1,032	£1,032	£688	£2,753
8	3		£2,344	30%	11	£50,823	20	10	138	£2,033	£2,033	£1,742	£5,808
9	4		£586	35%	8	£12,093	40	15	50	£967	£726	£912	£2,605
10	5		£146	40%	2	£814	80	20	6	£130	£65	£130	£325
11	6		£0	50%	1	£124	160	25	2	£40	£12	£52	£104
12	7		£0		0	£0			0	£0	£0	£0	£0
13	8		£0		0	£0			0	£0	£0	£0	£0
14	9		£0		0	£0			0	£0	£0	£0	£0
15				Total	27	£213,513			370	£5,183	£5,829	£4,260	£15,272
16													
17	Count	Part Number	Annual Usage or Demand	Cost Per Part	Value Class	Annual Spend Value £	Cycle Days	Safety Days	No of Orders	Average Cycle Inventory	Safety Inventory		
18	1	B78811ZD	1,324	£42.84	1	£56,720.16	5	5	50	£567.20	£1,134.40		
19	2	B78812ZF	987	£41.87	1	£41,325.69	5	5	50	£413.26	£826.51		
20	3	B78810741A	1,012	£18.50	2	£18,722.00	10	5	25	£374.44	£374.44		
21	4	N6554004M0256	523	£35.08	2	£18,346.84	10	5	25	£366.94	£366.94		
22	5	SK98751	46	£316.19	2	£14,544.74	10	5	25	£290.89	£290.89		
23	6	LE763	781	£11.11	3	£8,676.91	20	10	12.5	£347.08	£347.08		
24	7	D0883030014C	267	£27.54	3	£7,353.18	20	10	12.5	£294.13	£294.13		
25	8	C78810742A	360	£16.87	3	£6,073.20	20	10	12.5	£242.93	£242.93		
26	9	D0862060018Y	163	£33.26	3	£5,421.38	20	10	12.5	£216.86	£216.86		
27	10	C78810761A	567	£8.43	3	£4,779.81	20	10	12.5	£191.19	£191.19		
28	11	LE02	396	£11.09	3	£4,391.64	20	10	12.5	£175.67	£175.67		
29	12	B78812001B	458	£7.10	3	£3,251.80	20	10	12.5	£130.07	£130.07		
30	13	KN552130	10	£319.98	3	£3,199.80	20	10	12.5	£127.99	£127.99		
31	14	A0906030015	18	£150.22	3	£2,703.96	20	10	12.5	£108.16	£108.16		
32	15	B78810721A	749	£3.44	3	£2,576.56	20	10	12.5	£103.06	£103.06		
33	16	D0991020012	164	£14.60	3	£2,394.40	20	10	12.5	£95.78	£95.78		
34	17	D0862070019Y	60	£35.25	4	£2,115.00	40	15	6.25	£169.20	£126.90		
35	18	D0978040014	35	£57.63	4	£2,017.05	40	15	6.25	£161.36	£121.02		
36	19	A78810601E	450	£4.20	4	£1,890.00	40	15	6.25	£151.20	£113.40		
37	20	B78818AE	35	£49.57	4	£1,734.95	40	15	6.25	£138.80	£104.10		
38	21	C78810762A	199	£7.44	4	£1,480.56	40	15	6.25	£118.44	£88.83		
39	22	D0753100033	75	£15.36	4	£1,152.00	40	15	6.25	£92.16	£69.12		
40	23	D1017040014	10	£95.36	4	£953.60	40	15	6.25	£76.29	£57.22		
41	24	KDB300600	8	£93.75	4	£750.00	40	15	6.25	£60.00	£45.00		
42	25	A0889030013	52	£9.59	5	£498.68	80	20	3.125	£79.79	£39.89		
43	26	B30880112C	700	£0.45	5	£315.00	80	20	3.125	£50.40	£25.20		
44	2	B30880113C	105	£1.18	6	£123.90	160	25	1.5625	£39.65	£12.39		

Enter these formulae

Using Excel 7.9 add to the summary Table A5 to M15

Overage %age	D6 *then copy down to* D14	enter percentages as above
Planned Overage	L6 *then copy down to* L14	=+M6–J6–K6
Planned Inventory	M6 *then copy down to* M14	=(J6+K6)/(1–D6)

- Average Inventory = J15 / 2
- Average Cycle + Safety = J15/2 + K15
- Planned Inventory = Average Cycle + Safety + Overage = J15/2 + K15 + L15

Because we do not show *k* on the chart, it is not easy to see the relation between *k* and the inventory level.

In Table 7.6 we can see the *k* values in relation to the total inventory, thus if we were given a target to achieve £15,000 we would select a *k* value very close to 30; if the target was further reduced to £10,000 we can easily see that we would we need to reduce the *k* value to 10. From the discussion earlier in the chapter we know that the first step to confirming that the plan is possible will be to confirm our ability to process 370 orders in order to achieve an inventory of £15,000 and similarly our ability to process 596 orders to achieve an inventory level of £10,000.

Testing the different options for inventory classes

In this chapter we have made some default assumptions about Pareto and *k*-curve. For Pareto we assumed three value classes and for *k*-curve we assumed six. The default position for Pareto is to use three classes, however Wild (2002) and other authors identify that it may be logical/appropriate to extend to four or even five as the granularity is not sufficient when managing a larger group of parts. Similarly, Dupernex (1993) investigated the optimum number of classes when using *k*-curve. The conclusion typically was that 'it depends' on the group of parts being examined. We know from our discussion in this chapter that Pareto becomes more difficult as we increase the number of classes to be managed. We also know that *k*-curve, unlike Pareto, will populate/de-populate classes dependent on the parts annual spend, thus if we specified too many classes they may well not be used. If we look at our sample parts in Excel 7.10 and look at the population in each class for the *k* values used in Table 7.6 we would clearly see this de-population of the value classes. The population of each class as the value of *k* is varied as shown in Table 7.7; we can see that as the value of *k* increases so the population of parts in the higher value classes decreases and the parts migrate to the lower value classes. We know from looking at Table 7.6 that as the value of *k* increases the inventory increases and the number of orders decreases; the increase in inventory is the result of fewer parts in the higher classes where the order cycle is lower, ie fewer parts being ordered weekly, more ordered monthly.

It is possible to use to utilize the phenomenon shown in Table 7.7 to help decide which number of classes is the best option.

Table 7.7 Inventory class population

	No of Parts in Class								
Value Class	***k* = 1**	***k* = 5**	***k* = 10**	***k* = 20**	***k* = 30**	***k* = 40**	***k* = 60**	***k* = 80**	***k* = 100**
1	21	7	5	2	2	1	0	0	0
2	5	13	8	5	3	4	2	2	2
3	1	5	10	13	11	8	8	5	4
4	0	2	3	5	8	10	11	13	12
5	0	0	1	2	2	3	5	5	7
6	0	0	0	0	1	1	1	2	2

In Table 7.7 we can see that for certain *k* values there are no parts in either the first or last class; this would suggest that there is no point in having that class in the scenario. We can test, for example, different numbers of classes to see which may be the best fit for the selection of parts we are planning. For example, we could create exchange curves for the classic Pareto as well as *k*-curve using 4, 6 and 8 classes. Table 7.8 shows the layout of these possible scenarios we could consider testing.

Table 7.8 Possible scenarios for number of classes and order cycles

Classes	Scenarios				
	Pareto 80/20	4 Class	6 Class	6 Class – Lean	8 Class
1	5	5	5	1	1
2	20	20	10	2	2
3	125	40	20	5	5
4		125	40	10	10
5			80	20	20
6			160	80	40
7					80
8					160

Note 1: There are two differences between the 3 class and 4 class scenarios, one the addition of a 40 days of supply class and that Pareto uses the percentage split, whereas *k*-curve uses the class limit to define the class boundaries.

Note 2: The 6 Class, 6 Class – Lean and 8 Class have similar sequences of days of supply, but in different classes.

We can use the Excel 7.10 model to conduct the test but for simplicity we will only examine the effect on the cycle stock and number of batches. The results are best displayed as *k*-curves as it is easier to see which result is better. These results are shown in Figure 7.12.

The key to interpreting the curve is that the best position is where we can achieve the lowest inventory for the least number of batches. This is because, as we saw in the exchange curve, to lower inventory we need to process more batches, thus by selecting a position that delivers the lowest inventory for the lowest number of batches we are making the most effective use of our batching rules. What is clear is that the Pareto is significantly less effective than the 4 Class scenario, which is a combination of the addition of an extra class with 40-day cycle between the 20-day and 125-day B and C classes and the

Figure 7.12 Comparison of cycle stock scenarios using *k*-curves

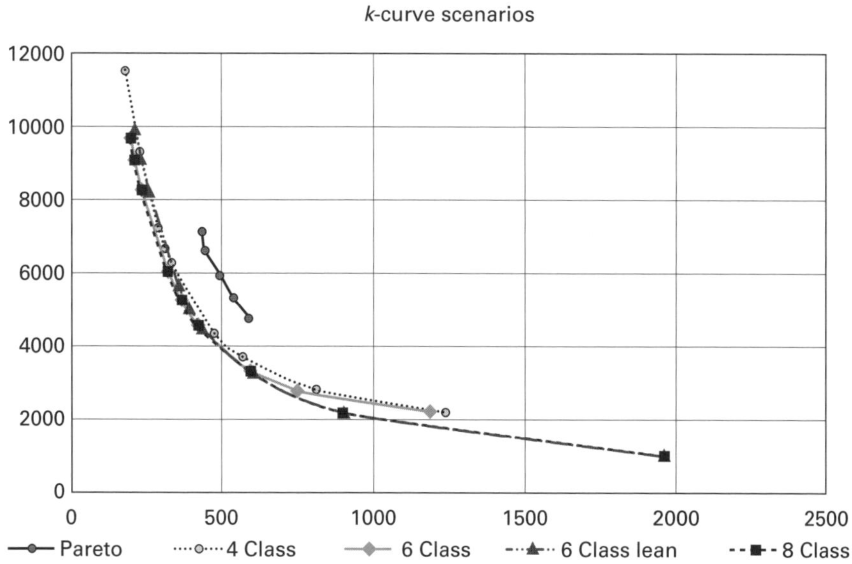

effect of using percentage split vs value class boundaries. Looking more generally at the remaining scenarios, the difference is much less significant. We need to get a closer view of the centre of the curve shown in Figure 7.12; this is shown in Figure 7.13.

Figure 7.13 Close up of *k*-curve Figure 7.12

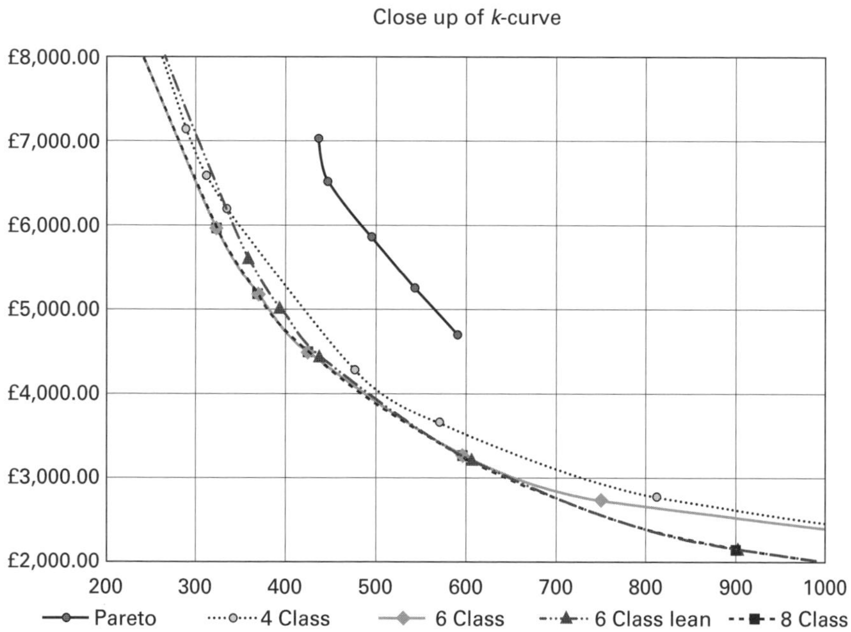

Looking at Figure 7.13, the central portion of Figure 7.12, we can see that in the top right corner of the curve the 6 Class and 8 Class scenario are on the same line. This is because there are no parts in Classes 1 and 2 in the 8 Class scenario and thus it will behave like the 6 Class scenario. At the bottom right of the curve the 8 Class and 6 Class Lean are on the same curve, again this is because the parts are migrating from the lower classes to the higher classes. By looking at these three scenarios in Table 7.8 it can be seen that they are similar based on the populations of the higher and lower classes. Thus the correct interpretation is that for this group, the best course of action is that Pareto and 4 Class are not effective. First, while the inventory is in the £7,000 region with the batch processing capability circa 300 batches per year the best scenario is to use 6 Class. Second, as we target inventory levels lower than £3,000 with a batch capability of 700, then using 8 Class, or 6 Class Lean becomes the most effective scenario. Thus by creating scenarios and plotting them we can visually identify which is the most effective for the group of parts. While in this above analysis we have focused only on the cycle stock, once this is done it is easy to add the safety stock and overage to create a complete *k*-curve policy for a given group of parts. The analysis of the exchange curve using only the cycle stock is recommended as there are a wide range of combinations of safety and overage values and they can mask the correct interpretation of the basic *k*-curve.

Create a plan group inventory plan

In Chapter 7 we have identified that a weakness of Pareto was that because it uses percentage, the first 20 per cent will always be given the lowest cycle stock irrespective of the annual spend for the items. What we have seen in Table 7.6 is that *k*-curve will de-populate the highest inventory class if it is not appropriate to the annual spend of the parts. We can therefore be confident, even if we are overly optimistic about reducing our batch sizes that the *k*-curve approach will adjust and balance our optimism, thus *k*-curve provides a robust and self-correcting technique. As it does not sub-optimize it means that you can with confidence plan different groups using different settings by specifying different numbers of classes, cycle stock ranges, safety stock techniques and levels of overage. For example, for new products you may specify higher levels of safety and overage as the demand is not yet fully understood. Similarly, for end of life you would be keen to keep overage and safety to a minimum.

In Chapter 7 we have discussed that the key difference between purchased and manufacturing was their ability to process batches, thus we may not have the same *k* values for each group.

Once we have made the decisions, we are able to model the inventory plan and compare to the business targets. It is useful to express the plan in sufficient detail to be able to replicate or recalculate if the source data, typically the demand data, were to change. Table 7.9 shows a typical plan statement which would summarize the outcome of the planning analysis.

Table 7.9 Typical plan statement for a plan group

Plan						
Classes	**Parts in Class**	**No of Batches**	**Cycle Stock**	**Safety Stock**	**Overage**	**Inventory**
1	1	50	5	5	10%	£1,891
2	4	100	10	5	20%	£4,647
3	6	75	20	10	25%	£1,710
4	12	75	40	15	30%	£5,831
5	3	9	80	20	40%	£2,754
6	1	2	160	25	50%	£104
$k = 45$	27	311	£6,221	£6,126	£3,927	£16,275
Inventory Target						£17,500
Capability: it has been confirmed with the machine shop manager that they can process eight batches per week, equivalent to 400 batches in a year.						400pa

Summary

In this chapter we have looked at the tools and techniques that can be used to analyse and plan groups of parts rather than focus on individual parts. This extends the capabilities of the planner to enable them to take a wider, more strategic view and role in the area of inventory planning.

The chapter looked at the history behind coverage analysis and the exchange curve principle and how the development of these tools took a more holistic approach to inventory planning. Murdoch (1965) first focused on the relationship between stock (cycle and safety) and number of deliveries, using the number of deliveries as the key. Later, authors Brown (1982) and Shah (1992) looked at combining the Pareto curve technique and the EOQ tool to make a tool to create an exchange curve that can be easily be used to test an inventory plan for viability before the plan is accepted. These base curves then added safety and overage to create a composite curve that was able to identify an envelope for an optimum inventory for a defined group of parts. This envelope could then be used to test any proposed plan for viability. Moreover, it could also test any proposed inventory reduction against the required improvements in supporting process by showing if there was sufficient ROI (Return on Investment) to support both the plan and the investments required to deliver the plan.

The key learning point in this chapter is that while the underlying theory may appear complex the use of the simplified EOP formula and resultant classification of each part into value classes based on EOP boundaries provides a very easy-to-manage analysis tool. The simplest exchange curve based only on cycle stock can easily be used to evaluate differing scenarios to find the most effective set of cycle days. The addition of safety and a guide as to the acceptable level of overage complete the generation of an exchange curve that is a good representation of the possible inventory for any group of parts. The chapter concluded by showing how we can use the *k*-curve to determine settings to meet a given target inventory. The next chapter will look at how this approach could be developed and used to create a credible inventory plan for a typical organization.

Tools and techniques discussed in this chapter

- Coverage analysis
- Inventory exchange curve
- Pareto exchange curve
- *k*-curve

References

Brown, R (1982) *Advanced Service Inventory Parts Control* (2nd edn), Material Management Science Inc, Norwich

Burcher, P, Dupernex, S and Relph, G (1996) The road to lean repetitive batch manufacture: modelling planning system performance, *International Journal of Operations and Production Management*, **16**(2), pp 210–19

Dupernex (1993) Improving Inventory Performance using *k*-curve Methodology, Masters, Sunderland University

Dupernex (1997) Inventory Parameter Management and Focused Continuous Improvement for Repetitive Batch Manufacture, Ph Thesis, Aston University

Handley, R (1999) Inventory Management, *Control*, pp 24–26

Lewis, C D (1975) *Scientific Inventory Control*, Butterworths, London

Murdoch, J (ed) (1965) Coverage Analysis: A new way of optimizing the stock ordering policy, Proceedings of One Day Conference, Cornfield

Relph (2006) Inventory Management in Business Systems, PhD Thesis, Manchester University

Schwarz, M (2000) Multi-Item Inventory Control: The *k*-curve Methodology, PhD Thesis, Hamburg University

Shah, S (1992) Setting Parameters in MRP for the is effective management of bought-out inventory in a JIT assembly environment, PhD Thesis, Aston University

Wild, T (2002) *Best Practice in Inventory Management* (2nd edn), John Wiley, Oxford

You do the maths

This exercise provides an opportunity to use the Planning model to examine the effect of changes to the planning rules and the effect of varying the constant *k* to achieve an inventory objective.

First, we need to extend the model to include actual stock and actual overage. To do this we will take the Excel 7.10 and add additional columns and summaries as shown in Excel 7.11.

Having established the model, we can now perform some scenario analysis.

The base plan conditions have been agreed with new targets for the planned overage. These are shown on Table 7.10. Update Excel 7.11 to reflect the new planning rules.

Table 7.10 *k*-curve planning table

Value Class	Cycle Days	Safety Days	Overage %age
1	5	5	10%
2	10	5	20%
3	20	10	25%
4	20	15	30%
5	80	20	40%
6	160	25	50%

Excel 7.11 Chapter 7 You do the maths exercise – Inventory model with actual stock and overage added

	A	B	C	D	E	F	G	H	I	J	K	L	M	N	O
1	Constant *k*	*45*													
2	Working Days	250													
3															
4															
5	Value Class		Class Limit	Overge Percent-age	No of Parts in Class	Annual Spend Value £	Cycle Days	Safety Days	No of Orders	Average Cycle Inventory	Safety Inventory	Planned Overage	Total Inventory	Actual Overage	
6	1		£37,500	20%	2	£98,046	5	5	100	£980	£1,961	£735	£3,677	£214	
7	2		£9,375	25%	3	£51,614	10	5	75	£1,032	£1,032	£688	£2,753	£4,016	
8	3		£2,344	30%	11	£50,823	20	10	138	£2,033	£2,033	£1,742	£5,808	£8,839	
9	4		£586	35%	8	£12,093	40	15	50	£967	£726	£912	£2,605	£11,079	
10	5		£146	40%	2	£814	80	20	6	£130	£65	£130	£325	£129	
11	6		£0	50%	1	£124	160	25	2	£40	£12	£52	£104	£55	
12	7		£0		0	£0			0	£0	£0	£0	£0	£0	
13	8		£0		0	£0			0	£0	£0	£0	£0	£0	
14	9		£0		0	£0			0	£0	£0	£0	£0	£0	
15				Total	27	£213,513			370	£5,183	£5,829	£4,260	£15,272	£24,332	
16															
17	Count	Part Number	Annual Usage or Demand	Cost Per Part	Value Class	Annual Spend Value £	Cycle Days	Safety Days	No of Orders	Average Cycle Inventory	Safety Inventory	Actual Stock	Planned Maximum	Overage	Overage Value
18	1	B78811ZD	1,324	£42.84	1	£56,720.16	5	5	50	£567.20	£1,134.40	58	53	5	£214.22
19	2	B78812ZF	987	£41.87	1	£41,325.69	5	5	50	£413.26	£826.51	20	39	0	£0.00
20	3	B78810741A	1,012	£18.50	2	£18,722.00	10	5	25	£374.44	£374.44	75	61	14	£259.00
21	4	N6554004M0256	523	£35.08	2	£18,346.84	10	5	25	£366.94	£366.94	75	31	44	£1,543.48
22	5	SK98751	46	£316.19	2	£14,544.74	10	5	25	£290.89	£290.89	10	3	7	£2,213.31
23	6	LE763	781	£11.11	3	£8,676.91	20	10	12.5	£347.08	£347.08	321	94	227	£2,522.66
24	7	D0883030014C	267	£27.54	3	£7,353.18	20	10	12.5	£294.13	£294.13	98	32	66	£1,817.91
25	8	C78810742A	360	£16.87	3	£6,073.20	20	10	12.5	£242.93	£242.93	7	43	0	£0.00
26	9	D0862060018Y	163	£33.26	3	£5,421.38	20	10	12.5	£216.86	£216.86	65	20	45	£1,496.56
27	10	C78810761A	567	£8.43	3	£4,779.81	20	10	12.5	£191.19	£191.19	3	68	0	£0.00
28	11	LE02	396	£11.09	3	£4,391.64	20	10	12.5	£175.67	£175.67	0	48	0	£0.00
29	12	B78812001B	458	£7.10	3	£3,251.80	20	10	12.5	£130.07	£130.07	15	55	0	£0.00
30	13	KN552130	10	£319.98	3	£3,199.80	20	10	12.5	£127.99	£127.99	2	1	1	£319.98
31	14	A0906030015	18	£150.22	3	£2,703.96	20	10	12.5	£108.16	£108.16	8	2	6	£901.32
32	15	B78810721A	749	£3.44	3	£2,576.56	20	10	12.5	£103.06	£103.06	251	90	161	£554.54
33	16	D0991020012	164	£14.60	3	£2,394.40	20	10	12.5	£95.78	£95.78	104	20	84	£1,225.99
34	17	D0862070019Y	60	£35.25	4	£2,115.00	40	15	6.25	£169.20	£126.90	39	13	26	£916.50

	A	B	C	D	E	F	G	H	I	J	K	L	M	N	O
35	18	D0978040014	35	£57.63	4	£2,017.05	40	15	6.25	£161.36	£121.02	91	8	83	£4,783.40
36	19	A78810601E	450	£4.20	4	£1,890.00	40	15	6.25	£151.20	£113.40	1117	99	1018	£4,275.60
37	20	B78818AE	35	£49.57	4	£1,734.95	40	15	6.25	£138.80	£104.10	14	8	6	£297.42
38	21	C78810762A	199	£7.44	4	£1,480.56	40	15	6.25	£118.44	£88.83	54	44	10	£74.40
39	22	D0753100033	75	£15.36	4	£1,152.00	40	15	6.25	£92.16	£69.12	34	17	17	£261.12
40	23	D1017040014	10	£95.36	4	£953.60	40	15	6.25	£76.29	£57.22	3	2	1	£95.36
41	24	KDB300600	8	£93.75	4	£750.00	40	15	6.25	£60.00	£45.00	6	2	4	£375.00
42	25	A0889030013	52	£9.59	5	£498.68	80	20	3.125	£79.79	£39.89	1	21	0	£0.00
43	26	B30880112C	700	£0.45	5	£315.00	80	20	3.125	£50.40	£25.20	566	280	286	£128.70
44	27	B30880113C	105	£1.18	6	£123.90	160	25	1.5625	£39.65	£12.39	125	78	47	£55.46

Enter these formulae

Actual Stock Quantity	Copy Data from Appendix B2 sorted to show highest to lowest Annual Spend Value use Actual Stock Cells E6 to E32	
Planned Maximum Quantity	Cell M17 then copy down to M44	=ROUND((C18/$B$2)*(G18+H18),0)
Actual Overage Quantity	Cell N17 then copy down to N44	=IF(L18-M18<=0,0,L18-M18)
Actual Overage Value	Cell O17 then copy down to O44	=N18*D18
Planned Overage	Cell L6 then copy down to L14	=M6-J6-K6
Planned Inventory	Cell M6 then copy down to M14	=(J6+K6)/(1-C6)
Actual Overage Value	Cell N6 then copy down to N14	=DSUM($E$17:$O$44,O$17,$A$5:$A6)-SUM(N$5:N5)

Questions

1 What would the Planned Inventory and Actual Overage be if we set constant *k* to 45 using the agreed *k*-curve planning rules plan in Table 7.10?

2 If we were asked to achieve a planned inventory below £14,500 what is the constant *k* value that would deliver a planned inventory below the target?

  a What would be the Planned Inventory and Overage levels? Look at the Planned Inventory levels and Actual Overage. What do you notice as you vary the value of *k*?

3 If you analyse the Actual Overage in Excel 7.13 what do you observe about where the overage is in the Value Classes and is the Actual Overage constant through all parts?

Notes for Excel 7.12 Answer 1

1 If we set constant *k* to 45 using the agreed *k*-curve planning rules plan in Table 7.10, the Planned Inventory would be £16,276 and the Actual Overage would be £23,126.

Notes for Excel 7.13 Answer 2

1 The nearest value of *k* to give a Planned Inventory below £14,500 is 33.

  a This would give a Planned Inventory of £14,342 and an Actual Overage of £24,098

2 The Inventory levels and Actual Overage are not directly related, the inventory has reduced by £1,934 but the overage has only reduced by £973.

  a In general, for both values of *k* the overage is not evenly spread over all the parts. Some parts have no overage, and some have very high values.

b When k is set to 33, the overage is concentrated in Classes 2, 3 and 4, a total of £22,446.29 of £23,216 (97%). The highest level of overage is in Class 4 – £12,593. There are 6 items with no overage and 7 items with overage over £1,000. Two items account for £9,058 of total overage.

An important feature of using planned inventory is that it allows the analysis of Actual Inventory based on the proposed Planned Inventory and can identify where the excess stock are to be fond prior to implementing the plan.

Excel 7.12 Chapter 7 You do the maths exercise answer 1

	A	B	C	D	E	F	G	H	I	J	K	L	M	N	O
1	Constant *k*	45													
2	Working Days	250													
3															
4															
5	Value Class		Class Limit	Overge Percent-age	No of Parts in Class	Annual Spend Value £	Cycle Days	Safety Days	No of Orders	Average Cycle Inventory	Safety Inventory	Planned Overage	Total Inventory	Actual Overage	
6	1		£56,250	10%	1	£56,720.16	5	5	50	£567.20	£1,134.40	£189.07	£1,890.67	£214.20	
7	2		£14,063	20%	4	£92,939.27	10	5	100	£1,858.79	£1,858.79	£929.39	£4,646.96	£4,015.85	
8	3		£3,516	25%	6	£36,696.12	20	10	75	£1,467.84	£1,467.84	£978.56	£3,914.25	£5,836.31	
9	4		£879	30%	12	£25,469.68	40	15	75	£2,037.57	£1,528.18	£1,528.18	£5,093.94	£12,593.21	
10	5		£220	40%	3	£1,563.68	80	20	9	£250.19	£125.09	£250.19	£625.47	£409.95	
11	6		£0	50%	1	£123.90	160	25	2	£39.65	£12.39	£52.04	£104.08	£55.46	
12	7		£0		0	£0.00			0	£0.00	£0.00	£0.00	£0.00	£0.00	
13	8		£0		0	£0.00			0	£0.00	£0.00	£0.00	£0.00	£0.00	
14	9		£0		0	£0.00			0	£0.00	£0.00	£0.00	£0.00	£0.00	
15				Total	27	£213,512.81			311	£6,221.24	£6,126.70	£3,927.43	£16,275.37	£23,124.98	
16															
17	Count	Part Number	Annual Usage or Demand	Cost Per Part	Value Class	Annual Spend Value £	Cycle Days	Safety Days	No of Orders	Average Cycle Inventory	Safety Inventory	Actual Stock	Planned Maximum	Overage	Actual Overage Value
18	1	B78811ZD	1324	£42.84	1	£56,720.16	5	5	50	£567.20	£1,134.40	58	53	5	£214.20
19	2	B78812ZF	987	£41.87	2	£41,325.69	10	5	25	£826.51	£826.51	20	59	0	£0.00
20	3	B78810741A	1012	£18.50	2	£18,722.00	10	5	25	£374.44	£374.44	75	61	14	£259.00
21	4	N6554004M0256	523	£35.08	2	£18,346.84	10	5	25	£366.94	£366.94	75	31	44	£1,543.52
22	5	SK98751	46	£316.19	2	£14,544.74	10	5	25	£290.89	£290.89	10	3	7	£2,213.33
23	6	LE763	781	£11.11	3	£8,676.91	20	10	12.5	£347.08	£347.08	321	94	227	£2,521.97
24	7	D0883030014C	267	£27.54	3	£7,353.18	20	10	12.5	£294.13	£294.13	98	32	66	£1,817.64
25	8	C78810742A	360	£16.87	3	£6,073.20	20	10	12.5	£242.93	£242.93	7	43	0	£0.00
26	9	D0862060018Y	163	£33.26	3	£5,421.38	20	10	12.5	£216.86	£216.86	65	20	45	£1,496.70
27	10	C78810761A	567	£8.43	3	£4,779.81	20	10	12.5	£191.19	£191.19	3	68	0	£0.00
28	11	LE02	396	£11.09	3	£4,391.64	20	10	12.5	£175.67	£175.67	0	48	0	£0.00
29	12	B78812001B	458	£7.10	4	£3,251.80	40	15	6.25	£260.14	£195.11	15	101	0	£0.00
30	13	KN552130	10	£319.98	4	£3,199.80	40	15	6.25	£255.98	£191.99	2	2	0	£0.00
31	14	A0906030015	18	£150.22	4	£2,703.96	40	15	6.25	£216.32	£162.24	8	4	4	£600.88
32	15	B78810721A	749	£3.44	4	£2,576.56	40	15	6.25	£206.12	£154.59	251	165	86	£295.84
33	16	D0991020012	164	£14.60	4	£2,394.40	40	15	6.25	£191.55	£143.66	104	36	68	£992.80
34	17	D0862070019Y	60	£35.25	4	£2,115.00	40	15	6.25	£169.20	£126.90	39	13	26	£916.50
35	18	D0978040014	35	£57.63	4	£2,017.05	40	15	6.25	£161.36	£121.02	91	8	83	£4,783.29
36	19	A78810601E	450	£4.20	4	£1,890.00	40	15	6.25	£151.20	£113.40	1117	99	1018	£4,275.60
37	20	B78818AE	35	£49.57	4	£1,734.95	40	15	6.25	£138.80	£104.10	14	8	6	£297.42
38	21	C78810762A	199	£7.44	4	£1,480.56	40	15	6.25	£118.44	£88.83	54	44	10	£74.40
39	22	D0753100033	75	£15.36	4	£1,152.00	40	15	6.25	£92.16	£69.12	34	17	17	£261.12
40	23	D1017040014	10	£95.36	4	£953.60	40	15	6.25	£76.29	£57.22	3	2	1	£95.36
41	24	KDB300600	8	£93.75	5	£750.00	80	20	3.125	£120.00	£60.00	6	3	3	£281.25
42	25	A0889030013	52	£9.59	5	£498.68	80	20	3.125	£79.79	£39.89	1	21	0	£0.00
43	26	B30880112C	700	£0.45	5	£315.00	80	20	3.125	£50.40	£25.20	566	280	286	£128.70
44	27	B30880113C	105	£1.18	6	£123.90	160	25	1.5625	£39.65	£12.39	125	78	47	£55.46

Excel 7.13 Chapter 7 You do the maths exercise answer 2

	A	B	C	D	E	F	G	H	I	J	K	L	M	N	O
1	Constant *k*	33													
2	Work Days	250													
3															
4															
5	Value Class		Class Limit	Overage %age	No of Parts in Class	Annual Spend Value	Cycle Days	Safety Days	No of Orders	Average Cycle Inventory	Safety Inventory	Planned Overage	Planned Inventory	Actual Overage Value	
6	1		£41,250	10%	2	£98,052	5	5	100	£981	£1,961	£327	£3,268	£214	
7	2		£10,313	20%	3	£51,613	10	5	75	£1,032	£1,032	£516	£2,581	£4,016	
8	3		£2,578	25%	10	£48,434	20	10	125	£1,937	£1,937	£1,292	£5,166	£7,613	
9	4		£645	30%	9	£14,487	40	15	56	£1,159	£869	£869	£2,897	£12,071	
10	5		£161	40%	2	£814	80	20	6	£130	£65	£130	£325	£129	
11	6		£0	50%	1	£124	160	25	2	£40	£12	£52	£104	£55	
12	7		£0		0	£0			0	£0	£0	£0	£0	£0	
13	8		£0		0	£0			0	£0	£0	£0	£0	£0	
14	9		£0		0	£0			0	£0	£0	£0	£0	£0	
15				Total	27	£213,524			364	£5,279	£5,877	£3,186	£14,342	£24,098	
16															
17	Count	Part Number	Annual Usage or Demand	Cost Per Part	Value Class	Annual Spend Value £	Cycle Days	Safety Days	No of Orders	Average Cycle Inventory	Average Safety Inventory	Actual Stock	Planned Maximum	Overage	Overage Value
18	1	B78811ZD	1324	£42.84	1	£56,726.63	5	5	50	£567.27	£1,134.53	58	53	5	£214.22
19	2	B78812ZF	987	£41.87	1	£41,325.69	5	5	50	£413.26	£826.51	20	39	0	£0.00
20	3	B78810741A	1012	£18.50	2	£18,722.00	10	5	25	£374.44	£374.44	75	61	14	£259.00
21	4	N6554004M0256	523	£35.08	2	£18,346.42	10	5	25	£366.93	£366.93	75	31	44	£1,543.48
22	5	SK98751	46	£316.19	2	£14,544.64	10	5	25	£290.89	£290.89	10	3	7	£2,213.31
23	6	LE763	781	£11.11	3	£8,679.28	20	10	12.5	£347.17	£347.17	321	94	227	£2,522.66
24	7	D0883030014C	267	£27.54	3	£7,354.28	20	10	12.5	£294.17	£294.17	98	32	66	£1,817.91
25	8	C78810742A	360	£16.87	3	£6,071.97	20	10	12.5	£242.88	£242.88	7	43	0	£0.00
26	9	D0862060018Y	163	£33.26	3	£5,420.88	20	10	12.5	£216.84	£216.84	65	20	45	£1,496.56
27	10	C78810761A	567	£8.43	3	£4,780.58	20	10	12.5	£191.22	£191.22	3	68	0	£0.00
28	11	LE02	396	£11.09	3	£4,393.19	20	10	12.5	£175.73	£175.73	0	48	0	£0.00
29	12	B78812001B	458	£7.10	3	£3,250.36	20	10	12.5	£130.01	£130.01	15	55	0	£0.00
30	13	KN552130	10	£319.98	3	£3,199.83	20	10	12.5	£127.99	£127.99	2	1	1	£319.98
31	14	A0906030015	18	£150.22	3	£2,703.97	20	10	12.5	£108.16	£108.16	8	2	6	£901.32
32	15	B78810721A	749	£3.44	3	£2,579.83	20	10	12.5	£103.19	£103.19	251	90	161	£554.54
33	16	D0991020012	164	£14.60	4	£2,393.59	40	15	6.25	£191.49	£143.62	104	36	68	£992.47
34	17	D0862070019Y	60	£35.25	4	£2,115.00	40	15	6.25	£169.20	£126.90	39	13	26	£916.50
35	18	D0978040014	35	£57.63	4	£2,017.10	40	15	6.25	£161.37	£121.03	91	8	83	£4,783.40
36	19	A78810601E	450	£4.20	4	£1,890.00	40	15	6.25	£151.20	£113.40	1117	99	1018	£4,275.60
37	20	B78818AE	35	£49.57	4	£1,734.95	40	15	6.25	£138.80	£104.10	14	8	6	£297.42
38	21	C78810762A	199	£7.44	4	£1,480.56	40	15	6.25	£118.44	£88.83	54	44	10	£74.40
39	22	D0753100033	75	£15.36	4	£1,152.00	40	15	6.25	£92.16	£69.12	34	17	17	£261.12
40	23	D1017040014	10	£95.36	4	£953.60	40	15	6.25	£76.29	£57.22	3	2	1	£95.36
41	24	KDB300600	8	£93.75	4	£750.00	40	15	6.25	£60.00	£45.00	6	2	4	£375.00
42	25	A0889030013	52	£9.59	5	£498.68	80	20	3.125	£79.79	£39.89	1	21	0	£0.00
43	26	B30880112C	700	£0.45	5	£315.00	80	20	3.125	£50.40	£25.20	566	280	286	£128.70
44	27	B30880113C	105	£1.18	6	£123.90	160	25	1.5625	£39.65	£12.39	125	78	47	£55.46

The practical application of *k*-curve

08

Introduction

This chapter brings together the tools and techniques for inventory planning from the previous chapters. In Chapter 2, we developed an understanding of the important role of MRP as a planning system, we examined its strengths and weaknesses, and now know that we must manage these parameters proactively. The tools described in Chapters 5 to 7 provide a good basis for the determination of these parameters at various levels and help focus on planning at strategic, tactical and detail levels. In summary:

- Focus on optimizing products by examining the inventory in the stack and flow: Chapter 5.
- Plan cycle stocks and safety stock for individual items: Chapters 6 and 7.
- Manage groups of items and build decision models that plan at an aggregate level: Chapters 6 and 7.

In this chapter we will now look at tools and techniques that will help us plan inventory at an aggregate level and then identify the actions required to implement the plan in detail. We have understood from earlier chapters that we are potentially dealing with a massive number of parts and parameters that we need to determine and manage. This chapter will use the four steps we identified in Chapters 4 for development of an inventory plan. We will build upon the inventory tools used in the previous chapter and expand the use of the *k*-curve approach, to show how it can be developed into a planning and implementation tool.

The four steps to the planning process developed in Chapters 4 are:

- Understand the current inventory position: *How much stock do I have on hand?*
- Identify the business targets for inventory: *What inventory do I need?*
- Create an inventory plan: *What do I have to do to achieve the business targets and how difficult will it be?*
- Implement the plan: *What actions must I take to achieve the plan?*

We will take these four steps and show how we can bring together the individual tools discussed in previous chapters into a coherent process. This will show how we can create an implementable inventory plan. An important key step we will look at is how to provide, in a practical way, information that can be implemented into the MRP planning system.

Figure 8.1 shows the overall inventory planning roadmap for the process, with links to the relevant chapters in the book. We have developed Figure 8.1 from Figure 4.19, and will now use the work from the previous chapter as the first step to 'identifying the business targets'. The chapter will look in detail at each of the four steps and, using a practical scenario, demonstrate the creation of an inventory plan.

Figure 8.1 shows how the four steps link to the previous chapters and develops a roadmap for an inventory planning process. It identifies the four steps and summarizes the key actions, which will be detailed in the following sections in this chapter:

- Understand the current inventory position: we need to extract data from the company's planning system, to determine the stock position and the parameters currently in use.
- Identify the business targets for inventory: the senior management will typically set targets and the planner needs to determine the new plan. To do this the planner needs to analyse current data; establish a current position; and then apply the *k*-curve model to show how the planning target can be met.
- Create an inventory plan: having created the model which represents the new plan we need to, using the model, specify in detail the actions required to achieve the new plan.
- Implement the plan: the detailed actions are typically expressed in two ways:

Figure 8.1 Overall planning process roadmap

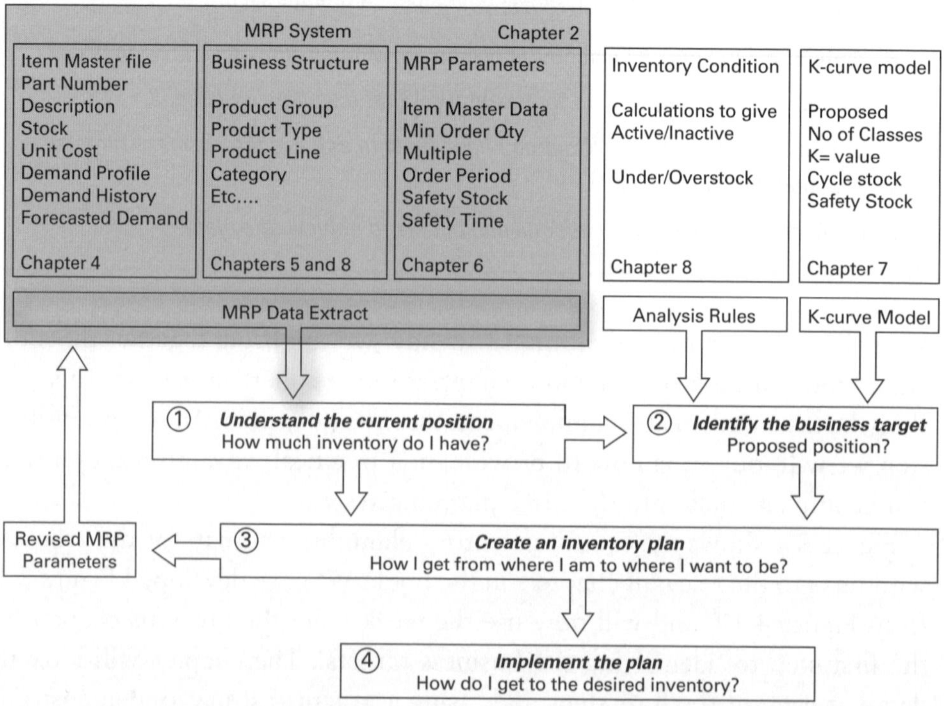

- First, systems-based actions that will drive the planning system to deliver the new inventory plan through revised cycle, safety and lead-time parameters which need to be implemented into the planning system.
- Second business-based actions that address the tasks identified during the analysis and planning stages that require changes to manufacturing and supply chain processes to improve the capability of the organization and allow the business to operate safely at a lower inventory level.

The best way to demonstrate the application of this technique is to use a real inventory planning situation. In this chapter we will use a database of about 5,000 parts, available from the online resources, which we shall call our scenario Division X. Should you wish, you will be able to follow the planning process and examples and then take a closer look at the data to aid your understanding.

By working through an example we want to show how to tackle the issue raised in Chapter 1, Figure 1.3, which is related to the implementation of inventory reduction programmes that are driven from the global senior management targets. Thus for our working example we shall assume that our management has requested a 20 per cent inventory reduction within the next

12 months. We will show how, when planning Division X, the tools identified in Chapter 6 which looked at planning parts individually can be used. We will then show how *k*-curve can plan a group of parts as described in Chapter 7. We know that in a real business we would want to subdivide the parts into groups because we cannot adopt a one-size-fits-all approach. Therefore when planning Division X we will look at how we can 'spread' the inventory reduction across the business. We will look at analysis techniques that allow you to understand the current position for a given group of parts and then create an exchange curve that will allow you to match the target inventory level and thus determine the *planning rule set* for that group of parts. Finally, we will step through the creation of a consolidated plan. As in previous chapters where it is appropriate we will show the Excel logic, however there is still a need for the reader to fully understand their own MRP system as each system has its own way of planning. Thus the use of Division X will show how to navigate the roadmap shown in Figure 8.1.

The scenario is as follows: Division X currently has £9.5 million of inventory, which is well managed and has a stock turn of around 10 turns. The business is doing well and predicts a cost of sales for the coming year of just below £100 million. The senior management would like to capitalize on the strong sales by reducing the inventory by 20 per cent. Thus our challenge is to achieve a planned stock level for year-end of £7.6 million.

Understand your current inventory position: how much have I got?

The first stage in any planning process is to understand where you are. There are four elements:

- First, identify the current inventory position: this is the obvious start point, ie how much inventory do we have and where is it? This will be a simple list of the quantity on the shelf, the unit cost, location (if appropriate) and its status: is it good stock, is it available for use, is it new or refurbished?
- Second, and almost as important, is to know what the MRP system is planning at the moment. This is so that we understand what inventory the MRP system is planning. These MRP parameters are normally in the 'item master data' and should not be too difficult to extract. They are, typically,

Minimum Order Quantity (MOQ), Order Multiple, Order Period, Safety Quantity, Safety Time, Lead Time and Shelf Life (if appropriate). These are important since they are the parameters used by MRP to raise purchase/manufacturing orders, which in turn drive deliveries into stores and the inventory held. We know from the discussions in Chapter 4 that if these are not managed they can cause significant problems in non-compliance.

- Next, we know from Chapter 2 that there is a direct relationship between the inventory and demand. It would be useful to determine both the past demand (historic) and the future demand (forecast). The importance of the historic demand will make it easier to understand why some parts are being held in stock, and the forecast will make it easier to determine the ideal level of future demand and which parts are still required to be stocked.
- Finally, most businesses will have developed reporting structures that divide the business into reporting groups. These are often based on MRP 'product groupings' and these help to segment the business performance data to match the structure of the business.

In combining these four elements we will get a much clearer picture of the current inventory position rather than a simple list of all the inventory, with the highest inventory item at the top of the list, as often suggested when using Pareto. To enable this analysis we will need to establish a database/spreadsheet which we can use as the basis of the analysis. The data required is shown in Table 8.1.

This is quite an exhaustive list and may not be easily assembled, however it is worth persisting in assembling this data into a single database (eg Excel workbook) as it will form the basis of the inventory plan. Demand is often a difficult area to determine and it may require some ingenuity with Excel or a skilled IT technician to extract the required data. Ideally it is useful to look back at least three years and to get the forecast that will cover the next 12 months. Once the database is established it can also be used on a regular basis in the future for tracking the current performance, thus it should be reasonable to justify the considerable IT effort if needed.

Generating an inventory overview

Once we have collected the data we will want to present it in a form that identifies the current inventory position. The data collected based on Table 8.1 has four sections: Item Master, Demand Profile, Business Structure and MRP Parameters; these will enable us to determine the current position.

Table 8.1 MRP Data Extract – key elements

Item Master / Inventory Module

- part number
- description
- number in stock
  - available
  - allocated
  - quarantine
- unit cost (to be used for all valuations)
- warehouse
- location

Demand Profile

- historic usage for previous years (three years)
- projected demand
  - usage for 12 months if possible, or as far into the future as is valid, then pro rata to be equivalent to 12 months' demand
  - or use the historic demand as a representation for future demand

Business Structure

- product group
- product type
- product category
- planner
- buyer

MRP Parameters

- cycle stock parameters
  - lot size
  - minimum order quantity
  - multiple quantity
  - economic order quantity – if defined
  - order period (in days, confirm if five-day week or seven days)
- safety stock parameters
  - safety stock quantity
  - safety time
- lead-time
  - manufactured
  - purchased
  - additional lead-times if used

We need to develop an Excel database to be able to bring these elements together, and a suggested structure is shown in Excel 8.1. Next we need to add some formulae to establish the detail behind the current inventory position.

First, we need to know if the part is active and valid. To be active we would expect stock and/or demand; to be valid we would expect to have a record for the three elements of stock, demand and unit cost. From these three elements we can determine if the part is both 'active/inactive' and valid.

Next, for all the active parts we need to evaluate if the current inventory is too much or too little. In Chapter 6 we looked at the inventory saw tooth and how we can base an analysis of the 'inventory condition' on the MRP parameters of cycle and safety. The MRP parameters identify the maximum and minimum planned stock levels and to do this we will need to calculate:

- MRP cycle stock – this evaluates the MRP parameters to determine the cycle stock.
- Number of batches – using the cycle stock to give an estimate of the number of batches.
- MRP safety stock – this evaluates the MRP parameters to determine the safety stock.

Once we have these calculations we can apply the rules set out in Table 6.14 to allocate the parts to their appropriate 'active condition'.

In the following sections we look in detail at how to create the Excel database based on the recommended structure shown in Excel 8.1, which shows each formulae in detail.

MRP cycle stock and safety stock

The first step to correctly interpreting the MRP parameters is to estimate what the MRP system would calculate when creating a planned order. To understand the logic applied by the MRP system we have used the typical logic applied by most MRP systems. It is important to check the exact logic that your MRP system uses as there may be subtleties in the way it interprets the individual parameters.

Excel 8.2 shows the logic for creating the cycle stock; typically MRP will calculate the demand for a specified order period, and then test to see if a minimum order quantity and multiple quantity need to be applied. If no order period is applied it is usually one day of demand. Thus if all the parameters are set to zero it should return a value equivalent to one day of demand.

Excel 8.1 Structure and logic of inventory planning database

	A	B	C	D
1	A	Part Number	Database	MRP Extract
2	B	Standard Cost		
3	C	STOCK		
4	D	Annual Demand Quantity		
5	E	MIN_QTY		
6	F	MAX_QTY		
7	G	ORD_MULT		
8	H	SFTY_TIME		
9	I	ORDER_PER		
10	J	SFTY_STOCK		
11	K	Product Group		
12	L	MRP Cycle Stock Quantity	Excel 8.2	MRP Rules
13	M	MRP Safety Stock Quantity	Excel 8.4	
14	N	MRP Over/Under Qty	Excel 8.7	
15	O	No of MRP batches	Excel 8.3	
16	P	Actual Stock Value	=B2*C2	
17	Q	Annual Demand Value	=B2*D2	
18	R	MRP Cycle Stock Value	=B2*L2	
19	S	MRP Safety Stock Value	=B2*M2	
20	T	MRP Net Overage Value	=B2*N2	
21	U	Days of Overage	Excel 8.8	
22	V	Plan Group	=VLOOKUP(K2,'Table 8.6'!A:B,2,FALSE)	Analysis Rules
23	W	Active / Inactive	Excel 8.5	
24	X	Active Condition	Excel 8.6	
25	Y	Value Class	Excel 8.9	*k*-curve logic
26	Z	Class Cycle Days		
27	AA	Class Safety Days		
28	AB	Proposed No of Batches		
29	AC	Proposed Cycle Quantity		
30	AD	Proposed Safety Quantity		
31	AE	Proposed Cycle Stock Value		
32	AF	Proposed Safety Stock Value		
33	AG	Cycle Stock Difference	=L2-AC2	Differences
34	AH	Safety Stock Difference	=M2-AD2	
35	AI	Cycle Stock Value Difference	=B2*AG2	
36	AJ	Safety Stock Value Difference	=B2*AH2	

Open new Excel workbook. Create sheets with names Database, *k*-curve.
Copy Excel 7.10 into *k*-curve.
Copy Database from online resources to Database columns A to K.

Once we know the estimate of the order size we can calculate the numbers of orders per year for each product by dividing the demand by the order size. Excel 8.3 shows the excel logic for calculating the number of batches based on the cycle stock.

Excel 8.2 Estimating cycle stock logic

<table>
<tr><td colspan="8">L2=IF((D2/'k-curve'!$B$2)*IF(I2<=1,'k-curve'!$J$2,I2)<=E2,E2,ROUNDUP(((D2/'k-curve'!$B$2)*IF(I2<=1,'k-curve'!$J$2,I2))/IF(G2=0,1,G2),0)*IF(G2=0,1,G2))
NB
Column B is Demand
Column I is Order period
Column E is Minimum Order Quantity
Column G is Order Multiple
Cell reference 'k-curve'!$B$2 is the number of work days in the year
Cell reference 'k-curve'!$J$2 is used to set a minimum cycle stock, often MRP is set to a batch days of 1, which is not representative of the reality of weekly deliveries which is the usual default
For calculating demand / day the assumption is there are 250 working days in a year, with a 5 day week
When applying this equation in Excel substitute the appropriate Column references
Assumes 1st line of data is Row 2</td></tr>
<tr><td>=IF((D2/'k-curve'!$B$2)*IF(I2<=1,'k-curve'!$J$2,I2)<=E2
Test to see if Order Period Qty is Greater than MOQ
Order period must be 1 not 0</td><td>True</td><td colspan="6" rowspan="2">False</td></tr>
<tr><td></td><td>E2,</td></tr>
<tr><td></td><td></td><td>ROUNDUP(</td><td colspan="5"></td></tr>
<tr><td colspan="3">Apply the Multiple to Quantities over MOQ by dividing and then rounding by the multiple</td><td>(((D2/'k-curve'!$B$2)*IF(I2<=1,'k-curve'!$J$2,I2))
Order Period Qty
Order period must be 1 not 0</td><td>/</td><td>IF(G2=0,1,G2)
Multiple Must be 1 not 0</td><td>,0)</td><td></td></tr>
<tr><td colspan="7">Correct for where Multiple is 0, which logically means 1.</td><td>*IF(G2=0,1,G2))
Multiple</td></tr>
</table>

Excel 8.3 Logic for calculating the number of batches

O2=IF(D2=0,0,ROUNDUP(D2/L2,0))
NB
Column D is Demand
Column L is Calculated Order Quantity
When applying this equation in Excel substitute the appropriate Column references
Assumes 1st line of data is Row 2

=IF(D2=0,	True	False		
	0, **No demand = no batches**			
		ROUNDUP(		
			D2/L2 **Demand divided by Order Qty**	,0))

Excel 8.4 Estimating additive safety stock logic

M2=ROUNDUP(J2+(H2*D2/'k-curve'!$B$2),0)
NB
Column D is Demand
Column H is Safety Time
Column J is Safety Stock Quantity
Cell reference 'k-curve'!$B$2 is the number of work days in the year
For calculating demand / day the assumption is there are 250 working days in a year, with a 5 day week
When applying this equation in Excel substitute the appropriate Column references
Assumes 1st line of data is Row 2

ROUNDUP(				
Add the Safety Quantity and Safety Time and round up the result.	(J2 **Safety Stock Qty**	**+**	(H2*D2/'k-curve'!$B$2) **Safety Time * Demand / Day**	,0)

The next element to determine is the safety stock. Excel 8.4 shows the logic here is slightly different as there are a number of key variations in logic that will need to be understood. The three options are:

1. Additive Safety Stock = Safety Time + Safety Quantity
2. Min Safety Stock = Lower of Safety Time or Safety Stock
3. Max Safety Stock = Higher of Safety Time or Safety Stock

It will need to be confirmed which is in use by the MRP system. The example is based on additive safety stock.

The next step in the creation of the database is to determine the condition of the stock. This is divided into two stages: the first is to identify if the part is valid and active; the second, if the part is active the 'active condition', eg comparing the actual stock with the planned stock based on the MRP parameters.

Active/inactive inventory

To be able to identify whether an item is active and inactive we need to consider three attributes: stock, demand and unit cost. The range of options for these three attributes and how the eight combinations can be classified are shown in Table 8.2.

Table 8.2 Active/inactive inventory

Name	Description	Stock	Demand	Cost
Active	Stock with Demand and Cost	Y	Y	Y
	No Stock with Demand and Cost	N	Y	Y
Inactive	Stock with No Demand but Cost	Y	N	Y
Dormant	No stock, No Demand but Cost	N	N	Y
Threat	Stock and Demand but No cost	Y	Y	N
	Stock with No Demand and No Cost	Y	N	N
	No Stock with Demand but No Cost	N	Y	N
Invalid	No stock, No Demand and No Cost	N	N	N

The inventory value will reside in the first two categories; dormant parts will indicate the number of parts in the database not being used. The threat category is important as it indicates that there are parts that cannot be valued and could potentially be a problem. These may be new products where the value has not been assigned, parts where the value has been written down to zero or an error. A possible logic statement that can be used to identify the inventory categories is shown in Excel 8.5.

A typical current position is shown on page 339 based on an Excel pivot table from the Division X database in Table 8.3.

Excel 8.5 Logic tree for identifying active/inactive inventory

W2=IF(B2>0,IF(D2>0,"Active",IF(C2>0,"Inactive","Dormant")),IF(D2>0,"Threat",IF(C2>0,"Threat","Invalid")))
NB
Column B is Unit Cost
Column D is Demand
Column C is Stock
When applying this equation in Excel substitute the appropriate Column references
Assumes 1st line of data is Row 2

<table>
<tr><td>=IF(B2>0,
Cost</td><td colspan="5">True</td><td colspan="5" rowspan="3">False</td></tr>
<tr><td>Cost and Demand</td><td>IF(D2>0,
Demand</td><td>"Active",</td><td colspan="3">False</td></tr>
<tr><td colspan="3">Cost but No Demand test for Stock</td><td>IF(D2>0,
Stock</td><td>"Inactive",</td><td>"Dormant")),</td></tr>
<tr><td colspan="6">No Cost but Demand</td><td>IF(D2>0,
Demand</td><td>"Threat",</td><td colspan="3">False</td></tr>
<tr><td colspan="8">No Cost and No Demand test for Stock</td><td>IF(D2>0,
Stock</td><td>"Threat",</td><td>"Invalid")))</td></tr>
</table>

Table 8.3 Division X analysis of 'active/inactive' inventory using Excel pivot table

Row Labels	Count of Part Number	Sum of Actual Stock Value	Sum of Stock	Sum of Annual Demand Value	Sum of Annual Demand Quantity	Sum of Cycle Stock Value	Sum of Cycle Stock Quantity	Sum of Safety Stock Value	Sum of Safety Stock Quantity
Active	3,991	£8,667,067.77	31,505,499	£86,900,221.13	196,810,241	£2,872,967.37	18,141,143	£3,306,812.94	6,347,855
Inactive	809	£789,365.20	1,538,343					£8,595.22	2,761
Dormant	13							£88.44	200
Threat	126		300,022		338,311		8,325		17,554
Invalid	14								
Grand Total	**4,953**	**£9,456,432.97**	**33,343,864**	**£86,900,221.13**	**197,148,552**	**£2,872,967.37**	**18,149,468**	**£3,315,496.60**	**6,368,369**

In the Table 8.3 sample we can see that there is a total inventory of £9.5 million held in 4,953 parts.

Active

There are 3,991 active parts representing an inventory of £8.7 million, with demand of £86.9 million.

Dormant

The next category is 'dormant'. Here we see just a few parts listed, however looking across we can see that the MRP parameters show some safety stock; if these parts are truly dormant then we should ensure that cycle and safety stock parameters in MRP are removed to prevent unnecessary ordering and stocking of the products, which have no demand or current stock.

Inactive

About 809 parts are 'inactive' with a value of £789K. This inactive inventory is not contributing to the business and if the demand used in the analysis represents the next 12 months, demand suggests that it will still be there in 12 months. More importantly, if the business target is based on reducing the inventory by, say, 20 per cent or £1.8 million then it will be made more difficult as at least £789K of the inventory will still be there in a year's time.

Invalid

These parts are the deadwood and in data terms are clogging up the system. These are often excluded from reports so they often go unnoticed.

Threat

The next category, 'threat', shows that we have 126 parts that have no unit cost, but have quantities of stock, demand and MRP parameters. This is a dangerous situation as it means that first the actual stock and demand values are understated and second MRP is potentially ordering materials without knowing the cost. This can be because these are new products, or alternatively the stock has been written down. In both cases it is important to know what these parts are and ensure that they are costed at the earliest opportunity.

Excel 8.6 Logic for determining the 'active condition'

X2=IF(P2=0,"Shortage",IF(P2<S2,"Underage",IF(P2<(S2+R2),"Optimum",IF(P2<2*(S2+R2),"Overage",IF(P2<Q2,"Severe Overage",IF(P2<2*Q2,"Excess","Surplus"))))))
NB
Column P is Stock Value
Column Q is Demand value
Column R is Cycle Stock Value
Column S is Safety Stock Value
When applying this equation in Excel substitute the appropriate Column references
Assumes 1st line of data is Row 2

Condition	Test	True	False
Stock Value = 0	=IF(P2=0,	True "Shortage",	False
Stock Value is less than Safety	IF(P2<S2,	True "Underage",	False
Stock Value is less than Maximum Stock (Cycle + Safety)	IF(P2< (S2+R2),	True "Optimum",	False
Stock value is less than twice Maximum Stock (Cycle + Safety)	IF(P2<2* (S2+R2),	True "Overage",	False
Stock Value is less than one year's demand	IF(P2<Q2	True "Severe Overage",	False
Stock Value is less than two years' demand	IF(P2<2 *Q2,	True "Excess",	False "Surplus"))))))

Inventory vs plan level: active/inactive inventory condition

The next stage is to use the MRP parameters to determine the overall health of the active stock, and take a closer look at the inactive. In Figure 6.14 we identified the different conditions of inventory, underage, overage optimum and how these are related to the cycle stock and safety stock. We can therefore easily classify the active stock into the seven categories specified in Table 6.14. To classify the stock we will need to create a classification column in the database. The logic for determining the inventory condition is shown in Excel 8.6.

The same essential logic can be used to determine the amount of stock that is in overage and underage. This will help in the evaluation of the current stock position. Excel 8.7 shows the logic.

Excel 8.7 Logic for determining overage and underage

<table>
<tr><td colspan="5">N2=IF(C2-L2-M2>0,C2-L2-M2,IF(C2-M2>0,0,C2-M2))
NB
Column C is Stock Quantity
Column L is Cycle Stock Quantity
Column M is Safety Stock Quantity
When applying this equation in Excel substitute the appropriate Column references
Assumes 1st line of data is Row 2
Explanation of Underage / Overage see Figure 6.14</td></tr>
<tr><td>=IF(C2-L2-M2>0,</td><td>True</td><td colspan="3" rowspan="2">False</td></tr>
<tr><td>Overage is quantity of stock over maximum</td><td>C2-L2-M2,</td></tr>
<tr><td colspan="2">Test to identify for underage or optimum value</td><td>IF(C2-M2>0,</td><td>0,
If inventory is within optimum range result is 0</td><td>C2-M2))
Underage</td></tr>
</table>

The final piece of logic is to determine how long the overage will last, as discussed previously in Figure 6.16, and extended in Excel 8.8 to show the logic for determining the number of overage days.

Once we have added this logic to the database we can begin the process of analysis. Excel has an excellent pivot table which will make analysis very easy.

Excel 8.8 Logic for determining overage days

U2=ROUNDUP(IF(N2<=0,0,IF(D2=0,0,(N2+L2)/(D2/'k-curve'!$B$2))),0)
NB
Column D is Demand
Column L is Cycle Stock Quantity
Column N is The Over/Under Quantity
Cell reference 'k-curve'!$B$2 is the number of work days in the year
When applying this equation in Excel substitute the appropriate Column references
Assumes 1st line of data is Row 2
Explanation of Underage / Overage see Figure 6.14

=ROUNDUP(						,0)
	IF(N2<=0,	True	False			
Test for Overage		0,				
Test for Demand			IF(D2=0,	True	False	
Calculates number of days till minimum stock, i.e. next delivery is due				0,	(N2+L2)/(D2/'k-curve'!$B$2)))	

In this analysis we are only concerned with the active inventory. Looking at Table 8.4 we can see that active stock is £8.7 million and cost of sales of £86.9 million, which confirms the turnover of 10. On the surface this is very respectable. If we are able to achieve the optimum inventory (½ Cycle + Safety stock), of £3.426m / 2 + £3.316m = £5.029m it would give us an inventory well below our target of £7.6 million and a possible stock turn of 17.3.

Shortage

Looking first at shortages there are 917 parts, which is approximately 22 per cent of the number of parts. It is reasonable to assume that not all are causing line stoppages, but they represent a significant workload for the planners, which will no doubt be the focus of the production and shipping meetings. What is interesting is that if all these parts were to become available it would increase the inventory by £544k.

Underage

Next underage items: these are not yet causing problems in production/sales, however the 'safety' is being utilized and the focus should be to ensure that the stock is delivered on time. Ideally the stock should be £1.202 million (£0.504 / 2 + £0.950 million) but it is currently only £0.527 million, some £675K short, the net result of getting the shortages and underage under complete control would be an increase in inventory of £1.2 million.

Table 8.4 Division X analysis of active inventory condition using Excel pivot table

Row Labels	Count of PART NUMBER	Sum of Actual Stock Value	Sum of Annual Demand Value	Sum of MRP Cycle Stock Value	Sum of MRP Safety Stock Value	Sum of MRP Net Overage Value
Active	3,991	£8,667,068	£86,900,221	£3,426,309	£3,316,579	£3,643,419
Shortage	917	£0	£22,508,495	£560,652	£274,253	–£274,253
Underage	248	£527,398	£18,798,506	£504,920	£950,260	–£422,863
Optimum	673	£890,535	£11,463,818	£1,144,318	£399,884	£0
Overage	504	£2,548,552	£18,076,428	£675,241	£1,100,427	£772,884
Severe Overage	1,111	£3,549,246	£15,594,513	£460,599	£567,285	£2,521,361
Excess	138	£422,478	£312,317	£29,171	£16,631	£376,677
Surplus	400	£728,858	£146,145	£51,408	£7,838	£669,613
Grand Total	**3,991**	**£8,667,068**	**£86,900,221**	**£3,426,309**	**£3,316,579**	**£3,643,419**

Optimum

The optimum stock should be £0.971 million (£1.144m / 2 + £0.399m but is £0.891 million, thus is running slightly under. It is worth noting that only 10 per cent of the inventory is in optimum.

Overage

If we now look at the overage, here we have said that overage only occurs above maximum, so the amount of overage should be measured from the maximum stock, Cycle Stock + Safety Stock, thus the maximum is £1.8m and £0.773 million is the actual overage. In the discussion in Chapter 6 we understood overage was to be expected; this is, however, counterbalanced by the understocks. These over and understock values really represent the problems of balancing the supply and demand and they are to be expected in most businesses. The lower the value the more control the business has over its supply and demand.

Overage days

It is useful to be able to evaluate overage in terms of the number of days of overage, particularly when identifying where to focus, for example we may have a part with £10,000 of overage that will take five days to consume, and another £10,000 part that the overage will take 50 days to consume. There is really no case for action on the first part, whereas it would be wise to investigate and ensure that no further orders were received for the second for at least 50 days.

Severe overage, excess and surplus

What is more of a problem is the remaining overstock conditions: severe overage, excess and surplus, although these values will take a lot longer to resolve and should be of significant interest to the organization. The severe overage, when the maximum stock of £0.941 million is removed is £2.393 million, and represents the bulk of the overstock problem.

Next, if we look at the excess, the correct working level for which is only £31K, £0.376 million is in 'excess', which means that this stock will take at least 12 months to be consumed.

Similarly for surplus the correct level is only £34K which means that the 'surplus' of £0.669 million is going to take at least two years to be consumed.

If we were to take the inventory conditions of severe overage, excess and surplus and investigate the top 10 per cent (only 170 items), we would get a very clear picture of the causes and thus actions to be put in place to improve the problem.

CASE STUDY

Comment

What we have found with clients is that there are numerous reasons why they are overstocked. There are two examples that come to mind: first, a company was managing a difficult contract where the supply for a particular motor was likely to put the project at risk. It was decided to purchase the entire estimated demand of 1,000 motors at £500. When the squeeze was put on inventory having £500,000 of insurance stock on an inventory of £3 million meant that finding inventory reductions is significantly harder as 10 per cent of £3 million is £300,000, whereas the true opportunity should be based on £2.5 million or £250,000, not only that but the £500,000 was going to take several years to be consumed.

In the second, during a long period of drought a company decided to purchase water storage tanks – needed to enable their equipment to be used during the hose pipe ban. The 25 tanks were purchased at £6,100 each, at which point the weather broke, the hose pipe ban lifted and only three were ever utilized. The result was that the £134,000 of stock, which was 10 per cent of the £1.4 million business's stock, remains waiting for next drought; meanwhile it limits the ability to reduce stock. In both cases the initial purchases were for sound business reasons, but when creating targets for inventory reduction it has to be accepted that these inventory items cannot be included. These inventory items need to be identified and classified as 'strategic stock' and handled outside the working stock.

In summary, through some simple analysis we can get a good view of our current position and we can make sure that when we set inventory reduction targets that we take into account inventory that can be reduced and specifically exclude those that for strategic reason we have decided to hold. This will result in credible targets and realistic plans. In summary, we would show the high-level analysis as described for Division X in Table 8.5.

Determine the business targets that relate to inventory: what do I have to achieve?

All businesses need to plan and this will often follow an annual cycle; as the business year ends there is a frenzy of activity to meet the business targets set for that year, whether they be the sales, production or inventory targets.

Table 8.5 Division X current inventory

Inventory	No of parts	Value	Over/Under Value	Comment/Action
Active	**3,991**	**£8,667,068**	**£3,643,419**	
• Shortage	917	£0	–£274,253	22% of parts to be improved
• Underage	248	£527,398	–£422,863	
• Optimum	673	£890,535	£0	10% of parts
• Overage	504	£2,548,552	£772,884	All overage 50% of stock
• Severe Overage	1,111	£3,549,246	£2,521,361	Severe demand changes in July on Far East
• Excess	138	£422,478	£376,677	
• Surplus	400	£728,858	£669,613	"Strategic stock = £450 for critical supply = £100 AB123455 Project Alpha"
Inactive	**809**	**£789,365**	**£746,592**	£200 for Cancelled Project Alpha, alternate use being investigated by engineering
Dormant	13	£0		
Threat	126	£0		100 new products being introduced costs due by M/E by mid Jan
Invalid	14	£0		
Grand Total	**4,953**	**£9,456,433**	**£4,432,784**	

Overall position has improved since last year, overage running at 50% of all stock key focus will be improvement in shortage control, overage management and disposal/reuse of Project Alpha stock

CASE STUDY

When working for IBM I recall a number of New Year Eve's being disturbed, as the plants inventory manager I was called in to adjudicate on the last minute arrivals from our sister plants, who were trying to reduce their inventory by shipping early, whilst conversely we were refusing to receive early deliveries to ensure that we met our inventory targets. Businesses are driven by planning, targets and the creation of action plans to ensure delivery of the target. This example shows how competing business KPIs within one organization can create extra work for the staff, all of whom are focused on their specific division/department when trying to meet their own targets.

A progressive business will begin the planning process before the end of the year and each department gets their targets and objectives. These are typically expressed at a high level and the departmental managers are expected to deploy the targets to a lower level; each business will have its own programme for this deployment, the methods used include:

- Quality functional deployment.
- Lean six sigma.
- Hosin Kanri.
- PDCA (Plan, Do, Check, Action).

The common feature is that they will look to link the actions of the business to the business targets to ensure that the focus is directed at what needs to be achieved. This effort is always in addition to the challenge of managing the day-to-day operations. Thus it is important to ensure that the inventory actions will assist in producing a more effective operation of the business system.

Inventory management from the top

As we stated in the introduction, senior management typically express the inventory target as a simple number, either × per cent or £y. For the operations manager we need to determine how this is to be achieved, which necessitates a detailed analysis of where we are and what is possible. The pressures within the business are often such that there is a constant pressure downwards on inventory and the need to consistently improve our 'on time performance' to the customer/manufacturing operation. These provide the key challenge to any manager responsible for inventory, often expressed as simple statements that completely belie their complexity.

> Quotes from Plant Inventory Manager at IBM in 1980s
> 'You can reduce the inventory as much as you like... but don't stop my production.'
> 'Reduce the inventory by 10 per cent but you must not fail to service the customer.'
>
> Quotes from case study research conducted during Inventory Management Research Thesis
> 'Don't purchase any safety stock.'
> 'Only purchase A & B Components.'
> 'The Maximum stock cover must be no greater than six weeks.'
> 'Base batch sizes on 1–2 weeks of components or a practical minimum will be set to compensate for set-up times.'
>
> (Relph, 2006)

If we are going to avoid the scatter-gun approach we need to be able to express the global targets in detail. Fortunately business often naturally divides the business into sub-groups – these will provide the best basis for inventory planning.

Identifying different groups

These sub-groups can often reflect what the business manufactures, or consider manufacturing process key stages such as:

- raw materials;
- components;
- sub-assemblies;
- machined parts/moulded parts; and
- finished products.

These stages fall into three types of process: purchased, manufactured and finished goods stock. In addition to these groups we may need to consider the phase that the part is in its product lifecycle. If our business is retail the natural groupings would essentially be based on finished goods stock that has been purchased. Thus they will have the same constraints; in addition to product lifecycle the following may be important considerations for managing the stock levels:

- product categories;
- volatility of demand;
- criticality to customer; and
- source.

And finally, if our business were a Repairs and Maintenance business, it would be similar to Manufacturing as it will contain manufacturing stages, however we could also consider:

- criticality to customer;
- reliability of product;
- field population; and
- availability of replacement parts.

All these factors may or may not affect the way in which the inventory should ideally be planned. If these groupings are summarized it is possible to identify which factors will require different inventory planning rule sets. Table 8.6 shows how they affect the rule set components.

Table 8.6 Product grouping considerations

Group	No of Classes	Cycle Stock	Safety Stock	Capability/ Throughput
Purchased	Product Range Spread of Annual Spend		Service level required	Resource Technology
Manufactured				Tools Line changeover
Finished Goods		Maximise customer variety		Variability
New Product			Respond to initial demand	

Table 8.6 *continued*

Group	No of Classes	Cycle Stock	Safety Stock	Capability/ Throughput
End of Life			Minimize stock investment	
Customer Critical			Maximize service level through statistical safety stock	
Volatile Demand			Statistical Safety Stock to respond to demand volatility	

Once the business structure is defined we can begin to break down the inventory target. If the business structure can be expressed by utilizing particular data fields from MRP it will make the planning task much simpler. Business always tend to divide inventory into sub-groups, which are often used for reporting status and summarizing the business position. MRP systems will often provide data fields to facilitate the creation of these sub-groups. Product group, product type, product line, product class, planner, buyer, category are just a few examples. The prime purpose of these fields is to enable management reporting and target setting. We will utilize these to form the basis of the plan groups as we develop the inventory plan. The issue will be that each of the plan groups must first relate to the way management wish to see the inventory and second that the parts within the group can be managed in the same way. If not, we may need to further divide the 'management groups' to make plan groups that can be set using the *k*-curve technique, eg A Class, Far East etc… New Products, End-of-Life Products, Machined or Purchased. Before commencing the next stage it is important to resolve two questions:

- Can I present and track the plan in a way that the management will recognize?
- Can I plan each group with a common set of rules for cycle stock, safety stock and overage?

Once the plan group decisions have been made we can progress to the next stage of planning.

In our scenario Division X we have used the Product Group (Column K) in the database and identified plan groups (Column V) based on the definition of the planning groups as shown in Excel 8.9.

The plan groups initially reflect the management reporting structure but also will be used by the *k*-curve planning tool to identify the target inventory levels.

Create inventory plan: how difficult will this be and what must I do?

Apportioning inventory target

In Chapter 4 we looked at the business problem of specifying a business target and being able to determine a credible plan, and then to execute the plan, and implement in the business system. This requires the tricky problem of looking at a total number of parts being managed and then determining how to spread the inventory reduction over the total inventory. Once we have identified in the database our plan groups we can summarize the inventory by plan group. We can now review the current inventory position of the Division X for each Plan Group based on an extension of Table 8.2 as shown in Table 8.7 below.

Table 8.7 shows the summary evaluating the stock, demand, current MRP parameters and the number of batches. The 'plan group' with the highest demand will be the most important to plan. If management are asking to achieve a 20 per cent reduction, that would mean finding £1.89 million. We can see that Group 1 is by far the largest demand, closely followed by Asia and Europe. We know from Table 8.4 that there is a significant amount of overstock; we should focus on the severe overage as this could be significantly reduced within the year. The excess should also be gone within the year: however, we can assume that at least half the surplus will remain. The inactive stock will not reduce unless specific actions are taken to dispose of the stock as, at present, the MRP system see no use for the parts.

To be able to provide targets for each group we can present the inventory condition by plan group. The results for Division X are shown in Table 8.8. If we look at the analysis we can see that Group 1 and Group 3 have relatively small amounts of inactive,

Excel 8.9 Product code/plan group structure for Division X product codes

	A	B
1	*Product Code*	Plan Group
2	1	Group 1 UK
3	2	Group 1 UK
4	3	Group 1 UK
5	5	Group 2 Europe
6	6	Group 2 Europe
7	7	Group 2 Europe
8	8	Group 4 End of Life
9	10	Group 2 Europe
10	11	Group 3 Asia
11	13	Group 1 UK
12	14	Group 4 End of Life
13	15	Group 6 Field Spares
14	18	Group 4 End of Life
15	19	Group 4 End of Life
16	20	Group 4 End of Life
17	21	Group 4 End of Life
18	22	Group 4 End of Life
19	23	Group 6 Field Spares
20	24	Group 4 End of Life
21	25	Group 4 End of Life
22	26	Group 4 End of Life
23	27	Group 4 End of Life
24	28	Group 4 End of Life
25	38	Group 5 New Products
26	41	Group 6 Field Spares
27	53	Group 4 End of Life
28	57	Group 4 End of Life
29	65	Group 4 End of Life
30	67	Group 4 End of Life
31	96	Group 4 End of Life
32	97	Group 4 End of Life
33	98	Group 4 End of Life
34	99	Group 4 End of Life

Excel Formula

Create a sheet called 'Table 8.6' with the Product Code in Column A and Plan Group in Column B
V2 =VLOOKUP(K2,'Table 8.6'!A:B,,FALSE)

whereas Group 2, Group 4 and Group 6 are 20 per cent, 72 per cent and 17 per cent respectively. Group 4, End of life, suggests problems with managing falling demand. New products inactive could be an indication that the demand for the products is not yet visible in the MRP system. From this analysis we can consider how we would express the targets for each plan group. Table 8.9 shows a strategy and

Table 8.7 Division X showing plan groups and current status using Excel pivot table

Row Labels	Count of Part Number	Sum of Actual Stock Value	Sum of Annual Demand Value	Sum of MRP Cycle Stock Value	Sum of MRP Safety Stock Value	Sum of MRP Net Overage value	Sum of No of MRP Batches
Group 1 UK	2,976	£5,864,409	£72,595,010	£2,575,729	£2,219,416	£2,430,787	102,508
Group 2 Europe	626	£611,355	£3,982,919	£226,140	£225,153	£299,893	13,859
Group 3 Asia	176	£1,883,980	£8,096,729	£473,799	£899,438	£653,571	2,747
Group 4 End of Life	826	£591,228	£674,632	£162,483	£25,785	£524,629	7,919
Group 5 New Products	65	£7,495	£156,282	£5,722	£9,159	–£3,496	2,148
Group 6 Field Spares	284	£497,966	£1,394,649	£75,314	£71,481	£374,735	4,661
Grand Total	4,953	£9,456,433	£86,900,221	£3,519,188	£3,450,432	£4,280,119	133,842

Table 8.8 Division X inventory plan groups and active inventory condition and totals for inactive parts using Excel pivot

Sum of Actual Stock Value				Column Labels			
Row Labels	Group 1 UK	Group 2 Europe	Group 3 Asia	Group 4 End of Life	Group 5 New Products	Group 6 Field Spares	Grand Total
Active	£5,717,780	£488,958	£1,881,810	£164,176	£261	£414,083	£8,667,068
Shortage	£0	£0	£0	£0	£0	£0	£0
Underage	£458,612	£26,844	£54,487	£1,456		£5,196	£546,595
Optimum	£673,462	£54,009	£132,935	£11,514		£24,999	£896,920
Overage	£1,487,822	£123,095	£1,081,979	£18,425		£25,253	£2,736,574
Severe Overage	£2,588,716	£146,998	£359,083	£42,804		£198,041	£3,335,642
Excess	£183,539	£9,359	£146,742	£8,062	£62	£74,713	£422,478
Surplus	£325,628	£128,653	£106,584	£81,914	£199	£85,881	£728,858
Inactive	£146,629	£122,397	£2,169	£427,052	£7,234	£83,883	£789,365
Grand Total	**£5,864,409**	**£611,355**	**£1,883,980**	**£591,228**	**£7,495**	**£497,966**	**£9,456,433**

action statement which would typically be the start point for a planning cycle, with key targets and concerns expressed from a management analysis of the summary reports.

Table 8.9 Division X plan group analysis and strategy

Plan Group	Division X Strategy for Plan Groups	Plan Group Actions / Targets
Group 1 UK	These are the flagship products and are about 83% of the demand. Product availability and optimum stock are key considerations.	Target for 20% overall reduction in inventory to about £4.5m
Group 2 Europe	The European sales have not performed well this year and there is now a significant proportion of surplus and inactive stock.	Target for 20% overall reduction. £250k of surplus and inactive to be investigated and dissipation to be prepared.
Group 3 Asia	Stock holding are high for the Asian product range and sales have held. Stock-turn performance poor when compared to UK products.	Target 20%+ £1.5m target stock level. Minimize safety to 20 days on all products.
Group 4 – End of Life	Major product range revision Products removed from website to prevent new sales.	Sales team to 'fire-sale' products direct with main customers. No new orders accepted. Minimize safety stocks
Group 5 New products	More rationalized range of new products introduced this year. To be released onto website as soon as production stabilized. Sales team to liaise with major customers for initial stock purchases.	Investigate 4 & 6 Class curves, Replicate Group 1 settings. Ensure parts transferred as to Groups 1, 2 & 3 as soon as production is considered stable.
Group 6 Spares	Field spares remain stable and a good source of high margin income, focus on availability	Maintain at £500k, need to support products in field

Excel 8.10 Division X product group 1 UK – inventory plan by class

	A	B	C	D	E	F	G	H	I	J	K	L	M	N	O	P	Q	R	S
1	k Value	140																	
2	Work Days	250							Minimum Cycle	5	Days								
3																			
4		Planning Rules					Base Data		MRP – Current parameters			Actual Performance			Proposed Inventory				
5	Plan Group	Value Class	Class Limit	Class Cycle Days	Class Safety Days	Overage %age	No of Parts in Class	Annual Demand Value	No of MRP Batches	MRP Cycle Stock Value	MRP Safety Stock Value	Actual Stock Value	MRP Net Overage value	Overage % age	Proposed no of Batches	Proposed Cycle Stock Value	Proposed Safety Stock Value	Planned Overage	Total Inventory
6	Group 1 UK	1	£175,000	5	5	10%	82	£37,961,380	3,942	£803,526	£986,251	£1,527,061	£270,452	18%	4100	£759,598	£759,598	£126,599.71	£1,265,997
7	Group 1 UK	2	£43,750	10	5	20%	231	£19,392,268	9,927	£525,329	£682,592	£1,667,875	£690,471	41%	5775	£776,601	£388,707	£194,251.92	£971,260
8	Group 1 UK	3	£10,938	20	10	25%	491	£10,814,534	19,682	£521,148	£400,417	£1,325,122	£613,509	46%	6383	£866,706	£434,290	£289,214.28	£1,156,857
9	Group 1 UK	4	£2,734	40	15	30%	598	£3,468,360	22,748	£379,035	£112,470	£711,269	£404,572	57%	4186	£555,908	£209,293	£208,820.24	£696,067
10	Group 1 UK	5	£684	80	20	40%	524	£782,846	17,386	£213,966	£29,501	£271,262	£156,132	58%	2096	£251,095	£63,109	£125,770.74	£314,427
11	Group 1 UK	6	£0	160	25	50%	879	£175,621	27,795	£90,659	£7,113	£215,191	£166,284	77%	1758	£113,766	£19,424	£76,307.47	£152,615
12	Group 1 UK	7	£0				0	£0	0	£0	£0	£0	£0	0%	0	£0	£0	£0.00	£0
13	Group 1 UK	8	£0				0	£0	0	£0	£0	£0	£0	0%	0	£0	£0	£0.00	£0
14	Group 1 UK	9	£0				171	£0	1,028	£42,066	£1,071	£146,629	£129,368	88%	0	£0	£0	£0.00	£0
15							2976	£72,595,010	102,508	£2,575,729	£2,219,416	£5,864,409	£2,430,787		24,298	£3,323,675	£1,874,421	£1,020,964	£4,557,223
16							4953	£86,900,221	133,842	£3,519,188	£3,450,432	£9,456,433	£4,280,119		31,262	£4,144,453	£2,277,029		

Enter these formulae

Cell C6 *then copy down to* C14	Class Limit	=IF($D7=0,0,+$B$1*$B$1*$B$2/($D6*$D7))
Cell G6 *then copy down to* G14	No of Parts in Class	=DCOUNTA(Database!A:AF,Database!A$1,$A$5:B6)-SUM(G$5:G5)
Cell H6 *then copy down to* H14	Annual Demand Value	=DSUM(Database!$A:$AF,Database!$Q$1,$A$5:B6)-SUM(H$5:H5)
Cell I6 *then copy down to* I14	No of MRP batches	=DSUM(Database!$A:$AF,Database!$O$1,$A$5:$B6)-SUM(I$5:I5)
Cell J6 *then copy down to* J14	MRP Cycle Stock Value	=DSUM(Database!$A:$AF,Database!$R$1,$A$5:$B6)-SUM(J$5:J5)
Cell K6 *then copy down to* K14	MRP Safety Stock Value	=DSUM(Database!$A:$AF,Database!$S$1,$A$5:$B6)-SUM(K$5:K5)
Cell L6 *then copy down to* L14	Actual Stock Value	=DSUM(Database!$A:$AF,Database!$P$1,$A$5:$B6)-SUM(L$5:L5)
Cell M6 *then copy down to* M14	MRP Net Overage Value	=DSUM(Database!$A:$AF,Database!$T$1,$A$5:$B6)-SUM(M$5:M5)
Cell N6 *then copy down to* N14	Overage % age	=IF(L6=0,0,M6/L6)
Cell O6 *then copy down to* O14	Proposed No of Batches	=DSUM(Database!$A:$AF,Database!$AB$1,$A$5:$B6)-SUM(O$5:O5)
Cell P6 *then copy down to* P14	Proposed Cycle Stock Value	=DSUM(Database!$A:$AF,Database!$AE$1,$A$5:$B6)-SUM(P$5:P5)
Cell Q6 *then copy down to* Q14	Proposed Safety Stock Value	=DSUM(Database!$A:$AF,Database!$AF$1,$A$5:$B6)-SUM(Q$5:Q5)
Cell R6 *then copy down to* R14	Planned Overage	=S6-(P6*0.5)-Q6
Cell S6 *then copy down to* S14	Total Inventory	=((P6*0.5)+Q6)/(1-F6)

Plan group planning (k-curve)

The next stage is to take the requirements set out in the strategy statement shown in Table 8.9, which has the business targets identified for each plan group. The planner's task is to create and determine the ideal *k*-curve and position on the curve for each plan group. Building on the Excel 7.10 model we can extend the 'summary' section to cover both current inventory, active and inactive, and also evaluate the current MRP parameters and number of batches for each plan group. To do this we need to add the extra fields that we have defined in Excel 8.1 and the logic for each element which we have described in the preceding sections of this chapter. The revised layout is shown in Excel 8.10 with the required formula for the summary tables. The DSUM Excel feature has been utilized to allow each plan group to be separately analysed and planned by the addition of the 'plan group' in Column A. Once the planning is complete the data will need to be copied and pasted to a separate sheet to summarize into a total plan.

As discussed in Chapter 7 the first step is to determine which number of classes and cycle stock policy is best for the group of parts. For Plan Group 1 UK, we shall assume for simplicity that we have completed this work and concluded that a 6 Class policy as shown in Excel 8.10 is to be used for the plan. Once this decision is made, the remaining decisions of safety stock and overage can be made. This will establish a working model for Plan Group 1 UK; the value of *k* can be varied as shown in Chapter 7 and the results collated.

Figure 8.2 shows the exchange curve that will be created from Excel 8.11. There is a lot of information contained in the chart which we will need to interpret carefully. There are four key elements to the chart: the two axes show the inventory values on the vertical and the number of orders on the horizontal.

- The current inventory position is shown with two horizontal lines:
  - (A) Total inventory – this is the total inventory including any inventory defined as inactive.
  - (B) Active inventory – this shows only the inventory defined as active.
- The current MRP planning is shown with the horizontal and vertical lines which represent what the current MRP system would be planning as well as an estimate of the current number of orders MRP would produce.
  - (C) MRP average cycle – this is the calculation of just the cycle stock.
  - (D) MRP average cycle + safety – this has the safety stock values added.

Excel 8.11 Detail layout for the creation of the Plan Group k-curve shown in Figure 8.2

From Excel 8.10, for each value of *k*, copy/paste values the following
No of orders = O15
Average Cycle = P15/2
Average Cycle + Safety Inventory = P15/2 + Q15
Planned Inventory = S15

	D	E	F	G	H	Z	A	B	C	D
19	K	No of Orders	Average Cycle	Average Cycle + Safety Inventory	Planned Inventory	Actual Inventory	Active Inventory	MRP Average Cycle	MRP Average Cycle + Safety	Plan Position
20	10	63,708	£813,580	£2,299,059	£2,608,139					
21	20	50,769	£907,256	£2,426,996	£2,808,948					
22	30	44,025	£991,283	£2,545,447	£2,994,282					
23	40	39,770	£1,066,903	£2,653,040	£3,163,512					
24	50	36,473	£1,141,608	£2,764,115	£3,336,749					
25	75	30,955	£1,315,361	£3,022,191	£3,740,740					
26	100	27,566	£1,466,517	£3,249,683	£4,098,118					
27	200	20,978	£1,941,282	£3,953,224	£5,230,120					
28	300	17,732	£2,344,936	£4,553,653	£6,208,707					
29	MRP	102,508				£0	£0	£0	£0	
30		102,508				£5,864,409	£5,717,780	£1,287,865	£3,507,280	
31		0				£5,864,409	£5,717,780	£1,287,865	£3,507,280	
32	Plan Position	24,298								£0
33		24,298								£4,557,223
34		0								£4,557,223

From Excel 8.10 copy from the summary table data is independent of *k*.
MRP No of Orders = I15
Actual Inventory = L15
Active Inventory = L15 – L14
MRP Average Cycle = J15/2
MRP Average Cycle + Safety = J15/2 + K15

From Excel 8.10 for the *k*-value selected
Plan Position No of Orders = O15
Actual Inventory = S15

Enter these formulae

Select range V19:AD34, Insert Chart type XY to create Figure 8.2

- (E) No of MRP Orders – this estimates the number of orders based on the MRP cycle stock.

- The three optimum inventory curves represent the build-up of the Planned Inventory for the various values of *k*:
  - (F) Average cycle – this curve shows the results of varying *k* for just the cycle stock.
  - (G) Average cycle + safety inventory – this curve shows the results of varying *k* for just the cycle stock and the safety stock policy chosen.
  - (H) Planned inventory – this has the estimate for the planned overage added.

- These horizontal and vertical lines show the value of result for the value of *k* that has been selected as the best fit to meet the business objective:
  - (I) Objective £4.5m.

If we look at Figure 8.2, which shows the planning curves for Plan Group 1 for Division X, we can compare the *k*-curve with the current MRP settings and actual and active inventory. What can be seen here is that the current number of MRP Orders (E) being processed is high when compared to the Plan Position (I) which suggest that there are a lot of parts being planned with small batch quantities, possibly lot-for-lot. We would need to be able to confirm this assumption by an analysis of the Division X database. A quick analysis of the Division X database indeed shows us that 544 of the 2,976 parts in Plan Group 1 UK have their order period set to one day. In reality this means that the planners must be making the batching decisions as they plan, rather than based on a pre-defined set of rules. This can be verified by finding out how many transactions are being processed by each plan group; this is typically verified by counting the actual deliveries to 'goods in' if they are all purchased or the 'works orders' processed by the manufacturing/assembly line if they are manufactured. To illustrate this issue, we have detailed a case study of a project that explains in more detail the story behind this point.

CASE STUDY

Kidde Graviner: resolving the lot-for-lot planning issue

Figure 8.3 shows a chart from a Kidde Graviner project where a similar anomaly of a high number of initial MRP transactions was identified. When this issue was discussed with the planners it was found that they had deliberately set the MRP parameters to lot for lot orders. They had wanted to review the MRP output in detail once MRP outputs were received, they then consolidated the orders themselves. They believed that this was an effective way of planning and a useful use of their time. Our project was able to show, through an analysis of the MRP output and simulation based on a *k*-curve parameter set, that the same amount of consolidation would take place if pre-set order periods were used in place of the lot-for-lot settings. The results of the analysis are shown in Figure 8.3. The client then instituted a project which included training the staff on MRP parameter management and followed through by providing the planners with tools to help with the correct batching rule decisions. Figure 8.3 shows the reduction in the number of transactions from over 162k

Figure 8.2 *k*-curve with guidance notes

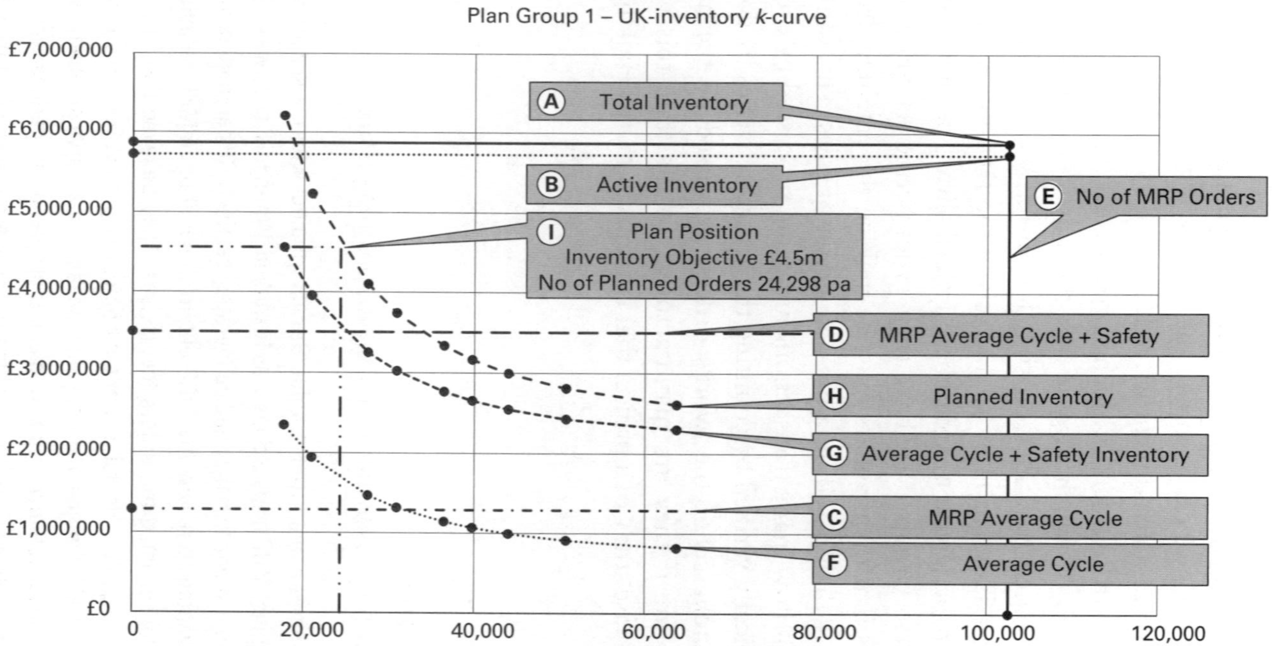

to under 30k, ie more than an 80 per cent reduction. It is also useful to note that the later increase from 22k to 29k transactions was matched by a decrease of almost a third in the planned inventory level from £2,382k to £1,610k.

Figure 8.3 Lot-for-lot recommendations

	No of Transactions	Planned Inventory Level
MRP Order transactions output from system	162,591	
MRP Orders after consolidation by Planners	22,305	£2,382k
Step 1 pre-set planning rules where K = 40	20,510	£1,889k
Step 2 pre-set planning rules where K = 20	26,851	£1,603k
Step 3 pre-set planning rules where K = 16	29,260	£1,610k

Reproduced with kind permission of Kidde Graviner

Returning to the Plan Group 1, Figure 8.2, having now understood why the number of MRP orders (E) and Plan Position (I) are different we can now be confident that proposed Plan Position is achievable. If we were to set the plan at the point where the current MRP Cycle Stock (C) and Average Cycle (F) intersect, the cycle stock would remain the same and we would make a significant reduction in the number of batches processed, thus reducing the workload.

The Plan Position (I) selected represents a setting of k = 140 and shows that the intersection with MRP Cycle Stock (F) means that the Cycle Stock is a little higher but fewer batches are planned to be processed. The key challenge for Division X will be how to deal with the order period of 1 day for 544 parts which appear to be in the Class 1 to 3 parts.

The model shows the addition of the safety stock decision and allows comparisons between the current MRP Average Cycle + Safety Values (D) and the Average Cycle + Safety Optimum Curve (G); when we look at the intersection between these two lines we can see that whilst the amount of cycle stock would increase, the safety stock recommended by the *k*-curve is slightly lower than the current MRP settings. This shows that there is a potential to re-balance the inventory and focus it more on cycle stock, compensating with a reduction in safety stock. Finally, by adding planned overage, a level of £1.0 million will allow enough headroom for managing any difficulties in plan.

Having set the plan conditions we can refer back to Table 8.8, which is based on the selected plan. We can see that there will be a need to be a focus on severe overage to ensure the plan is met. Group 1 has a fair share of the 20 per cent inventory reduction at £1.2 million. This process needs to be repeated for the remaining plan groups and then consolidated into a total plan.

Consolidating the plan

Once the current position is established for each of the plan groups they can in turn be planned using the *k*-curve model for each of the plan groups as in Figure 8.2, working from highest inventory to lowest. This will easily identify the gap, which can then be prioritized until a consensus on the proposed plan is achieved. This will mean that for each plan group a statement like Excel 8.10 can be determined. The total lines from each individual analysis can then be consolidated into a total plan as shown in Table 8.10. This can be viewed as three separate tables:

- planning rules;
- MRP current parameters, actual inventory and overage performance; and
- proposed inventory.

In describing the plan for each group we have now determined the target, identified where the key issues are and will have begun to understand the areas for concern.

In describing the plan for each group we have now determined the target, identified where the key issues are and will have begun to understand the areas of concern. In addition to the detail plan group numbers – an example is shown in Table 8.11 – an assumptions statement will also be vital. The Division X planner will need to prepare a summary assumptions statement to support the numbers, which should list the current business environment, agreed actions for inactive inventories, and an outlook for the reduction of excess and surplus stocks. This will be important later in the year if the targets are not met, which may be due to events that were not initially predicted; the assumptions will be able to show what was expected and what was unexpected.

Table 8.10a Total plan by plan group – detail

	Planning Rules					Base Data	
Plan Group	**Planned k-value**	**Number of Value Classes**	**Planned Value Class Cycle Days**	**Planned Value Class Safety Days**	**Planned Overage as a %age**	**No of Parts in Class**	**Annual Demand Value**
Group 1 UK	140	6 Class	5,10,20,40,80,160	5,5,10,15,20,25	10,20,25,30,40,50	2,976	£72,595,010
Group 2 Europe	140	6 Class	5,10,20,40,80,160	5,5,10,15,20,25	10,20,25,30,40,50	626	£3,982,919
Group 3 Asia	100	6 Class	5,10,20,40,80,160	20,25,30,35,40,45	10,20,25,30,40,50	176	£8,096,729
Group 4 End of Life	150	6 Class	5,10,20,40,80,160	0,0,0,0,5,5	10,20,25,30,40,50	826	£674,632
Group 5 New Products	100	4 Class	5,10,20,80	5,5,10,20	10,20,30,50	65	£156,282
Group 6 Field Spares	150	6 Class	5,10,20,40,80,160	5,5,10,15,20,25	10,20,25,30,40,50	284	£1,394,649
Total						**4,953**	**£86,900,221**

Table 8.10b Total plan by plan group – detail (B) current MRP parameters, actual inventory and overage performance

	Base Data		MRP – Current parameters			Actual Performance		
Plan Group	**No of Parts in Class**	**Annual Demand Value**	**No of MRP Batches**	**MRP Cycle Stock Value**	**MRP Safety Stock Value**	**Actual Stock Value**	**MRP Net Overage Value**	**Net Overage as a % age**
Group 1 UK	2,976	£72,595,010	102,508	£2,575,729	£2,219,416	£5,864,409	£2,430,787	41%
Group 2 Europe	626	£3,982,919	13,859	£226,140	£225,153	£611,355	£299,893	49%
Group 3 Asia	176	£8,096,729	2,747	£473,799	£899,438	£1,883,980	£653,571	35%
Group 4 End of Life	826	£674,632	7,919	£162,483	£25,785	£591,228	£524,629	89%
Group 5 New Products	65	£156,282	2,148	£5,722	£9,159	£7,495	–£3,496	–47%
Group 6 Field Spares	284	£1,394,649	4,661	£75,314	£71,481	£497,966	£374,735	75%
Total	**4,953**	**£86,900,221**	**133,842**	**£3,519,188**	**£3,450,432**	**£9,456,433**	**£4,280,119**	**45%**

Table 8.10c Total plan by plan group – detail (C) proposed inventory

	Base Data		Proposed Inventory				
Plan Group	**No of Parts in Class**	**Annual Demand Value**	**Proposed No of Batches**	**Proposed Cycle Stock Value**	**Proposed Safety Stock Value**	**Planned Overage**	**Total Inventory**
Group 1 UK	2,976	£72,595,010	24,298	£3,323,675	£1,874,421	£1,020,964.35	£4,557,223
Group 2 Europe	626	£3,982,919	2,530	£296,040	£131,149	£109,534.36	£388,703
Group 3 Asia	176	£8,096,729	2,694	£270,861	£732,277	£172,896.41	£1,040,604
Group 4 End of Life	826	£674,632	1,135	£83,815	£2,858	£26,723.99	£71,490
Group 5 New Products	65	£156,282	171	£9,382	£4,374	£3,779.09	£12,844
Group 6 Field Spares	284	£1,394,649	898	£107,055	£45,423	£38,684.75	£137,635
Total	**4,953**	**£86,900,221**	**31,726**	**£4,090,827**	**£2,790,503**	**£1,372,583**	**£6,208,499**

Table 8.11 Summary plan showing all inventories and assumptions

	Current Actual	Plan based on New Planning Rules	Inactive Inventory	Assumptions & Comments
Group 1 UK	£5,864,409	£4,557,223	£146,629	UK business to remain steady Target of about £4.5m achieved
Group 2 Europe	£611,355	£388,703	£122,397	Target for 20% overall reduction £250k of surplus and inactive investigated and dissipation plan prepared as part of Surplus and Excess plan
Group 3 Asia	£1,883,980	£1,040,604	£2,169	Far East business to grow by 10% Minimize safety to 20 days on all products £1.0m stock level set lower than target of £1.5m or > 20%
Group 4 End of Life	£591,228	£71,490	£427,052	Sales team to 'fire-sale' products direct with main customers No new orders accepted Safety stocks set 0 for all except class 5 & 6
Group 5 New Products	£7,495	£12,844	£7,234	4 Class curve proposed as best option
Group 6 Field Spares	£497,966	£137,635	£83,883	Parameters same as Plan Group 1 Budget of £500k, need to support products in field, will transfer end-of-life products to field spares
Total	£9,456,433	£6,208,499	£789,365	
Total Active and Inactive Inventory		£9,456,433		

Table 8.11 *continued*

Inventory not included in the Optimum Plan Calculations		
Scrap Disposal	–£500,000	Finance approved £500 of £789 inactive inventory
Severe Overage	£750,000	Improved management of suppliers re-schedules
Excess	£100,000	Outlook for Excess by Y/e is £100k based on current demand
Surplus	£500,000	Outlook for Surplus by Y/e is £500k based on current demand
Total Plan	£7,847,865	Target for Y/e was £7.6m
Saving	£1,608,568	Equivalent to 17% reduction

The demand for each plan group over the plan period:

- *It is expected that UK business will remain steady.*
- *The Far East business will grow by 10 per cent.*

- The disposal of the inactive stock:
  - *Finance have approved a budget of £500,000 for scrap of inactive materials.*
- The consumption of surplus and excess:
  - *Outlook for Excess by Y/e is a reduction to £100,000.*
  - *Outlook for Surplus by Y/e is a reduction to £400,000.*
  - *Assumes no change in the Alpha Project consumption of Motors.*
- The management of supply/demand:
  - *Overage performance will reduce severe overage to £1.5.*
  - *Training of staff on supply demand management 1Q.*
  - *S&OP meeting to be held monthly from Jan.*

The importance of keeping a clear record of the assumptions is that if there are any changes to them, that result in a significant effect on inventory, then it will provide an important audit trail.

Implement the plan: what actions must I do to achieve the plan?

Creating the deployment plan

Now that we have created this plan statement, which is the result of a technical analysis, we need to be able to articulate how we can implement this plan. There are three types of actions we are required to organize:

- deployment of the inventory actions;
- deployment of the capability actions; and
- deployment of the MRP parameter actions.

Create deployment plan for inventory actions

Planning the inactive/surplus/excess

In the initial analysis we identified the inactive, surplus and excess inventories. We know these are the longer-term problems and will take most of the year ahead to resolve. We need to ensure there is a regular review or re-focus throughout the year to keep the focus. When starting this process for the first time the history of why parts got into their current overstock may not be easily determined. It is important this process is managed on a monthly basis, as when new items are identified it will be easier to find an explanation as it will be fresh in the minds of the planners/buyers and corrective actions may still be possible.

What is important with the inactive parts is to understand if they are truly wanted, that is why having up to three years history will be useful. It may be that the parts have only just stopped being used or that they have not been used for a long time. Whichever is true, once it has been confirmed that the parts are not wanted, then they should be disposed of. This is not a trivial process; it is not as simple as putting the parts into a skip. The engineering and finance departments will need to be closely involved to ensure that parts are scrapped in an effective and controlled way, and that the financial decrease in inventory value is managed correctly so as not to affect the business profit.

For the surplus and excess the most urgent action is to ensure that no further stock of these items is being purchased. Next the validity of the future demand needs to be understood to be sure that the stock will be used up.

Looking at alternative usage of the parts as well as getting the sales team to focus on the products will all help. The database can be used to identify the inactive parts and identify a hit list based on the highest values. Our experience is to avoid producing long lists which will invariably not be completely actioned. A good rule is to only list one page with the highest value first. For example:

Inactive inventory report for Division X:

- All items over £5,000 of stock.
- Total report value £325,000 of £789,000 inactive stock (41 per cent).
- Total items listed 36 items of 810 (4 per cent).
- This would provide a good start to the achievement of the business target to dispose of £500,000.

Create a deployment plan for the capability actions

The deployment plan for capability needs to look at the business process side of the business to create a credible plan. In the Division X example, the issue of order period being set to one day has a significant effect on Plan Group 1. There will be good reasons why this happened and a 'capability project' should be established to understand why this decision was made. The Kidde Graviner case study shows how this issue was resolved in a particular client. The project will not directly benefit the inventory level, however it will ensure that the planners make the most effective use of their time and their decisions will sit within the guidelines required to achieve the proposed inventory level. It may be that what is required is to increase the capability of a particular manufacturing or supply chain process; in these cases it would be appropriate to use Lean implementation tools, some of which are described in Richards and Grinsted (2013). This book provides a simple guide to the many Lean tools that can be used to identify problems and focus on providing solutions.

Create deployment plan for MRP parameter changes

The *k*-curve analysis is based on making decisions about the cycle and safety stock coverage; first at an aggregate level, which identifies the inventory classing limits, these decisions then define for each part the value class, cycle and safety parameters, essentially reversing the aggregating process to set parameters at a part level for a given plan. Once we have made decisions for the number of classes and the value of *k*, we have in effect set the cycle stock and safety stock for each item.

The importance of parameter maintenance in MRP

In Chapter 2 we identified the importance of maintaining parameters. What is important here is that we can use the MRP parameters, calculated for each plan group to re-tune MRP to drive the business towards the new inventory plan. We know from earlier discussion about the planning process that unless we change the parameters the results that MRP produces will not change. We also know from Chapter 4 that keeping parameters up to date has a beneficial effect on compliance. The challenge is how to implement parameters for 5,000 parts. We know from the creation of the logic for Excel 8.2, Excel 8.3 and Excel 8.4 that there are at least five parameters that affect the cycle and safety stock:

- Cycle stock (Excel 8.2 and Excel 8.3):
  - minimum order quantity;
  - order multiple;
  - order period.
- Safety stock (Excel 8.4):
  - safety quantity;
  - safety periods.

Any or all of these parameters may need to be altered to bring the current MRP parameters into line with the proposed inventory plan. Thus, this means that there are up to 25,000 parameters that we potentially may need to change. We could adopt an approach of uploading all the new parameters to the system. This would be potentially reckless as it takes no account of the reason why the parameters are currently set to their values in the first place. The second issue is more sensitive: the planner has traditionally been responsible for making the parameter decisions, and could easily resent advice from a computer/management system. They may argue that each decision has to be examined on the individual item and cannot be applied as blanket rules. Both are extremely valid points and ignoring them would mean taking a considerable risk.

There are two different strategies that we have found work well and can be adopted to facilitate implementation of MRP parameter change.

Guide the planner

The first is to provide a reference guide, which the planner can be asked to consider when making parameter decisions.

This table is a simple set of guidelines as shown in Excel 8.12 that will allow the planner to make the final decision within a set of rules that corresponds to the inventory plan, which will in effect drive the MRP parameters in the required direction. This has proved very effective with experienced planners.

Request planner permission

An alternative, slightly more prescriptive approach is to produce a report which compares the current parameters with the proposed parameters and identifying parts where there is a difference. As we rebalance the inventory the MRP parameter differences can be either an increase or a decrease, and if all the differences were listed would cover most parts. Rather than listing all parts, which would be rejected as too much work, we can create an exception report to identify the highest value changes. Table 8.12 shows an action exception report which has been filtered to identify the top eight increases and top eight decreases in cycle and safety stock. Looking at the detail we can see that in some cases, mostly Value Class 2 parts, the quantity shift of from cycle stock to safety stock, this is in line with what we saw in Figure 8.2 and the increase in cycle stock and reduction of safety stock.

Parameter investigation report for Division X

Top 16 Parts with Cycle Stock changes
8 Parts with Cycle stock reduction = £139k
8 parts with Cycle Stock increases = £ 52k
Net reduction = £ 87k

Top item	Reduction £19,782	Increase £6,754
Part Number	= AB03279	= AB00845
Annual demand	= 71,318	= 15,063
MOQ	= 0	= 90
Multiple	= 13,320	= 0
Order Period	= 5 days	= 5 days

Proposed Cycle stock		
Class	= 2	= 2
Order Period	= 10 days	= 10 days
Cycle Quantity	= 2,853	= 603

For AB03279 – what is clear here is the multiple is very high, the recommendation is to reduce this by a factor of five. Reducing this to the proposed value would potentially save £20,000 of inventory so it would be worthwhile spending time investigating and if necessary negotiating a reduction in batch size. It may be that this parameter was set some years ago when the demand for the product was higher – the multiple will create an order for 50 days of stock. There is also a possibility that it could even be a typo, as the 1,320 would match the order period of five days.

For AB00345 we can see it would be possible to increase the order period to reflect that this part is a Class 2 part; this will possible counterbalance the fact that we will be increasing the number of batches of AB03279.

Excel 8.12 Planner guidance table based on Excel 7.4 with added columns

	A	B	C	D	E	F	G	H	I	J
1	*K Value*	140								
2	Work Days	250								
3										
4										
5	Value Class	Cycle Days	Class Limit	Max Order value	Minimum Order Value	Class Safety Days	Maximum Safety Value	MOQ Round to nearest	Multi to nearest	Overage %age
6	1	5	£72,000	N/A	£1,440	5	£1,440	1	1	10%
7	2	10	£18,000	£2,880	£720	5	£360	1	1	20%
8	3	20	£4,500	£1,440	£360	10	£180	1	1	25%
9	4	40	£1,125	£720	£180	15	£68	10	10	30%
10	5	80	£281	£360	£90	20	£23	10	10	40%
11	6	160	£0	£180	£0	25	£0	100	100	50%
12	7									
13	8									
14	9									

Enter these formulae

D8 *then copy down to* D11	Maximum Order Value	D7 = B7*(C6/$B$2)
E6 *then copy down to* E11	Minimum Order Value	E7 = B7*(C7/$B$2)
G6 *then copy down to* G11	Maximum Safety Value	G7 = F7*(C7/$B$2)

Values in Columns B, F and J are from *k*-curve
Values in Columns H and I are the planners' decision

Table 8.12 Planner action exception report: showing greatest differences in cycle and safety stock parameters

Part Number	Standard Cost	STOCK	Annual Demand Quantity	Min Quantity	Max Quantity	Order Multiple	Safety Time	Order Period	Safety Stock	MRP Cycle Stock Quantity	MRP Safety Stock Quantity	Value Class	Class Cycle Days	Class Safety Days	Proposed Cycle Quantity	Proposed Safety Quantity	Cycle Stock Difference	Safety Stock Difference
AB00711	£8.66	2,592	39,225	36	0	36	10	5	0	792	1,569	2	10	5	1,569	785	–777	784
AB00741	£5. 02	15,860	50,480	0	0	5,292	30	5	0	5,292	6,058	2	10	5	2,020	1,010	3,272	5,048
AB00759	£15.59	1,384	21,843	16	0	16	10	5	0	448	874	2	10	5	874	437	–426	437
AB00827	£10.34	36	32,400	36	0	36	10	5	0	648	1,296	2	10	5	1,296	648	–648	648
AB00845	£22.74	324	15,063	90	0	18	10	5	0	306	603	2	10	5	603	302	–297	301
AB00919	£5.32	3,640	3,024	0	0	3,700	30	5	0	3,700	363	4	40	15	484	182	3,216	181
AB00921	£5.94	11,410	23,427	0	0	3,700	30	5	0	3,700	2,812	2	10	5	938	469	2,762	2,343
AB01931	£46.75	48	336	0	0	416	25	5	0	416	34	4	40	15	54	21	362	13
AB01935	£13.67	238	927	0	0	1,440	25	5	0	1,440	93	4	40	15	149	56	1,291	37
AB02342	£4.74	2,466	65,784	0	0	0	10	5	0	1,316	2,632	2	10	5	2,632	1,316	-1,316	1,316
AB02952	£8.04	6	390	0	0	2,142	30	5	0	2,142	47	5	80	20	125	32	2,017	15
AB03279	£1.89	1,339	71,318	0	0	13,320	0	5	20	13,320	20	2	10	5	2,853	1,427	10,467	–1,407
AB03288	£1.08	11,622	278,671	0	0	0	0	5	0	5,574	0	2	10	5	11,147	5,574	-5,573	–5,574
AB03685	£0.55	8,874	40,895	0	0	560	10	250	0	41,440	1,636	4	40	15	6,544	2,454	34,896	–818
AB04203	£9.13	0	36,624	0	0	0	0	5	0	733	0	2	10	5	1,465	733	–732	–733
AB04481	£7.92	4,779	42,581	60	0	60	10	5	0	900	1,704	2	10	5	1,704	852	-804	852

NOTE Cycle and safety stock differences are shown as negative where there is an increase in the required parameter. This is because the report focuses in on 'decreasing' inventory thus negative values signify an increase in inventory.

What can be seen from the parameter investigation report for Division X is that the implementation does not always require a wholesale review of all the parameters. Although all the parameters may be adjusted the inventory effect of many is quite small. By focusing on high value, both up and down we can have the greatest impact for a small effort. If we analyse the Division X data based on the plans we have created then we can see in Table 8.13 that 68.5 per cent are under ±£1,000 and 94.2 per cent under ±£5,000. Thus it is clear that we would only need to really focus on a small percentage to make significant impact.

CASE STUDY
Hozelock

Hozelock first implemented the approach by generating and reviewing the exception report, and examining the items. From this analysis they identified where they disagreed and why, which helped improve the selection criteria for the parameters to be adjusted. Once this process had been used for a couple of years there was sufficient confidence in the report output that the reported items were uploaded directly to the MRP system.

Linking the inventory plan to MRP parameters

The importance of this part of the process cannot be overstated, as traditionally parameter maintenance has been seen as the key cause of failure in MRP implementations. By using the *k*-curve process to determine a recommended position we are providing a challenge to the status quo. Without this challenge it is unlikely to expect all but the most diligent planners to continuously review their parameters. From the earlier discussions in Chapter 2 and 4 on non-compliance we can see how well-maintained parameters help to improve compliance. This process of feeding the output of the planning process back into MRP will close the loop between MRP and inventory management. Thus driving the execution of the inventory plan through changes in the MRP system. What we have described in this chapter is a process that can take a top-down request for inventory reduction and generate a detailed part level plan that can quickly and efficiently focus on the 'inventory' issues.

The processes described in this chapter have focused on selecting parts for action principally based on the inventory value of the action proposed. This

Table 8.13 Comparison of value of parameter change with number of parts affected

Value of Change	No of Parts Affected	Percent of Parts Affected
20,000	11	0.2%
10,000	23	0.5%
5,000	216	4.4%
1,000	99	2.0%
500	503	10.2%
0	2260	45.6%
–500	628	12.7%
–1,000	1172	23.7%
–5,000	41	0.8%
–10,000	0	0.0%

will focus on the valuable few rather than the trivial many. The operations manager will always have to apply the 'local' knowledge and not all the recommendations will be readily accepted as value is not the only rational for taking action. The chapter has built a complex Excel-based model; the overall architecture of the model is summarized in Figure 8.4.

This model has three worksheets:

- database;
- pivot table; and
- *k*-curve model.

The key function and relationship of the modules can be summarized as follows:

It is important to note that the process described in this chapter is focused on inventory principally based on value – the actions are identified based on value. The operations manager will always have to apply the 'local' knowledge and not all the recommendations will be readily accepted.

Figure 8.4 Architecture of the Excel inventory model

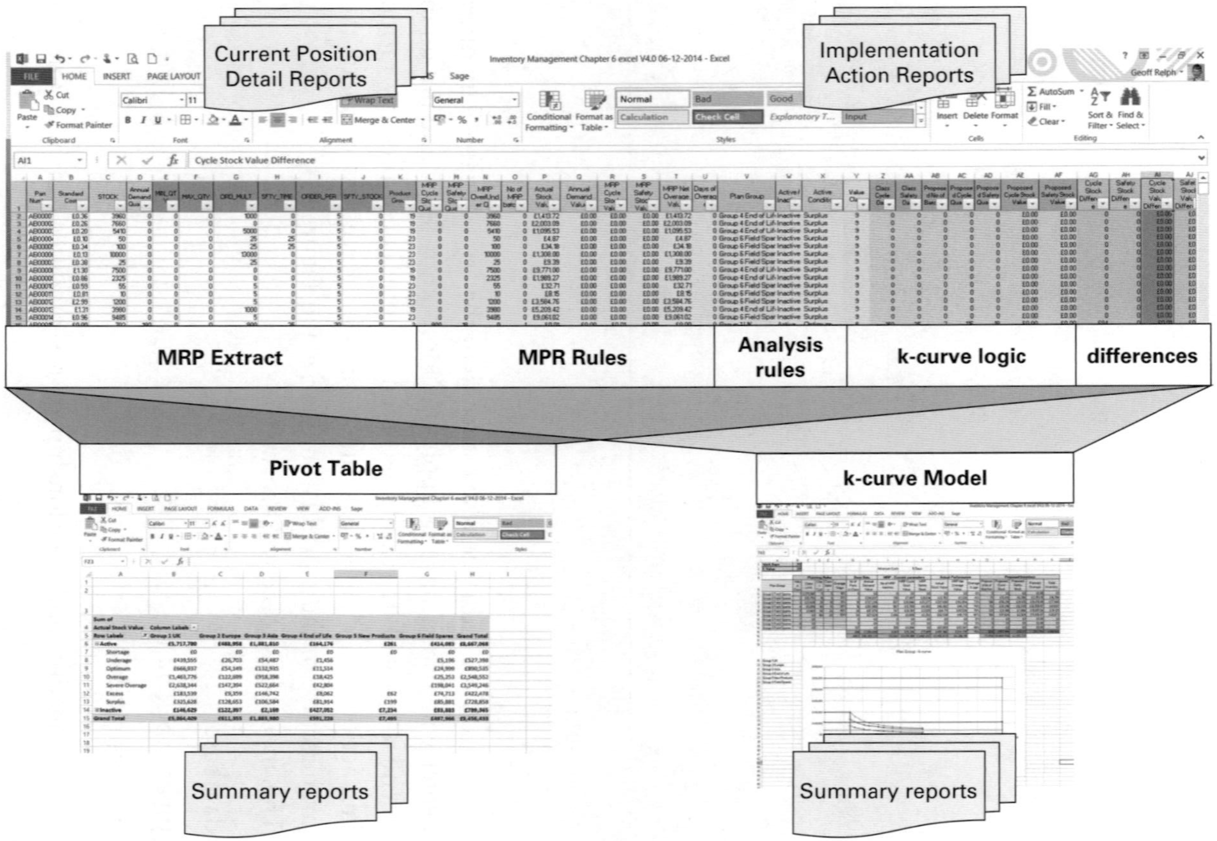

The database

The database is structured:

- The extracted data from the MRP system (Excel 8.1).
- The MRP rules for evaluating the current parameters (Excel 8.2 to Excel 8.4).
- The analysis rules for identifying what is:
  - Active/inactive (Excel 8.5)
  - Inventory condition (Excel 8.6)
  - Over and understock (Excel 8.7 and Excel 8.8)
  - Business reporting rules (Table 8.10)
- The *k*-curve logic applying the *k*-curve model to the extracted data (Excel 8.10) and (Excel 8.11) to create a k-curve as shown in (Figure 8.2).
- Differences – identifying the difference between current and proposed (Excel 8.1 rows AG to AJ).

The database can be used to create detail part number level reporting for the current position and implementation action reports using the standard Excel filter feature.

Pivot table

This utilizes the standard Excel feature to provide an analysis tool that can summarize the database. The summaries can be used to create summary level reports, both to summarize the current position and the proposed plan.

The k-curve model

The *k*-curve model, shown in Excel 8.10, summarizes the data from the database. This can be represented as a *k*-curve shown in Figure 8.2, which is created using Excel 8.11 and allows the planner to:

- evaluate the most appropriate number of classes;
- evaluate the cycle stock, safety stock policies;
- compare current position to the *k*-curve; and
- set the appropriate target.

The calculated plans can then be copied and collated into a total plan.

Plan cycle checklist

- Understand your current inventory position – *How much have I got?*
  - MRP settings
  - determine inventory condition
  - active–inactive
  - over/understock
  - actual throughput rates
  - what is the business structure
  - list plan groups in descending order
  - add commentary and compare with previous assumptions
- Determine the business targets that relate to inventory – *What do I have to achieve?*
  - identify business targets
  - inventory
  - service level
  - identify constraints – limits to batch throughput rates
  - what is the business structure and where is the priority
  - allocate target to each group
  - list assumptions about targets and business direction
- Create inventory plan – *How difficult will this be and what must I do?*
  - plan group planning (*k*-curve)
  - separate active and inactive inventory
  - create scenario curves for active inventory
  - determine which curve is most effective
  - add safety stock policy – either days or statistical or hybrid
  - add overage limits
  - generate overall *k*-curve
  - identify current actual position
  - add actual inventory and number of batches
  - identify best scenario and value of *k*
  - consolidate plan
  - create consolidated plan of all plan groups

- create plan for inactive, excess, surplus
- identify gap between plan and actual
- identify improvement required for each plan group
- list assumptions about each group plan

- Implement the plan – *What actions must I do to achieve the plan?*
  - create parameter list for input to MRP
  - create deployment plan for capability improvement
  - create deployment plan for inventory actions
  - list assumptions about implementation challenges

Summary

In this chapter we have looked in detail at the inventory planning process and how the business targets, which are usually set at a high level, can be taken and broken down. By analysing the business targets and making rational decisions, a credible inventory plan can be developed. Once the plan is confirmed, the data used to create these plans can be converted into detailed actions both specific and by part number, and where necessary business process improvements. The problem first articulated in Chapter 1 in Figure 1.3 (where directors of a business require inventory levels to be reduced by X% or £Y, and which has to be converted into specific changes at the item and parameter level) remains a key headache for most operations managers today: this chapter has focused on developing a business process to enable the development of a robust and credible inventory plan.

Thus, the focus of this chapter has been to utilize established theories to build (Excel-based) models that help the operations managers, with a little help from IT professionals, to create inventory modelling tools that can express inventory at both detail and summary levels. These modelling tools can then be used as a basis for a rational planning process and provide both detail-level instructions and prepare reports that identify the key actions that need to be taken.

The chapter has taken us through the four key steps of the inventory planning process first shown in Figure 1.5. These steps are:

- Understand your current inventory position – *How much have I got?*
- Determine the business targets that relate to inventory – *What do I have to achieve?*

- Create inventory plan – *How difficult will this be and what must I do?*
- Implement the plan – *What actions must I do to achieve the plan?*

In summarizing the four steps, the first step shows the importance of understanding what inventory we have got and how by evaluating the MRP parameters we can explain why we have got the inventory levels we have.

In the second step, we see how the business targets, given in summary form, represent our planning challenge and how to manage the development of an inventory plan. Step three focuses on how we can use the *k*-curve modelling tool to calculate a plan to achieve the business targets. The final step looks at both the specific, ie how to identify detail part number parameter changes, and the wider problem of getting the more generalized planning actions implemented by working with the operations team.

Tools and techniques discussed in this chapter

- *k*-curve modelling
- MRP cycle stock and safety stock evaluation
- Application of active/inactive inventory rules
- Application of inventory active condition rules
- Excel pivot tables
- Quality functional deployment.
- Lean six sigma.
- Hosin Kanri.
- PDCA (plan, do, check, action).

References

Relph, G (2006) Inventory management in business systems, PhD thesis, Manchester University

Richards, G and Grinsted, S (2013) *The Logistics and Supply Chain Toolkit*, Kogan Page, London

Case study examples of *k*-curve planning approach

09

Introduction

In the previous chapters we outlined the tools and techniques for planning inventory at a product level (Chapter 5), at an item level and aggregate level using Pareto (Chapter 6) and then developed the aggregate planning technique using the exchange curve/*k*-curve methodology (Chapters 7 and 8). In this chapter we will review a number of case studies where the *k*-curve approach has been used. These illustrate the approaches used and the issues that arose during implementations.

The case studies from the exchange curve/*k*-curve implementations are covered in this chapter together with essential lessons learnt from each one. The case studies cover:

- the importance of process improvement before inventory reduction;
- benefits of embedding the logic eg *k*-curve into the MRP planning process;
- nobody noticed;
- when to stop 'inventory reduction';
- we do it anyway;
- we know better than the system.

In addition, key pointers for successful implementation of new approaches are identified from the case studies, and the importance of the triumvirate of process + organization + technology is reviewed.

Emerging from the analysis of these case studies is the continued importance of the planners' decisions, which greatly benefit from being aligned to the focus of the business. To achieve this communal focus, planner control and alignment tools to assist in parameter management are discussed at the end of the chapter.

Exchange curve/*k*-curve case studies

CASE STUDY

The importance of process improvement before inventory reduction

Business-case-driven inventory planning

We have talked throughout the book about the need to understand the business, the need to drive costs down, and the implication of this at detailed, part level. It is important for a business to know when to stop – when its stock turns are high enough and when its inventory levels should no longer be decreased. It is to be expected that there will be a continued and relentless pressure on inventory, but there is a fine line between lean and anorexic.

Figure 9.1 Typical lean implementation approach (Slack, Chambers and Johnston, 2010)

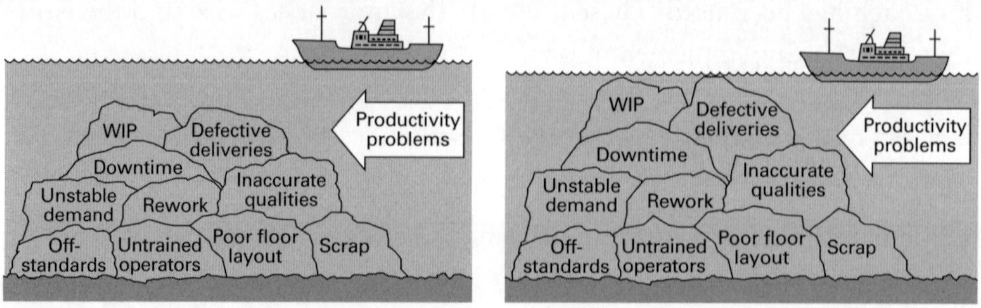

Reducing the level of inventory (water) allows operations management (the ship) to see the problems in the operation (the rocks) and work to reduce them

Inventory initiatives, unless properly handled, can often create a failure cycle:

Reduce inventory → service level fails → production disrupted by short-term priority → safety re-applied → loss of confidence of customer demand falls → pressure to reduce inventory.

This failure cycle is difficult to break. But by utilizing the *k*-curve method, reductions can be made progressively in planned stages, rather than the typical vertical drop often caused by simply removing all the safety stock.

Lean approach to inventory reduction

Traditional Lean thinking can lead a company into danger, if the philosophy of removing the water to expose the rocks is followed blindly. When the rocks (the business problems) are exposed the business will need to improve the process. The assumption is that there is time to improve the process before each exposed rock causes a significant problem, which could potentially sink the boat (the business). If this is followed to the letter, then lowering the inventory will cause problems in the business. Case study – Automotive details a case in point. Figure 9.1 shows the typical Lean approach as a ship in rocky waters.

CASE STUDY

Automotive: Lean production

A new manufacturing manager wanted to focus the organization on Lean production. His strategy was to remove all safety stock from the products in order to reduce the inventory in the process. As is the case in most complex moulding equipment the production equipment was subject to failure. Although the organization was focused on improving these failures the effect was that production was disrupted. These disruptions would normally have been smoothed out by the safety stock. With the removal of the safety stock, more emergency changeovers needed to be arranged, which in turn reduced capacity utilization and finally decreased the customer service level. Only when the safety stock was put back into the process could the organization focus on real improvements to the equipment rather than wasting time on firefighting.

CASE STUDY

Automotive: process improvement before inventory reduction

The *k*-curve approach to inventory reduction

Another example is of a client who manufactures front and rear bumpers for the automotive industry. This company used the *k*-curve approach and focused on capability improvements hand-in-hand with the inventory reductions. In this case study, the company didn't expose any 'rocks', since the problems were identified and resolved before the inventory reductions had reached the critical levels.

The company moulded and painted front and rear bumpers for a number of local automotive manufacturers. They would receive the pull signal four hours prior to the required sequenced delivery. In order to improve flexibility and reduce inventory they completed an inventory–capability analysis using *k*-curve. The study used a particular safety stock algorithm that took account of the batch size, supply reliability and demand variation. The study showed that as the batch sizes reduced there was a point when the safety stock increased in order to protect against the risk of supply failure. This clarified that unless the processes were reliable, and it was known that the paint colour changeover was particularly problematic, then it was unwise to lower the safety stock further. This case study was presented at Manufacturer Live in 2004 and subsequently published in *The Manufacturer* in August 2004. The punchline was simple: 'If the paint changeover process is not capable don't take the inventory out, but when process becomes capable then take inventory out.'

Lesson learnt: process improvement before inventory reduction

In both these case studies the lesson learnt was that in the drive for continuous improvement through batch size reduction, as the key to inventory reduction, pushing beyond the capability of the process eventually caused an unacceptable failure rate. By understanding the link between capability and inventory it will focus on improving capability in advance of the inventory reduction. In summary, if you contrast the two case studies, the approach of the manufacturing manager in the first case felt that 'taking out the safety' inventory would focus the attention on the process improvement. This is shown on the left of Figure 9.2, and the difference between the two approaches can be summarized as follows:

- The pure Lean approach is to take out the inventory to find the problem, then fix it (ie the left-hand side of Figure 9.2).
- The *k*-curve approach is to balance the inventory with the capability and then remove inventory as the improvement in capability is achieved (ie the right-hand side of Figure 9.2).

Figure 9.2 Comparison of lean and inventory capability on a *k*-curve

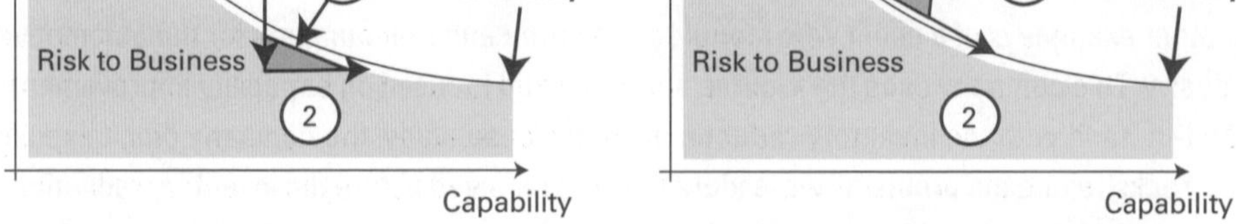

1. Lean / Agile initiatives – 'take out inventory expose the rocks'
2. Fix the process problems
3. Result – business exposed whilst learning new skills

1. Optimized Inventory – understand and balance inventory with capability
2. Continuous process improvement synchronizing inventory reduction with increased capability
3. Result – business protected whilst learning new skills

Business-case-driven inventory planning as an approach shows that linking the inventory reductions to the business process capability improvements is a much safer path than using inventory reduction as a mechanism to expose the process problems.

CASE STUDY

An aerospace company: embedding the logic into the MRP process

In this case study the company was already a mature user of MRP and had a well-trained planner team and management.

When working with an aerospace company as part of doctoral research by Relph (2006), the case study carried out during the research led to a project to implement the *k*-curve approach through the use of DIOS, which was embedded into the companies BaaN ERP system. The project succeeded because it was supported and sponsored by the general manager and led by a highly experienced MRP user.

Pilot/implementation

In 2004 the company had recently completed the implementation of a new ERP system which was not achieving the expected inventory benefits. The volatility of the market was driving the inventory value up. There were significant challenges in controlling the supply chain. The research project had shown the benefits of a formalized approach to planning inventory at the item level. There were difficulties in translating inventory planning objectives from senior management to the detailed level needed by the planning function.

Approach

The underlying business processes were analysed and processes' breakages were determined.

The project wanted to integrate the parameter management processes with the planning objectives. It was identified that embedding the *k*-curve planning engine DIOS into the MRP process, BaaN, and using it to give parameter actions directly to the planner would bring order and structure to the parameter maintenance process. Figure 9.3 shows a typical action screen.

Summary of benefits to date

In this case study, an aerospace company had recently implemented a new ERP system and the focus was now moving to achieving business benefit. There was pressure on the resource and when a study on the *k*-curve approach was completed, the conclusion was that whilst it was a beneficial approach, the planners did not have the time to devote to another additional process that would be required. However, it was considered worthwhile

Figure 9.3 Computer screen showing AIM action codes

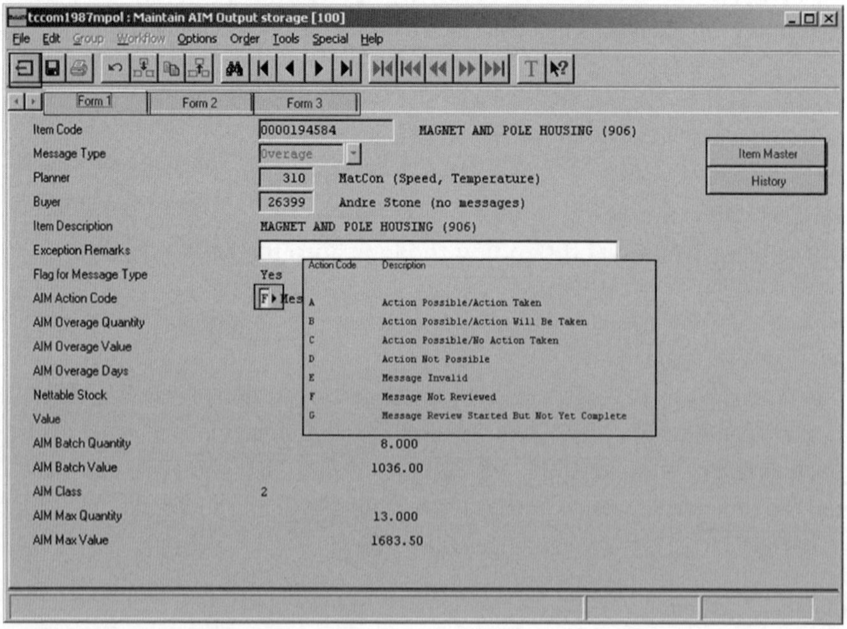

Reproduced by kind permission of Esterline Corporation

to invest in automating the process so that the planners were only required to act/review the outcome of the process. This was achieved by completely embedding the logic as part of the MRP process, using the action messaging process already in the existing ERP recommendations processes. The planners simply saw the output as additional action messages which were part of the daily routine. Thus, use of *k*-curve methodology was embedded into the ERP system. Parameter evaluation and exceptions were calculated weekly and delivered to the planners as actions via the ERP system. The improved inventory planning process reduced overage and was a significant contributor to the 25 per cent reduction in inventory.

Embedding the logic into the MRP planning process: lesson learnt

The key observation here is that by embedding it into the ERP system, the planners were not involved in any additional actions that needed to be completed after their normal processing. It was simple part of the daily routine, in the same way as with the MRP logic; once they understood and accepted the *k*-curve logic the system did all the number crunching and simply presented the planner with actions, which they then applied to their knowledge. The planner remained the final arbiter of the acceptance of the action and thus felt in control of the process.

CASE STUDY

Computer hardware manufacture: nobody noticed

Business background

As a newly appointed inventory specialist in the 1980s, my predecessor had been in post for a long time and was considered the guru; the author had to present at the annual planning review the outcome of research with Aston University and the proposals for the inventory plan for the following year. The presentation was to the eight first-line managers, the two second-line managers and the head of manufacturing planning, all seasoned veterans. The research, prompted by my predecessor's retirement, received a warm welcome, with a lot of questions. However, when the inventory plan for the following was shown to be based on the research the concerns came thick and fast, with requests for additional work to demonstrate that 'production' would not be put at risk. To bring the lengthy discussion to a close, at this point the head of manufacturing made a remark that has stayed with me all my inventory career: *'You can reduce inventory as much as you like but don't stop my production lines, is that clear?'*

Outcome

The eight first-line managers insisted on a final review of the proposed changes and we were faced with more work on justification of the plan. However, my line manager got agreement from the head of manufacturing to change key 'plant level' parameters on the understanding that if any of the first-level managers noticed then they would be reverted back. Only one manager noticed the change, and he was my former boss. He simply winked and said, 'Shall we see who else notices?'

Lesson learnt: nobody noticed

A clear lesson here is that it is always easier to find a reason not to make change, even in a progressive company. My predecessor had told me that his evaluation of the plant level setting had been based on science and a large lump of 'judgement' rather than pure science, as the manufacturing team thought.

CASE STUDY

Kidde Graviner: when to stop

Business background

Kidde Graviner is part of Hamilton Sundstrand/UTC. In 2010 it was weathering the downturn well. Sales in 2008 were £28.7 million to 414 customers and the business balance was 70 per cent into the aerospace market and 30 per cent into the vehicle market. The S&OP process was able to identify that 70 per cent of demand was known at start-of-month. The customer lead time was 8–16 weeks for build. The expected spares lead time for aerospace was much shorter. Kidde used Forth Shift to manage manufacturing and inventory. In addition, there was extensive use of Excel spreadsheets for forecasting. The business had between 10,000 and 20,000-part numbers, with 190 suppliers accounting for approximately £9.6 million spend, of which approximately £5.6 million was inter-company trading. Like many companies Kidde had an active and successful business improvement initiative called ACE (Achieving Competitive Excellence) in operation.

Business performance

- Over the last three years stock turns had been increased from 3.5 to 5.
- This was considered to have taken the 'low-hanging fruit'.
- Kidde Graviner held safety stocks for some customers.
- £2,700k stock today split:
  - £2,000k in raw materials (including £500k safety);
  - £600k is WIP;
  - £100k is FGS (2,500 items).

Project scope

The project wanted to identify the effort required to achieve the stock turn of 10 by end of 2011, estimating that it would significantly increase activity across many of the current improvement initiatives. Kidde wanted to understand how to accelerate the rate of improvements by thinking outside the box, prioritizing and obtaining new skills.

Outcome

The goal of the inventory capability study was to address the challenge of achieving a stock turn of 10. The project identified that some of the product areas had achieved optimum inventory and process capability; these were sunset products where there was no business benefit in focusing on further improvement. The optimal parameter settings for the sunrise products were identified using *k*-curve, and analysis of the capability requirements identified a path that would achieve the goal of stock turn of 10. Based on sales forecasts for 2010–2012 it required a reduction in inventory to less than £1.6 million by Y/E 2012. The project identified process weaknesses which were translated into 17 capability improvement projects. The 17 projects were then divided into three groups: inventory drivers, capability enablers and ACE improvements (ACE was the corporate improvement programme). A key capability enabler project was MRP parameter training, which covered the use of *k*-curve methodology, parameter management and non-compliance as an MRP management process. The key success was a clear understanding of the relationship between the inventory and capabilities in the business and a re-focus on the effective use of MRP. The case study has also been discussed in Chapter 8 when looking at the use of planner guidance tables as described in Excel 8.12.

Lessons learnt: when to stop

Key in this case study is the understanding of the position of the *k*-curve and when further improvements will cost more than they will achieve in benefit. Also linking back, the discussion in Chapter 8 on this case is the use of a planner guidance table which gives a basic set of rules to be observed. This is not dissimilar to the use of simple Pareto planning rules and the matrix approach discussed in Chapter 6. A key characteristic is in all cases that the planner remains the final arbiter of the application of the rules.

CASE STUDY

Electro-mechanical assembly: mature business

Planner's discretion: we do it anyway!

In the case studies so far, we have seen that involvement of the planner in the implementation and leaving the planner as the final arbiter has a strong relation to success. This is underlined in this case study, where the approach to the project appeared to threaten the position of the planner.

Business background

In one of the four 26-week case studies conducted as part of the research for Inventory Management in Business Systems, in the discussions with the planners about their parameter management practices, they stated that 'we change parameters regularly'. However, part of the research had monitored the MRP database for 13 weeks prior to involvement of the planners and the data showed that not one parameter had been changed during these 13 weeks. The following 13 weeks' parameters were changed based on the recommendations of *k*-curve-based reports. At the concluding reviews, when discussing the parameter changes the planners' view was that 'we would have made that change anyway' (Relph, 2006).

Lesson learnt: we do it anyway!

This shows that planners in general see making the parameter decision as part of their raison d'être, and removing this decision can appear a direct threat to their job security. Thus, when implementing a new concept that appears to 'do their job', a more softly-softly approach is more likely to deliver success, as this next case study at Hozelock shows.

CASE STUDY

Hozelock: management commitment

The implementation of the *k*-curve methodology occurred in stages. The first stage was to recommend to the planner any proposed changes calculated by the *k*-curve assessment. The planner then approved the adjustment. Second, when confidence had been established in the *k*-curve analysis, recommendations were uploaded, after a management review of the summary report.

Lesson learnt

The key learning points from this project were:

- maintain the management commitment;
- allow the planner to test and gain confidence in new practices;
- keep a sustained focus on embedding the new practices; and
- ensure that all departments understand and support the MRP improvements.

Summary of case studies and lessons learnt

In looking through these case studies it is useful to tease out the key points. We can categorize them into three areas: process, organization and technology.

Process

- The importance of process improvement before inventory reduction.
- When to stop 'inventory reduction'.

The importance of linking inventory reduction to the capability of the business process, using *k*-curve, exchange curve or Pareto, is that it provides a rational argument that breaks the cycle of relentless reduction. Without this rational argument the business risks continuing inventory reduction until there is a failure in customer service, when management reverse the policy and it is all put back.

Organization

- Push back from planners.
- Nobody noticed.
- We do it anyway.
- We know better than the system.

There is a very significant lesson to be learnt in that it must be understood that the planner will always remain core to the successful operation of any ERP/MRP system. New advanced applications of systems may change the nature of the planner's role, but the fundamental point is that they will inevitably still make the decision. The risk will always be that if the planner is not trained and educated in the new technology, they will always resort to experience and point to any failures of the new system to deliver as proof that 'the planner' knows best. A key point is to be sure that the planner 'understands' the role of the new technology/process and more importantly their part in it, which is usually more significant and important. The importance of 'understanding' as well as training, education and experience was shown in the conclusion to a master's research project on BOM accuracy presented at the Logistics Review Network in 2017 by Relph, Malins and Sorsby. In conclusion, it is important with any new process that we involve and bring the planner along with the implementation of new technology as highlighted in the previous point.

We need to ensure that:

- we involve the planner in the organizational changes;
- we educate the planner to the appropriate level;
- the planner understands the reasons and consequences for any action required;
- we train the planner to use the new systems, ensuring that each transaction is understood.

Technology

Benefits of embedding the logic, eg *k*-curve into the MRP planning process

When a new system is introduced it is important to ensure that it does not add to the workload. The Baan example shows us the success of embedding the inventory management and parameter maintenance activity with the routine action of MRP recommendations. Without this built-in capability the careful use of Excel and upload features should be considered. This shows that the application of technology needs to go hand in hand with process and organization changes. It is, at this point, worth discussing current applications that offer *k*-curve as embedded logic.

Software applications

There are a wide range of software products that focus on inventory optimization. A majority still use Pareto ABC classification, Runner-Repeater-Stranger, and Volatility to classify the parts. In addition, these advanced optimization tools use forecasting, forecast error and statistical safety stock to manage safety stock levels. However, they will still rely on the planner to specify the batch size. To our knowledge there are only two software products that explicitly use *k*-curve methodology in their inventory optimization approach.

DIOS (dynamic inventory optimization software)

IBM developed inventory management software based on the *k*-curve methodology in the mid-1990s in their UK and Swiss offices. It was used by IBM Consulting to support consulting projects and the software was also made available to clients.

CASE STUDY

Mann+Hummel

Mann+Hummel is a major German retailer quoted by IBM as a case study.

The implementation: a classic supply chain dilemma

In reviewing operations, the Mann+Hummel management team noticed that its central distribution centre was 'out of balance'. The centre was carrying excess inventory, but it was missing its targeted customer service levels. The company gave IBM a goal: identify upwards of 15 per cent to 30 per cent in inventory reductions – freeing up valuable working capital and keeping order line service levels at 97 per cent or above for all products. IBM was also asked to study the effect that other factors might have on the facility's inventory, such as shorter production lead times, stock build-ups that occur before production holidays, and expected increases in market share.

Benefits

IBM was able to show how Mann+Hummel could lower its current stock by 30 per cent using DIOS while keeping customer service levels at 97 per cent and reducing order lines for production per year by 18 per cent. The resulting benefits quoted were:

- reduced inventory levels and material handling costs;
- increased customer service level performance;
- improved demand forecasting (IBM, 2014).

Amis-delta

Inventory Matters developed amis-delta, an inventory planning tool based on *k*-curve principles, in 2008. It is used both as a consulting tool and operationally by clients.

CASE STUDY

Hozelock: we know better than the system

This case study starts back in 2002 when Hozelock wanted to improve service levels to their customers. Hozelock work in the demanding UK DIY retail sector and wanted to reduce lost business and improve the seasonal planning process.

Background

Hozelock were a mature MRP user with an established system. Lean/agile manufacturing techniques were established but the management wanted further service levels improvement. There was a recognition that the business needed to be 'make to stock'-driven to meet the demands of their customers. Forecast was owned by the sales function; the quality was unreliable as the product demand was highly influenced by the weather. The planners were using arbitrary parameters policies and did not believe the forecast from sales. Supply/demand planning was not fully synchronized with significant manual progressing activities.

Approach

With the help of Inventory Matters, the business took a critical look at existing business processes and identified where there were breakages in the processes and scope for improvement. A critical area was the maintenance of safety stock parameters which were causing visibility and capacity issues as there were large changes on a quarterly basis. The MRP planning cycle needed to be aligned to the customer demand cycle. The weakness of the quarterly MRP seasonal planning process was identified and understood. A detailed analysis of seasonal demand patterns based on three years' history helped balance the distribution of the safety stocks.

A re-evaluation of safety stock techniques using *k*-curve methodology improved the visibility and capacity utilization. The use of *k*-curve was supported using a planning tool based on *k*-curve methodology, called amis-delta. The development and implementation of the amis-delta monthly stock-planning process improved the overall stock effectiveness. Initially the output from amis-delta was reviewed by the planners and, if approved, input by them into their MRP system. Once confidence had been built up the parameters were then uploaded directly into the planning systems.

Summary of benefits to date

There has been a significant and sustained reduction in lost business. There has also been an improved visibility of demand in the seasonal cycle, resulting in better utilization of stock and improved capacity planning.

Continuous evaluation and adjustment of safety stock parameters has become a routine practice, which helps to ensure that end-of-season stocks are minimized. The planning in amis-delta focuses on the 'B' Class parts, leading to higher MRP compliance. This in turn means that the business can focus on detailed manual planning of the A-Class stock parts. Hozelock were the winners of the Manufacturer of the Year Award 2009.

SOURCE www.amis-delta.co.uk

Parameter alignment tools and techniques

What emerges from the analysis of these case studies is the importance of the planner's decision. Despite massive technological changes the systems generally require the planner to define the parameters for each product. Some systems provide defaults that can be applied at a group level, but these can be dangerous and apply parameters inappropriately. Planner(s) are human and as such will be influenced by prevailing conditions. In simple terms, when you consider how many parameters are typically managed by a planner or group of planners it is difficult to expect consistency. Shortage of supply of products, poor performance of suppliers will influence them to increase safety stocks. Pressure to reduce inventory will drive the planners to reduce parameters. Pressure from manufacturing and purchasing to increase batch sizes will compete with the drive for a 'lean' organization. Each planner will be influenced to a greater or lesser extent by these competing factors. The result will be, as shown in Figure 9.4, that each planner will apply their own rules, influences and personality to the parts they control. Whilst this may not result in chaos it will mean that there is often no common or consistent standard applied across the business. The most common guidance tool used to assist planners is Pareto and many authors like Wild (2017) and Silver, Pyke and Thomas (2017) assert that what this effectively does is align the planners through a common set of rules. As we discussed in Chapters 6 and 7, Pareto has its place but as the number of parts increases, more sophisticated alignment tools are needed.

Figure 9.4 Planners setting parameter without common rules

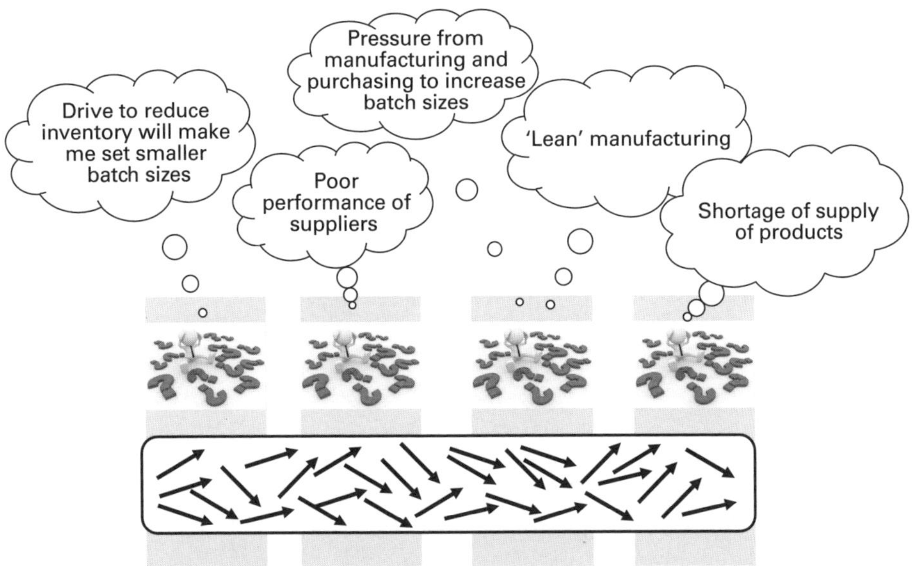

It is necessary to recognize that although alignment tools are an important guidance, they do not require blind compliance. The alignment of the parameters can be through:

- planner tables to provide guidance;
- system-based classifications (pareto/*k*-curve);

- parameter uploads based on off-line analysis (*k*-curve);
- embedded rules/filters based on classifications.

Most MRP systems will offer a hierarchy of default parameters or simple tools like ABC Pareto to classify products and pre-allocate parameters. Pareto/Matrix are useful tools but, as discussed, for large organizations the level of granularity and inherent weakness of Pareto will mean that the result will tend to be sub-optimal. The next logical step from Pareto is the use of an inventory matrix as discussed in Chapter 6: an example is shown in Table 6.13. The matrices again can be applied manually or automatically. It is possible to develop sophisticated matrices that would allow the setting of parameters similar to the one developed in Chapter 8 – see Excel 8.12. The benefits of the use of alignment tools (shown in Figure 9.5) are that by using an alignment tool we can moderate the pressures from external influences. The Hozelock case study shows that planners respond to the use of guidance if they retain the role of the 'final arbiter'.

Figure 9.5 Planners setting parameters with a common table like Excel 8.12

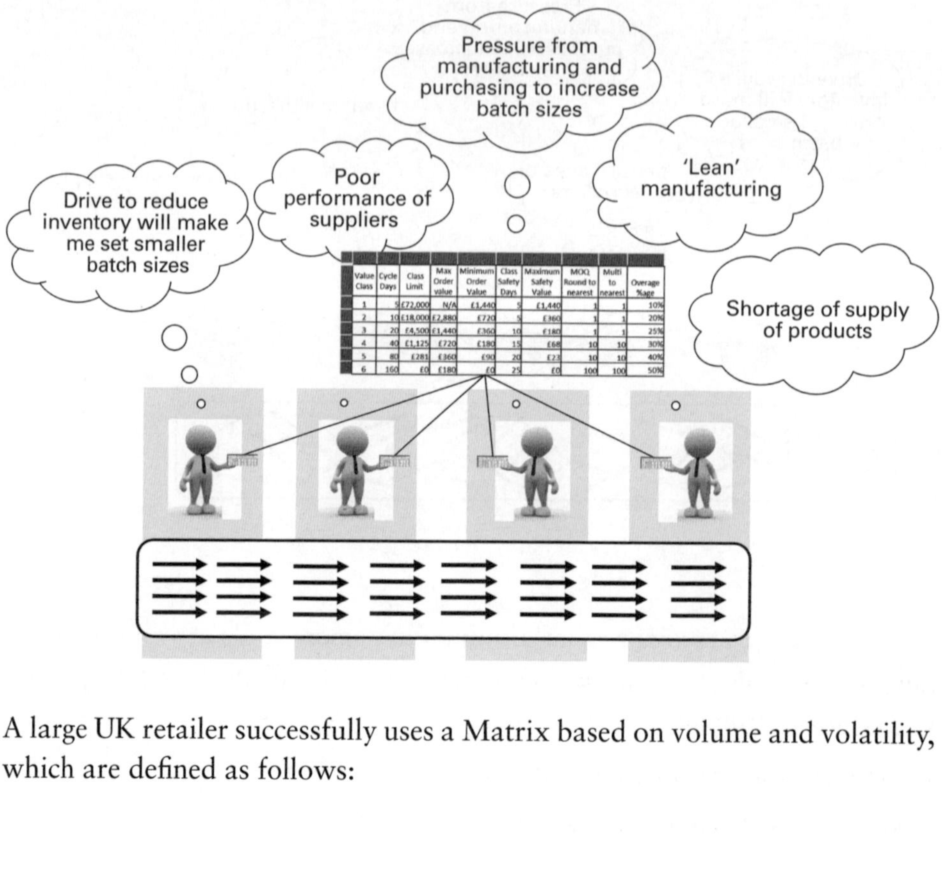

A large UK retailer successfully uses a Matrix based on volume and volatility, which are defined as follows:

- volume is based on quantity sold in a year;
- volatility is based an analysis of the variability of the demand.

They use two key matrices: one determines the classification of the part as either ABC for Volume and XYZ for Volatility – this classification determines the order/replenishment policy – and the other sets limits on the forecast accuracy for volume and variability.

Many systems now allow 'mass updates' via an upload of parameters via Excel or CSV files. Mass updates will work well if the process that surrounds them involves the planner through an approval cycle.

Summary

In this chapter we looked at the implementation of the *k*-curve approach and more generally the issues related to the role of the planner in the management and maintenance of parameters in any MRP system. Emerging from this are a number of useful lessons:

1. Planners need to be educated, system-trained and must understand the role and importance of each of the parameters they set. The role of the system implementor is principally to train, specifically the 'how and where' of transacting the daily operations. Education to ensure good understanding of the process (for example inventory planning) is often omitted: not educating or ensuring that planners understand their role in the new system will inevitably lead to failure.
2. The more sophisticated the system the more important the role of the planner in managing the input parameters to ensure that the output is realistic and correct. To ensure the planners are 'pulling together' an aligned focus is essential.

Tools and techniques discussed in this chapter

- Pareto ABC
- Matrix for parameter policy decisions
- Parameter alignment

References

IBM (2013) IBM Dynamic Inventory Optimisation Solution [online] www.ibm.com/downloads/cas/AZLZBLPV [accessed 2019]

Relph, G J (2006) Inventory Management in Business Systems, PhD thesis, Manchester University

Relph, G J, Malins, M and Sorsby, K (2017) The real cost of poor-quality BOM in manufacturing, LRN Conference Proceedings 2017, pp. 200–209, Southampton Solent University: Chartered Institute of Logistics and Transport

Silver, E A, Pyke, D F and Thomas, D J (2017) *Inventory and Production Management in Supply Chains* (4th ed) CRC Press, Taylor Francis Group, London

Slack, N, Chambers, S and Johnston, R (2010) *Operations Management*, Financial Times/Prentice Hall, London

Wild, T (2017) *Best Practice in Inventory Management* (3rd ed) Routledge, New York

Review, summary and what to do next 10

Introduction

This book has discussed the many facets of inventory management in business systems. And for those of you who have considered every chapter – even the scary maths – as well as for those of you who have only selected parts of the book to read so far, it's time to bring it all together with examples of how these are used in the real world.

Following the calculations closely in this book will have brought great value to some of you. However, it's not necessary for everyone to get into the maths: understanding the meaning and rationale used, and how to use the output from the methods brings great value to the business.

This chapter briefly revisits some of the key messages from the book, and covers:

- three pillars of inventory management: plan, control, balance;
- four steps to inventory heaven;
- five milestones in the journey through the book, with case studies to illustrate the five steps;
- the business systems (MRP and ERP) in which:
  - the inventory plans have to be implemented;
  - orders are raised and transacted;
- impact of new technology on the future of inventory management;
- toolbox review;
- summary.

This chapter is a review of the whole book. It brings together the key messages. We start off by returning to the three pillars of inventory management.

The three pillars of inventory management

In Chapter 1 we refer to these three pillars as a three-legged stool – plan, control, balance – and show that where any one of these three fails the whole process fails.

Control

In Chapters 1 and 3 we discussed technologies and tools (eg bar-coding and RFID) which can be used both to increase business capability and to improve data accuracy. If we consider the complexity described in the Airbus case study in Chapter 5 we can see that it would be common to need to pick a list of 100 parts (see Table 10.1). Were we to accept a 90 per cent chance of the items being correct, we know that failure is guaranteed, as can be seen in the table in Chapter 9. That is why very high levels of accuracy equivalent to 'parts per million' (PPM) need to be applied; 90 per cent accuracy may appear, incorrectly, to be reasonable, whereas 100,000 PPM errors immediately grab our attention.

It is important to apply the same philosophy used for product quality to the data quality of parts, for example six-sigma.

Balance

As systems increase their ability to update more often – or even go real time – it is much easier to provide the planner with up-to-date information and instructions as to what needs to be done to keep the inventory in balance. We know that as technology improves both interconnectivity and the speed of reaction times, the time needed to rebalance inventory according to the plan should also decrease. This doesn't, however, decrease the time needed to plan for optimum inventory. Sadly, the increased efficiency of these systems has seen a reduction in the numbers of planners in organizations, leaving them little time to 'think' and truly plan the products for which they are responsible.

Planning

The professionalism of the planning community is important. There is a much higher level of education/skills available and needed in the planning community. However, as Table 10.1 shows, inventory planning is still largely

Table 10.1 Probability of picking a kit with 100 parts

Accuracy of data	Probability of shortage free kit of 100 parts	No of failures per million
90.0000%	0.003%	100,000
95.0000%	0.592%	50,000
99.0000%	36.603%	10,000
99.9000%	90.479%	1,000
99.9990%	99.999%	10
99.9999%	99.999%	1

determined by the planner's skill and judgement, which we believe to be a key inefficiency in managing MRP effectively. By giving the operations managers the ability to ensure that planners are working to common rules and guidelines we are not de-skilling the planner but linking the high-level plans to the detail decision. For most companies MRP is only successful when the painstakingly detailed adjustments carried out by planners is aligned to the common goal of the business. As Einstein said, the definition of insanity is 'doing the same thing over and over again and expecting different results'. In this context:

1. If you do not change MRP parameters how can you expect the inventory level that MRP is driving the business towards to change?
2. If you do not change how parameters are calculated – ie moving from individual decisions to coordinated decisions that relate the value and importance of parts to one another – how can you expect to influence the direction of travel?
3. If you do not link the high-level target to the detail parts, how can you expect to exert any power over MRP and the inventory level that MRP is driving the business towards?

Batch, safety, lead time

In Chapter 4 we explained how MRP is critically dependent on three decisions being made:

- Batch: How much?
- Safety: How important is it to protect against service level failure from both supply side and customer demand?
- Lead time: How long must I allow for the resupply of the item?

The option is to plan inventory within MRP or to manage 'ad-hoc', often using Excel or home-grown reports designed by the planner. Lack of confidence in the system is a key reason why planners often plan outside the system. If these plans are not loaded back into the system, including changes to parameter settings, the recommendations then made by the system are likely to be incorrect.

We return again to inventory management within business systems, in ERP and MRP, which is a fundamental theme within this book, later in this chapter. Here we continue with the key planning points in the book.

Inventory/MRP complexity

In the book we have examined the dilemma of planning at aggregate vs detail level. It is an inescapable problem within business that it is necessary to consider both the total value of the inventory as well as which individual parts are affected. If we must reduce inventory by 20 per cent or £1 million, how do we decide which parts to reduce? Most businesses will have thousands of parts and if they use MRP there are many parameters to adjust. If a business decides to reduce inventory then it must be that there is more inventory than is needed, either:

- I have too much inventory, ie we have *overage*; or
- I plan too much inventory, ie the plan is incorrect.

What is obvious is that you cannot identify if you have too much inventory unless you have already defined your target inventory level. To define the target level, some form of economic model is needed to tell us when we are planning for too much inventory.

The 'exchange curve' shows that inventory can only be reduced *whilst still maintaining the correct inventory level* if the business is capable of managing smaller batches in greater frequency, ie by exchanging inventory for a faster process. If you can define the plan level then MRP will help to manage overage, but the planner must comply with the recommendations.

Item-level planning tools

In the book we have looked at the well-known and largely understood economic order quantity (EOQ) approach, which is often challenged and modified. The EOQ logic is fundamentally sound but lacks credibility because key elements required are showing to be indeterminate. Safety stock is often considered more theoretically solid ground; however, looking at the wide range of safety stock algorithms, which vary from simple to very complex, very quickly the data required to execute the formulae becomes too difficult to gather and maintain.

Product planning

The set-back or stick chart was explored in Chapter 5 in the discussion of the P:D ratio (ie the stacked production time: the time the customer is willing to wait). The gap between the P and the D identifies the 'at risk' time where forecasts are essential and planning is based on this uncertainty. This gap may be increased where customers want to shorten the delivery time (ie reduce the D time), or decreased where purchasing, production, delivery times etc are reduced. The stick chart is built upon the BOM, thus informing the way the BOM is set up in the MRP system. It focuses on the product and the issues related to the P:D ratio.

Product value profile

The product value profile helps to identify where in the production process the greatest value of inventory is held. Once it is understood what items/ sub-assemblies etc comprise the greatest inventory value, and what stage in the process these are tied up in, a business may be able to work towards introducing high inventory value later in the process. For example, when assembling a car, the production process is designed to add in low-value parts first, adding the engine, which is a very valuable part of the vehicle, at the last moment possible.

These ideas were also explored in the book with regard to the benefits of late customization, for example with the snow shovel and the control boxes. It has been shown that the design of the product itself may be modified to improve the production process and to achieve a low cost inventory value profile.

Strategic planning

Strategic planning happens at a gross level. Here we consider the total sales of a business and total business capacity, from which we derive the resulting inventory requirements.

One example of this is an e-commerce company who start their business planning process by identifying the total sales objective for the year. From this they determine the cost of sales, and thereby determine the precise amount and type of inventory they want to invest in. The result of this is to identify the budget, against which the buyers have to buy.

A second example is fast-fashion company Zara, whose business strategy is to respond quickly to changing fashions. This requires high levels of capacity for their fashion production lines, and low levels of inventory to remain agile and flexible.

These two examples show that the strategic plan is based on the three lines – P & S & I (production, sales, inventory). As we saw in Chapter 2, this relationship remains inviolate and applies at all levels.

Aggregate planning tools

Pareto The requirement of a business to plan from aggregate to item is facilitated by the use of Pareto, a widely understood and used tool. It is one of the few inventory planning tools that is generally available as a planning tool in MRP. The book examined the Pareto weaknesses (Relph and Newton, 2014) and how they are resolved by developing the exchange curve principle.

Exchange curve and *k*-curve The extension of Pareto into the *k*-curve methodology has been developed through the book, and an inventory planning model has been created to enable the reader to use the *k*-curve approach within their own business.

Inventory capability planning In this chapter we have looked at how the *k*-curve approach can improve the Lean approach by ensuring that the capability is improved before the 'water is lowered', preventing the business from floundering on the rocks. The *k*-curve approach takes fewer risks and can indicate when to stop. The four steps to inventory planning are summarized below.

CASE STUDY

Zara

Business strategy and inventory category both affect inventory management

Globally, Zara is considered a leading clothes retailer and manufacturer. Starting in A Coruña, Spain in 1975, Zara developed a vision of bringing style to the high street at affordable prices and are attributed with the phrase 'democratization of fashion'. Their strategy is based on 'fast fashion' where speed to market is essential. They capture ideas and trends direct from their customers in stores and from the wider market and are able to translate them into new or modified products. From starting a design their target is for a new product to reach stores in three to four weeks.

Zara's 'democratization of fashion' and strategy results in them producing a vast array of products each year. Divita and Yoo tell us that Zara produces '11,000 items in five to six colours and five to seven ranges annually... [whilst] H&M and Gap produce 2,000 to 4,000 items per annum' (Divita and Yoo, 2017).

Managing operating costs is essential to all businesses. Retailers in the fast-fashion industry benefit from frequent deliveries of small quantities of a large number of designs to their stores. This ensures that stores are constantly receiving fresh stock. Inventory is not often left in overage at the stores either, since items are either shipped to different stores where there is demand, or put 'on sale'. However, this costs fast-fashion retailers less than traditional retailers, and Fernie tells us that 'fast-fashion retailers sell approximately 15 per cent of their merchandise on markdowns as opposed to 50 per cent for traditional apparel retailers' (Fernie, 2015).

However, for Zara to be able to achieve their strategy, they need access to agile and flexible production capacity resulting in 'fast-fashion methods' which are not the cheapest. Zara use an integrated network of both independent and company-owned facilities to 'produce in small batches at short notice' (Christopher, 2016). This allows Zara to access additional capacity as required.

Costs for producing fast-fashion items are brought down in Zara, however, by medium- and long-term forecasting for material (as well as capacity). Thus, material can be planned and manufactured using greater economies of scale, with the final cutting and sewing carried out within a short time of the item being available to customers in store and online.

Zara offer a small range of standard or classic items alongside the fast-fashion items, eg white t-shirts. The white t-shirt has a timeless element to it and can be forecast to the item level. This allows Zara to benefit from greater economies of scale in the production of the final item than for the fast-fashion items. Table 10.2 shows some of the different requirements in managing the business and planning the inventory for classic and fast-fashion items.

Table 10.2 Key attributes of Zara products need managing differently based on inventory category

	Classic items	Fast fashion items
Product range	Narrow: few colours eg white T-shirt	Wide: many styles eg jacket, dress, suit
Design changes	Infrequent	Constant
Price	Everyday low price	Premium prices
Quality	Consistency, conformance to reasonable spec	Perception of good grades of material and workmanship
Sales volumes	Consistent sales over time	Low volumes of each item, high volumes in total
Order winners	Price	Time to market Brand – alike High fashion
Order qualifiers	Quality, availability	Price (affordable when compared with premium brands), availability
Logistics priorities	Cost Dependability Quality	Speed Flexibility Quality

Developed from Harrison *et al* (2014) p. 29

Zara, along with its parent company Inditex and most other fast-fashion companies, is working to ease some of the environmental issues that have resulted from fast fashion and the buying habits of the general population, some of which were explored in Chapter 3.

Zara has achieved great success in its fast-fashion offering to the marketplace. This has led to a clear strategy and the development of a responsive supply chain. Within this, the recognition of managing inventory according to the production stage and inventory category has been key.

Four steps to inventory heaven

These four steps have been a common theme within the book. The diagrams in Chapter 6 show the relationship between them and their progression. The steps are:

- Understand your current inventory position – *How much have I got?*
  - What inventory is active and which of the active parts have I got too much of?
  - What inventory is inactive, how long has it been inactive, and can I dispose of it or use it elsewhere?
  - Is there a strategic reason why I acquired the inventory and is that reason still valid?
- Determine the business targets that relate to inventory – *What do I have to achieve?*
  - The business will of necessity need to reduce costs and inventory will invariably come into focus. Inventory targets are always broad brush expressed as percentages or monetary values. For the business to understand what it needs to achieve it needs to know where the constraints are. The constraints can be expressed as an inventory level or in the capability of the business processes.
- Create an inventory plan – *How difficult will this be and what must I do?*
  - Plan at group level first, using a combination of Pareto and *k*-curve. Using a combination of Pareto and *k*-curve, individual groups can be planned, and individual constraints for each group identified and listed in an action plan. Thus, each active group can then be planned separately.
  - Consolidate plan: these individual plans can be brought together before adding back the inactive stock to create a consolidated total plan.
- Implement the plan – *What actions must I do to achieve the plan?*
  - The planning process will have identified actions:

    What parameters need changing?

    Where am I overstocked?

    Plan and agree disposal of inactive stock.

    Where do I need to improve the process?
  - The plan is supported by a detailed list of assumptions that will ensure that when changes happen the plan can be adjusted with confidence.

The five milestones were introduced in Chapter 1, and are reviewed here to recap the journey through the book. The milestones are illustrated with case studies.

Five milestones

The journey through the book has five milestones, as shown in Figure 10.1. The milestones and associated 'lessons learnt' from case studies are titled:

1. Milestone 1: Managing inventory and the business systems.
   - Coordinating the business with the system needs educated people.
2. Milestone 2: The impact of inventory throughout the business.
   - Strong leadership and cross-business support are essential.
3. Milestone 3: Effective, measurable inventory planning.
   - Measuring compliance reinforces proactive parameter management.
4. Milestone 4: The inventory management toolbox.
5. Milestone 5: People and aligning the business needs.
   - Don't fiddle with the trivial many but focus on the precious few – changing habits.
   - System training vs education (don't presume the recipient understands basic mechanisms).

Figure 10.1 Five milestones

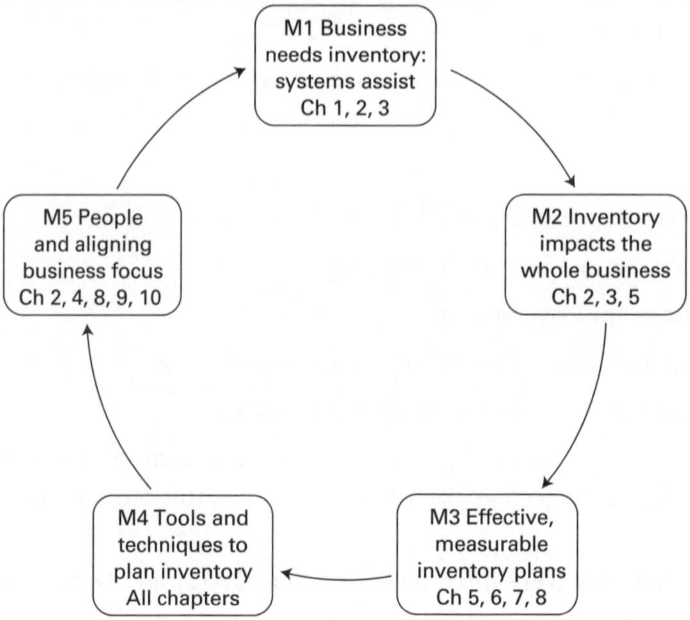

Here is the route we have taken.

Milestone 1: Managing inventory and the business systems

We have considered both the business needs relating to inventory and the systems together and separately:

- The business needs inventory:
  - available;
  - in the right place;
  - at the right time;
  - in the right quantity and quality;
  - costs to be minimized;
  - to be well managed – ie planned, controlled and balanced.
- The systems:
  - are used to communicate and coordinate throughout the business;
  - assist planning and manage the products and services complexity;
  - are used to control:

    including physical control in warehousing and elsewhere;

    data so that it matches the actual physical parts;
  - are used to balance real-time progress and situations.

Milestone 1 is discussed specifically in Chapters 1, 2 and 3.

CASE STUDY
Toiletries

In a conversation with a business systems manager it was stated, 'Our planning system did not plan so we created our own planning report... It takes the gross requirement – subtracts the stock and then the orders. When it has done that it places new orders...' Our reply was, 'Why do you not use the MRP module that is usually supplied with most planning systems...?' The business systems manager's reply was, 'What is MRP...?' Subsequent investigation of the system showed that there was an MRP module available. The operations planners, who had used the old system for several years, found when comparing with the 'off the shelf' MRP that the recommendations were incorrect. The planners were shown how to use the standard MRP and the old system was switched off.

Case study toiletries: lessons learnt

Coordinating the business with the system needs educated people

The company took an early decision to build their own system to create planning reports and to calculate what orders were necessary. They had no background knowledge about MRP and were unaware that their existing ERP system could create the reports and the orders to do this for them.

It is important to understand what a business system can do for you. Thus, prior to implementing a system a business will benefit greatly if it audits existing knowledge and educates its people about production planning and control, inventory management, etc.

During and after implementation, system training remains essential. But system training without prior inventory management education will be vastly sub-optimal.

Milestone 2: The impact of inventory throughout the business

In the book we have discussed how inventory impacts businesses at strategic, tactical and operational levels, as well as impacting many parts of the business from commercial to production and customer service to operations. This was shown at a basic level with the snow shovel, wherein even the simplest businesses, holding inventory is highly likely to be necessary.

Chapter 1:

> The dichotomy of inventory is that inventory held ties up working capital (because it costs money and therefore less is better) but it is needed in order to have something to add value to and sell (because we need the inventory to ensure product availability).

The concept of 'stockless production' was detailed by Robert W. Hall (Hall, 1983) in *Zero Inventories*. He recognized that 'instantaneous conversion of raw material to finished product is, of course, not literally possible' (Hall, 1983, p. 2), but the phrase 'zero inventory' led to a misconception that it is possible for businesses to operate without inventory. In his book, Hall discusses inventory reduction through 'reduction of set-up times' and 'as inventory shrinks and operations become more tightly linked, production rates at all work centres need to become more closely coordinated'. This is also shown in this book in the exchange curve, relating the reduction in inventory to the increased capability of the business.

Milestone 2 was introduced in Chapters 2 and 3 and discussed further in Chapter 5.

CASE STUDY

Where implementation projects fail

It is always easy to talk of success, but not so easy to talk of failure. This example is from a company which was making equipment for trains and tanks. The company had had a mature MRP implementation, but due to staff turnover the level of MRP understanding within the business had declined. In addition, there was a strong focus on working capital reduction, of which inventory reduction was a significant component.

The improvement project initially focused on MRP training together with an independent analysis of the inventory using *k*-curve. The project developed inventory plans and identified the need to focus on non-compliance.

The project was initially successful. However, following changes in senior management and the planning manager, the success was not sustained. There was a strong solo mentality within the organization which meant the required level of inter-departmental cooperation was not forthcoming. Once the original management support for the project waned the planners quickly reverted to the old habits.

Lessons learnt: where implementation projects fail

Strong leadership and cross-business support are essential

It is essential to have excellent leadership, good management support, strong change management and clear direction for all system implementations and improvement projects to have a chance to succeed. When these are removed before a change in system and process has been embedded in people's daily work activity, the temptation, as in this case study, is to revert to the old, comfortable habits.

Planners have always been depended upon to set parameters. Consequently, it is easy for them to feel defensive if given any external help or advice. This example shows that the early loss of the project leaders caused the improvement project to fail.

Milestone 3: Effective, measurable inventory planning

Inventory needs to be planned as effectively as possible to ensure best value add, relating reasonable cost to the greatest benefit possible. Measuring planning effectiveness is essential. Compliance (measuring the accuracy and acceptance of system-generated orders/instructions) is a key measure necessary in all ERP systems.

Milestone 3 is discussed specifically in Chapters 5, 6 and 7.

CASE STUDY

Pumps

We worked with a client who had just implemented SAP in 17 plants worldwide. When their compliance level was analysed it was found to be as low as 25 per cent. When the planners were challenged they stated: 'We have no time to maintain our parameters because we are too busy firefighting'. The improvement project created a 'parameter sickie', which in effect meant that the planner was assumed not to be available and his colleagues covered for him as though he were sick. This gave the planner time and space to properly review the parameters, based on an analysis of their non-compliance. This returned huge benefits, with compliance increasing from 25 per cent to 75 per cent in six weeks and eventually to 90 per cent.

Lessons learnt: measuring compliance reinforces proactive parameter management

Compliance is an essential measurement for all businesses running an MRP/ERP system. Compliance is a measure of how well the system is performing (ie whether the orders recommended by the system are accepted as correct or not).

Understanding that their compliance levels were low allowed the Pumps company to quantify their existing problem of *not managing* their system parameters in a timely and accurate way. Consequently, they identified that time was needed to maintain parameters, hence their 'parameter sickie'.

The consequence of poorly maintained parameters is that system-recommended orders will be incorrect. It is all too common for planners to become habituated to adjusting orders frequently, and it is easy for them to believe that this is where they are adding value. The real value is not by constantly adjusting the system output but added by managing the *input*:

- Are the parameters and the data correct?
- Do they result in the correct output (eg orders)?
- Do they reflect the current goals of the business?

Once the Pumps company understood that measuring compliance would help them to manage their business and their system, they recognized the importance of managing parameters and allocated time to achieve this.

Milestone 4: The inventory management toolbox

We've considered that there are several ways to effectively plan inventory, including Pareto, inventory management matrices, and EOQ. Ultimately, we believe that each business should utilize the most appropriate tools to plan their inventory. For some this is the use of *k*-curve methodology.

Tools and techniques have been summarized at the end of each chapter. Milestone 4 relating to *k*-curve is discussed in detail in Chapters 7 and 8.

> A summary of the tools used in each chapter is given in Appendix C.

Milestone 5: People and aligning the business needs

We've talked about how systems assist us, the people. Inventory planning and decisions originate with us: the system needs people to set parameters, bills of materials, etc before it can work. We've talked about the best way of using MRP within ERP systems to implement our plans, exploding the plans down from the independent demand into the dependent, detailed levels.

Some inventory planning decisions will be carried out outside MRP and these decisions are then fed back into the ERP systems. It is essential to ensure people are aligned, and all planners are focused on the same business goals and working to achieve the same, correct direction. Pareto is a simple tool to assist with this alignment. *k*-curve is a more sophisticated and ultimately more effective tool to ensure planners are aligned.

The person who is the planner has and will continue to have a pivotal role in managing inventory – ensuring the system settings remain correct according to the changing needs of the business is essential.

Milestone 5 is discussed specifically in Chapters 2, 4, 9 and 10.

CASE STUDY

EDF – setting up systems correctly

Background

The Supply Chain and Logistics group of EDF Energy Networks, a major power supplier in the UK, were having difficulty implementing their Inventory Optimization Software as an add-on to their SAP system. The initial implementation and re-implementation had not succeeded and as a result the system was not being used by the planners.

Project objective

The project examined the processes, organization and technology. The *k*-curve methodology was used to analyse the existing settings. These settings were challenged, and an alternative set of values proposed. The organization and the planners' non-compliance were investigated. By examining the reasons for their non-compliance, the project was able to identify process improvements and training to help ensure that the software was properly understood. The parameter settings were reviewed to ensure that they were in alignment with the business targets.

The outcome

The project identified a revision to the existing parameter settings and approach. It also identified where there were opportunities to increase compliance by focusing on high-value components. The manager's view of the completed project was:

> The main aim was to reduce the inventory value while improving service to our customers. The structured manner in which the final report was submitted along with the suggested project plan will enable my team and I to implement and track progress moving forward. (Paul Farmer, Inventory Demand Manager)

Lessons learnt: don't fiddle with the trivial many but focus on the precious few – changing habits

Independent expert help from a non-threatening (and non-competitive) source resulted in a re-setting of the system. This brought about improvements in EDF's inventory management.

The hard-working planners had previously been making frequent adjustments to the system-generated forecasts and to the output of orders. This is akin to firefighting: greater value is added by the up-stream management of the system.

The key lessons learnt were:

- Up-stream management of parameters and data accuracy is critical.
- Don't fiddle with the trivial many but focus on the precious few.
- Without the people involved understanding the process and accepting new ways of working, improvements will not be implemented:
  - ensure time is spent with the planners;
  - deal with the necessary politics and move past it.

CASE STUDY

Education and training: Morrisons

Background

Morrisons is a well-known UK retailer that was implementing a new ERP system as part of a five-year IT improvement programme. Morrisons were particularly keen to ensure that the staff were properly trained in the use of the new system as it represented a significant change in the business operation, through automation of the ordering process. The ERP systems provider was contracted to provide the transactional training. Morrisons identified that there was an additional need to provide 'theoretical training' or 'education' for the planning team to ensure that they understood the mechanics of the transactions and the reasons behind this. The training covered the operation of the forecasting and planning processes and the key requirements for managing the parameter settings.

Objective

To educate the supply chain analysts and planners to understand the business requirements from the forecasting and inventory planning systems, and their critical part in this by rigorous management of parameters.

Outcome

The training programme was initially developed and piloted using a group of the senior planners and first-line management to confirm that the level of complexity in the material was appropriate for the target audience. All the planners were asked to complete a 'test' to determine their knowledge of supply chain planning principles. The planners were tested again at the end of the training and an average improvement of 10 per cent on their test score was achieved. As expected, the planners were then able to approach the new system with confidence and were able to adjust to the new role easily. What was not so expected was that it almost completely removed the 'fear of job loss' associated with the new systems as the planners were able to see that the benefits of the automation were to enable them to become planners and not just order processors.

Lessons learnt: training verses education

The Morrisons case study builds on the lessons learnt in the Toiletries case study. What is important is to understand and appreciate the difference between system training and education that focuses on the essential theory behind the systems being implemented. It is a mistake to assume the recipient understands the basic mechanisms involved in the new transactions.

Morrisons educated their people in advance of the system implementation, thereby giving them the understanding and proper tools to do their work well. In addition, any feeling that the system might threaten jobs disappeared, since they realized that the role of the planner – decision making, parameter settings, etc – would remain essential.

These milestones are reflected also in the 'Overall planning process roadmap' diagram which was shown at the beginning of Chapter 8 in Figure 8.1.

The business systems MRP and ERP

Managing inventory within the business systems has been a common theme in this book. It is MRP and ERP in which:

- the inventory plans have to be implemented;
- orders are raised and transacted.

MRP in relation to ERP

MRP is still the most common materials planning technique at the centre of most ERP systems, even though it may be enhanced by advanced planning systems, which still rely on the same cycle, safety and lead-time planning parameters. There have been continuous developments and advances in the capabilities of ERP and the planning function in MRP. What continues to surprise us when visiting companies is that parameters – specifically those that define the cycle stock, safety stock and lead times – remain manually assessed and maintained by the planner. This means that the business planning system is subject to planners making thousands of individual decisions that are, in effect, not necessarily linked. If you recall, Figure 2.9 shows the ERP configuration with MRP at the heart of the operations. This demonstrates just how fundamental it is that these decisions are correct and linked to the business operations through the planning process and the wider ERP functions that then rely on the MRP and MRPII planning decisions.

Current management of MRP

A study of MRP parameter management practices over two decades by Jonsson and Mattsson (2006) is shown in Table 10.3. It shows that 64 per cent of lot-sizing parameters were set by the planner. This was a high and significant proportion, which is likely to have improved by only a small amount since then. Of the three categories, planners/operations managers will argue that lot-for-lot is a Lean approach and therefore a good thing. What is worth challenging is that lot-for-lot requires the planner to review at the time of ordering.

We need to question whether this is a good thing or a bad thing – or perhaps a bit of both. Does my observation that the 'setting of ordering parameters to lot-for-lot' give the planner a sense of control and adding value, since it offers them the chance to review quantity at time of ordering and then to consolidate with other orders using skill and expertise? With the advance of computer planning systems that continue to threaten the role of the production/operations planner, it is no wonder they want to maximize control over the decisions required. However, this is a false sense of control

Table 10.3 Frequency of company using each lot-sizing method (Jonsson and Mattsson, 2006)

Method Identifier	Lot-sizing method	Percentage of companies
A	Lot-for-lot	24
B	Experience-based number of periods covered	29
C	Experience-based Fixed Quantity	11
D	EOQ	31
E	Dynamic optimization method	5

since it forces the planner to review every order placed, whether each individual order is a good use of their time or not, creating additional workload for an already busy planner. The result is that 64 per cent of the decisions are experienced-based. Without negating the benefit of this experience, just consider the difficulties in getting a group of planners making in the region of 30,000 decisions to remain rational and coordinated.

In spite of a wealth of knowledge and experience, business systems implementations are still failing and for the same reasons. In Chapter 2 we summarized the many studies since the 1980s which show that the underlying cause of failure and thus the CSF (Critical Success Factors) for good ERP implementations remain the same.

Impact of new technology on the future of inventory management

The business focus continues to manage the cash flow in the business. This requires continuous improvement on all aspects of inventory management as a key driver of the cash flow. The need to continuously improve puts ever more pressure on the effective use of business tools to manage the supply chain. Technology advances have significantly improved the interconnectivity of the supply chain. An understanding of the inventory within the business is key, both the high-level business numbers and how they relate to the detailed inventory at part and parameter level.

It is essential to know how to identify and drive down overstock, and how to optimize cycle stock without reducing it too far to a point where the business would become anorexic. Most businesses rely on some form of computer-based planning system, of which ERP packages, cloud-based or otherwise, are still the most common, with MRP remaining at the core of these systems.

New technologies will not change the fundamental requirements of inventory management – the three pillars, the four steps to heaven, and the five milestones will remain true and valid. They may, however, allow us to change some of the business processes and increase the capability of the organization (thereby reducing inventory held).

The IoT (Internet of Things) and Industrie 4.0 have the potential to continue to increase the capability of our organizations, thereby reducing inventory held. They allow devices and equipment to communicate with each other and to business systems, thereby improving data speed and accuracy and reducing manual input. Consequently, improved cyber-security requirements will continue to be needed on ever greater scales.

3D printing has changed and will continue to change business processes. One example of this is in the spares business. The vast cost of producing and storing large quantities of spare parts has started to reduce in some organizations; with access to the relevant electronic files, spooled plastic or powdered metal raw material, 3D printing can create items needed on demand. The 'economies of one' has the potential to create great changes in inventory management in certain industries.

New technologies like these have the potential to affect the way that inventory is managed but do not change the fact that inventory will still be needed in business, together with planning and control systems to calculate inventory requirements.

Toolbox review

Many tools have been discussed and there have been plenty of calculations throughout the book. In addition to the extensive use of Excel, key tools in each chapter were:

- Chapter 3
  - Lean tools: Three 3-Mu; Five S; Seven Wastes; Poke Yoke.

- Automated item identification and data capture: RFID & QR/bar codes.
- Consignment stock; vendor-managed inventory (VMI); two bin system.
- Customer relationship management (CRM).
- Non-compliance measurement.
- Pareto by frequency of issue/by total inventory value of item.
- Sales and operations plan (S&OP).
- Warehouse management systems (WMS).

- Chapter 4
  - MRP (materials requirements planning) and ERP (enterprise requirements planning).
  - KPI – key performance indicators.
- Chapter 5
  - Product planning tools: weighted average profile (WAP); set-back chart/stick chart; product value profile.
  - Strategic inventory planning tools: stock turnover; planning calendar.
- Chapter 6
  - Inventory saw tooth.
  - Order/batch size: economic order quantity; economic order period; order period.
  - Safety stock: statistical safety stock; safety time; hybrid safety.
  - Parts classification: Pareto ABC; runner, repeater and stranger; classification matrix.
  - Inventory condition.
- Chapter 7
  - Overage analysis.
  - Inventory exchange curve.
  - Pareto exchange curve.
  - *k*-curve.
- Chapter 8
  - *k*-curve modelling.
  - MRP cycle stock and safety stock evaluation.
  - Application of active/inactive inventory rules.

  - Application of inventory active condition rules.
  - Excel pivot tables.
- Chapter 9
  - Alignment.

Summary

Figure 10.2 Journey from three pillars to five milestones

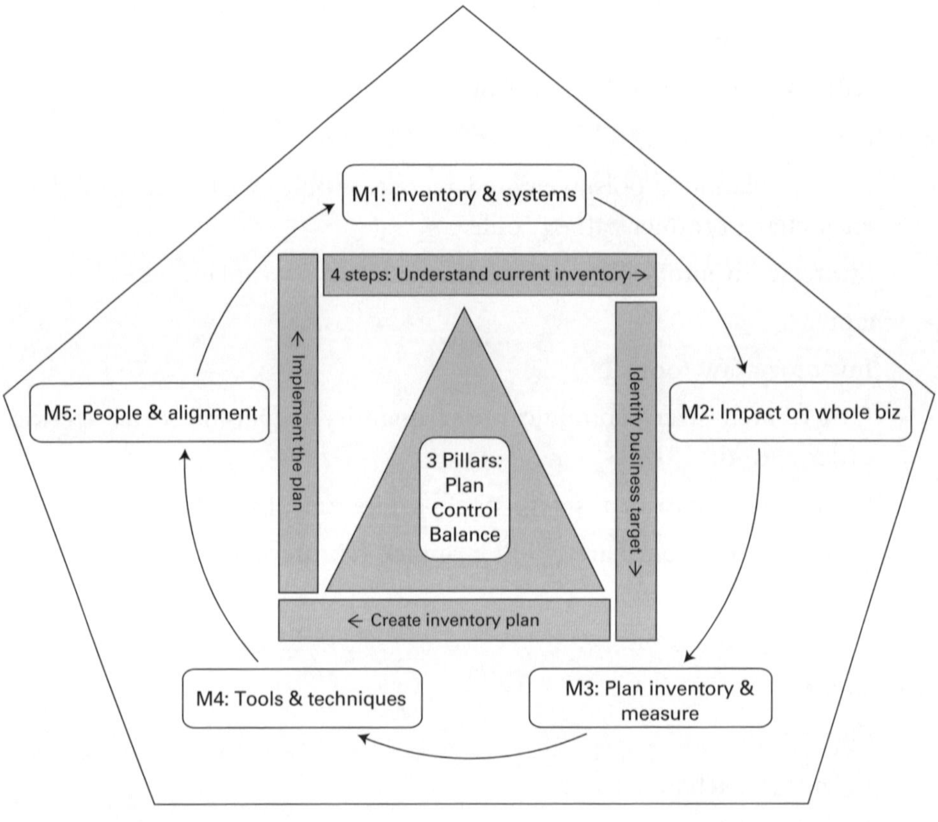

Inventory management has been important ever since people first gathered and stored grain to carry them through the winter. Forecasting consumption and replenishment of the grain was vital to survival. Today the success of our businesses means understanding the relationship between inventory management and organizational capability. Our business systems need to link the strategic decisions of senior management with the practical ability of the planner to make it happen at a part level.

This book aims to achieve exactly that, with the progress from the three pillars of inventory management, through the four steps to inventory heaven, to the five milestones of the journey, as shown in Figure 10.2.

It is hoped that the tools and techniques used throughout this book will assist in making your organization's journey easier and to help shed light on some of the many improvement opportunities.

References

Christopher, M (2016) *Logistics and Supply Chain Management*, Pearson Education, Harlow

Divita, L and Yoo, J J (2017) Examining global retailing's innovators, in T-M Choi (ed) *Fast Fashion Systems*, CR Press

Fernie, J G (2015) *Fashion Logistics*, Kogan Page, London

Hall, R W (1983) *Zero Inventories*, Dow Jones and Irwin, Illinois

Harrison, A *et al* (2014) *Logistics Management and Strategy*, Pearson

Jonsson, P and Mattsson, S (2006). A longitudinal study of materials planning applications in manufacturing companies, *International Journal of Operations Production Management*, **26**, pp. 971–95

Relph, G J (2006) Inventory Management in Business Systems, PhD Thesis: Manchester University

Relph, G J and Newton, M (2014) Both Pareto and EOQ have limitations: combining them delivers a powerful management tool for MRP and beyond, *International Journal of Production Economics*, **157**, pp 24–30

APPENDIX A

You do the maths control box exercises general briefing

In Chapters 2 to 5 we have provided 'You do the maths' exercises that are designed to enable the reader to review the key points covered in the chapter by working through a relevant exercise. These exercises are designed to reinforce the tools and techniques covered. In the same way that these chapters use the snow shovel as an example, all the exercises are based around a common set of manufacturing products that are typical of most batch manufacturing companies.

Figure A.1 Control boxes with 2/4 inputs and 5/9 outputs

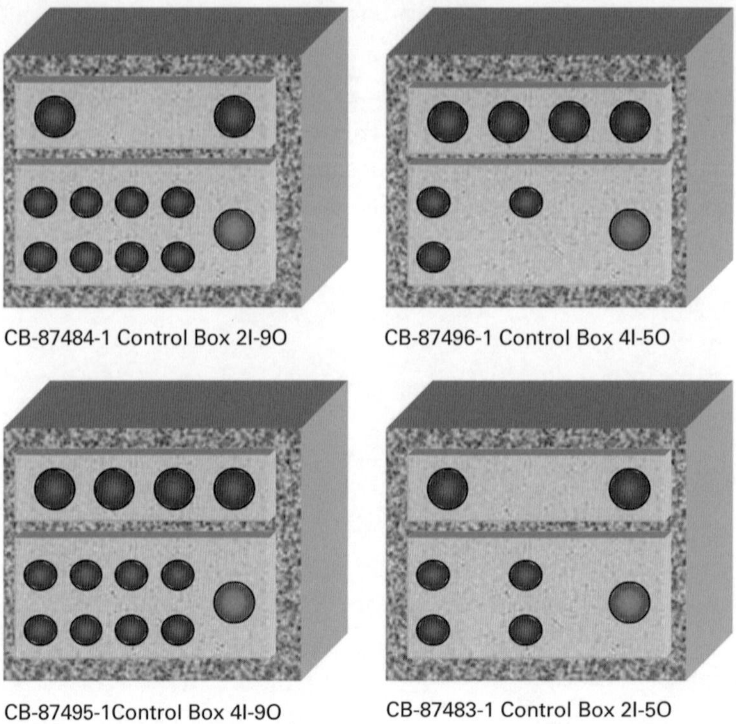

© Reproduced with kind permission of Inventory Matters Ltd

Control Box UK PLC is a company that manufactures and assembles control boxes. They have a range of control boxes that have four variants, shown in the picture opposite. These products are:

- CB-87495-1 Control Box 4I-9O: this has 4 inputs and 9 outputs (4 positive, 4 negative, 1 grounding).
- CB-87483-1 Control Box 2I-5O: this has 2 inputs and 5 outputs (2 positive, 2 negative, 1 grounding).
- CB-87496-1 Control Box 4I-5O: this has 4 inputs and 5 outputs (2 positive, 2 negative, 1 grounding).
- CB-87484-1 Control Box 2I-9O: this has 2 inputs and 9 outputs (4 positive, 4 negative, 1 grounding).

Multilevel BOMs are provided in this appendix for each of the four products, and available for download from www.koganpage.co.uk.

The products have been designed to utilize as many common components as possible, for example they use the same components for the Input/Output panels. These panels are machined to suit the input or output hole configurations based on the customer orders/forecasts.

The company operates a 13-week quarter with 4/4/5 accounting months.

Exercises are based on training materials developed by Inventory Matters Ltd and are reproduced with their kind permission.

Table A.1 CB-87495-1 Control Box 4I-9O

Indented BOM for CB-87495-1 Control Box 4I-9O

4 Input Channels Red)- 4I
4 Output Channels Red)
4 Output Channels Black)- 9O
1 Ground (Green))

Part Number	Description	Qty	UOM	Type	LLC	Lead-time
CB-87495-1	Control Box 4I-9O	1	ea	F	02	5
.BC-24919-6	Base Casting Common	1	ea	P	03	60
.TC-57843-4	Top Cover	1	ea	P	03	60
.LC-87650-4	Logic Card	1	ea	X	03	5
..RC-67896-8	Raw Card	1	ea	P	04	30
..LD-25376-2	Logic Device	2	ea	P	04	30
..RV-23458-7	Resistor 1Meg	8	ea	P	04	10
..WR-14259-2R	Wire – Red	6	mtr	R	07	5
.IP-4682-A4I	Input Panel Assy 4I	1	ea	S	03	5
..IP-23572-4I	Input Panel 4I	1	ea	C	04	15
...IC-25376-1	Input Panel Casting	1	ea	R	05	60
..IP-3654-A2R	Input Socket – Red Assy	4	ea	A	04	15
...CB-47898-7	Connector – Common	4	ea	P	05	15
...IP-35367-2R	Input Socket – Red	4	ea	P	05	15
...FS-56124-1	Fixing Screw	8	ea	P	05	10
..GT-25833-1	Gasket 4I	1	ea	C	04	5
...GP-42317-4	Gasket Paper (2″ Strip)	4	in	R	05	15
..FS-56124-1	Fixing Screw	4	ea	P	07	10
.OP-67236-A9O	Output Panel Assy 9O	1	ea	S	03	15
..OP-89712-9O	Output Panel 9O	1	ea	C	04	15
...IC-26345-1	Output Panel Casting	1	ea	R	05	60
..OL-26877-19O	Output Lead Assy 9O	1	ea	A	04	5
...OC-25369-1R	Output Connector – Red	4	ea	P	05	15
...OC-25679-1B	Output Connector – Black	4	ea	P	05	15
...OC-25754-2G	Output Connector – Green	1	ea	P	05	15
...WR-14259-2R	Wire – Red	4	mtr	R	07	5
...WB-14625-5B	Wire – Black	4	mtr	R	07	5
...WG-14765-5G	Wire – Green	1	mtr	R	07	5
...SS-32992-2	Shrink Sleeve	3	mtr	R	07	5
...FS-56124-1	Fixing Screw	18	ea	P	07	10
..GT-46573-2	Gasket 9O	1	ea	C	04	5
...GP-42317-4	Gasket Paper (2″ Strip)	4	in	R	05	15
..FS-56124-1	Fixing Screw	4	ea	P	07	10
.FS-56124-1	Fixing Screw	4	ea	P	07	10

Table A.2 CB-87483-1 Control Box 2I-5O

Indented BOM for CB-87483-1 Control Box 2I-5O

2 Input Channels Red)- 2I
2 Output Channels Red)
2 Output Channels Black)- 5O
1 Ground (Green))

Part Number	Description	Qty	UOM	Type	LLC	Lead-time
CB-87483-1	Control Box 2I-5O	1	ea	F	02	5
.BC-24919-6	Base Casting Common	1	ea	P	03	60
.TC-57843-4	Top Cover	1	ea	P	03	60
.LC-87650-4	Logic Card	1	ea	X	03	5
..RC-67896-8	Raw Card	1	ea	P	04	30
..LD-25376-2	Logic Device	2	ea	P	04	30
..RV-23458-7	Resistor 1Meg	8	ea	P	04	10
..WR-14259-2R	Wire - Red	6	mtr	R	07	5
.IP-4682-A2I	Input Panel Assy 2I	1	ea	S	03	5
..IP-23572-2I	Input Panel 2I	1	ea	C	04	15
...IC-25376-1	Input Panel Casting	1	ea	R	05	60
..IP-3654-A2R	Input Socket - Red Assy	2	ea	A	04	15
...CB-47898-7	Connector - Common	2	ea	P	05	15
...IP-35367-2R	Input Socket - Red	2	ea	P	05	15
...FS-56124-1	Fixing Screw	4	ea	P	05	10
..GT-25834-1	Gasket 2I	1	ea	C	04	5
...GP-42317-4	Gasket Paper (2" Strip)	4	in	R	05	15
..FS-56124-1	Fixing Screw	4	ea	P	07	10
.OP-67236-A5O	Output Panel Assy 5O	1	ea	S	03	15
..OP-89712-5O	Output Panel 5O	1	ea	C	04	15
...IC-26345-1	Output Panel Casting	1	ea	R	05	60
..OL-26877-15O	Output Lead Assy 5O	1	ea	A	04	5
...OC-25369-1R	Output Connector - Red	2	ea	P	05	15
...OC-25679-1B	Output Connector - Black	2	ea	P	05	15
...OC-25754-2G	Output Connector - Green	1	ea	P	05	15
...WR-14259-2R	Wire - Red	2	mtr	R	07	5
...WB-14625-5B	Wire - Black	2	mtr	R	07	5
...WG-14765-5G	Wire - Green	1	mtr	R	07	5
...SS-32992-2	Shrink Sleeve	3	mtr	R	07	5
...FS-56124-1	Fixing Screw	10	ea	P	07	10
..GT-46574-2	Gasket 5O	1	ea	C	04	5
...GP-42317-4	Gasket Paper (2" Strip)	4	in	R	05	15
..FS-56124-1	Fixing Screw	4	ea	P	07	10
.FS-56124-1	Fixing Screw	4	ea	P	07	10

Table A.3 CB-87496-1 Control Box 4I-5O

Indented BOM for CB-87496-1 Control Box 4I-5O

4 Input Channels Red)- 4I
2 Output Channels Red)
2 Output Channels Black)- 5O
1 Ground (Green))

Part Number	Description	Qty	UOM	Type	LLC	Lead-time
CB-87496-1	Control Box 4I-5O	1	ea	F	02	5
.BC-24919-6	Base Casting Common	1	ea	P	03	60
.TC-57843-4	Top Cover	1	ea	P	03	60
.LC-87650-4	Logic Card	1	ea	X	03	5
..RC-67896-8	Raw Card	1	ea	P	04	30
..LD-25376-2	Logic Device	2	ea	P	04	30
..RV-23458-7	Resistor 1Meg	8	ea	P	04	10
..WR-14259-2R	Wire - Red	6	mtr	R	07	5
.IP-4682-A4I	Input Panel Assy 4I	1	ea	S	03	5
..IP-23572-4I	Input Panel 4I	1	ea	C	04	15
...IC-25376-1	Input Panel Casting	1	ea	R	05	60
..IP-3654-A2R	Input Socket - Red Assy	4	ea	A	04	15
...CB-47898-7	Connector - Common	4	ea	P	05	15
...IP-35367-2R	Input Socket - Red	4	ea	P	05	15
...FS-56124-1	Fixing Screw	8	ea	P	05	10
..GT-25833-1	Gasket 4I	1	ea	C	04	5
...GP-42317-4	Gasket Paper (2" Strip)	4	in	R	05	15
..FS-56124-1	Fixing Screw	4	ea	P	07	10
.OP-67236-A5O	Output Panel Assy 5O	1	ea	S	03	15
..OP-89712-5O	Output Panel 5O	1	ea	C	04	15
...IC-26345-1	Output Panel Casting	1	ea	R	05	60
..OL-26877-15O	Output Lead Assy 5O	1	ea	A	04	5
...OC-25369-1R	Output Connector - Red	2	ea	P	05	15
...OC-25679-1B	Output Connector - Black	2	ea	P	05	15
...OC-25754-2G	Output Connector - Green	1	ea	P	05	15
...WR-14259-2R	Wire - Red	2	mtr	R	07	5
...WB-14625-5B	Wire - Black	2	mtr	R	07	5
...WG-14765-5G	Wire - Green	1	mtr	R	07	5
...SS-32992-2	Shrink Sleeve	3	mtr	R	07	5
...FS-56124-1	Fixing Screw	10	ea	P	07	10
..GT-46574-2	Gasket 5O	1	ea	C	04	5
...GP-42317-4	Gasket Paper (2" Strip)	4	in	R	05	15
..FS-56124-1	Fixing Screw	4	ea	P	07	10
.FS-56124-1	Fixing Screw	4	ea	P	07	10

Table A.4 CB-87484-1 Control Box 2I-9O

Indented BOM for CB-87484-1 Control Box 2I-9O

2 Input Channels Red)- 2I
4 Output Channels Red)
4 Output Channels Black)- 9O
1 Ground (Green))

Part Number	Description	Qty	UOM	Type	LLC	Lead-time
CB-87484-1	Control Box 2I-9O	1	ea	F	02	5
.BC-24919-6	Base Casting Common	1	ea	P	03	60
.TC-57843-4	Top Cover	1	ea	P	03	60
.LC-87650-4	Logic Card	1	ea	X	03	5
..RC-67896-8	Raw Card	1	ea	P	04	30
..LD-25376-2	Logic Device	2	ea	P	04	30
..RV-23458-7	Resistor 1Meg	8	ea	P	04	10
..WR-14259-2R	Wire - Red	6	mtr	R	07	5
.IP-4682-A2I	Input Panel Assy 2I	1	ea	S	03	5
..IP-23572-2I	Input Panel 2I	1	ea	C	04	15
...IC-25376-1	Input Panel Casting	1	ea	R	05	60
..IP-3654-A2R	Input Socket - Red Assy	2	ea	A	04	15
...CB-47898-7	Connector - Common	2	ea	P	05	15
...IP-35367-2R	Input Socket - Red	2	ea	P	05	15
...FS-56124-1	Fixing Screw	4	ea	P	05	10
..GT-25834-1	Gasket 2I	1	ea	C	04	5
...GP-42317-4	Gasket Paper (2" Strip)	4	in	R	05	15
..FS-56124-1	Fixing Screw	4	ea	P	07	10
.OP-67236-A9O	Output Panel Assy 9O	1	ea	S	03	15
..OP-89712-9O	Output Panel 9O	1	ea	C	04	15
...IC-26345-1	Output Panel Casting	1	ea	R	05	60
..OL-26877-19O	Output Lead Assy 9O	1	ea	A	04	5
...OC-25369-1R	Output Connector - Red	4	ea	P	05	15
...OC-25679-1B	Output Connector - Black	4	ea	P	05	15
...OC-25754-2G	Output Connector - Green	1	ea	P	05	15
...WR-14259-2R	Wire - Red	4	mtr	R	07	5
...WB-14625-5B	Wire - Black	4	mtr	R	07	5
...WG-14765-5G	Wire - Green	1	mtr	R	07	5
...SS-32992-2	Shrink Sleeve	3	mtr	R	07	5
...FS-56124-1	Fixing Screw	18	ea	P	07	10
..GT-46573-2	Gasket 9O	1	ea	C	04	5
...GP-42317-4	Gasket Paper (2" Strip)	4	in	R	05	15
..FS-56124-1	Fixing Screw	4	ea	P	07	10
.FS-56124-1	Fixing Screw	4	ea	P	07	10

APPENDIX B

The table below is to be used in conjunction with Excel 6.8.
Sample parts for exercise in highest to lowest order.

Table B.1 Sample parts for exercise in part number order

Count	Part Number	Annual Usage or Demand	Actual Stock	Cost Per Part	Annual Spend Value £	Actual Stock Value
25	A0889030013	52	1	£19.59	£1,018.88	£19.59
14	A0906030015	18	8	£150.22	£2,703.97	£1,201.77
19	A78810601E	401	1117	£5.20	£2,085.20	£5,808.40
26	B30880112C	700	566	£1.19	£835.28	£675.38
27	B30880113C	650	125	£1.18	£767.00	£147.50
15	B78810721A	749	251	£3.44	£2,579.83	£864.54
3	B78810741A	1012	75	£18.50	£18,722.00	£1,387.50
1	B78811ZD	1324	58	£42.84	£56,726.63	£2,485.00
12	B78812001B	458	15	£7.10	£3,250.36	£106.45
2	B78812ZF	987	20	£41.87	£41,325.69	£837.40
20	B78818AE	35	14	£59.41	£2,079.36	£831.74
8	C78810742A	360	7	£16.87	£6,071.97	£118.07
10	C78810761A	567	3	£8.43	£4,780.58	£25.29
21	C78810762A	230	54	£8.44	£1,941.66	£455.87
22	D0753100033	75	34	£22.84	£1,713.04	£776.58
9	D0862060018Y	163	65	£33.26	£5,420.88	£2,161.70

Table B.1 *continued*

Count	Part Number	Annual Usage or Demand	Actual Stock	Cost Per Part	Annual Spend Value £	Actual Stock Value
17	D0862070019Y	60	39	£38.98	£2,338.96	£1,520.32
7	D0883030014C	267	98	£27.54	£7,354.28	£2,699.32
18	D0978040014	39	91	£57.63	£2,247.62	£5,244.45
16	D0991020012	164	104	£14.60	£2,393.59	£1,517.89
23	D1017040014	15	3	£104.23	£1,563.49	£312.70
24	KDB300600	8	6	£193.37	£1,546.99	£1,160.24
13	KN552130	10	2	£319.98	£3,199.83	£639.97
11	LE02	396	0	£11.09	£4,393.19	£0.00
6	LE763	781	321	£11.11	£8,679.28	£3,567.29
4	N6554004M0256	523	75	£35.08	£18,346.42	£2,630.94
5	SK98751	46	10	£316.19	£14,544.64	£3,161.88
	Totals				**£218,630.61**	**£40,357.77**

The table below is to be used in conjunction with Excel 6.8.

Table B.2 Sample parts for exercise in highest to lowest annual spend value order

Count	Part Number	Annual Usage or Demand	Actual Stock	Cost Per Part	Annual Spend Value £	Actual Stock Value
1	B78811ZD	1324	58	£42.84	£56,726.63	£2,485.00
2	B78812ZF	987	20	£41.87	£41,325.69	£837.40
3	B78810741A	1012	75	£18.50	£18,722.00	£1,387.50
4	N6554004M0256	523	75	£35.08	£18,346.42	£2,630.94
5	SK98751	46	10	£316.19	£14,544.64	£3,161.88
6	LE763	781	321	£11.11	£8,679.28	£3,567.29
7	D0883030014C	267	98	£27.54	£7,354.28	£2,699.32
8	C78810742A	360	7	£16.87	£6,071.97	£118.07
9	D0862060018Y	163	65	£33.26	£5,420.88	£2,161.70
10	C78810761A	567	3	£8.43	£4,780.58	£25.29
11	LE02	396	0	£11.09	£4,393.19	£0.00
12	B78812001B	458	15	£7.10	£3,250.36	£106.45
13	KN552130	10	2	£319.98	£3,199.83	£639.97
14	A0906030015	18	8	£150.22	£2,703.97	£1,201.77
15	B78810721A	749	251	£3.44	£2,579.83	£864.54
16	D0991020012	164	104	£14.60	£2,393.59	£1,517.89
17	D0862070019Y	60	39	£38.98	£2,338.96	£1,520.32
18	D0978040014	39	91	£57.63	£2,247.62	£5,244.45
19	A78810601E	401	1117	£5.20	£2,085.20	£5,808.40
20	B78818AE	35	14	£59.41	£2,079.36	£831.74

Table B.2 *continued*

Count	Part Number	Annual Usage or Demand	Actual Stock	Cost Per Part	Annual Spend Value £	Actual Stock Value
21	C78810762A	230	54	£8.44	£1,941.66	£455.87
22	D0753100033	75	34	£22.84	£1,713.04	£776.58
23	D1017040014	15	3	£104.23	£1,563.49	£312.70
24	KDB300600	8	6	£193.37	£1,546.99	£1,160.24
25	A0889030013	52	1	£19.59	£1,018.88	£19.59
26	B30880112C	700	566	£1.19	£835.28	£675.38
27	B30880113C	650	125	£1.18	£767.00	£147.50
	Totals				**£218,630.61**	**£40,357.77**

APPENDIX C
Tools and techniques

- 3-Mu: in Lean/JIT the identification of activities which add no value to a system, based on MUDA, MURA and MURI (Chapter 3).
- 5S: the five steps of the Gemba Kanri process to promote good teamwork, standard working practices and clear visual management of stock-holding areas (Chapter 3).
- 7 wastes of Lean: Lean processes work to maximize value whilst minimizing unnecessary work (too early or overly complex), movement (both transport and motion by equipment or people), waiting, product, mistakes. Wastes are also referred to as MUDA (Chapter 3).
- Alignment: Parameter Alignment method of keeping MRP parameters aligned with agreed policies (Chapter 9).
- Application of active/inactive inventory rules (Chapter 8).
- Application of inventory active condition rules (Chapter 8).
- Automated item identification and data capture: use of 2D and 3D (or QR) bar codes and RFID tags to aid in processing and handling goods at all stages of holding and movement (Chapter 3).
- Bar code (1D): a rectangle containing a series of numbers and most commonly a pattern of parallel white and black bars of different thicknesses used to aid with the automatic identification of items (Chapter 3).
- Bar code (2D): a square or rectangle containing many bars or dots of different thicknesses used to aid with the automatic identification of items. 2D barcodes include QR codes, DataMatrix and PDF417 (Portable Data Format) and hold significantly more information than a 1D bar code (Chapter 3).
- Bar code (3D): most commonly similar to a 2D bar code with the lines and dots at different physical depths or in different colours (Chapter 3).
- Classification Matrix (Chapter 6).

- Consignment stock: inventory is held on an organization's premises and is managed by the customer. Levels of service are agreed, and stock remains the property of the supplier until used (Chapter 3).
- Customer relationship management (CRM): systems for managing the relationship with the customer (eg customer data, customer communication and interaction, marketing, sales automation), which benefits from good integration with other business systems (eg ERP) (Chapters 2, 3).
- Customer service levels: linking safety stock considerations to customer service levels (Chapter 6).
- Economic order period: a way of calculating batch or order quantity in inventory planning (Chapter 6).
- Economic order quantity: a way of calculating batch or order quantity in inventory planning (Chapter 6).
- ERP: enterprise requirements planning (Chapters 2, 4).
- Excel pivot tables (Chapter 8).
- Gemba Kanri: see 5S.
- Hybrid safety: calculating safety stock using a combination of methods (Chapter 6).
- Inventory condition: a useful way to provide generalized categories of inventory, ie Shortage, Underage, Optimum, and Overage that can be used for inventory reporting (Chapter 6).
- Inventory exchange curve (Chapters 3, 5, 7).
- Inventory saw tooth (Chapters 2, 3, 6).
- *k*-curve principle (Chapter 7).
- *k*-curve modelling (Chapter 8).
- KPI: key performance indicators (Chapters 1, 4).
- Lean tools: see 3-Mu; 5S; 7 Wastes; Poke Yoke (Chapter 3).
- MRP: materials requirements planning (Chapters 2, 4).
- MRP cycle stock and safety stock evaluation (Chapter 8).
- Non-compliance measurement: used to identify where incorrect system parameters and/or data are creating the most correctable mistakes, and what correction and improvement steps are needed to the system and/or the process (Chapters 2, 3, 4).
- Order/batch size: different ways of calculating batch or order quantity in inventory planning (Chapter 6).

- Order period: a way of calculating batch or order quantity in inventory planning (Chapter 6).
- Overage: stock above maximum stock, ie total of safety stock and batch stock (Chapters 3, 6).
- Overage analysis: identification of causes and required action of parts in overage (Chapter 7).
- Parameter alignment: a method of keeping MRP parameters aligned with agreed policies (Chapter 9).
- Pareto ABC: used to classify parts by total inventory value (Chapter 6).
- Pareto by frequency of issue: used to identify location of part in warehouse (Chapter 3).
- Pareto by total inventory value of item: used to determine each item's warehouse stock checking frequency (Chapter 3).
- Pareto exchange curve (Chapter 7).
- Parts classification: different methods for classifying parts in inventory planning (Chapter 6).
- Planning calendar: used as a strategic inventory planning tool (Chapter 5).
- Poke Yoke: also known as 'fail-safe-ing' or 'mistake-proofing'. Errors are prevented by a process designed to prevent them happening, or to easily identify when a flaw or error occurs (Chapter 3).
- Product planning tools (Chapter 5).
- Product value profile (PVP): a product planning tool (Chapter 5).
- Quick response (QR) codes: a matrix bar code, first designed in 1994 and used to aid the automatic identification of items (Chapter 3).
- Radio frequency identification (RFID): tags which hold electronically stored information. They are read through the use of electromagnetic fields and do not have to be physically visible. Tags are either active (and have their own power source) or passive (and do not). Some tags, most commonly the active tags, are re-used (Chapter 3).
- Runner, repeater and stranger: an inventory classification by frequency of use often used in business (Chapter 6).
- Safety stock: various ways of calculating safety stock. Related to customer service levels (Chapter 6).
- Safety time: an often-used method to calculate safety stock using time periods (Chapter 6).

- Sales and operations plan (S&OP): a process for balancing supply and demand at all levels within an organization (ie strategic, tactical, operational). It is relevant in inventory balancing and control at the operational level to identify how the supply/demand relationship is working and to look for improvements (Chapters 2, 3, 5).
- Set-back chart/stick chart (Chapter 5).
- Statistical safety stock: an often-used method to calculate safety stock. Several different calculations can be used (Chapter 6).
- Stock turnover: the number of times stock is used or sold, usually measured over a year. A strategic inventory planning tool (Chapter 5).
- Strategic inventory planning tools (Chapter 5).
- Two-bin system: a simple visual system in which items are re-ordered when the first bin is emptied. Whilst the new order is being waited for, items from the second bin are used. Similarly, there are also three-bin systems used, with the third bin being considered safety stock (Chapter 3).
- Vendor-managed inventory (VMI): inventory is held on an organization's premises and is managed and controlled by a supplier. Agreed minimum and maximum levels of inventory are agreed, and stock remains the property of the supplier until used. The two-bin system is a frequently used process in VMI (Chapter 3).
- Warehouse management systems (WMS): systems for managing the warehouse which benefit from good integration with other business systems (eg integral to ERP or interfaced with it) (Chapter 3).
- Weighted average profile (WAP): a product planning tool (Chapter 5).

USEFUL WEBSITES

http://www.apics.org/

http://www.appriseconsulting.co.uk

https://ciltuk.org.uk/

https://www.demanddrivenmrp.com/

http://goldratt.co.uk/

http://www.inventorymatters.co.uk

https://www.koganpage.com/

https://www.oliverwight-eame.com/

INDEX

The index is filed in alphabetical, word-by-word order. Numbers and acronyms are filed as spelt out. Page locators in italics denote information contained within a figure or table.